BOB DYLAN

Photo by John Young.

BOB DYLAN
A Bio-Bibliography

William McKeen

Popular Culture Bio-Bibliographies
M. Thomas Inge, Series Editor

GREENWOOD PRESS
Westport, Connecticut • London

Library of Congress Cataloging-in-Publication Data

McKeen, William, 1954-
    Bob Dylan : a bio-bibliography / William McKeen.
      p.   cm.—(Popular culture bio-bibliographies, ISSN
0193-6891)
    Discography: p.
    Includes bibliographical references and index.
    ISBN 0-313-27998-5
      1. Dylan, Bob, 1941- . 2. Dylan, Bob, 1941- —Bibliography.
3. Rock musicians—United States—Biography. I. Title.
II. Series.
ML420.D98M25   1993
782.42162'0092—dc20   92-32212
[B]

British Library Cataloguing in Publication Data is available.

Copyright © 1993 by William McKeen

All rights reserved. No portion of this book may be
reproduced, by any process or technique, without the
express written consent of the publisher.

Library of Congress Catalog Card Number: 92-32212
ISBN: 0-313-27998-5
ISSN: 0193-6891

First published in 1993

Greenwood Press, 88 Post Road West, Westport, CT 06881
An imprint of Greenwood Publishing Group, Inc.

Printed in the United States of America

The paper used in this book complies with the
Permanent Paper Standard issued by the National
Information Standards Organization (Z39.48-1984).

10 9 8 7 6 5 4 3 2 1

To my children
Sarah, Graham and Mary

with love

Contents

Preface ix

Part I: Portrait of the Artist

Chapter 1. Boy from the North Country 3
Chapter 2. The Whole World Is Watching 31
Chapter 3. Song and Dance Man 57

Part II: Bob Dylan's Songs and His Influence

Chapter 4. Writing on His Favorite Wall 85
Chapter 5. Something Is Happening Here 123

Part III: Bibliography

Chapter 6. Words and Music 137

Part IV: Performances

Chapter 7. Recordings 183
Chapter 8. Film, Television and Video 241
Chapter 9. Concerts 265

Part V: Chronology

Chapter 10. Bob Dylan's Life-in-Progress 287

Index 303

Preface

MY FRIEND LUCIA WORSHIPPED BOB DYLAN. The famous Milton Glaser poster of the musician was framed over her couch, and there were pictures of Dylan taped to her bedroom door. Lucia had all his albums and a small collection of bootleg records, and she knew the words to all of his songs--no mean feat. She had never seen him, but that was all right. Very few people had seen him in a long time.

Then, in the winter of 1973, Bob Dylan announced that he would be making a concert tour with The Band. This was a shock. Dylan was the Greta Garbo of rock 'n' roll. *He wanted to be alone.* In fact, there had been rumors of his death following a nasty motorcycle accident some years before. But Dylan was alive and coming to our town.

We ordered tickets (at a then-outrageous $9.95) and planned for concert day: We would listen to Dylan's albums in chronological order, have some manicotti and wine, and then go to the concert arena to commune with the Great Man. But things did not proceed according to plan. When I arrived at Lucia's home that morning, she was sullen. She moped the whole day and threatened to back out of attending the concert. Finally, she confessed her problem: Seeing Dylan would somehow ruin him for her, or so she thought. The *intimacy* (her word) between them would forever be shattered if he sang not only to her but to thousands of other spectators as well.

Luckily, good sense prevailed and Lucia was persuaded to attend the concert. Sitting in the audience when Dylan and The Band took the stage and cranked into "Most Likely You Go Your Way (and I'll Go Mine)" was an overwhelming experience, like standing next to a jet at takeoff: *krrriiissshhh*. I was both deafened and inspired and I swear I smelled exhaust fumes. In the seat next to me, Lucia held my hand and laughed. That concert remains the best performance I have ever witnessed.

Somehow, Lucia's relationship with Dylan survived, but her concern shows something about the typical Dylan fan's feelings about the artist. For most Dylan devotees, the relationship is personal: He's been singing to them--and only them--for much of their lives.

It may seem rather silly to make all this fuss over a singer, but Bob Dylan's admirers are wont to have such attachments to him. I ought to know.

The concert Lucia almost missed took place February 3, 1974, in Bloomington, Indiana. Dylan returned to Bloomington 14 years later to record at John Mellencamp's studio outside town. The bus was early and he arrived unexpectedly. He called the Mellencamp home but was told it would be a while before someone could pick him up. Would he mind waiting. Consequently, Dylan sat on the curb in front of a Domino's Pizza next to the bus station and began to blow on his harmonica. Two kids walked by. "Who's that guy think he is?" one of them asked the other. "Bob Dylan?"

As a matter of fact, he does think he's Bob Dylan--and he has been doing so for more than three decades. Throughout that time, he has been a most unusual public figure. One of the world's most famous entertainers, he is still able to keep much of his life private--to blend in, sit on a sidewalk and play his harmonica. This book is devoted to this talented, frustrating, brilliant and baffling man, who is unique in American popular culture. I do not purport to understand him, nor do I wish to analyze or categorize him. However, I do hope to add to the knowledge about his life and work.

This book is divided into five parts. It starts with three chapters of biography. Dylan's work and its influence is the subject of the second part, while his extensive song catalog and the works about him comprise the third. The majority of the reference material--discography, concert itineraries and film work--is in part four. The work ends with a chronology.

Bob Dylan did not sanction this book (he has sanctioned few of the scores of books about him), but his representative did call to say, "Although Mr. Dylan declines to participate in this project, he wishes you good luck." I *was* lucky to find so much credible, reliable material. This book, by its nature, owes a tremendous debt to several earlier authors. Anthony Scaduto, Robert Shelton, Bob Spitz and Clinton Heylin were the primary sources for the biographical material, while a good deal of the reference material was confirmed by a marvelous book by Michael Krogsgaard called *Positively Bob Dylan*.

The nature of the writing inspired by Dylan and his work is unlike that inspired by any other popular musician. Some of the best criticism of rock 'n' roll, whether by Jon Landau, Greil Marcus, Dave Marsh or Paul Williams, has been written about Bob Dylan. Reading and re-reading all this material has been a pleasure. Moreover, there exist true Dylan scholars. Heylin and

PREFACE / xi

his partner, John Bauldie, of the Wanted Man organization (England's Dylan Information Office) are the most reliable. Their publication, the *Telegraph*, is single-minded in its pursuit of Bob Dylan's art. Krogsgaard has meticulously tracked Dylan's recordings, while Betsy Bowden and Wilfred Mellers brilliantly analyzed Dylan's performances. Marsh, Shelton, Tim Riley and Robert Christgau offered intriguing analyses of the artist's work. Again, it has been a pleasure to be immersed in the writing devoted to Dylan.

I wish to thank my friends and associates, who have been patient and kind. Lucia Howe really did need to be talked into going to see Dylan in concert in 1974, but she has remained a devotee of his work and a friend of mine for more than 20 years. Lynne Walker is another great friend whom I wish to thank. Lynne discovered Dylan's work when he revolutionized contemporary Christian music, and I would have never appreciated his effect on that genre without Lynne's analysis. Lucia and Lynne are among the greatest friends I have ever had, and I hope they meet someday.

I thank my colleagues and students at the University of Florida for advice and support: William Alexander, Kathleen Bennett, Steve Carney, Lester Carson, Jean Chance, David Chalmers, Meg Cornwell, John Griffith, Jon Roosenraad, and Laurie Schammel. They have all been patient with me. There are some other people to thank: Andrea Billups read the manuscript, John Young and Tim Detore helped with the reference section, and Scott Wilson was a terrific music-industry source.

My office neighbors deserve special mention. I have Dylan's complete works in my office and I fear that the thundering opening chords of "Series of Dreams" have frequently interrupted scholarly reveries (and probably a few naps). I therefore tender this public apology. Forgive me. I could not help myself. Please excuse me for having been so enthusiastic about my research.

In addition, I thank my friends in the newspaper business who read parts of the manuscript and/or helped with the research: Peter Couture, Michael Foley, Neville Green, John Oudens and Jerry Stockfisch of the *St. Petersburg Times*; Bill DeYoung of the *Gainesville Sun*; and Rebecca Brown of the *Orlando Sentinel*.

Thomas Inge, editor of this series, and the staff at Greenwood Press-- Marilyn Brownstein, Julie Cullen and Nicole Balant--worked hard on my manuscript and I appreciate their care, professionalism and enthusiasm.

Lisa Waitcus put up with me during the two years I researched and wrote this book. She is a woman of extreme tolerance and unflagging good humor, who listened to every twist and turn of the composition process and never complained, even when I repeatedly sang "Subterranean Homesick Blues."

My children, Sarah, Graham and Mary, also had to endure a great deal. I thank them for letting me play my tapes in the car in between Paula Abdul and Boys II Men. I think I'm getting them to come around (Sarah listened to Dylan's "Please Mrs. Henry" and thought it was one of the funniest songs she ever heard).

My parents and my brother and sister have always encouraged me and I appreciate their confidence. That does not mean they share my interest in the subject. Once, when I was a teenager, my father stuck his head in my room while I was listening to Dylan's *Blonde on Blonde*. "That guy can't sing," he said. "Right, Dad," I responded. "He *can't* sing . . . but he's a great singer." If he were alive, my father would be both proud of my work on this book and baffled by its contents.

William McKeen

Part I

Portrait of the Artist

Chapter 1

Boy from the North Country

IF YOU BELIEVE THE LEGEND, Robert Johnson went down to a crossroads on Highway 51 in the Mississippi Delta and forged a contract with the devil, signing his soul over for eternity. In exchange, Johnson became the greatest guitarist of his time, the king of the Delta blues singers, and one of the forefathers of rock 'n' roll. If you want to believe another legend, Woodrow Wilson Guthrie was a scrawny hobo and populist poet whose enduring songs of the struggle between good and evil during America's midlife crisis, the Great Depression, were the works of a functional illiterate.

There is both truth and falsity in these legends. Johnson was a gifted guitarist, but he made no such pact with the devil. Guthrie's paeans to the working class showed the possibilities of the topical song during the 1930s, but he was also an urbane and literate man.

Nonetheless, these tall tales became part of the men's considerable legacies. As a character said in director John Ford's 1962 film, *The Man Who Shot Liberty Valance*, "When the legend becomes fact, print the legend."[1] The folklore of popular music encourages us to perpetuate these stories.

It is no accident that Robert Allen Zimmerman, known to the world for more than three decades as Bob Dylan, cites Johnson and Guthrie as his major influences. His first book of lyrics is dedicated to them ("the magnificent Woody Guthrie and Robert Johnson")[2] and their work in the folk and blues idioms deeply affected the younger man's music. Like them, Dylan built a legend for himself and dwelled in the realm of myth.

For a man who has spent most of his life as a public character, we really know little of Bob Dylan's private life. There are the facts of his birth and schooling, and statistics of his marriage and parenthood. There are the details of his career: the lists of albums and singles, the videos, the television performances and the film appearances. Beyond that, however, there is much speculation.

Listeners cannot assume they have learned about Dylan's private life through his music. Even though the songs on his 1975 album, *Blood on the Tracks*, record the dissolution of a relationship, Dylan has denied that they reflect his then-crumbling marriage to Sara Lowndes Dylan. Rather, he asks to be credited with the artist's imagination, saying that his songs do not come from his private journals.

Few artists of Dylan's renown have so successfully guarded their private lives, yet it is Dylan's upbringing that shaped him, making him an artist who, in his early manhood, would find hundreds of thousands of those from his generation listening to his every public word.

Clean Cut Kid

Robert Allen Zimmerman was born May 24, 1941, in Duluth, Minnesota, the port town from which Lake Superior springs at the convex of Minnesota and Wisconsin. Ore mining was the principal industry of northern Minnesota and southern Canada, and Duluth bore the stench of industry, being the principal site for the mineral's transport. His parents were Abraham Zimmerman and Beatty Stone Zimmerman, who had wed in 1936. They lived in a small apartment in Duluth while Abe Zimmerman worked his way up from messenger boy to a department supervisor at the regional office of Standard Oil.

The Zimmermans were not wealthy, but by 1940 they felt comfortable enough to think they could afford to start a family. Their first son, Robert, was a difficult birth owing to his large head. As a small child, he was known as Bobby Allen. Neighbors fawned over his looks: bountiful, curly blond hair and a smile that displayed an early form of showmanship. Beatty Zimmerman told her son he was so beautiful that he should have been a girl, and even tied ribbons in her son's locks.[3]

Abe Zimmerman was excluded from military service during World War II because his work at Standard Oil was deemed essential by the government. He took his son to his office occasionally, and once, when Bobby was three, he stood on his father's desk to perform for coworkers and marveled at the sound of his voice on his father's dictating machine. Abe was a proud father, always showing off his son or bragging about him.

At a family reunion on Mother's Day in 1946, the children performed for an audience of relatives. Bobby took his role seriously and demanded respect from his listeners. After mounting the stage, he stamped his feet until silence fell over the gathering. "If everyone is this room will keep quiet," he told them, "I will sing for my grandmother."[4] Thus, long before he began his recording career, Bobby was a star in his family circle.

Abe Zimmerman lost his job not long after the war's end, which had slowed demand for Standard Oil's products. A second son, David, was born in 1946, a year in which Abe spent half his time bedridden with polio. The following year, with economic drought spreading through Duluth, Zimmerman moved his family inland to Hibbing, Beatty Zimmerman's hometown, where her family owned a clothing store and two movie theaters, the Victory and the Garden. Hibbing's tradition was that of an immigrant town, comprised of transplanted Croats, Serbs, Slavs and a number of Scandinavians. Abe Zimmerman became part owner of Micka Electric, a hardware and appliance store downtown. Abe, Beatty, six-year-old Bob and the infant David shared a small apartment house with three other families. After a year of frugality, Abe bought a home in a Hibbing suburb, a neighborhood of confusingly similar houses and symmetrically planted trees. However, the Zimmerman home was different, standing out in the cookie-cutter suburb, looking like a combination bunker and hacienda. It was newer than the other houses and uglier than most.[5]

Iron ore had been discovered near Hibbing in 1890 which fired an economic boom that would resound through the early 1950s. The town's great years were those just following World War I. The Works Progress Administration and wartime contracts during World War II allowed Hibbing to coast along in relative comfort until 1953, when most of the ore had been removed from the earth.[6] The town, which was known as the world's largest open pit, was circled with craters, the residue of the mining, and looked like it had been bombed during a war.[7] The land was used up, leaving little for the next generation. For the first time in decades, the young people of Hibbing began to flee: There was nothing left to hold them.

Bob Zimmerman, like the other children of Hibbing, was restless. Television, that great new toy, showed that there was a world beyond the North Country and contributed to the inherent dissatisfaction with the dying town. However, young Bob was no one out of the ordinary. Neighbors remembered him as a quiet, normal boy. For the emergence of a talent that no one could see, he needed to be inspired by the heroes of music and film.

Abe worked long days at Micka Electric, and Beatty sold clothes part-time at Feldman's, a department store. After school, Bob turned to the family radio for companionship, listening to music and voices from far-distant places like Minneapolis, Chicago, Nashville and Denver. Because his mother's family owned two movie houses, Bob spent much time there, admiring the huge images of Marlon Brando and Montgomery Clift, whose new acting styles electrified audiences.[8]

As a young boy, Bob felt the pull of popular music. From down South, he heard country music on his radio. Hank Williams ("my first idol," he once wrote) was a strong influence.[9] Williams sang about the world of railroads, the pain of loss, and the need to move. His restlessness echoed Bob's own. However, the songs also appealed to Bob on an intellectual level; they made him want to express his feelings through writing. Emulating Williams, Bob began composing poetry when he was 11.[10]

Like others of his generation, Bob Zimmerman could not help but be affected by the enormous cultural changes in the 1950s, which might not have been obvious at the time but whose influence would shadow all other developments for a decade. One of the harbingers of this change was the film *Blackboard Jungle*, which was released in 1955. It starred Glenn Ford as a schoolteacher who is terrorized by thuggish students, played by young actors Vic Morrow and Sidney Poitier. Despite the drama on screen, it was the soundtrack of the film that had the greatest effect on Bob and the rest of the audience. The theme song was "Rock around the Clock" by Bill Haley and the Comets. Haley never became a huge star and served out his career as a journeyman musician, but the impact of "Rock around the Clock" should not be undervalued: It signaled the commercial beginning of a musical revolution.

At night, when the radio band offered stations from all over the country, Bob began to hear the new music. It came not from the usual signals in Duluth or Minneapolis, but from down South, from Little Rock and Tallahassee.[11] It had the same sound as Bill Haley, except it was rawer and rougher. It was something Bob had never heard before: The announcers called it rock 'n' roll.

Soon, Bob learned the names of the voices he admired: Elvis Presley, Chuck Berry, Little Richard, Fats Domino and Buddy Holly. (He saw Buddy Holly on his last tour in 1959, when Holly played Duluth three days before his fatal plane crash.) Bob liked them all, but there was something special about Richard Penniman, who performed under the name Little Richard. Penniman was the rawest of the rock 'n' roll performers, personifying the freedom that this music represented. Clapping, gallivanting, and ranting and raving his way through nonsensical songs that were pure, unvarnished emotion, Penniman became Bob's second idol.[12]

The coming of rock 'n' roll in the mid-1950s contributed to Bob's restlessness, and the records he heard on the radio became his new religion. When he bought the singles and albums, he learned that he could easily play along with them, even though he had had no musical training. Thus, while still a young teenager, Bob decided that he would be a rock 'n' roll star.[13]

The piano pounding of Little Richard was inspirational to Bob, who learned he did not have to practice for hours and make certain that each note was exactly as some great master had written it. Richard Penniman's chords were simple; the music and the emotion were vital. "To thine own feeling be true": Bob could worry less about technique.

Traditional singing was also falling by the wayside. In music class at school, Bob was given exercises that demanded a wide vocal range and found climbing the upper registers somewhat precarious. In rock 'n' roll, however, the feeling and the power of the middle range was explored. Thus, it held more possibilities for him. No doubt this was one of the appeals of the honky tonk sound of early country and western music. Bob was enamored of Hank Williams's hillbilly yodel. Williams's painful songs of loves won and lost provided most of the terminology that Nashville tunesmiths would explore for a generation (frequently without Williams's style and wit). The rawness of Williams's laments was influential--not just for Bob Zimmerman, but for a whole school of country music artists.

The songs of Williams and Little Richard, both unschooled musical geniuses, played constantly in Bob's head. He heard them as he walked, he sang them to himself, and he played them on the piano. The tunes were relatively nondescript: It was the emotion that was so distinctive. Often, Bob played the tunes while substituting his own words: "I got a yeah . . . she can yeah yeah all the time."[14]

Bob had other infatuations beyond Hank Williams and Little Richard. Actor James Dean put a face on the alienation of young America with his film performances in *East of Eden* and *Rebel without a Cause*. Even after his death in a car crash in September 1955, Dean's persona lived on, influencing a generation of admirers, including Bob, for whom Dean's tough-guy pose symbolized a growing contempt for society.[15]

Bob soon eschewed his mother's concept of clothing--polo shirts, chinos, and related accouterments--in favor of jeans, boots, and other forms of apparel that Marlon Brando would find suitable. Bob began to grease his hair, to slick it up until it formed a waterfall above his eyebrows. He also adopted the patented James Dean scowl. He was 15, and he was a rebel.

Bob was now ready to share his music. With a couple of friends from Hibbing High School, he formed a band called The Golden Chords. Unfortunately, the other boys whom he recruited for the group did not share Bob's musical tastes. The clarinet player was from the school band and liked jazz, while a trumpet player became a second guitarist. "None of us had ever heard the music he wanted us to play," a band member said.[16]

The Golden Chords practiced at Bob's house after school, turning the living room into a rehearsal hall. Bob ruled the group like a benevolent dictator. He played the records he wanted the band to mimic, and then told them how to perform. The band had rehearsed for only a short time when Bob judged it ready for its first public performance: a concert at Hibbing Community College. However, the audition got in the way.[17] While Bob pounded the piano and sang like a Little Richard possessed ("Jenny Jenny" was the song), the producers of the college talent show laughed at his manic performance. They had never really heard rock 'n' roll, and Bob was too much for them. The Golden Chords were rejected, having been judged inappropriate for the annual College Capers.

Rock 'n' roll had not reached Hibbing. Bob heard it on radio stations late at night, but the Zimmermans' radio was probably one of the few in the town that was tuned to those frequencies. The Golden Chords' audition may have been the town's first brush with the new music. Bob was ahead of the crowd, which was the way he liked it. The band broke up soon after the failed audition, mostly because Bob had developed an interest in rhythm and blues and the other members of the band wanted to play the more successful (and safe) pop music.

Already, Bob was unable to exist as part of a group. Being in a group required a democratic decision-making process, while Bob's vision and determination did not allow for compromise.

Minstrel Boy

Dreaming of fame occupied Bob's days. He saw himself as a rock 'n' roll star, acting the part long before he played any professional gigs. His infatuations were legion: Hank Williams, Little Richard, Elvis Presley, Marlon Brando, and James Dean. Dean, perhaps more than the others, contributed to the formation of Bob's identity as he expressed a certain anger and resentment that Bob was, at yet, unable to voice. Determined to be famous, Bob sat in school dreaming of glory. In English class one day, he wrote a note to a friend: "I'm going to make it big. I know it for sure, and when I do, you bring this piece of paper and for two months, you can stay with me, no matter where I'm at."[18]

Bob began, slowly, to break away from Hibbing. When he was 16, he took a bus to Minneapolis, supposedly to attend the state basketball tournament. However, his real mission was to investigate the big city's music stores, which were bursting with the sorts of records he had only heard about up north. Regular trips to Minneapolis followed.

In 11th grade, Bob met Echo Helstrom. She had seen him before but paid little attention to him because he had appeared to be such a goody-goody, a kid from the right side of the tracks who probably would not pay attention to her. That fall, however, when Bob and Echo started their junior year, he came to school transformed. His look was different and his absorption in music dominated his life. One day, Echo met him at a cafe after school and he lit up when he began talking about music. He was delighted that Echo loved the same music. She said few people could understand Bob and his passion the way she could.[19] Eager to impress her, he broke into a room upstairs from the cafe and played the piano.

He had found a kindred spirit, another kid whose ambitions exceeded the city limits. But there was some tension at first. As Bob used Echo's pocket knife to break into the rehearsal room, she asked if he was Jewish. He said nothing, but later one of Bob's friends counseled Echo not to talk about Bob being Jewish. He was sensitive about his faith, the friend told her.[20]

Bob soon learned that Echo Helstrom didn't care about his heritage; she had merely been making conversation. Thus began their relationship, which consisted in the early days of many after-school listening sessions, as they shared their musical interests. He asked about her unusual first name; she said she had earned it by being born exactly 14 years after her brother.[21] Soon they were going steady and Bob gave her an identification bracelet. They made a pact: Whoever became famous first would help the other. Bob was going to be a rock 'n' roll star and Echo was going to be an actress. Before the year was out, Echo had decided she would marry Bobby Zimmerman one day.[22]

Bob once played a prank on Echo. He called her and said he wanted her to listen to him sing. Presumably setting down the phone and sitting at a piano, he pounded out a raucous version of "Do You Wanna Dance?" Echo believed him, but it was a hoax: Bob had merely played Bobby Freeman's recording of the song.[23] Bob's parents were not fond of Echo. They were cordial to her, but did not take her seriously. First of all, she was not Jewish, and the Zimmermans assumed that their son would marry within the faith. She was also poor, which distressed the Zimmermans. As David Zimmerman said, "Bobby always went with the daughters of miners, farmers, and workers in Hibbing. He just found them a lot more interesting."[24]

Echo helped Bob survive high school, which before had been barely endurable. Constantly at war with teachers as he cultivated his James Dean "bad boy" image, he now had found a compadre in academic misery. He circulated a petition to "impeach" a teacher who crossed him, but--with Echo now in his life--he spent less time dwelling on his discontent and more time opening up to his new soul mate.

He spent a lot of time at the Helstroms' house, a shack south of town. Bob would hitchhike there after school and spend the afternoons listening to music and talking with Echo. Echo lounged on the porch swing while Bob played guitar and made up verses. He mainly sang the blues. Echo and Bob also spent time with classmate John Bucklen, whom Bob called "my main man."[25] Bob did what he wanted and ignored his parents. He was frequently on the road, hitchhiking with Echo and John. No longer would he endure a summer in exile at a Zionist camp at the behest of his parents. "His family was trying too hard to form him and he wasn't about to be formed in any manner," Echo said.[26]

High school was painful for Bob. He was not anti-intellectual, he just disapproved of the school's curriculum. He loved to read, but like others of his generation, he preferred books such as *The Catcher in the Rye* by J. D. Salinger to the usual English class fare. His discovery of John Steinbeck-- *Cannery Row* was his first experience with the author--started him on a course of reading that included *East of Eden*, to which he had first been attracted because James Dean starred in the film version. Eventually, his interest led him to *The Grapes of Wrath*, which intersected with his interest in the works of Woody Guthrie. (Guthrie wrote a song called "Tom Joad," about the protagonist of Steinbeck's novel.)

Bob began riding a motorcycle and completed his transformation from the goody-goody Echo first saw to the "cool" guy he was by the time they started dating. His restlessness moved him to include weekend trips to Minneapolis, and Echo suspected he was dating other girls downstate.

Music helped him make a connection with another young woman: Bonnie Beecher. Bonnie frequented the same Minneapolis coffeehouses as Bob and shared his affinity for the blues. As rock 'n' roll entered a creative drought--Elvis was in the army, Chuck Berry was in trouble with the law, and Little Richard was going into the ministry--this other, rawer form of music was exacting a tremendous pull on Bob. First it had been country, then rock 'n' roll, and now his absorbing interest was in the blues. Eventually, this path brought him to urban folk music.

His fascination with the blues kept Bob spinning his radio dial. Eventually, he found a black disk jockey in Virginia, Minnesota, a town even further north than Hibbing. Not content with listening to the broadcaster, whose "air name" was Jim Dandy (he was born James Reese), Bob and Echo made a pilgrimage to Virginia and visited Dandy's home, listening to his records and absorbing the whole experience of the culture. Bob heard Son House, Bukka White and Leadbelly (Huddie Ledbetter).[27] Dandy also introduced him to the music of Robert Johnson.[28] Bob visited Dandy frequently and benefited from the disk jockey's tutorials. Of all the many stages in the evolution of his music as Bob Dylan, the blues would be the one constant in his career.

However, Bob was unwilling to say goodbye to rock 'n' roll. One of his last exploits before officially leaving home for college was as a piano player in a rock 'n' roll band. Staying with relatives in Fargo, North Dakota, he joined a local boy's band. Bob had been working as a busboy and was happy to go on a small tour of the North Country with Robert Velliene, who would eventually gain fame as teen idol Bobby Vee. "He was a kind of scruffy little guy," Vee later said, "but he was really into it."[29] Bob adopted the first professional stage name of his career: Elston Gunn.

The Zimmermans held a graduation party for their son (against his wishes). Few of Bob's real friends were invited; the guests were mostly friends of his parents. It was a miserable experience for him, but it did reap one important reward. One of the graduation presents was a set of 78 rpm recordings by Leadbelly.[30] Huddie Ledbetter, known as Leadbelly, thus provided Bob with a personal history of traditional American music. Still, Bob's last months at home were rough. There was constant friction with his father, and Beatty Zimmerman had to serve as mediator, which was a frustrating task. Bob was rarely home, although occasionally Abe Zimmerman asserted his parental authority, once sending his son briefly to a school in Pennsylvania for troubled youths. Bob did not stay long. He was 18 and began to break his bonds to home.

The countdown to leaving Hibbing was agonizingly slow for Bob. He was determined to escape his father and his father's small-town view of the world. "I had to get out of there and not come back," Bob said.[31]

Restless Farewell

How much of Bob Dylan's early life is fact and how much is fantasy is something perhaps only he knows. His tales of hitchhiking, traveling with Woody Guthrie as a teenager, and being a hobo at age 13 are mostly exaggerations. However, it does appear that he went as far west as Colorado as a very young man. Biographer and friend Robert Shelton suggests that Bob made this trip before officially "leaving home" in the fall of 1959. Anthony Scaduto, the first Dylan biographer, puts the trip in the summer of 1960. Whichever the case--and Bob Dylan does not make it a habit to clarify what others write about him--he apparently performed in coffeehouses in Central City, Colorado, spending time with influential blues singer Jesse Fuller.[32] On his return to Hibbing, Bob told his parents he had been a big hit with audiences.[33] His parents had vainly hoped that going to college would rid him of his performing ambitions. The wild tales of his youthful travels, spun for gullible journalists early in his professional career, and even his new performing names may have been manufactured. His restlessness was not.

The University of Minnesota represented freedom, and when Bob Zimmerman went there in the fall of 1959, he briefly reverted to the goody-goody personality that Echo Helstrom had first observed. He toyed with the idea of joining a fraternity, Sigma Alpha Mu, and stayed at the frat house for a while during the fall semester. However, Abe Zimmerman was not eager to pay his son's fraternity fees.[34]

Fraternity brothers recall Bob Zimmerman as being antisocial, solitarily pounding the piano in the lounge at hours the brothers found inappropriate. Sometimes, his music was appreciated, and he played at a couple of fraternity dances. However, one frat member suggested that if Bob's membership had ever come to a vote, no one would have been in favor of permitting his entry.[35] Instead, the matter resolved itself; Abe Zimmerman did not have to pay any dues for his son. Bob quit after a couple of months, already feeling too "cool" for a fraternity. There was a mutual parting of the ways, but Bob usually said the fraternity brothers had kicked him out.

On his weekend visits from Hibbing, Bob had gone to the Ten O'Clock Scholar cafe in the Dinkytown section of Minneapolis which bordered the university. That was where he met Bonnie Beecher, who called the Scholar the "only beatnik cafe in the Midwest."[36] She was a student at University High School, a laboratory for the education program at Minnesota. Like

Echo, she loved the blues and connected with the North Country truant who often skipped school to hitchhike down to Minneapolis to hang out around the campus. Now, Bob was finally a legitimate student at the university. Almost immediately upon his arrival in the city, he showed up for an audition at the Scholar. The coffee shop was offering entertainment, mostly folk singers, although the singers were not paid. Owner David Lee asked Bob his name. "Bob Dylan," he said.

Dylan later claimed that the name simply came to him when Lee asked the question. However, Echo Helstrom said he had used the name tentatively a few times in Hibbing.[37] She said he had come over with a friend one day in 1958 and said, "I know what I'm going to call myself. I've got this great name--Bob Dillon."[38] Bob's fascination with the West was showing. He liked the name of the TV marshal Matt Dillon of the "Gunsmoke" program. "Dillon" was not an uncommon name in Hibbing and Bob may have preferred its rough sound to his somewhat more cumbersome name, which did not lend itself easily to show business. (Indeed, Broadway star Ethel Merman, who began life as Ethel Zimmerman, explained her name change by saying that "Zimmerman" would look ridiculous on a marquee.)[39] Bob once claimed that "Dillon" was a family name, taken from an uncle who was a Las Vegas gambler.[40] Whatever his name, Bob began attracting a lot of attention around the university and the surrounding communinity.

He made his first public performances as Bob Dylan in the Scholar during the fall of 1959. Cheered on by Bonnie Beecher and Judy Rubin (a girl he had met years before at summer camp and become reacquainted with in Minneapolis), Bob sang faithful versions of the rural blues he had learned through his listening parties at Jim Dandy's house.[41] Some suggest he was the first white performer to combine guitar with harmonica using a frame holder around his neck. He probably first saw this distinctive device in photographs of blues singer Sonny Terry, and observed it first hand in performances with Jesse Fuller during his trip to Colorado.

Dylan began extensively rewriting his history, a practice that he has carried on throughout his professional career. He may have done it in part to romanticize a rather conventional upbringing. Perhaps he did it to accentuate the material he chose to perform. He might also have done it to preserve his privacy. The last tactic appears to have worked: Bob Dylan has protected himself better than most other artists of his stature, and much about his background remained cloudy for years, affording him the opportunity to maintain a life outside the fish bowl in which most rock 'n' roll stars dwell.

Bob inhabited the student ghetto called Dinkytown, not only making connections with young women like Bonnie Beecher and Judy Rubin, but also ingratiating himself with music aficionados such as Paul Nelson and Jon Pankake, editors of the *Little Sandy Review*, and a married couple, Dave and Gretel Whitaker. "Dave was an intellectual," Beecher said, "and we were all very impressed that he was an intellectual."[42] Dave Whitaker said he taught Bob to read for himself and excited him about the arts.[43] These older enthusiasts provided Bob with an education in music, and they watched him grow with every performance, perfecting his style with each new addition to his repertoire. A friend compared him to blotting paper.[44] Bob was gorging himself on experience, sponging up stories from his new friends, digesting what he needed and expelling the rest.

He began writing songs. A too-short haircut, administered at the hands of Bonnie Beecher, became the fodder for a song: "Why'd You Cut My Hair?"[45] Some friends recall hearing an early version of "Song to Woody" during his Minneapolis party performances. Often, he reworked traditional songs with his own lyrics. And one of the staples of his repertoire was the work of Woody Guthrie. Dylan's discovery of Woody Guthrie was a central moment in his life. He knew of Guthrie and had heard the songs, but reading the singer's autobiography affected Bob deeply. Dave Whitaker had urged him to read Guthrie's *Bound for Glory* and Bob sat for hours in the Ten O'Clock Scholar, reading and rereading the story of Guthrie's experiences on the road.[46] Dylan's stories of life as a wandering minstrel began to evolve. He even claimed he was from Oklahoma, like Guthrie.[47]

Bob first mimicked Guthrie, and then he nearly became him, all as part of the process of artistic reinvention. He was good at it. Other performers who had befriended the kid came to resent him because he surpassed them on stage, earning fierce praise. When guitarist Rolf Cahn, an actual recording artist, came to town and heaped compliments on Bob, calling him "the most talented guy around," the jealousies were enhanced.[48] The fascination with Guthrie increased. Bob and his friends learned that Guthrie was hospitalized and tried to call him, getting as far as the doctor on Guthrie's ward. The singer was too ill to come to the phone, but Bob vowed that night to make a pilgrimage to see his hero.[49]

From the moment that Whitaker introduced Bob Zimmerman to Woody Guthrie, Zimmerman was, in a real sense, dead. Bob Dylan was now in ascendancy. It also meant that his days in Minneapolis were numbered and his formal education was over. Bob now saw himself as a student in a larger classroom. He hit the road for New York, to find Woody Guthrie. "I stood on the highway during a blizzard snowstorm believing in the mercy of the world," Dylan said. "I didn't have nothing but my guitar and suitcase."[50]

Hard Times in New York Town

He took a circuitous route, stopping (and mooching) off acquaintances in Madison, Wisconsin, and Chicago. To these new crowds, he spun stories about his friendship with Guthrie and his adventures on the road as a hobo. He talked as if he had been on the road for a decade, yet his boyish face betrayed his youth as Bob Zimmerman.

Bob Dylan arrived in New York City in December 1960 and began hanging out in Greenwich Village the following February. He claimed to have spent the intervening months as a Times Square hustler, working with a partner and making $250 a night.[51] He told Shelton he lived this way for two months before taking the subway down to the Village, where he was received as an endearing orphan in need of nurturing. As the Dinkytown crowd had adopted him, so did another coterie of friends in the Village's art and music community. Other biographers, including Clinton Heylin, entirely discount the hustling story and suggest that Dylan went directly to the Village upon his arrival on Manhattan Island on January 24, 1961.[52]

Guthrie was not in New York but rather was a patient at Greystone Hospital near Morristown, New Jersey, where he was slowly dying from Huntington's chorea. Dylan became a regular visitor, singing the old man his songs: "This Land Is Your Land," "Rambling Round," "Pastures of Plenty" and others. Guthrie smiled to show his appreciation; speaking was painful for him.

Two Guthrie fans, Bob and Sidsel Gleason, checked Guthrie out of the hospital on Sundays for afternoon socials at their home. Soon Dylan was a regular at these gatherings, working his way into another crowd and exciting the nurturing spirit in these older music fans. Through the Sunday parties, he began to rapidly make a number of friends in the folk music community, including Pete Seeger, Ramblin' Jack Elliott (who lived with Guthrie's family), Odetta and other performers.

Guthrie loved Dylan's attention and looked forward to his visits, asking the Gleasons--upon arrival on Sunday afternoons--if "the boy" was going to show up. "That boy's got a voice," Guthrie said once. "Maybe he won't make it with his writing, but he can sing it."[53] Dylan also made friends in the Guthrie household. Dylan hitchhiked to Queens and finagled his way inside the Guthrie home, teaching young Arlo Guthrie how to play the harmonica his way.[54] He visited Woody's hospital bed frequently, and the older man appreciated the attention and the music. At one of the Sunday afternoons with the Gleasons, Dylan riveted the attention of the audience by playing Guthrie a song he had written, "Song to Woody." It was a paean, a note of thanks to an idol, and a sharing of experience. It was also courageous. To one of America's greatest songwriters, Dylan was proclaiming that he, too, could write songs. "That's good, Bob," Guthrie croaked. "Damn good." After all the other guests had left, Guthrie told the Gleasons, "Pete Seeger's a singer of folk songs, not a folk singer. Jack Elliot is a singer of folk songs, not a folk singer. But Bobby Dylan is a folk singer. Oh, Christ, he's a folk singer all right."[55]

Dylan sponged off the Gleasons and a host of acquaintances in the Village and performed at the various music clubs: Cafe Wha?, the Bitter End, and Gerde's Folk City. Mike Porco, the Folk City proprietor, signed Dylan to share the bill with bluesman John Lee Hooker. Dylan was paid for performing; it was his first genuine job. Since Dylan was under 21, Porco signed the musicians union papers as Dylan's guardian.[56] Porco even tried to groom Dylan, offering him a comb for his tangled locks. However, Dylan responded that he had so many thoughts inside his head that the hair came shooting out of that crowded space.

Dylan began attracting a lot of attention. Robert Shelton of the *New York Times* recalled an early Dylan performance:

> He was only 19 then, looking, with his thin, pale face, as if parts of a choir boy and parts of a beatnik had gone astray in one of the tunnels from Jersey and been hastily reassembled before the Manhattan exit .... In the Village clubs, Dylan touched the audience occasionally with his bluesy songs and his emerging poetic statements, but mostly he made them laugh. He had a curious set of Charlie Chaplin tramp mannerisms that were irresistible. His shamble would send him way past the target of the microphone and there was a lot of stage business with his hat, his hair, his harmonica.[57]

Dylan quickly sought a recording contract. He approached Folkways Records, the most-respected company recording folk artists. However, he was turned away with little consideration, which left him angered and bitter.

Ramblin' Jack Elliott and another singer, the physically intimidating Dave Van Ronk, schooled Dylan further in folk music. Elliott had been performing Guthrie's music for so long that he was almost more like Guthrie than Guthrie himself. Van Ronk took over the Dave Whitaker role in Dylan's life, tutoring the younger man on poetry, introducing him to the works of Francois Villon, Guillaume Appollinaire and Arthur Rimbaud, whose ideas would resonate through Dylan's music for decades.[58]

One of the other musicians Dylan met was John Hammond, Jr. Hammond was following in a family tradition, exploring the blues and performing in clubs throughout the Village. He heard Dylan sing on several occasions and was impressed enough to tell his father. His father, John Hammond, was a legend in the music business. In 1961, he was the director of talent acquisition for Columbia Records, a position he had earned through his "discovery" of such legendary singers as Billie Holliday and Bessie Smith. He also played a vital role in the careers of Benny Goodman, Teddy Wilson, Count Basie and other jazz greats. As a producer and talent scout, Hammond was part of the history of blues, jazz and folk music.

Hammond had heard about Dylan from his son by the time he was producing a recording session for folk singer Carolyn Hester. Hester had booked her friend Dylan to play harmonica on the record. (It was his second such recording as a side man; earlier, in June 1961, Dylan had played harmonica on Harry Belafonte's "Midnight Special.") Hester's album was a sign that Columbia, one of the world's largest and most prestigious record companies, was interested in folk music. The genre had formerly been confined to smaller, esoteric labels. Now, even the industry giants were becoming concerned with tapping the audience for the boom in folk music.

Dylan met John Hammond on September 14, 1961, at Columbia Studios in New York, during a rehearsal for Hester's album.[59] He next saw him on September 29, the day the *New York Times* had printed a review of Dylan's performance at Folk City. The piece, by Robert Shelton (later to become one of Dylan's biographers), heralded the young singer as a "bright new face in folk music ... literally bursting at the seams with talent."[60] Naturally, Dylan had a copy of the review in his back pocket, which he presented to Hammond.[61]

Hester was a little upset by Hammond's obvious interest in Dylan. The session proceeded, with Hammond pulling Dylan aside and suggesting he show up at his office to discuss his musical future.[62] Something about Dylan impressed Hammond enough to make some demonstration recordings with the young man. Hammond did not think highly of Dylan's musicianship, considering him only passable on guitar and harmonica, but he liked Dylan's approach, his view of the world, and his anger. Bob's rebellious attitude was something that Hammond wanted to record.[63] Soon, Hammond offered Bob Dylan a deal with Columbia Records. When Hammond presented Dylan with the contract, he asked that Dylan get his parents to cosign since he was only 20. "I don't have any parents," Dylan said. Hammond went ahead and secured the deal.[64] Dylan's version of the story suggested that Hammond signed him before the recorded audition, and that version was perpetuated by some of the Dylan biographies. However, Hammond said that the offer was not made until after the demos were cut. Whatever the case, signing with Columbia thrilled Dylan:

> I couldn't believe it. I left there and I remember walking out of the studio. I was like on a cloud. It was up on 7th Avenue and when I left I was happening to be walking by a record store. It was one of the most thrilling moments of my life. I couldn't believe that I was staring at all the records in the window, Frankie Laine, Frank Sinatra, Patty Page, Mitch Miller, Tony Bennett and so on and soon I, myself, would be among them in the window. I guess I was pretty naive.... I wanted to go in there dressed in the rags like I was and tell the owner, "You don't know me now, but you will."[65]

After the signing of the contract but before his debut album was recorded, Dylan performed his first major New York concert. The Folklore Center presented Dylan at Carnegie Chapter Hall on November 4, 1961.

Fifty-three people (most of them friends) paid $2 to hear [...] tion of Guthrie tunes and traditionals and perform his c[...] tween songs.[66]

Dylan on stage could be quite funny. Early critics often cited [...] of his body as an instrument of comedy. His was a spontaneous sar[...] humor, which endeared him to audiences. A fellow performer said Dylan's "flair for the comic gesture" helped form his stage personality. "It is not a contrived, play-acted personality," said singer Gil Turner. "One gets the impression that his talk and storytelling on stage are things that just come into his head that he thought you might be interested in."[67]

Changing of the Guards

Hammond recorded Dylan's first album in two sessions, on November 20 and 22, 1961. Only two originals were performed, "Song to Woody" and a Guthriesque talking blues about Dylan's early days in the city, "Talkin' New York." The rest of the material was blues with a few folk touches, such as "Man of Constant Sorrow," which he had heard as "Maid of Constant Sorrow," performed by Judy Collins, during his trip to Colorado. This was typical of Dylan's repertoire. He did few originals in his 1961 performances, relying instead on Guthrie material and folk and blues standards. Occasionally, in the middle of a 25-song performance, he would introduce an original, such as "The Story of East Orange, New Jersey," "Man on the Street" or "Talkin' Bear Mountain Picnic Massacre Blues."

By early 1962, as he impatiently awaited the release of his album, he adapted his performances to include more new songs: "Ballad of Donald White," "Rambling, Gambling Willie," "Poor Boy Blues" and "Ballad for a Friend." Many of these, of course, were adaptations of traditional tunes with new lyrics. It was standard practice within the folk music community to borrow a tune in homage. So quickly was he writing that by the time *Bob Dylan* was released on March 19, 1962, he had already grown far beyond that record. He no longer even resembled the errant choir boy on the cover. Dylan stared from the album confidently, like a child posing as a tough guy. The contents of the record, like the photograph, were merely a representation of what Dylan had *been* when the record was made. Before the album hit the stores, however, he had begun furiously writing original material.

A song about a human being's dignity in the face of an imminent nuclear holocaust, "Let Me Die in My Footsteps," had already been written by the time the first album was released. (The song was sometimes performed under the title "I Will Not Go Down under the Ground.") He also wrote "Blowin' in the Wind" during this period.

The album earned polite reviews but sold few copies. Behind the celebrated producer's back, other Columbia Records officials called Dylan "Hammond's Folly." Disappointed but relatively unfazed by the poor sales, Dylan continued to make an impression in New York, performing three powerful new songs on "The Broadside Show" on WBAI-FM radio. He had sung "Ballad of Donald White" before. However, his specific finger-pointing song, "The Death of Emmett Till," and the more encompassing "Blowin' in the Wind," were given their first wide exposure during the May 1962 broadcast.

Between the release of his first album in March 1962 and his brilliant second album, *The Freewheelin' Bob Dylan*, in May 1963, Dylan became a fixture in Greenwich Village, playing at the usual assortment of pubs and coffeehouses. Recordings of performances at the Gaslight Cafe exist and have circulated among collectors for years, later becoming available as bootlegged recordings. Perhaps his most important show was his Town Hall concert of April 12, 1963, a month before the second album's release. The album had been largely recorded the previous summer and fall, with four new songs cut in the spring of 1963. However, his Town Hall show included only two songs from the imminent album.[68] He was writing songs faster than he could get around to recording them.

He recorded demos of his songs for his music publisher, M. Witmark and Sons, a division of Warner Bros. Inc. These were made primarily so that the songs could be transcribed for sheet music and made available for recording by other artists. Dylan never released official versions of these songs, so they also circulated on unauthorized recordings for years until he began issuing his own bootlegs in order that he, rather than the bootleggers, would profit from his work. A performance at Montreal's Finjan Club was also recorded, circulated, and later bootlegged. However, the trip to Montreal was rare. Most of Dylan's performances from 1961-1963 were in New York City, though he also ventured to Rutgers, New Jersey, and Saratoga Springs, New York.[69] He generally kept within the environs of Greenwich Village, still sleeping on couches and staying with friends.

Dylan returned to Minneapolis for a concert in August 1962 and strolled through the University of Minnesota campus. At the Sigma Alpha Mu house, there was a sign over the front door that read "Bob Dylan: Our Alumni Makes Good." Bonnie Beecher said Dylan was furious because they had kicked him out and, now that he was becoming famous, wanted to take credit for him.[70] The trip back to Minneapolis had convinced him that his long-distance relationship with Bonnie was doomed. Dylan returned to New York where he met Suze Rotolo, a 17-year-old from the Village who inspired several of his most beautiful and desperate love songs. Dylan virtually exploded with songs in 1962, and Suze was responsible for many of them.

Dylan was staying with a woman named Miki Isaacson, whom Shelton described as a "folk den mother," since she often housed Dylan, Jean Redpath and Ramblin' Jack Elliott, when he was not at the Guthrie home. The musicians played songs all night, sleeping on air mattresses in Isaacson's living room. Suze Rotolo, with her mother and sister, lived in the same apartment building.[71] Suze became a soul mate, as Echo and Bonnie had been, and she learned how diverse were Dylan's interests. Though he was still in his "folkie" period, Dylan and Suze listened to a lot of rock 'n' roll when they were alone together, and she was aware that his interests went well beyond the constricting arena of the folk music community.[72]

Early in the relationship, Dylan endured a long separation from Suze, as she bowed to the wishes of her mother and stepfather and went to Italy to study art. The anxiety was reflected in one of his reworkings of a blues song, "Down the Highway," which showed up on *The Freewheelin' Bob Dylan*. The summer of separation was productive for Dylan as a songwriter. The previous winter, a new magazine of folk music, *Broadside*, had debuted with a Dylan parody, "Talkin' John Birch Paranoid Blues." The sixth issue of the mimeographed publication featured the lyrics to "Blowin' in the Wind" on the cover. No less an authority than Pete Seeger, who had become America's preeminent folk singer in the wake of Guthrie's illness, embraced Dylan as a brilliant talent. Seeger believed Dylan's topical songs were the best of the genre since the era of Guthrie at his greatest. Soon, Seeger began performing the tunes himself.

The *Broadside* contributors met, shared notes and songs, and performed. During these meetings in 1962 and early 1963, Dylan presented a number of striking songs, including "Masters of War," "Blowin' in the Wind," "A Hard Rain's A-Gonna Fall" and "With God on Our Side." Seeger, who was signed to Columbia Records, began to include these songs in his performances and publicly hailed Dylan as the most important songwriter of the time.[73]

He was not going unnoticed, despite the nonsuccess of his first album. Obviously, he needed a professional manager and Hammond was quick to suggest Harold Leventhal, whose ties to Guthrie were strong and who also managed Seeger and Judy Collins. He seemed like a natural choice. However, a comment by Noel Stookey--who became the "Paul" of Peter, Paul and Mary--also made Albert Grossman take notice of Dylan. Grossman managed Odetta and Peter, Paul and Mary. He seemed to be interested in managing big-money acts (at least, that was the impression he gave Dylan), but still, after Stookey's recommendation, Grossman attended one of Dylan's coffeehouse shows and conveyed a genuine interest in the young man and his music. Eventually, after the release of the first album, Grossman offered his services, vowing to take care of all the business aspects of Dylan's career and allowing him to concentrate on songwriting and performing. It was time for Dylan to move away from the coffeehouses, Grossman told him, and begin to consider himself a concert performer.[74]

Grossman became the bad guy, refusing gigs he thought unworthy of Dylan, insulating the performer from promoters and taking the blame for any faux pas, whether it was his fault or not. Grossman believed in protecting his artists. His role in Dylan's career was large but Grossman rarely exaggerated his part. "He would have made it without anyone," he said of Dylan.[75]

Bob Dylan's Dream

It was Grossman who secured the music publishing deal with M. Witmark and Sons, a prestigious older company that had recently been brought under the Warner Bros. aegis. It was Grossman who began making the business decisions that allowed Dylan to maintain his artistic mystique. Grossman kept his promise, managing Dylan's business affairs and allowing the artist to concentrate on nurturing his talent and getting his life in order. Dylan even settled into an apartment of his own, on West Fourth Street in the Village.

Thus, the young man's dream of becoming a star was realized, thanks to Grossman, a large man who was known in music circles as the Bear. As an example of Grossman's contributions, Dylan felt a gulf between himself and John Hammond, but rather than broach the subject, he had Grossman handle the affair. As a result, before the second album was completed, Dylan had a new producer. Grossman was upset by the Columbia contract. After examining it, he learned that Dylan earned more money when other artists recorded his songs rather than when he released his original versions. Grossman wanted to get Dylan out of the Columbia deal, which was ironic considering that Dylan's first album sold poorly and that Dylan had little assurance his talents would be employed elsewhere. The royalty rate also displeased Grossman, so he brought up to the Columbia lawyers the fact that Dylan was underage when he signed the contract, thereby rendering it invalid. However, by that time Dylan was 21, so it was a moot point.

The second album was a long time in coming, but certainly not because Dylan faced any form of writer's block. Dylan spewed out songs, but the disaffection with Hammond had made it difficult for him to record. Eventually, Hammond backed down voluntarily and urged Tom Wilson, another Columbia staff producer, to take over the Dylan album. Wilson, who was the record label's only black producer, was a tremendous fan of Dylan and the relationship worked--for a while.

At his second-to-last session with Hammond, on November 14, 1962, Dylan recorded an original tune called "Mixed Up Confusion," which was released as a single. The song and its flip side, the traditional "Corrina, Corrina," featured rock 'n' roll backing: electric guitars, bass, drums and piano. Musically reminiscent of Elvis Presley's recording of "Mystery Train," the song indulged in classic Dylan wordplay. He recorded several other songs that day, some of which turned up on promotional copies of *The Freewheelin' Bob Dylan* in 1963. These sessions demonstrate that Dylan's move into rock 'n' roll in 1965 had an antecedent.

Dylan recorded with Hammond again in December but did not finish his second album until late April, in his first work with Tom Wilson. In one day, they recorded "Girl from the North Country," "Masters of War," "Bob Dylan's Dream," "Talkin' World War III Blues" and "Walls of Red Wing." Pleased with the results, Dylan and Grossman pronounced the album completed, and it was released in late May, with Hammond credited as the sole producer. Unlike the first album, virtually all the songs were originals. (The exceptions were his rearrangement of "Corrina, Corrina" and a reworking of Henry Thomas's "Honey, Just Allow Me One More Chance," which is sometimes credited to Dylan/Thomas, in an interesting juxtaposition of names.)

Suze was with him on the cover, slogging through the winter slush of Greenwich Village, and this album truly announced Dylan's arrival in the music world. Of his first album he told the *New York Mirror*, "That's not me. There was only a couple of my stories on it." Now, however, he told the reporter, he needed to tell his own stories. "Because Dickens and Dostoyevski and Woody Guthrie were telling their stories much better than I ever could, I decided to stick to my own mind."[76]

Peter, Paul and Mary's hit version of "Blowin' in the Wind" helped spur interest in *The Freewheelin' Bob Dylan* and that, of course, jump-started sales on Dylan's second record. Controversy also aided the album. Dylan was to perform on "The Ed Sullivan Show" on May 12, a premier spot for any entertainer but particularly for a young artist such as Dylan. The Sunday night CBS program was a staple of American broadcasting for years, offering viewers a miscellany of dancing bears, Borscht Belt comedians, vaudevillians gone to seed and rock 'n' roll stars. Sullivan's show boosted the careers of Elvis Presley, The Beatles and The Rolling Stones.

It was not Dylan's first encounter with Ed Sullivan. The previous year, after an advance copy of the first album had been circulated, a talent agent arranged for Dylan to audition for Sullivan's show. Dylan did not like the idea but acquiesced when Hammond urged him to do so. Dylan sang "Man of Constant Sorrow," "Pretty Peggy-O," "Song to Woody" and a few others. The representatives of the Sullivan show (the host was not present) were visibly unimpressed, and the experience gnawed at Dylan. He snarled at the talent agent and, back in the safety of Greenwich Village, angrily denounced the experience. "I'm not going up there again," Dylan told a friend. The friend cautioned, "They'll call you. Just wait."[77]

Finally, "The Ed Sullivan Show" had called. No audition was required this time. Dylan was to appear on the same broadcast with Irving Berlin, puppet Topo Gigio and comedian Myron Cohen. At a mid-week runthrough, Dylan had performed "Talkin' John Birch Paranoid Blues" for Sullivan and a producer, and both had approved of the song. However, during the afternoon dress rehearsal for the live broadcast on Sunday night, a CBS censor told Sullivan and the producer that the song could not be used as it could offend members of the John Birch Society who might, in turn, sue CBS. Sullivan was annoyed but wanted the show to go on live at eight o'clock as scheduled. He asked Grossman and Dylan to substitute another song. The stories differ on what happened next. Two writers claim that Dylan calmly told Sullivan that if he could not sing "Talkin' John Birch Paranoid Blues," he would not appear on the show, while another account has Dylan screaming "Bullshit!" at the censor and stalking from the studio.[78]

The newspapers jumped on the story and Ed Sullivan, a former columnist, was eager to talk. Any publicity was good publicity for his show. While not portraying himself as a selfless proponent of free speech, he did tell reporters that he had fought for the song and was deeply disappointed by the CBS decision.

The incident also affected the album, which had been scheduled for imminent release. "Talkin' John Birch Paranoid Blues" was on it. Columbia Records was a subsidiary of CBS Inc. and the news of the song's notorious reputation wafted through the executive suites. Then an order came down: Remove the song from the album. All the stories agree on this point: Dylan was incensed by the decision. The record company told him that any member of the John Birch Society could sue for libel since Dylan's song compared its members to Nazis. Dylan demanded to see the record company's legal affairs adviser, a 31-year-old attorney named Clive Davis, who was later to become president of Columbia Records. "What *is* this?" Dylan demanded of Davis. "What do you *mean* I can't come out with this song? You can't edit or censor me." Davis, who believed Dylan's song to be brilliant satire, still had to speak the company line. "God, I hate to do this," he told the singer, but it was a simple legal issue. "It's all bullshit," Dylan screamed, and stalked from the office.[79]

The song was deleted from the album when it was released two weeks later, though extremely rare early copies contained the Birch song as well as four others that were deleted. (These were cut not by censors, but by Dylan.) Of the original album, he said, "There's too many old-fashioned songs in there, stuff I tried to write like Woody. I'm going through changes. Need some more finger-pointin' songs in it, 'cause that's where my head's at right now."[80] The finger-pointing songs were perfectly married to the times. The so-called folk-protest movement, of which Dylan was becoming a part, allied with the civil rights movement in that era, and Bob Dylan's music became a significant part of that social revolution.

The civil rights movement may have begun with the integration of Major League Baseball. In 1947, baseball became the first American institution to disavow segregation when black athlete Jackie Robinson was signed to play for the Brooklyn Dodgers. Soon, President Harry Truman began pushing for the integration of the armed forces, which finally occurred in the early 1950s. In 1954, the United States Supreme Court ruled that the "separate-but-equal" schools that an earlier group of justices had declared fit and proper for children were no longer appropriate. Separate schools for blacks were inherently unequal, the court ruled, and so the long process of school integration was begun.

However, it was an event the following year, on December 1, 1955, that gave the civil rights movement its focus and its hero. Rosa Parks, a black seamstress in Montgomery, Alabama, was arrested for violating that city's busing segregation ordinance: She had refused to give up her seat to a white passenger. This incensed the black community and an organization called the Montgomery Improvement Association was formed to stage a boycott of the city's buses. Martin Luther King, Jr., a 26-year-old minister, was elected president of the group. Putting to use the principles of civil disobedience as espoused by Henry David Thoreau, and the tactics of Mahatma Gandhi, King staged a yearlong economic boycott of the city's public transportation. Eventually, the city caved in and the busing segregation ordinance was thrown out.

That victory showed how King's nonviolent strategy could work. The Montgomery Improvement Association gave birth to the Southern Christian Leadership Conference and King (as well as hundreds of others who never gained his level of celebrity) staged a series of demonstrations and events that resulted in nonviolent demonstrators being met with violence by the white power structure.

Perhaps the seminal moment of King's involvement in the civil rights movement occurred in Birmingham, Alabama, in the spring of 1963, around the time that Dylan was becoming well known because of his second album. King recruited schoolchildren to march in demonstrations protesting the city's racial policies. The children were met by police attack dogs and the fire department's water hoses, which sprayed the young marchers with a force of 100 pounds of pressure per square inch. Television cameras from the three networks recorded the event and put a face on the concept of racism. The face was that of Theopolis Eugene Connor (generally known as Bull Connor), the city's police commissioner. Driving through the streets of Birmingham in a white tank, he ordered the dogs unleashed and the hoses turned on.

Dylan was not the only white musician to become active in the civil rights movement. While he was still back in Minneapolis, a number of white entertainers had joined other celebrities to sponsor an ad in the *New York Times* soliciting funds for Martin Luther King and the Southern Christian Leadership Conference. Peter, Paul and Mary were among the most visible performers participating in the movement. Pete Seeger was also a fixture at such demonstrations, as was Joan Baez, whose whole career has been dedicated to activism. There were many others as well.

Dylan, however, emerged in the summer of 1963 at the forefront of activist artists. His songs were topical and therefore reflected the nation's struggle to guarantee rights to all its citizens. One of his early songs, "The Death of Emmett Till," told the story of a 15-year-old black youth from Chicago who was murdered during a visit to Mississippi for whistling at a white girl. That murder, in 1955, had attracted national attention, and Dylan summarized the facts of the case accurately and succinctly in his song. "Oxford Town," which had appeared on *Freewheelin'*, was another news account, this time of the furor that occurred when black student James Meredith enrolled at the all-white University of Mississippi in September 1962. "Blowin' in the Wind," his series of questions about the nature of justice and truth, was not overtly about the movement; it made no specific references. However, it, too, was a finger-pointing song in the sense that it asked the questions and implied that the answers were easily apparent.

He did not drop these themes after the release of *Freewheelin'*. He appeared at a voter registration rally on July 6, 1963, near Greenwood, Mississippi. Standing in the yard of black farmer Silas Magee, Dylan, Seeger, Theodore Bikel and the Freedom Singers entertained an audience of 300 people, mostly blacks, and three car loads of white men who watched the front-yard concert from a distance. Seeger had brought Dylan to Greenwood to allow him to see, up close, the struggle about which he had been writing. It was Dylan's first trip to the South.[81] Dylan, who was obviously nervous and distracted, debuted another topical song. "Only a Pawn in Their Game" was about Medgar Evers, a civil rights activist in Greenwood who had been murdered the month before. Evers was state field secretary for the Mississippi chapter of the National Association for the Advancement of Colored People (NAACP). Returning home one night, he was shot as he opened his front door. A Greenwood man, Brian de La Beckwith, was indicted in the shooting. Strangely, however, Dylan's song offered Beckwith--whom he did not identify by name--some sympathy. "Only a Pawn in Their Game" concludes that the assassin was also a victim, harmed by a system that teaches hate. That approach made it an unusual song and its immediacy heightened its effect.[82] (Incidentally, a *New York Times* story about the event referred to the singer as "Bobby Dillon.")

Dylan performed "Only a Pawn in Their Game" frequently that summer while joining Joan Baez onstage during her concerts. Baez became something of a benefactor for Dylan, sharing him with her large audience. She was an extremely popular entertainer, the reigning queen of folk music, and drew large crowds in concert arenas. She had met Dylan two years before in Folk City but found him uninteresting, and when Baez met him again, Dylan paid little attention to her and instead focused his energies on her sister, singer Mimi Farina. However, when Baez heard *Freewheelin'*, she was impressed by Dylan's writing. She heard him at a club and thought him an enaging performer. Their paths crossed again in early summer, at the Monterey (California) Folk Festival, in the heart of the land about which Dylan had read so much in Steinbeck's novels.[83] Baez then invited him to her home in Carmel, California, where he ended up spending a couple of weeks.

Dylan had other obligations and could not enjoy a long California idyll. Along with Suze Rotolo, her sister and her mother, he attended a Columbia Records convention in Puerto Rico. He performed "With God on Our Side," his desperate antiwar plea, leading the sales representatives in the audience to wonder how they would be able to sell copies of such a depressing song.[84] Nonetheless, Dylan got the attention of company president Goddard Lieberson, who began to let him feel that his record company appreciated him and his talent.

In late July 1963, Dylan showed up at the Newport Folk Festival, where Baez had hoped to spend time with him. However, he brought along Suze Rotolo, which scotched Baez's plan. He did share the stage with Baez, duetting on "With God on Our Side," and after Newport, they embarked on a brief tour together. Dylan was an unbilled guest, and reactions were mixed when Baez introduced him midway through the shows. "I was getting audiences of up to ten thousand at that point," she said, "and dragging my little vagabond out onto the stage was a grand experiment."[85] The experiment was largely successful, and Dylan's stock as a performer was boosted by their concerts. Their joint tour culminated with their appearance in Washington, D.C., as part of the massive civil rights march on August 28, 1963. The celebrated March on Washington included a number of speakers and performers but is, of course, most remembered for King's "I have a dream" speech.

The artists who performed before the 200,000 people at the Lincoln Memorial comprised a virtual *Who's Who* of folk music: Odetta, Seeger, Baez, and Peter, Paul and Mary. Dylan, who was still perceived as a newcomer, made his presence known. Peter, Paul and Mary had had an enormous hit with "Blowin' in the Wind," and they asked the composer to sing it with them. He also sang "Only a Pawn in Their Game" and joined in on the choruses of "We Shall Overcome" and "Keep Your Eyes on the Prize." It was an impressive sight--the thousands of people around the reflecting pool, the speeches, the music. Nonetheless, Dylan wondered aloud to a friend what effect it would have on America, on the millions watching the event on television. "Think they're listening?" he asked, nodding toward the dome of the Capitol in the distance. "No, they ain't listening at all."[86]

When the Ship Comes In

Dylan had arrived. *The Freewheelin' Bob Dylan* was on the charts and he was being recognized as a unique voice in popular music. The concerts with Baez had broadened his base and he gained recognition as an activist for his Mississippi trip. Finally, the summer had been capped by his triumphant appearance at the March on Washington. He was a star: a star unlike any other, but a star nonetheless.

As the fall of 1963 began, Dylan was busy professionally (recording material for a new album, performing at Carnegie Hall) and personally (repairing his relationship with Suze Rotolo on the East Coast, and getting to know Joan Baez at her home on the West Coast).

Dylan flew Abe and Beatty to New York for the Carnegie Hall show. "We knew he was gifted when we went to Carnegie Hall," Beatty said. "We flew in for the concert and we stayed for a few days and we knew that he was enjoying what he was doing and that was important to us."[87] To friends, Dylan did not denounce his parents or insist that he was an orphan.

Nonetheless, he was angry when *Newsweek* revealed that he was from a middle-class background and that much of his performing mystique was based on falsehood.[88] Aside from poking holes in his carefully constructed public persona, the article made some claims that infuriated Dylan. It was on the streets within days of the Carnegie Hall triumph and included an implication that Dylan did not write "Blowin' in the Wind." (The article suggested Dylan had purchased the song from a high school student. The student, Lorre Wyatt, eventually repudiated the story.)

The experience left Dylan wary of journalists for the rest of his career. Months later, while speaking to Chris Welles of *Life*, he said, "Why did they do that? Man, they're out to kill me. What've they got against me?"[89] Robert Shelton came to Dylan's defense, writing *Newsweek* editor Osborn Elliott and accusing the magazine of doing a hatchet job on the young singer.[90] Grossman made some noises about libel for the "Blowin' in the Wind" charge, but he never sued the magazine. This outcome further goaded Dylan to adopt a sardonic attitude toward the press, impaling reporters with his sarcastic wit.

Dylan began moving away from political music, perhaps in reaction to the *Newsweek* article, which typed him as a seriocomic folk singer. Perhaps the drift began as a reaction to the assassination of President John F. Kennedy in November, as he saw a progressive leader slain. Perhaps it came about because of his disastrous confrontation with the old guard of liberalism at an awards ceremony in New York that December. Dylan was to end his breakthrough year, 1963, with an honor and yet he ended up causing a furor. A long-standing liberal group called the Emergency Civil Liberties Committee gave him its Tom Paine Award at a ceremony on December 13. Arriving at the dinner, Dylan saw only bald, fat men in the audience. He began to drink heavily, wondering what he had gotten himself into. He did not realize these were true civil libertarians, many of whom had paid a dear price for speaking up on behalf of personal freedom. A great number in the audience had been blacklisted and denied work, but Dylan thought they were all rich, hypocritical liberals, and so he filled his acceptance speech with venom. He was greeted with boos for his insulting remarks. Only later did he realize his error.[91]

Making albums was easier than making speeches--or so he thought. However, working with his new producer, Tom Wilson, proved nearly as frustrating as working with Hammond. Both producers were great technicians and vital in the recording of blues and jazz music, but neither Dylan nor Grossman believed they understood their young charge. Some songs were recorded in August, and more were cut in October. Together, these sessions would form the bulk of Dylan's third album. The Carnegie Hall concert, which was held in the main auditorium, rather than the Chapter Hall, was a triumph. There was significant new material; it was not just another concert performance of *Freewheelin'*. However, most of the new songs were not to appear on Dylan's next album.

The concert was recorded and, along with several songs from his Dylan's Town Hall concert in April, the tracks were arranged for a live album. Acetates for *Bob Dylan in Concert* were pressed and circulated in an album jacket that showed Bob looking like a hillbilly and standing resolutely on stage, alone. Although it was catalogued and scheduled for release, the album never hit the stores. There were eight songs and a long prose poem called "Last Thoughts on Woody Guthrie," none of which would appear on a Dylan album for nearly 30 years. Dylan scholars assume the album was scrapped because by the time it was ready for release, it had become ancient history.[92]

The new album, which he recorded in the fall, was finally released in January 1964. The cover of *The Times They Are A-Changin'* showed a staunchly proletariat Dylan, jaws clenched, who appeared caught in contemplation. Dylan was so bursting with words that he included a sheaf of poems titled "11 Outlined Epitaphs." It began on the album's back cover and continued as an insert. (When the album was released on compact disc in 1989, this clumsy method of packaging, which threatened the continuity of the poem cycle, was solved by adapting the work to the CD's booklet format.)

These unusual album notes set the tone for the record even before it was played. The songs matched the solemn cover photograph. The title song conveyed anger and impatience with an older generation that had not done well by civilization, but at least Dylan *politely* asked his elders to step aside for the young. He also recorded "Only a Pawn in Their Game" and the antiwar ballad, "With God on Our Side." Once again, a news story inspired one of Dylan's songs, "The Lonesome Death of Hattie Carroll," which concerns the killing of a black woman by a young member of the white aristocracy. Listening to the album just prior to its release, Dylan said of "Hattie Carroll," "That's the one, that's the song I really like."[93] Other songs dealt with the devastation of a mining town ("North Country Blues"), a farm family slowly starving to death ("Ballad of Hollis Brown") and musical description of the hope that lies couched in the spirit of the Book of Revelation, "When the

Ship Comes In." This song spoke of the eventual triumph of the just over the unjust, at a time when "the whole wide world" would be watching. It was a chant picked up on the streets of Chicago four years later, as police clashed with antiwar demonstrators outside the Democratic National Convention, a riot broadcast into millions of American homes. Dylan had given the movement its slogan: "The whole world is watching."

A couple of his antilove love songs ("One Too Many Mornings" and "Boots of Spanish Leather") filled out the album. The final song, "Restless Farewell," seems, in retrospect, to indicate that Dylan was tiring of his identity as a protest singer. Dylan was changing, but it took some of his followers more than a year to notice. The outpouring of songs continued unabated, but few were political in tone. Instead, he was concentrating on his intricate love songs almost completely.

He took a long car trip with road manager Victor Maimudes, singer Paul Clayton and writer Pete Karman. They visited Kentucky coal mines and made it to New Orleans in time for Mardi Gras. There was a brief, uneventful meeting with the poet Carl Sandburg in North Carolina. Dylan performed in Atlanta, Jackson, Denver and Berkeley, thus singing his way across the country. Something happened out West. Dylan was driving through the mountains in Colorado when he heard The Beatles over the car radio singing "I Want to Hold Your Hand." Dylan began pounding on the car's dash, slapping his hand in time to the beat. It was a revelation and it pointed him back to rock 'n' roll. "They were doing things nobody was doing," he said of The Beatles. "Their chords were outrageous, just outrageous, and their harmonies made it all valid."[94] It made Bob Dylan want a band.

Notes

1. John Ford, *The Man Who Shot Liberty Valance* (1962); quoted in Joseph McBride and Michael Wilmington, *John Ford* (New York: DaCapo Press, 1975), p. 188.
2. Bob Dylan, *Writings and Drawings* (New York: Knopf, 1973), p. iii.
3. Robert Shelton, *No Direction Home: The Life and Music of Bob Dylan* (New York: Ballantine Books, 1987), p. 30.
4. Ibid.
5. Bob Spitz, *Dylan: A Biography* (New York: McGraw-Hill, 1989), p. 20.
6. Shelton, *No Direction Home*, p. 27.
7. Spitz, *Dylan*, p. 19.
8. Ibid., p. 24.
9. Bob Dylan, "Joan Baez in Concert, Part 2," in *Lyrics, 1962-1975* (New York: Alfred A. Knopf, 1985), p. 15.
10. Anthony Scaduto, *Bob Dylan: An Intimate Biography* (New York: Grosset and Dunlap, 1971), p. 13.
11. Spitz, *Dylan*, p. 28.
12. Scaduto, *Bob Dylan*, p. 13.
13. Spitz, *Dylan*, p. 37.
14. Ibid., p. 38.
15. Scaduto, *Bob Dylan*, p. 16.
16. Spitz, *Dylan*, p. 39.
17. Scaduto, *Bob Dylan*, p. 19.

18. Robert Hilburn, "Dylan Now," *Los Angeles Times Magazine*, 9 February 1992, p. 42.
19. Shelton, *No Direction Home*, p. 42.
20. Scaduto, *Bob Dylan*, p. 22.
21. Shelton, *No Direction Home*, p. 42.
22. Ibid., p. 41.
23. Scaduto, *Bob Dylan*, p. 29.
24. Shelton, *No Direction Home*, p. 42.
25. Ibid., p. 39.
26. Ibid., p. 45.
27. Clinton Heylin, *Bob Dylan: Behind the Shades* (New York: Summit Books, 1991), p. 30.
28. Spitz, *Dylan*, p. 47.
29. Heylin, *Behind the Shades*, p. 30.
30. Shelton, *No Direction Home*, p. 52.
31. Heylin, *Behind the Shades*, p. 32.
32. Ibid., p. 42.
33. Shelton, *No Direction Home*, p. 62.
34. John Bauldie, editor, *Wanted Man: In Search of Bob Dylan* (New York: Citadel Underground Press, 1991), p. 24.
35. Ibid., pp. 16-17.
36. Ibid., p. 18.
37. Heylin, *Behind the Shades*, p. 33.
38. Shelton, *No Direction Home*, p. 44.
39. Ibid.
40. Scaduto, *Bob Dylan*, p. 33.
41. Heylin, *Behind the Shades*, p. 35.
42. Bauldie, *Wanted Man*, p. 22.
43. Heylin, *Behind the Shades*, p. 43.
44. Ibid., p. 57.
45. Michael Krogsgaard, *Positively Bob Dylan: A Thirty Year Discography, Concert and Recording Session Guide* (Ann Arbor, Mich.: Popular Culture, Ink, 1991), p. 3.
46. Heylin, *Behind the Shades*, p. 43.
47. Scaduto, *Bob Dylan*, p. 38.
48. Ibid., p. 49.
49. Ibid., p. 58.
50. Cameron Crowe, Notes to *Biograph* [sound recording] (Columbia Records, 1985), booklet, p. 7.
51. Shelton, *No Direction Home*, p. 96.
52. Heylin, *Behind the Shades*, p. 49.
53. Joe Klein, *Woody Guthrie: A Life* (New York: Knopf, 1980), p. 444.
54. Scaduto, *Bob Dylan*, p. 69.
55. Ibid., p. 69.
56. Shelton, *No Direction Home*, p. 103.
57. Robert Shelton, "The Charisma Kid," *Cavalier*, July 1965, cited in Shelton, *No Direction Home*, p. 325.
58. Shelton, *No Direction Home*, p. 107.
59. Spitz, *Dylan*, p. 162.
60. Robert Shelton, "Bob Dylan: A Distinctive Folk Song Stylist," *New York Times*, 29 September 1961, cited in Craig McGregor, editor, *Bob Dylan: The Early Years* (New York: DaCapo Press, 1990), p. 17.
61. Spitz, *Dylan*, p. 167.
62. Ibid., p. 169.
63. Shelton, *No Direction Home*, p. 126.
64. Scaduto, *Bob Dylan*, p. 117.
65. Crowe, *Biograph*, p. 8.
66. Shelton, *No Direction Home*, p. 141.
67. Sy Ribakove and Barbara Ribakove, *Folk Rock* (New York: Dell, 1966), p. 26.
68. Krogsgaard, *Positively Bob Dylan*, p. 19.
69. Shelton, *No Direction Home*, p. 142.

70. Bauldie, *Wanted Man*, p. 24.
71. Shelton, *No Direction Home*, p. 147.
72. Ibid., p. 146.
73. Ibid., p. 157.
74. Ibid., pp. 160-163.
75. Ibid., p. 163.
76. Sidney Fields, "Only Human," *New York Mirror*, 12 September 1963, in McGregor, *Early Years*, p. 35.
77. Scaduto, *Bob Dylan*, pp. 129-130.
78. Shelton, *No Direction Home* (p. 189) and Spitz, *Dylan* (p. 217) support the calm, unruffled version of the tale, while Scaduto, *Bob Dylan* (p. 164) reports the tirade. Spitz speculates that Dylan fueled the tirade version through Scaduto in order to better fertilize his image as an angry young man.
79. Clive Davis, with James Wilwerth, *Clive: Inside the Record Business* (New York: Morrow, 1975), pp. 48-49.
80. Scaduto, *Bob Dylan*, p. 165.
81. Taylor Branch, *Parting the Waters: America in the King Years* (New York: Simon and Schuster, 1989), p. 718.
82. Details of the front-yard performance are offered in Krogsgaard, *Positively Bob Dylan*, and in "Northern Folk Singers Help Out at Negro Festival in Mississippi," *New York Times*, 7 July 1963, reprinted in McGregor, *Early Years*, pp. 38-39. The performance is also featured in D. A. Pennebaker's documentary, *Don't Look Back* (1967).
83. Shelton, *No Direction Home*, p. 194.
84. Ibid., p. 196.
85. Joan Baez, *And a Voice to Sing With* (New York: Summit Books, 1987), p. 91.
86. Scaduto, *Bob Dylan*, p. 177.
87. Ibid., p. 185.
88. "I Am My Words," *Newsweek*, 4 November 1963.
89. Scaduto, *Bob Dylan*, p. 186.
90. Shelton, *No Direction Home*, p. 215.
91. Ibid., pp. 222-224.
92. Paul Williams, *Bob Dylan: Performing Artist* (Novato, Calif.: Underwood-Miller, 1991), p. 98.
93. Scaduto, *Bob Dylan*, p. 179.
94. Ibid., p. 203.

Chapter 2

The Whole World Is Watching

IT WOULD BE A WHILE BEFORE BOB DYLAN formed another rock 'n' roll band, but the events of summer 1964 led Dylan further from his position as the king of protest music. In March, his affair with Suze Rotolo ended. He went to Europe in May, performing in England and vacationing in France and Greece. Back in the states, he recorded his fourth album in one wine-influenced evening and then showed up at the Newport Folk Festival in July, where he disappointed his fans by offering no protest songs.

It was Mississippi Freedom Summer, a massive voter-registration effort in the state that symbolized the segregation of the Deep South. Three civil rights workers were murdered by members of the Ku Klux Klan. Nonetheless, Dylan did not have a topical song for the occasion, no "Only a Pawn in Their Game" or "Death of Emmett Till." It had only been a year since he debuted the song about Evers in the front yard of the Mississippi farmhouse, but he had changed a lot more than his listeners had realized. Apparently, they were not listening carefully enough.

Another Side of Bob Dylan, which was released two weeks after Newport, was a clear sign of changing direction. Dylan had recorded 15 songs straight through, finishing the last take of "My Back Pages" at one-thirty in the morning. Dylan told journalist Nat Hentoff, who was profiling him for the *New Yorker*, that there were no finger-pointing songs on his new album. He had gone beyond merely pointing out injustice and on to a larger issue. "What's wrong goes much deeper than the bomb," he said. "What's wrong is how few people are free. Most people walking around are tied down to something that doesn't really let them *speak*, so they just add their confusion to the mess."[1]

Musically, he was still alone, accompanying himself on guitar, harmonica and piano. (The rock 'n' roll band was still to come.) The new songs no longer dealt with news events. They were not topical in any global sense, or, if they sniffed of any relevance, they were too obscure to be directly "useful" to the protest crowd. "Chimes of Freedom" had a couple of lines that voiced dissent and "Black Crow Blues" could be read in a certain way to refer to segregation. However, by and large, the songs were personal, dealing with his deteriortating relationship with Suze Rotolo. One of the most bitter was "Ballad in Plain D," a direct attack on Suze's mother and "parasitic sister." Nonetheless, other moments on the album were bright and happy. He even broke down laughing on a couple of the takes, and the false starts were kept on the album by Tom Wilson.

The album did not do as well as his previous records, which put Dylan on the defensive. He had broken from the formula. He protested the title, believing the "another side" angle to be record company cornball, which had, unintentionally, set him up for criticism. Still, he was proud of the record, calling the songs "insanely honest."[2] "Chimes of Freedom," for its part, was one of the first songs to show the dense lyricism that would pervade his mid-1960s recordings. The relative disappointment of the album did not overly discourage his fans. Many believed it to be an abberation, a brief detour on his path as spokesman for his generation. His concerts remained popular and he retained his place in the pantheon of popular music.

Dylan began to associate more with rock 'n' roll musicians. Meeting The Beatles in New York that August, he introduced the Fab Four to marijuana. He was startled that they had never smoked dope before, as he had assumed they were singing "I get high! I get high!" in the middle of "I Want to Hold Your Hand."[3] (It was "I can't hide! I can't hide!")

His concert tour that fall began to showcase the works of Dylan's new identity. He stopped performing "Only a Pawn in Their Game" after a Philadelphia appearance in September. New, darker, and more obscure material, like "Gates of Eden" and "It's Alright Ma (I'm Only Bleeding)" began to show up in his sets. Introducing "Gates of Eden" as a "sacriligious lullaby" at an October 31 show in New York, he said afterward, "It's just Halloween. I have my Bob Dylan mask on."[4] He performed with the old mask--the mask of protest--throughout that fall and into the spring, when he appeared in Europe. Visibly impatient with the old persona, he was preparing to don a new one when he finally entered the recording studio in the early months of 1965.

Working again with Tom Wilson, Dylan tried to record his new songs acoustically during their first session on January 13. The next day, however, sessions with a band produced usable takes. Two guitarists, a bass player (John Sebastian, who was later to form The Lovin' Spoonful), a drummer and two keyboardists augmented Dylan in his first appearance with a group since his final Hammond sessions in 1962. The first rock tune he recorded, "Maggie's Farm," set the tone: It was piercing, distinctive and raucous, unlike any rock 'n' roll to that time with its marriage of jackhammer lyrics and backbeat. The next day, with a different set of studio musicians, he rerecorded "Subterranean Homesick Blues." He had tried it on the first day with no accompaniment, but the band version defined Dylan's new style. Released as a single in April, this may have been one of the first rock 'n' roll songs to drive listeners to take notes. The words were so rapid-fire, so clever, and so forcefully sung that listeners had to pay attention. This was not background music.

The bulk of *Bringing It All Back Home* was recorded with a band in those two days, January 14 and 15. Nonetheless, Dylan still appeared solo in concert, accompanying himself on guitar and harmonica. To many of his fans, he was still the old Dylan wearing the old mask. In concert, he performed songs from the earlier era ("The Lonesome Death of Hattie Carroll," which would be a staple throughout his performing career, "With God on Our Side," and "Don't Think Twice, It's All Right"), along with the acoustic material from his forthcoming record ("Gates of Eden," "Mr. Tambourine Man," "It's Alright Ma (I'm Only Bleeding)," and "It's All Over Now, Baby Blue"). The near-journalism of the finger-pointing songs had been easy for listeners to follow, but this new material required a level of concentration previously unrequired of concert audiences. The allusions were complex, with the lyrical leaps demanding a knowledge of history and literature. One almost needed a required reading list to keep up.

The album was released in late March, and even its packaging was unique. For the first time, the front cover did not list the song titles. Dylan was the first major artist in the American market to make album covers more an artistic statement and less of an advertisement. Even albums released in America by The Beatles continued to hawk songs on the front cover, an utterly pointless exercise since they were also listed on the back.

Dylan's cover for *Bringing It All Back Home* was a carefully staged and organized work of art. Dylan sat in some fine living room, the center of a swirling controversy (represented by the blurred edges of the photo). Staring dead into the viewer's eyes, he appears challenging, even menacing. Behind him sits a confident young woman in a red lounge suit. She is smoking a cigarette and also staring down the camera. One writer described her as a "frosty-looking babe," and, indeed, her look is intimidating.[5] (The model was Sally Grossman, the wife of Dylan's manager.) Dylan is stroking a cat and he is surrounded by magazines bearing pictures of President Lyndon Johnson and Jean Harlow, albums by Robert Johnson, Lotte Lenya and The Impressions; and, deep in the background, *Another Side of Bob Dylan* (as if to say, "I'm way beyond that now").

The title was also a mystery. What was he saying? What was *It*? Was he referring to the Vietnam War, to poverty, to concern for humanity? Most likely, Dylan was making a reference to rock 'n' roll, a statement of his return to roots. The album notes were spectacular, perhaps Dylan's best writing outside song lyrics. It was a statement of definition and a profoundly moving self-examination by an artist. Everything about *Bringing It All Back Home* was revolutionary.

The audience would have to work hard to catch up with him, yet Dylan remained a crowd pleaser. His seminal concert tour of England in April and May 1965 showed Dylan chafing at the bit, eager to move forward yet held back by an audience with maddeningly unrealistic expectations of him. Luckily, there is a film record of that experience. Albert Grossman met D. A. Pennebaker, a filmmaker who was associated with Time, Inc., and suggested he come along on Dylan's brief European tour to "do some filming."[6] Grossman had ambitions for a film career for his charge, as he assumed that the "shelf life" of a pop star was short. Dylan did not object to any foray into film, since he enjoyed movies and frequently called on cinematic memories for inspiration.[7]

Pennebaker had made a few documentaries and had been hoping to center his new work on popular music. It was perfect timing for Pennebaker in terms of his career, but it was also perfect in terms of his art. He was able to show an artist in transition--an artist trying desperately to move into a new arena. The film was not released until 1967, but *Don't Look Back* is best considered in the context of 1965, when it was shot. Much of public knowledge about Dylan would be formed by this film, which offered telling glimpses of its 24-year-old star. Backstage, after an English concert, he was approached by members of a rock 'n' roll band who apologized for themselves and said he had set them thinking about the importance of words in songs. Dylan, however, asked them about their amplifiers.

He was clearly feeling frustrated and imprisoned by his past. Onstage, he opened shows with "The Times They Are A-Changin'." The song was then a huge hit in England, but it was well over a year old to Dylan and he was too much of a chameleon for any song to define him for longer than a couple of months at most.

Dylan skewered reporters throughout the tour, and some of these bloodless assassinations are shown in the film. He also turned cold on Baez. In reality, their relationship was doomed before the filming began as Dylan had already begun seeing Sara Lowndes, the woman he would marry later in the year. Perhaps Baez was aware of this, yet she went along with Dylan, assuming he would return her many favors. She had, largely, introduced him to mass audiences in America when he was an unknown singer. Now, she assumed, he had invited her along for the English tour in order to do the same for him with a European audience. To her surprise, she waited in the wings while he performed, and was never summoned to the microphone.

One of Dylan's new songs from the album, which he performed on stage during the tour, seemed a particularly sharp barb at Baez. "She Belongs to Me" made specific references to Baez and offered the tale of a woman who had been left with no options. Apparently finding herself in agreement, Baez left the tour and gave up her relationship with Dylan.

It's All Over Now, Baby Blue

Sara Lowndes flew to England to join Dylan at the end of the tour and vacationed with him on the Continent while he recovered from a slight illness which had been fueled by exhaustion. Once back in New York, he went into the studio (on June 15) to continue expanding his rock 'n' roll sound. He had a new song, "Like a Rolling Stone," which he called "very vomitific in its structure."[8] He took six pages of typed notes into the studio, and the words poured out, apparently in a diatribe against a well-protected, insulated person learning to live on her merits as an individual rather than the accomplishments or wealth of her parents; or was it about something else? Dylan once suggested it was aimed at himself.

The song was punched with cannon-like drums, and featured a majestic interplay between guitar and organ and a steady, rock-bottom bass. Still, Dylan said simply, "It started with that 'La Bamba' riff."[9] The comment was typical of Dylan's shrugging self-deflation, as he compared one of rock 'n' roll's most complex songs with one of its simplest. Nonetheless, Dylan did borrow the chords from the traditional Mexican tune, which had been updated and turned into a pop hit by Richie Valens.

Tom Wilson had arranged to hire the musicians for the session, including young blues guitarist Mike Bloomfield. Dylan showed up, plugged in his Telecaster, and played the song once for his musicians. Then he said he was ready to record.[10] Unhappy with the song after the first run-through, Dylan asked organist Paul Griffin to move to the piano. Another musician, Al Kooper, was attending the session as a guest of Wilson. When Griffin moved, Kooper sat down at the organ, an instrument he had never played publicly before. As the song began, Kooper added what flourishes he could manage on the alien instrument. At the mixing session following the take Dylan told Wilson, "Turn up the organ."

"That cat's not an organ player," Wilson said, nodding toward Kooper.

"Don't tell me who is an organ player," Dylan said. "Just turn up the organ."[11]

Released as a single, "Like a Rolling Stone" became the biggest hit of Dylan's career to date, and the longest (clocking in at six minutes) Top 10 song in popular music history to that point. The length made it an anamoly in an era when few songs went past the sacred three-minute mark to which the radio programmers held. Nonetheless, the demand for the cataclysmic song was great, and thus fell the three-minute barrier, thanks to Dylan and the celebrated record producer Phil Spector. (That summer, Spector had incorrectly listed the timing on the label of a Righteous Brothers single, "You've Lost That Lovin' Feeling," as three minutes when it was actually a half-minute longer. When disk jockeys realized the ruse, which caused them to fall behind on their play lists, it was too late: The song was already a hit.)

The "Like a Rolling Stone" session was one of the last with Tom Wilson. During later recording sessions that summer, Dylan began his long association with Bob Johnston, a songwriter and freelance producer who had just signed on with Columbia. He would prove to be Dylan's greatest collaborator in the studio.

The sessions were interrupted by Dylan's ritual appearance at the Newport Folk Festival. He wanted to unveil his new sound to an audience that, he could safely assume, would be hostile. Certainly, the audience should be wise to his new direction: *Bringing It All Back Home*, "Subterranean Homesick Blues" and now, "Like a Rolling Stone" were all top sellers. Amplified music had been played at Newport before, primarily by blues musicians, so Dylan was not breaking entirely new ground.

He hired three members of the the Paul Butterfield Blues Band for the occasion, including guitarist Bloomfield, who was key to Dylan's new sound. Al Kooper was recruited for the show when Grossman found him wandering in the crowd. After an all-night rehearsal, Dylan and his band performed on Sunday at the festival. The group ripped through "Maggie's Farm," "Like a Rolling Stone" and "It Takes a Lot to Laugh, It Takes a Train to Cry" before the boos and cries of "sell out" became too loud to allow the musicians to continue.

Backstage, there had been a frenzied response to electrified Dylan music. Pete Seeger, who was on the festival board, had been outraged from the first amplified notes of "Maggie's Farm" and threatened to pull the plug on the instruments.[12] The outcry was so great that Dylan and the band left the stage and, after a long interval, he returned alone, playing "Mr. Tambourine Man" and his classic kiss-off song, "It's All Over Now, Baby Blue."

Back in the studio later that week, Dylan recorded another kiss-off song, this one directly aimed at the folk music establishment. With rock 'n' roll backing, Dylan taped "Positively 4th Street," referring to all his former cronies from his Greenwich Village days, and labeling them as intransigent, stuck in their outmoded ways, and unwilling to change. In a sense, it was the message of "The Times They Are A-Changin'" on a personal, rather than societal, level. The song also contained accusations of jealousy and envy on the part of his former associates, who, Dylan claimed, disavowed his success but secretly wished they had attained that level of acceptance. It became his next single, and he and Johnston continued their work, cutting several more fierce blues and rock 'n' roll tunes. By the end of the summer, the new album, *Highway 61 Revisited*, was released.

There were no vestiges of folk music on the album. From the first crash of the drum at the beginning of "Like a Rolling Stone," it was clear that Dylan was reaching for the throne of rock 'n' roll king. The first side of the album (in its original long-playing configuration) was relentless, crashing through blues ("Tombstone Blues") and standard rock ("From a Buick 6") and ending with his vindictive trashing of a journalist, "Ballad of a Thin Man."

The second side contained another presumed attack on Baez, "Queen Jane Approximately," and two approaches to the apocalypse, "Highway 61 Revisited" and the 11-minute "Desolation Row," his first experience with a Nashville musician. Johnston, whose connections in country music were considerable, had recruited guitarist Charlie McCoy from Tennessee, bringing him to New York for an attempt at the epic after Dylan remained dissatisfied with an earlier recording. McCoy's guitar flourishes perfectly meshed with Dylan's chugging acoustic work, and the experience was good enough to convince Dylan to follow Johnston's urging and record in Nashville for his next album.

First, however, there was a tour and the attendant press interviews. Dylan was now entirely uncooperative with journalists. He became a put-on artist, spoofing everything. As Pauline Kael wrote:

> He was derisive, and even sneering . . . freaking out those who weren't worthy of being talked to straight. Implicit in the idea of the put-on was the idea that the Establishment was so fundamentally dishonest that dialogue with any of its representatives (roughly, anyone who wore a tie) was debased from the start.[13]

In press conferences, these sorts of exchanges took place between the put-on artist and the tie-wearing representatives of the Establishment:

> *Question*: Who is "Mister Jones" [the abused character in "Ballad of a Thin Man"]?
> *Answer*: He's a real person. You know him . . . . I saw him come into the room one night and he looked like a camel. He proceeded to put his eyes in his pocket.
> *Question*: Who is Queen Jane?
> *Answer*: Queen Jane is a man.
> *Question*: Do you think of yourself primarily as a singer or a poet?
> *Answer*: Oh, I think of myself more as a song-and-dance man.
> *Question*: How would you define folk music?
> *Answer*: As a constitutional replay of mass production.
> *Question*: If you were going to sell out to a commercial interest, which one would you choose?
> *Answer*: Ladies' garments.[14]

Journalists expected fun and witticism. After all, the previous year, The Beatles had turned their press conferences into joke fests. However, reporters did not expect the unabashed weirdness of Bob Dylan.

Dylan hit the road steadily, from the end of September 1965 through the end of May 1966. (The concerts on this legendary tour are discussed in Chapter 9.) He recorded when he had the chance, squeezing the sessions in between his demanding concert dates, which covered the United States and, beginning in April 1966, the Pacific and Europe as well. His traveling band included a regular group of musicians that had performed under the name Levon and the Hawks. Canadians who had once backed rockabilly star Ronnie Hawkins, the group had retained the Hawks stage name after leaving Hawkins and adding drummer Levon Helm, an Arkansan whose musical tastes were close to their own. This band would enjoy a long association with Dylan and become a successful concert draw in its own right, as The Band.

That season, Dylan ruled rock 'n' roll. Even The Beatles were following his every move, emulating him with their music. Their songs "You've Got to Hide Your Love Away" and "I'm a Loser" had shown early Dylan influences on The Beatles and the subsequent *Rubber Soul* and *Revolver* albums owed him a large debt.

"Like a Rolling Stone" had been a huge hit in the summer of 1965, and it was followed in rapid succession by "Positively 4th Street," "Can You Please Crawl Out Your Window?," "One of Us Must Know (Sooner or Later)," "Rainy Day Women #12 & 35" and "I Want You," all released between September 1965 and June 1966. All were moderately successful, with "Positively 4th Street" reaching No. 7 on the charts, "Rainy Day Women" making it to No. 2, and "I Want You" squeaking into the top 20.

As part of Dylan's assault on the music world, a rock 'n' roll band called The Byrds scored a huge hit with an electric version of his *Bringing It All Back Home* track, "Mr. Tambourine Man." To describe the new sound of both Dylan and The Byrds, the term folk rock was coined by the music industry. The form was not universally hailed, and one folk musician, Tom Paxton, referred to the new music of Dylan and his imitators as "folk rot." Nevertheless, the string of hits made it clear that Bob Dylan could be a pop star.

Dylan was in demand, and Grossman's office could barely keep up with denying all the requests for interviews. Maintaining privacy was even more of a concern for Dylan, and being a popular music star made that increasingly difficult. Dylan's romance with Sara Lowndes had blossomed, and they were able to attain some privacy when they journeyed to Woodstock, in upstate New York, where they stayed in the guest house at Grossman's estate. Since signing on with Grossman, the village haven had been Dylan's peaceful home away from the city. He cherished the times he could spend there with Sara, far away from the craziness of his career. Sara Lowndes was a divorced mother of a young daughter and may have represented the stability Dylan obviously could not find elsewhere in his life. A former Playboy bunny and model, she was a beautiful woman and an intelligent, ethereal companion.

On November 25, 1965, a rare night off between concerts, Bob Dylan and Sara Shirley Lowndes were married in front of a judge in Mineola, New York. Remarkably, news of the marriage was kept secret. Even several of Dylan's closest friends were not aware he was married for months after the private ceremony. The night after the vows, he was on stage at Chicago's Aire Crown Theater.

That winter Dylan spent several sessions taping a *Playboy* interview with journalist Nat Hentoff, one of the few reporters he trusted. When the magazine sent galley proofs of their conversations to Dylan and Hentoff in the spring, the two men were so dissatisfied with the magazine's transcription of the interview that they concocted an entirely new and tremendously weird "new interview," a collection of jokes and puns, thus turning a routine interview with a rock 'n' roll star into a masterpiece of the put-on.[15] It was not Dylan's only literary work: He had signed a contract with Macmillan Publishers in 1965, to produce a novel. He employed the "vomitific" approach he used in songwriting, and now, as he traveled the world on concert tour, he found himself with the daunting task of editing the galleys of this novel, which he called *Tarantula*. It was scheduled for publication in 1966.

He had also contracted with ABC Television for a segment of its "Stage 67" series, which was set to begin that fall. Consequently, Pennebaker came along on tour again, filming many of the performances with the Hawks. The reaction that Dylan had faced at the Newport Folk Festival had been repeated all around the world, as he and The Hawks faced rude, jeering audiences nearly every night. Pennebaker filmed several of these often-confrontational concerts.

To maintain his schedule, Dylan used amphetamines. When confronted with that accusation years later, he did not deny the drug use, but merely said that he needed them to stay awake and keep pace with his commitments. In the midst of this madness, Dylan managed to record what many critics believe to be his masterpiece, *Blonde on Blonde*. If not his finest work, it is certainly the culimination of his goals of the mid-1960s. Dylan himself has professed admiration for the album, which has a seamlessness to it that belies the conditions under which it was recorded.

The sessions were wedged in between concert dates from October 1965 and March 1966, in New York and Nashville. The musicians vary from track to track, from The Hawks (relative novices in the studio) to the legendary Nashville session pros. (Other future Nashville legends were also present: A janitor named Kris Kristofferson emptied ashtrays during the nightlong sessions.) Despite all these starts and stops, the revolving-door studio bands and the considerable strain under which Dylan was working, *Blonde on Blonde*, which was issued as a then unheard-of two-record set, was like an extended work, a rock 'n' roll symphony. Even Dylan was pleased:

The closest I ever got to the sound I heard in my mind was on individual bands [cuts] in the *Blonde on Blonde* album. It's that thin, that wild mercury sound. It's metallic and bright gold, with whatever that conjures up. That's my particular sound. I haven't been able to succeed in getting it all the time.[16]

When the grueling tour had finally finished, Dylan and Sara took a brief vacation in Spain, and then retreated to Woodstock where they contemplated another year full of commitments: recording, filming and performing. He felt worn and drained but was booked to get back onto the treadmill. The pastoral life with Sara beckoned. There was her daughter, Maria, and a new child, Dylan's first, a son named Jesse.

Even with this relative peace, the respite in Woodstock also demanded work. Dylan edited *Tarantula* and the television special, staying up at one point for three days in a row. Even away from the road, he could not stop living the full-speed life, but that would change on July 29, 1966.

Time Passes Slowly

Dylan followers came to speak of two periods in his early life, B.A. and A.A.: Before the Accident and After the Accident. According to press reports, Dylan was hurt in a motorcycle accident near Woodstock on July 29, 1966. The extent of his injuries was not immediately known, but it did force the cancellation of some impending concert dates.[17]

The account released to the press said that Dylan was riding his Triumph 500, taking it to a repair shop. Sara followed in the car. The Triumph's wheels locked and the bike skidded, dragging Dylan over the pavement.[18] Dylan himself later told playwright/actor Sam Shepard that he had been blinded by the sun and lost control of the bike.[19] The seriousness of Dylan's injuries was not directly reported, so there were rumors that he had been crippled or disfigured, even paralyzed. Dylan's neck was also reported to be broken.

Bob Spitz, in *Dylan*, his biography of the artist, offers a minority report of the accident: It never occurred. Spitz and others have claimed that it was merely a tool Dylan used to back away from a life-style that would have led to an early death. However, the consensus is that Dylan did have some kind of motorcycle accident and then went into a long period of recovery and seclusion. The publication of *Tarantula* was, therefore, delayed, and the television special was put on hold. Grossman expected Dylan to lay off for a couple months and then get back on the treadmill, but Dylan demurred.

As the months passed, he enjoyed time with his family and settled into the house that he and Sara had purchased in Woodstock. He worked occasionally, sorting through the film of his tour (he never produced anything that was acceptable to ABC) and writing songs. His pace did not approach the mad scale of the earlier part of the year. His new songs were not as apocalyptic as they were apologetic. They were songs of plea, humor, and hope. They included some moving ballads, but many of the new songs were lighthearted and silly. He decided that he wanted to play these songs, but not on stage or for a wide audience.

Members of The Hawks had settled near Dylan, renting a big pink house in nearby West Saugerties, New York. When they had begun playing with Dylan, they did not know much about him. They were young, rough and experienced only as a bar band. With Dylan, they had toured the world and played in some of the major concert venues of three continents, and their roughness naturally showed through.

The lead guitarist--known then as Jaime R. Robertson, but later to become famous as Robbie Robertson--said that Dylan was pressured by promoters to fire the backing group and hire more professional musicians. (Robertson added that there were times when he would have urged Dylan to do the same.) Nonetheless, Dylan had stood by the group, and the 1965-1966 tour had been a great experience for both the singer and the backing musicians. Robertson said:

> It was like thunder, with his Elmer Gantry speaking, going on, talking these words, singing them, preaching them. He was no longer doing this nasally folk thing. He was screaming his songs through the rafters, and it was like thunder. It was very dynamic, very frightening, and very exciting.[20]

Because of Dylan's belief in The Hawks, it was with a deep sense of gratitude that the musicians moved to rural New York to be near him following his injury. Beginning in the fall of 1966 and into the spring of 1967, Dylan and the musicians spent the afternoons playing his new songs, taping them with a home recorder in the basement of the big pink house. Many were intended as demos for Dylan's music publishing company. Some were offered to other artists: Peter, Paul and Mary recorded "Too Much of Nothing"; The Byrds used two of the songs, "You Ain't Goin' Nowhere" and "Nothing Was Delivered" on their seminal *Sweetheart of the Rodeo* album; and England's Manfred Mann had a top hit with "The Mighty Quinn." These were Dylan songs, but the message was delivered by other artists. Dylan had been on a schedule of producing two albums a year, and by the spring of 1967, his followers had had to endure a year without him. Columbia released *Bob Dylan's Greatest Hits*, which included only one song that had not previously been on an album ("Positively 4th Street") and was most noticeable for the enclosed poster, in which artist Milton Glaser showed Dylan in silhouette with a billowing mushroom cloud of multi-colored hair. It was a classic image of the

1960s and one of the distinguished artist's best works. (He later adapted it for the cover of his career retrospective, *Milton Glaser: Graphic Designer*.)

There was friction between Dylan and Columbia Records. While Dylan recuperated and played his new songs in the basement of the house, which was now dubbed "Big Pink," Grossman busied himself with trying to negotiate a new contract for his client. Dylan actually signed with MGM Records, in a deal that would have made the lightweight label a major contender in the rock 'n' roll market. However, Columbia fought back. Its new president was Clive Davis, the former legal affairs adviser who had justified the company's decision to keep "Talkin' John Birch Paranoid Blues" off *Freewheelin'*. Davis was determined to keep Dylan, and he approached MGM with the news that the Dylan catalog was not a big seller. MGM began to have second thoughts and meanwhile, Davis negotiated with the Columbia board to get a better deal for Dylan, including a tremendous increase in the royalty rates. Dylan, Davis said, was "a bulwark of Columbia Records."[21] As a result, Dylan returned to the Columbia fold.

Throughout 1967, Dylan's fans were curious about their reclusive idol but had to make do with rumors and the *Greatest Hits* album, which became Dylan's first gold record. With no new Dylan, the audience had to content itself with the old. In May 1967, D. A. Pennebaker's documentary of Dylan's tour of England two years before was finally released. *Don't Look Back* showed Dylan delivering brilliant performances and skewering journalists. It was the Dylan everyone remembered--and either loved or hated. Another film, Murray Lerner's *Festival*, showed another old face of Dylan--the rebellious young star of the Newport festivals of 1964 and 1965.

Finally, in the autumn, the new Dylan was ready. Dylan was so secretive that there was little written about his trip to Nashville in October and November to record a new album. Working with Bob Johnston and a stripped-down band of session pros, Dylan quietly recorded the 12 somewhat subdued songs that would make up *John Wesley Harding*. The album did not include any of the songs he had recorded in the basement of Big Pink.

While he had been disengaged from the wheels of the music machine, rock 'n' roll had apparently gone crazy. Records had become more ornate and, some would say, more pretentious. A move to more elaborate productions might be traced from The Beach Boys' *Pet Sounds* album in May 1966 and their subsequent (and never-released) *Smile*, which had aspirations of being, in the words of head Beach Boy Brian Wilson, "a teenage symphony to God."[22] The Beatles, citing the influence of *Pet Sounds*, set to work on a concept album called *Sgt. Pepper's Lonely Hearts Club Band*, which was released in June 1967. After that, a door flew open and rock 'n' roll bands began including gimmicks and studio trickery on their records.

John Wesley Harding flew in the face of that trend. It was a quiet oasis in the midst of cacophony. However, the quiet sound of the album did not reflect the record's theme. As Dylan said, "*John Wesley Harding* was a fearful album--not just dealing with fear, but dealing with the devil in a fearful way, almost. All I wanted to do was get the words right."[23] On the cover, Dylan appeared fit and smiling, with no visible disfigurement from the accident.

Dylan's album sent a signal to other artists, who began a move back to the basics. Soon, The Beatles were recording *The White Album* (officially known as *The Beatles*) and *Let it Be*, two records celebrating the simplicity of rhythm and blues. The Byrds presented country and western music with *Sweetheart of the Rodeo*. The Rolling Stones abandoned the pretentiousness of *Their Satanic Majesties Request* and recorded the blues-influenced *Beggars' Banquet* and The Beach Boys made a belated discovery of rhythm and blues with *Wild Honey*.

The new Dylan album was not supported by a tour. Dylan made only one public appearance. When Woody Guthrie died in October 1967, Dylan had called Guthrie's manager and suggested that something be done to honor his idol. With Dylan's participation promised, Guthrie associates quickly organized a concert featuring Guthrie's songs and selections from his autobiographical books. Carnegie Hall was booked for matinee and evening performances. Actors Will Geer (a close friend of Guthrie) and Robert Ryan agreed to do the readings, and an army of singers signed on.

Dylan's appearance turned the benefit shows into a media event. Wearing a suit but no tie, with a scruffy beard and a truly weird hairstyle (he looked as if he had not combed in the previous week), he was not immediately recognized by the audience.[24] With The Hawks (or The Crackers, as they sometimes called themselves), he performed three songs: "Dear Mr. Roosevelt," "I Ain't Got No Home" and "The Grand Coulee Dam." Then, with the full cast, Dylan joined in singing "This Train Is Bound for Glory."[25] It was January 20, 1968, a full year and a half since Dylan and The Hawks had performed over choruses of boos, but this audience, numbering many of the people who had disdained Dylan for his move away from folk music (including Tom Paxton and Pete Seeger) cheered as Dylan and his band played their noisy interpretations of Guthrie.[26] The times, indeed, were a-changing.

Well-reviewed though it may have been, the Guthrie concert did not signal a return to the stage for Dylan. Instead, he retreated to his wooded seclusion in upstate New York and audiences had to make do with morsels of information about him. Photographer Elliott Landy took a picture of a barefoot Dylan, looking like a backwoods guitar picker, sitting in a tire swing. It appeared on the cover of the *Saturday Evening Post*, which, just two years before, had profiled the long-haired and angry Bob Dylan, symbol of rebellion. Now he looked like a man of peace. However, all was not peaceful, despite Woodstock's serenity and Dylan's apparent distance from the problems of the world. There was increasing friction between Dylan and Grossman. The artist chose to stay at his country retreat and concentrate on raising his growing family. For a full year after the Carnegie Hall show, Dylan did little on the professional front.

On June 5, 1968, Abe Zimmerman suffered a heart attack and died. Dylan considered staying away from the funeral, but not out of disrespect to his father. Rather, he feared his presence would turn the services into another media event, another chance for the press to hound the "reclusive Bob Dylan." In the end, he could not stay away and so he flew into Hibbing, where he was upset to discover that the family home was filled with socializing relatives and friends. His brother David was struck by how serene Bob was, as if much older than his 27 years.[27] Seeing his father's body in the funeral home moved Dylan deeply. His mother told him that his father had been proud of him and of his accomplishments and what he had become. As Shelton wrote, "The 'saintly' son who came home to bury Abe was proof that [Abe] and Beatty had not failed."[28]

The nation was divided in the fall of 1968, by its split over the Vietnam War and social issues, such as the continuing battle of integration. As antiwar demonstrators and police clashed on the streets of Chicago, the young protesters chanted Dylan's words "The whole world is watching" and television showed the police riots to millions of American viewers. Dylan chose not to play an active role in war protests, although his former lover, Joan Baez, was at the vanguard of the movement.

That fall, amid the noise of chaos, Dylan's former backing group released a comparatively quiet album called *Music From Big Pink*, in honor of the house in which they and Dylan had recorded. They had signed with Capitol Records but did not have an official name. They told Capitol that they wanted to call themselves The Crackers, but the company executives nixed that idea. Finally, the album was released and credited to The Band. With a Dylan painting on the cover and three of his songs inside, the album assumed a prominent place in the new music of 1968. It included Dylan's hymnlike "I Shall Be Released," along with the generational ballad, "Tears of Rage" (a collaboration with pianist Richard Manuel) and the menacing "This Wheel's on Fire" (which Dylan wrote with bassist Rick Danko).

Dylan himself did not return to the studio until the spring of 1969. Back in Nashville, he produced an album of songs that were even more innocuous than those he had recorded with The Band in Big Pink. *Nashville Skyline* would contain songs with the "moon-and-june" rhymes that Dylan had disdained with his earlier work. He defended himself against the criticism, saying, "These are the type of songs that I always felt like writing when I've been alone to do so.... [They] reflect more of the inner me than the songs of the past."[29] If that statement was to be believed, it would prove discouraging to longtime admirers. What if this slick and superficial songwriter was the "real" Dylan?

Few, however, could complain about the musical quality of the album.

Again featuring superb session musicians, *Nashville Skyline* was like a musical soufflé: light and perfect. Some critics read between the lines of the songs, seeking in this simplicity a cover for some deeper message. Another surprising element of the album was Dylan's voice, which had become smooth and honeyed. He later told *Rolling Stone* editor Jann Wenner that it was because he had given up smoking during the sessions. (Soon he would again pick up the habit.) However, friends from Dylan's Minneapolis days recall him singing in the same voice in his early appearances, before he adopted the Guthrie vocal style.[30]

Again, the album's release did not signal a return to the stage. Except for a few appearances, Dylan stayed out of the public eye. He performed on "The Johnny Cash Show" on ABC, returning a favor, as Cash, a country and western star and longtime admirer, had performed a duet with Dylan on *Nashville Skyline* (a new version of "Girl from the North Country") and had written the album notes (for which he won a Grammy). Looking nervous, Dylan sang the duet with Cash and also performed "I Threw it All Away" and "Living the Blues." (Dylan and Cash had recorded an album's worth of duets, but released only the one song.)

In the summer of 1969, a song from *Nashville Skyline* became a hit. It was Dylan's first major chart performance since 1966. "Lay Lady Lay" had been written for the movie *Midnight Cowboy*, but Dylan missed the deadline to include the song in the film, which starred Jon Voight and Dustin Hoffman as two New York City hustlers. Dylan used it on the album and was surprised when Davis insisted it be issued as a single. Davis' decision was wise: The song reached No. 7 on the American charts and No. 5 in Britain.

Dylan made a brief return to Hibbing in early August 1969 for the tenth reunion of his high school class. Echo Helstrom was there, hiding Dylan-like behind dark glasses, and wondering what sort of reaction she would elicit from her former boyfriend. She had recently discussed their relationship with a reporter from the *Village Voice* and she feared Dylan would accuse her of aiding the invasion of his privacy. He showed up late, with Sara. He was thin, with short hair, unlike the Bobby Zimmerman whom Echo remembered. She asked him to autograph the reunion program. "You probably don't remember me," she said, "but I'd like your autograph." He looked up. "Hey," he said warmly. "I talk about you all the time." Then, turning to Sara, he said, "This is Echo." They talked a little, but a crowd had gathered and they could not say much. "I wrote you a song," Echo said. "What do you call it?" Dylan asked. "'Boy from the North Country,'" she replied.[31]

Although he did not perform, his presence was felt at the Woodstock Music and Arts Festival that summer. The Woodstock festival was the largest rock concert of its kind, drawing nearly a half million people to Max Yasgur's farm in upstate New York. Although it was not actually held in Woodstock, it was close enough for promoters to use the village's name, which had special significance for music fans as the town to which Dylan had retreated. Dylan himself had skipped town. He reemerged on the Isle of Wight, off the English coast, at a rock concert that drew half as many fans as Woodstock. Backed up by The Band, Dylan performed a 17-song set that included several of his hits as well as some songs he had never performed before, including the traditional "Wild Mountain Thyme" and his version of "The Mighty Quinn," which he called "Quinn the Eskimo." He also debuted a song called "Minstrel Boy." Dylan made $75,000 for the hourlong show, but the performance was sloppy and, apparently, poorly rehearsed. (Dylan had only "practiced" with The Band by making a three-song appearance with the group at an Edwardsville, Illinois, performance earlier in the month, where he was introduced as "Elmer Johnson.") The Isle of Wight Festival did not renew Dylan's enthusiasm for live performances.

Watching the River Flow

Dylan returned to live in Greenwich Village in the summer of 1969, yet he still hoped to retain his anonymity in the city. He visited some of his old friends, perhaps in an effort to regenerate atrophied alliances, but things had changed. He now owned a townhouse and was married, with a home full of small children. (In addition to Sara's daughter by her first marriage, the couple had four sons.) Dylan was now soft-spoken. He dressed differently, and he looked, at times, like a rabbinical student.

Indeed, Dylan had changed. That fall, *Rolling Stone* put him on its cover to announce its "exclusive" interview inside. Dylan had sat for an extended talk with editor Jann Wenner during the summer. Throughout the interview, Wenner pressed Dylan about his role in the world and his importance to his peers. Dylan professed ignorance of his status. Fans who had been disappointed with *Nashville Skyline* had begun to think the album was a joke they could not understand, or perhaps a sophisticated hoax. The "real Dylan" was laughing at the way in which the audience had bought into his smug exercise.

Some fans wondered if it was just another practical joke perpetrated by the celebrated put-on artist. Was he toying with people as he had during those 1965 press conferences when he answered reporters' questions with gibberish? Had he merely refined the put-on by making *Nashville Skyline* and releasing it with a straight face, insisting he stood behind it as a work of art? The interview might have given many readers the impression that his new, superficial songsmith was the "real Dylan." He spoke in commercial terms about selling albums, about being cut out of his share of the profits of *Don't Look Back*, and about the craft of the professional songwriter. The angry, questioning, political Bob Dylan was not in evidence. Indeed, the new Dylan casually dismissed much of the work of the old. He offered a fuller explanation to another interviewer.

> I believe that at certain periods in a person's existence, it's necessary, if not vital, to bring about a change in your life so as not to go under . . . I have children and I want to watch them grow up--to get to know them and for them to get to know me and know that I'm their father.[32]

Things continued to be unsettling for Dylan fans. In the spring of 1970, he finished an album rumored to be titled *Blue Moon*, and to feature the Rodgers and Hart song of that name. Word had it that Dylan had recorded an album of Tin Pan Alley standards. Many fans thought it could not be true.

Then in June, Dylan accepted an honorary doctorate from Princeton University, in the company of journalist Walter Lippmann and civil rights activist Coretta Scott King. Wearing an academic robe (but no mortarboard), Dylan endured an academician's induction speech calling attention to the fact that he was approaching the "perilous" age of 30, a comment that caused him to smile ruefully. Was this acceptance of the degree another sign that Dylan, in the language of the times, had "sold out" to the Establishment, or was it a put on?

Fans thought that the Dylan they knew would have refused the honor. Nonetheless, there he stood, on stage with the symbols of the Establishment against which he had, in part, inspired a rebellion. He wore a white armband on his robe which included the peace sign, his silent protest against the Vietnam War.

Then, his new album was released. Titled *Self Portrait*, it was the culmination of many fans' fears. Dylan ranged over a number of styles in the course of the double album, crooning "Blue Moon," *humming* a tune called "Wigwam" and merely strumming guitar behind a female chorus that repeated a phrase suggesting a severe case of writer's block in "All the Tired Horses." That song, which opened the double album, was heavily orchestrated and immaculately sung by the women. It seemed to be offered primarily as an apology for what followed. Unfortunately, if its intention had been to justify the album's inclusion of other people's songs and thereby deflate criticism, the effort failed. "What is this shit?" critic Greil Marcus asked in the opening line of *Rolling Stone*'s long-winded brutalization of the record.

Many theories abounded. The record might be another put-on, but surely Dylan would have tired of such jokes by now. Was this "self portrait" his way of displaying all the disparate elements and styles that meshed in his brain and came out as "Dylan songs," or was it a calculated effort to keep the mass audience at bay, a deliberate move to alienate people and thereby deflate the pressure under which Dylan worked. (This would make the album a metaphorical motorcycle accident, if one follows the logic of Bob Spitz.) Later,

Dylan came to regard *Self Portrait* as an unprofessional effort.[33]

Whatever the case, Dylan's reputation was now in serious trouble with the rock 'n' roll establishment. To many longtime fans, the new album was just the latest in a series of betrayals since the grand days of *Blonde on Blonde*.[34]

His work had almost single-handedly made possible the serious consideration of this music as an art form. He had offered critics the raw material that had allowed them to establish a rock 'n' roll intelligentsia. Thanks in large part to Dylan's work, there were now bona fide rock music critics, and in the summer of 1970, they turned en masse on Bob Dylan. Nonetheless, the album was a commercial success. Within two months, it was the No. 4 record on the American charts and No. 1 in Great Britain.

Dylan quickly followed *Self Portrait* with another album optimistically titled *New Morning*. He stubbornly maintained some of the elements of *Self Portrait*, notably the female singers, but the songs were all originals and he performed them with fierce conviction. Dylan played a lot of piano and was reunited for the sessions with Al Kooper, who directed a young studio band. As Ralph J. Gleason, the sage of American rock 'n' roll critics, exulted in *Rolling Stone*, "We've got Dylan back again."[35]

Even the cover of *New Morning* had a "so there" look to it. On the front, a 29-year-old Dylan glared. On the back, a decade-younger Dylan, hugged by blues singer Victoria Spivey, insouciantly smiled a challenge to record buyers. After a couple of years in the Nashville wilderness, the old Dylan did appear to be back, with a New York album that provided a tough, assertive taste of rock 'n' roll. Some of the songs ("New Morning," "Father of Night" and "Time Passes Slowly") had been written for a play by Archibald MacLeish called *Scratch*, based on a story by Stephen Vincent Benet called "The Devil and Daniel Webster." They had been rejected by the producer, so Dylan used them on the album.[36] Consequently, fans searching for autobiographical clues in those songs might have been baffled.

Not all of his fans were satisfied with *New Morning*. It was an improvement over *Self Portrait*, but to some followers, something appeared seriously wrong with their leader. One of these fans, A. J. Weberman, had begun a pursuit of his idol upon Dylan's return to the city, as he was convinced that evil forces were manipulating Dylan. Weberman was a radical who had deified the Dylan of an earlier phase and disparaged him now that he was a married man, a father and, apparently, less willing to strike out in anger at people and things that troubled him. Dylan's crime, in Weberman's view, was attaining contentment.

Weberman formed the Dylan Liberation Front, appointed himself "minister of defense," and dedicated his energies to bringing back Dylan from the "domestic wilderness." When Dylan quickly followed *Self Portrait* with the more vital *New Morning* and then issued a "political" single the following year ("George Jackson"), Weberman took credit.[37]

Weberman taught an alternative curriculum class on Dylan's work at New York University, where he proffered bizarre reinterpretations of Dylan lyrics. He hounded the artist, haranguing him in print (primarily in the *East Village Other*), and accusing him of being a heroin addict who was so strung out that he could no longer write songs of power. It was all a government conspiracy, Weberman theorized, to remove Dylan from the pinnacle of the youth world. Weberman also harangued Dylan in person, taking his students on field trips to Dylan's brownstone, where class members stood outside yelling, "Hey, Bobby--*please* crawl out your window" and "Open the door, Bobby."[38] Others chanted, "Free Bob Dylan! End rock rip-off! Free Bob Dylan!"[39]

Then Weberman's Dylan obsession took its wackiest turn: He began sifting through the garbage Dylan put out at the curb of his MacDougal Street home, analyzing it for clues about what troubled the artist. He found a half-finished letter to Johnny Cash, disposable diapers, copies of rock 'n' roll magazines, a used ticket from a cross-country flight, a ripped-up photo of Jimi Hendrix (which Weberman discovered the day after the guitarist's death from a drug overdose), a bill from the Book of the Month Club and a postcard from Dylan's grandmother.[40] After a while, Weberman also began to file wrapped-up collections of dog feces prepared by Dylan and his family.[41] Dylan had hoped that this would discourage the "garbologist" from further research.

Even at the height of Weberman's attacks, Dylan tried to shrug them off as "the price of fame," but it was hard for the artist to turn the other cheek when faced with a constant assault on his privacy.[42] In a hostile interview, which was begun during a street-corner confrontation and concluded later, Weberman accused Dylan of being a capitalist pig, of making money off of the poor and the oppressed, and then turning his back on them. (Actually, Dylan was not greedy. By choosing seclusion over continual offers to perform concerts, he declined millions of dollars during this era.)[43] Weberman told Dylan: "Bob . . . the kids on the street think you've turned into a fucking sellout . . . . People are saying you've turned into a capitalist pig, that your wealth has corrupted you . . . . You ripped off their music! *You owe them quite a bit!*"[44]

Weberman continued to scream at Dylan, citing debts supposedly owed by him to the American radicals. Dylan said he owed no such debts, and remained calm despite Weberman's hectoring. Finally, Weberman said that he and the members of the Dylan Liberation Front were going to "do a number" on Dylan. "We got some shit planned that's gonna blow your mind," he told him. Later, Weberman concluded: "Talking to Dylan was like talking to a ghost. The old Dylan, full of ideas and stories, was gone, replaced with a shell. It was also like talking to a con man who was really conning himself."[45]

Weberman had been circulating bootleg copies of Dylan's long-delayed novel, *Tarantula*. Dylan's income was being undercut by pirates of both his novel and his recorded work. Bootleg recordings of Dylan's 1967 basement sessions with The Band were selling in college-town record stores (under the title *The Great White Wonder*, so named because of its plain cover), and a profitable trade of the novel was contributing to the incomes of print bootleggers. Dylan dealt with the novel's pirates first. In 1971, Dylan finally allowed Macmillan to publish the novel, a decision that was no doubt made with great resignation. If anyone was to profit by its sale, some critics said, it should be the artist. Critic Robert Christgau, in the *New York Times*, said it was being published merely "to acknowledge the loss of a battle in his never-ending war for privacy."[46] The book baffled many critics, yet few could not marvel at the wordplay. Dylan's writing was, most critics noted, better when sung, but his writing on the page also was music of a sort.

Dylan's Greenwich Village lethargy continued as he remained besieged by radical fans and a music press that still expected a new testament. Years later, Dylan said he had come to regard that period in the early 1970s as one of the most unhappy of his life. It was also one of his least productive, and Weberman's harassment could have only worsened a troubling situation. Dylan produced no new albums.

He had made two quiet trips to Israel with his family in 1969 and 1970, but his trip in May 1971--in conjunction with his 30th birthday--made news as Dylan was photographed strolling through Jerusalem. Dylan and his wife spent part of his birthday in a theater, watching a Gregory Peck film. "I'm quite a fan of his," Dylan told a reporter from the *Jerusalem Post*. However, some saw these visits as more than simple family vacations. As with every other movement of Dylan's, these trips were analyzed and interpreted. Charges were made, by his followers in the United States, that he was a Zionist and was funneling money to the Israeli Army. When Dylan re-emerged as a concert performer three years later, Weberman was not alone in suggesting the tour was intended to raise money for Israel's defense budget. Joan Baez's sister, singer Mimi Farina, also voiced that opinion. Dylan adamantly denied the charges, though he was clearly taken with Israel and even investigated the possibility of moving there in 1972.[47]

He released two singles in 1971. "Watching the River Flow" suggested that Dylan was content to stand by and let others participate in the madness of contemporary society, in which he had once been awash. "George Jackson" was an overtly political song about a black leader who was murdered in prison. The only album released that year was a collection of "hits" (few had been true hits for Dylan). *Bob Dylan's Greatest Hits Vol. II* was a double album that featured "Watching the River Flow" and his one other recent hit, "Lay Lady Lay." "George Jackson" did not appear, but then, it had not been much of a success. Its lyrics included the word *shit*, and it was therefore given limited airplay. Other songs on the collection included Dylan's sloppy Isle of Wight version of "The Mighty Quinn" (a hit for Manfred Mann), "Don't

Think Twice, It's All Right" (a hit for Peter, Paul and Mary), "All I Really Want to Do" (a hit for Cher), "My Back Pages" (a hit for The Byrds) and "All along the Watchtower" (a hit for The Jimi Hendrix Experience). Dylan recorded some of his songs from the basement sessions with The Band ("I Shall Be Released," "You Ain't Goin' Nowhere" and "Down in the Flood"), accompanied by a friend, guitarist Happy Traum. The one gem pulled from the Columbia vaults was Dylan's performance of "Tomorrow Is a Long Time," from his April 12, 1963 Town Hall concert. Dylan also appeared that fall on *A Tribute to Woody Guthrie, Part One*, from the January 1968 Carnegie Hall tribute.

Throughout 1971 and 1972, Dylan confined his recording to works by other artists. He collaborated with Allen Ginsberg on television and record projects (some of these recordings were not released until the 1980s), and appeared as a side man on sessions with Steve Goodman and Doug Sahm (he gave Sahm a song called "Wallflower"). If he wrote other songs, he generally saved them, rarely offering them to other artists. From the release of *New Morning* in late 1970 until *Planet Waves* in early 1974, Dylan recorded little new material. He also began to sever his relationship with Grossman, a long process that would keep him in court for years.

In 1971, Dylan finally released his documentary of the 1966 tour with The Hawks, *Eat the Document*. The film had been intended for showing on ABC, but the network had rejected it. Edited by Dylan and Howard Alk (with the assistance of Robbie Robertson), the film was released on February 8, and credited D. A. Pennebaker as the director. Pennebaker's original version (which he called *Something is Happening*) was so different from the version released by Dylan and Alk that he disavowed the finished product. *Eat the Document* never earned a wide release and was shown mostly in art theaters and college auditoriums.

Dylan made only a few concert appearances during this fallow period: the celebrated Concert for Bangladesh in August 1971 and a New Year's Eve appearance with The Band on the crest of 1972. He was a side man and guest star for The Band's concerts, but he was the main attraction of the Bangladesh performances (matinee and evening shows) on August 1, 1971, in Madison Square Garden. Hosted by George Harrison, the benefit was intended to raise money for the refugees of Bangladesh. The superstar band that was assembled included Harrison's fellow ex-Beatle, Ringo Starr, the brilliant guitarist Eric Clapton, Indian sitarist Ravi Shankar, the flamboyant keyboardist Billy Preston and the multi-instrumentalist Leon Russell. However, the unbilled guest, Bob Dylan, stole the show. Dylan performed five songs at each concert, none of which was newer than *Blonde on Blonde*'s "Just Like a Woman." Dylan had eschewed his white suit from the Isle of Wight in favor of denim. He gave a masterful performance and appeared on the three-record set that was drawn from the concert, and released in time for the 1971 holiday season. In addition, a film of the concert was released in March 1972. Technically, Dylan was back on top of the charts.

Still, it had been a long time since the release of a real Bob Dylan album. Greatest hits anthologies, benefit concert performances and media events like the Bangladesh shows still did not render Dylan active as an artist. There was no motorcycle accident to blame this time, and Dylan's fans were notoriously impatient. Few were as extreme as A. J. Weberman in voicing their impatience, but gaps of years between albums were indeed rare in that era. (Later, of course, fans grew to expect albums from artists such as Bruce Springsteen only as frequently as presidential election years.)

Dylan had always been interested in film, yet it was not until 1973 that he found himself actually acting in one. *Don't Look Back* and *Eat the Document* had whetted his appetite, so when he was approached about becoming involved in a new western being made by director Sam Peckinpah, Dylan was intrigued. The film itself would be an unhappy experience for him, but it did lead him back into the public world.

The screenplay for *Pat Garrett and Billy the Kid* had been written by Rudolph Wurlitzer, a friend and admirer of Dylan. Wurlitzer, in turn, had asked Dylan to think about writing and performing the music for the film. Considering Dylan's attraction for films in general, and the western myth in particular, this was not an outrageous request, even for such a reclusive artist. The musician began studying Peckinpah's films, including *The Wild Bunch*, *The Ballad of Cable Hogue* and *Ride the High Country*. He soon found himself admiring Peckinpah's interpretation of the Old West. Dylan wrote a ballad, titled "Billy," which he played for Wurlitzer. Wurlitzer then introduced Dylan to the eccentric director. Peckinpah was ignorant of Bob Dylan. In fact, Peckinpah had been considering hiring country singer Roger Miller to do the score. The stars of the film, James Coburn and singer Kris Kristofferson (the former janitor turned singer and actor), were mildly horrified. (Miller was not such a completely outlandish suggestion; he later won a Tony Award for *Big River*, his adaptation of Mark Twain's *Adventures of Huckleberry Finn*.) However, Peckinpah was persuaded that Dylan's involvement might open the film to a wider audience.

Peckinpah insisted that Dylan perform "Billy," and was reportedly so moved that he cried. He also allowed Wurlitzer to expand a sidekick role in the script to a part that was suitable for an artist of Dylan's stature.[48] At first, Dylan was wary and had to be talked into taking the role. "If I do it, then they *got* me on film," he told Kristofferson. "Hell," Kristofferson drawled, "they already got you on records."[49]

Dylan moved his wife and children to Durango, Mexico, for three months, from November 1972 through the end of January 1973. Dylan found himself playing comic relief in the film. Wurlitzer and Peckinpah had been willing to expand the role of Alias, Billy the Kid's sidekick, out of respect for Dylan, but

Dylan kept the role small, perhaps concerned about his untested acting abilities. As a beginner in a film with so many veterans, he may have felt out of his element and sought help. If so, he got little guidance from Peckinpah, who was so distracted by his battles with the film company, MGM Studios, that he could not assist his novice. Dylan turned to Kristofferson for help, but he, too, was relatively inexperienced as an actor, having at that time made only three films.

The film featured a miscellany of character actors, including Slim Pickens, Chill Wills and Jack Elam, who were familiar faces from scores of westerns. However, these actors were not verbal; they were instinctive. Dylan was on his own. As if he did not have enough trouble before the cameras, he also had a small crisis to deal with off-camera: His wife and children were miserable in Durango. Kristofferson said that Dylan went days without speaking to Sara.[50] Dylan respected Peckinpah and identified him as an artist struggling against a corporation, but that did not make the director any easier to work for.

Two excursions allowed Dylan some release from the turmoil in Durango. The first occurred over the film company's Christmas break, when Dylan and family flew to England to spend the holiday with George and Patti Harrison, and the second came a month later when Dylan escaped the set for a recording session in Mexico City. Dylan had planned to record "Billy" and other film music, but a problem arose when the film's stars, Coburn and Kristofferson, along with several of members of the company, decided to accompany Dylan. Peckinpah had planned a screening of his new film, *The Getaway* starring Steve McQueen and Ali MacGraw, for that night, only to discover that most of his stars were playing hooky. In Peckinpah's view, this was a power play by Dylan, and, as a result, their relationship soured.

Dylan and family retreated to the West Coast after filming had been completed and he did further recording at the Burbank Studios for the film's score. (One of Dylan's children had become ill in Mexico and his father had reasoned that the best medical care would be found in Los Angeles, which prompted the move to California.) By April, Dylan had settled in Malibu.

Doing his first movie score, Dylan needed assistance with his music. Film composer Jerry Fielding was assigned to help Dylan put his songs together with the action on film. It was an arduous process and Dylan and Fielding did not work well together. Despite this friction, Dylan's music was often perfect for film: It underscored the action on the screen, matching the mood perfectly, but never distracting from the vision. An example was a piece Dylan wrote for the death of the old sheriff, who was played by Slim Pickens. After Pickens was shot, he staggered to the riverside, followed by his wife, played by Katy Jurado. As Pickens sat, slowly dying, Jurado comforted him. On the soundtrack, Dylan sang the dirge, "Knockin' on Heaven's Door." (Released as a single in August 1973, it became a Top 20 hit.)

That scene survived, but after all Dylan and Fielding's work, the initial version of *Pat Garrett and Billy the Kid* to be released showed evidence of studio brutalization of Dylan's music. Tunes that had been written for specific scenes were removed and placed elsewhere in the narrative, and Dylan saw little evidence that his labors on the film score had been of any use. Critics were not kind to the film, and several commented on the disjointed nature of the story, which resulted from the studio's re-editing of Peckinpah's version. Dylan's acting was largely dismissed but several writers noted his screen presence. When Dylan was on screen, they agreed, it was difficult to watch anyone else.

After the harassment in New York and the agony of working on the film, Dylan and his family enjoyed the respite in their leased home on the Pacific Coast Highway in Malibu. Dylan told reporters that Malibu would be only a temporary stop, but within a couple of years, he had begun building a castle by the ocean. He was all the way across the country from upstate New York and far removed from the little village of Woodstock, yet he had retained the same neighbors. Robbie Robertson and other members of The Band had moved to Malibu, building a recording complex called Shangri-La Studios. It was a state-of-the-art facility, and was far removed, both geographically and technically, from the basement of Big Pink. Soon, Dylan was back in the studio recording with his old backup band. He was ready to return to the public arena.

Notes

1. Nat Hentoff, "The Crackin', Shakin', Breakin' Sounds," the *New Yorker*, 24 October, 1964, cited in Craig McGregor, editor, *Bob Dylan: The Early Years* (New York: DaCapo Press, 1990), p. 44.
2. Clinton Heylin, *Bob Dylan: Behind the Shades* (New York: Summit Books, 1991), p. 107.
3. Peter Brown and Steven Gaines, *The Love You Make* (New York: McGraw-Hill, 1984), pp. 154-58.
4. Patrick Humphries and John Bauldie, *Absolutely Dylan* (New York: Viking Studio Books, 1991), pp. 180-81.
5. Bob Spitz, *Dylan: A Biography* (New York: McGraw-Hill, 1989), p. 274.
6. Ibid., p. 279.
7. John Bauldie, editor, *Wanted Man: In Search of Bob Dylan* (New York: Citadel Underground Press, 1991), pp. 203-4.
8. Robert Shelton, *No Direction Home: The Life and Music of Bob Dylan* (New York: Ballantine Books, 1987), p. 319.
9. Bob Dylan, Notes to *Biograph* [sound recording] (Columbia Records, 1985).
10. Spitz, *Dylan*, p. 298.
11. Joe Smith, *Off the Record: An Oral History of Popular Music* (New York: Warner Books, 1988), p. 269.
12. Shelton, *No Direction Home*, p. 348.
13. Pauline Kael, "The Calvary Gig," the *New Yorker*, 13 February 1978, in Elizabeth Thomson and David Gutman, *The Dylan Companion* (New York: Delta, 1990), p. 224.
14. These are drawn from interviews with Nora Ephron and Susan Edmiston of the *New York Post* and from a San Francisco press conference, both excerpted in Shelton, *No Direction Home*, pp. 324-25. The Ephron-Edmiston interview is available in McGregor, *Early Years*, pp. 82-90.
15. Heylin, *Behind the Shades*, pp. 151-52. The edited interview appears in McGregor, *Early*

Years, pp. 124-25.
16. Ron Rosenbaum, "Playboy Interview: Bob Dylan," *Playboy*, January 1978.
17. "Dylan Hurt in Cycle Mishap," the *New York Times*, 2 August 1966, cited in McGregor, *Early Years*, p. 192.
18. Anthony Scaduto, *Bob Dylan: An Intimate Biography* (New York: Grosset and Dunlap, 1971), p. 282.
19. Sam Shepard, "True Dylan," *Esquire*, July 1987, p. 68.
20. Smith, *Off the Record*, p. 247.
21. Clive Davis, with James Wilwerth, *Clive: Inside the Record Business* (New York: Morrow, 1975), p. 57.
22. Steven Gaines, *Heroes and Villains: The True Story of The Beach Boys* (New York: New American Library, 1986), p. 160.
23. Humphries and Bauldie, *Absolutely Dylan*, p. 191.
24. Shelton, *No Direction Home*, p. 453.
25. Michael Krogsgaard, *Positively Bob Dylan: A Thirty Year Discography, Concert and Recording Session Guide* (Ann Arbor, Mich.: Popular Culture, Ink, 1991), p. 65.
26. Shelton, *No Direction Home*, p. 455.
27. Ibid., p. 57.
28. Ibid., p. 59.
29. Humphries and Bauldie, *Absolutely Dylan*, p. 194.
30. Bauldie, *Wanted Man*, p. 23.
31. Scaduto, *Bob Dylan*, pp. 301-2.
32. The interviewer was Michele Enghien and the piece is cited in Humphries and Bauldie, *Absolutely Dylan*, p. 196.
33. Shelton, *No Direction Home*, p. 481.
34. Ibid., p. 473.
35. Ralph J. Gleason, "We've Got Dylan Back Again," *Rolling Stone*, 26 November 1970,
36. Shelton, *No Direction Home*, p. 483.
37. Ibid., p. 473.
38. A. J. Weberman, "Dylan Meets Weberman," from the *East Village Other*, 19 January 1971, reprinted in McGregor, *Early Years*, p. 379.
39. Spitz, *Dylan*, p. 404.
40. Listed in Kevin Stein and Dave Marsh, *The Book of Rock Lists* (New York: Dell/Rolling Stone Press, 1981), p. 340.
41. Shelton, *No Direction Home*, p. 471.
42. Ibid.
43. Ibid., p. 473.
44. Spitz, *Dylan*, p. 404.
45. Weberman, "Dylan Meets Weberman," pp. 387-88.
46. Robert Christgau, "Tarantula," the *New York Times Book Review*, reprinted in McGregor, *Early Years*, p. 390.
47. Shelton, *No Direction Home*, p. 474.
48. Heylin, *Behind the Shades*, pp. 219-20.
49. Shelton, *No Direction Home*, p. 491.
50. Ibid., p. 492.

Chapter 3

Song and Dance Man

BOB DYLAN WAS READY TO COME OUT OF HIDING by the fall of 1973. His daily Malibu jam sessions with The Band led to recording, which, in turn, led to rehearsals for a concert tour.

It happened quickly by Bob Dylan's standards. He began by playing at Robbie Robertson's Shangri-La Studios with The Band, unveiling new material. Robertson, The Band's principal songwriter, was himself suffering writer's block and appreciated the opportunity to sink back into the comfortable role of Dylan's lead guitarist.

Dylan had ended his long winter of discontent and was ready for action. Clive Davis had been fired as president of Columbia Records over charges of payola, and so Dylan had lost his major ally at the record company. (Davis went on to resurrect himself professionally, building Arista Records into a major record industry power.)

Dylan's relations with Columbia were chilled and he was dissatisfied with the way the company treated him. He felt that Columbia released his albums but did not put as much push behind them as behind other artists. Dylan's contract with Columbia had ended after the *Pat Garrett and Billy the Kid* soundtrack, and he began shopping around.

David Geffen had made his name as a manager of California rock 'n' roll artists and had recently started the appropriately named Asylum Records label, which he intended as an artists' haven from the monolithic record industry. After the giant Columbia/CBS corporate structure, the small, artist-driven Asylum seemed perfect for Dylan. He forged a handshake contract with Geffen, who was enthusiastic about Dylan's possible return to the concert stage. Dylan, in turn, enjoyed Geffen's personal attention after the shrugged indifference of the new Columbia officials.

Columbia executives were aware of Dylan's activities: that he was plotting a major tour and planning to record a new album for probable release on another label. In response, Columbia rush-released an album of outtakes recorded during the *Self Portrait* sessions. Dylan fans would perhaps have salivated in anticipation of outtakes from *John Wesley Harding* or *Highway 61 Revisited*, but little could be gained from an album that was nothing more than a *Self Portrait, Jr.* (Its official title was *Dylan*, but it was released in Europe years later as *A Fool Such as I*.) The sole intent of the album appeared to be revenge. To warm up for the *Self Portrait* recording sessions, Dylan had crooned his way through the Elvis Presley standard "Can't Help Falling in Love," Joni Mitchell's "Big Yellow Taxi" and Jerry Jeff Walker's "Mr. Bojangles." These exercises were never intended for release. Other songs, notably Peter LaFarge's "The Ballad of Ira Hayes" and the traditional "Spanish Is the Loving Tongue" were more acceptable and would have made excellent substitutes for some of the tracks on *Self Portrait*, yet the *Dylan* album served mostly to further sour the relationship between the artist and his former record label.

In October, Dylan flew to New York to finish composing songs and returned to Malibu in early November for his recording sessions with The Band. Although it had been three full years since his last real album, he felt at ease in the studio and recorded quickly. Originally titled *Ceremonies of the Horsemen* (from a line in "Love Minus Zero/No Limit"), the title was changed at the last minute to *Planet Waves*, which delayed the album's release.

Simultaneously, a huge concert tour had been organized by Bill Graham, rock 'n' roll's most celebrated promoter. Graham had established the Fillmore auditoriums, first in San Francisco, and then in New York, in the 1960s. These halls became splendid showcases for rock 'n' roll, places where musicians and audiences alike were treated with respect. They differed from concert halls that were really intended for other purposes but occasionally tolerated rock 'n' roll shows. Although Graham had closed both Fillmores to concentrate on other commitments, he was delighted to organize a joint tour for Dylan and The Band, which was set to begin early in 1974, along with the release of the new album. Graham was rock's principal showman and Dylan knew the concert producer would present him properly.

It was the first major tour of rock 'n' roll's adulthood. Previous tours--those in the early 1960s--had featured caravans of stars performing for brief periods. Later, with The Beach Boys and The Beatles, concert tours had consisted of a 30 to 45 minute set of hits, which were preceded by lots of supporting acts. In the late 1960s, with bands such as Cream and The Jimi Hendrix Experience, concerts had taken on the aura of an extended jam session. However, the Dylan/Band tour recognized that rock 'n' roll music was art, but also show business, and Graham allowed the musicians to achieve that delicate balance. Every aspect of the tour was handled carefully. All of the concert arenas had been booked anonymously in the fall of 1973, to avoid leaking news of Dylan's reemergence. Rather than long lines at ticket windows, a new process was employed: Tickets were available only by mail. There were 658,000 tickets; 12 million people applied for them.

In the tremendous glare of the national media, the tour began in Chicago on January 3, 1974. For two months, almost every one of Dylan's public movements was monitored, photographed, and interpreted. The reclusive artist had, at last, come out of hiding. The press greeted him like a god come back to life and the tour as a virtual second coming of rock 'n' roll. "Never in the history of American rock has a tour aroused so much public interest," *Time* magazine wrote. It was "a moment for a legend--and an era--to live again."[1] The *Village Voice* called it "the quintessential American event."[2]

Dylan started his first show with "Hero Blues," a song written ten years before but never released. Dylan and The Band opened the show jointly, ripping through several rockers before Dylan left the stage for The Band's set and then returned to play some solo acoustic numbers. Reunited, Dylan and the group then closed, generally, with "Blowin' in the Wind" and "Like a Rolling Stone." Although the set list settled into an identifiable pattern within a couple of weeks--Dylan both opened and closed the shows with "Most Likely You Go Your Way (and I'll Go Mine)"--each performance had a surprise: "Song to Woody" in Philadelphia, "Desolation Row" in St. Louis, a new song called "Nobody 'Cept You" in Chicago. Little material was played from *Planet Waves*. Dylan's inclusion of "It's Alright Ma (I'm Only Bleeding)," from *Bringing It All Back Home*, seemed staggeringly appropriate in the spring of 1974. The song's line about the president of the United States having to stand naked reflected the Richard Nixon presidency, which was then crumbling. Dylan did most of his famous songs, spitting the words and relinquishing to the stadium format of the tour any attempt at subtlety. It was a rock 'n' roll show, and Dylan was backed by a superb rock 'n' roll band.

They played 40 concerts in six weeks. Although it lasted only two months--not long by later standards, it was an exhausting tour as Dylan and The Band often performed two shows a day. Despite the coverage (it was a public relations delight, as Dylan was featured on the cover of most of the major magazines), Dylan managed to maintain his mystique. He rarely spoke during performances and remained aloof, granting few interviews.[3] Only Dylan could pull off the most publicized tour in the history of popular music and remain an enigma.

The tour with The Band was a retrospective: Much of the music belonged to Dylan the young man. Although the middle-aged Dylan had reinterpreted the songs and offered them up as fresh new material, they were still old songs. Nonetheless, the look back offered him a chance to put the seal on his youth and begin writing new works. *Planet Waves*, as it turned out, would become a mere warm-up for a creative period that would rival--some would say eclipse--the earlier work held so dear by his fans (who still quoted his earlier words, analyzed his every statement and sifted through his trash for clues to the mystery of life on earth). Dylan was about to experience a renaissance.

Buckets of Rain

Dylan was disappointed that *Planet Waves* did not sell well, and he believed that part of the problem was his association with a small record company like Asylum, which appeared inadequate after his experience with an arm of the mighty CBS corporation. There had been, after all, 12 million applications for the Dylan/Band tour. Why, then, had only a half-million copies of the album sold? He was disturbed, but David Geffen pressed him for a moral obligation: a live album of the tour. Dylan, Robertson and the engineers from *Planet Waves* constructed a reasonable document of the tour, a two-record set called *Before the Flood*, which was released by Asylum in June. He then opened negotiations with Columbia Records and soon returned to the company's roster.

Back in New York, and relieved, in a sense, of the burdens of his past, Dylan again revisited his old haunts. He was talked into performing at a benefit in May by his old mates, singers Dave Van Ronk and Phil Ochs. Ochs had organized the concert to aid the Friends of Chile and Dylan had casually agreed to perform. However, Ochs did not announce Dylan's appearance, figuring he might very well back out or forget to show up. Surprisingly, Dylan was there, somewhat inebriated, joining in on Woody Guthrie's "Deportees (Plane Wreck at Los Gatos)" and singing the lead on "North Country Blues," "Spanish Is the Loving Tongue" and "Blowin' in the Wind."[4]

It was a successful night, yet it was only another visit to the past. To deal with the future, Dylan sought out an art teacher named Norman Raeben. He had learned of Raeben during his time in California and had wanted to work with him during his New York stay. Friends said Raeben had taught them to define in the indefinable concepts of truth and love and beauty. In Dylan's account, he "dropped in" to see Raeben and stayed for two months.[5] Although Dylan had dabbled in painting (two works had appeared as the covers of *Music from Big Pink* and *Self Portrait*), he was not concerned with growing as that sort of artist. He came to regard the period with Raeben as a turning point in his career. Beyond the technique of painting, Dylan said Raeben taught him about uniting his abilities as a creative artist. "My mind and my hand and my eye were not connected up," Dylan said. "I had a lot of fantasy dreams. He doesn't respect fantasy. He respects only imagination."[6] If Raeben recognized Dylan's celebrity, he did not bow to it, and Dylan was treated like any other student. Raeben was often abusive to his students, saying they were idiots who lacked vision, because they had not learned to see.[7] Dylan studied with Raeben for a few months and began applying some of the techniques he learned from his teacher. The new ways of seeing that Raeben had tried to teach his painting students were now adapted by Dylan for use in writing lyrics. Dylan said Raeben taught him "to do consciously what I unconsciously felt."[8]

The result was *Blood on the Tracks*, which Dylan began recording in New York that fall. Still, home on his new Minnesota farm over the Christmas holiday, Dylan listened to the acetate recording of the impending album and was dissatisfied, so he asked his brother David (himself a musician) to help him arrange recording sessions at Sound 80 Studios in Minneapolis. Backed by a local band, Dylan rerecorded several key songs ("Tangled Up in Blue," "You're a Big Girl Now," "Idiot Wind," "Lily, Rosemary and the Jack of Hearts" and "If You See Her, Say Hello"), seriously altering the sound of the album. The New York version of "Idiot Wind," for example, was quiet and meditative, while the Minneapolis version was accusatory, like a menacing hurricane. The North Country sessions were much more relaxed and easygoing than the recording in New York. Dylan even sang the complicated lyrics to "Idiot Wind" off of a series of pink phone-message slips.[9]

Working without an outside producer (none was credited, as had also been the case with *Planet Waves*), Dylan made a superbly recorded and well-crafted record on his own. Although he and Bob Johnston apparently had a satisfying relationship, Dylan's spontaneous approach to recording put off most traditional producers. Dylan's revision of *Blood on the Tracks* delayed the album's release until after the holiday season, but it did not harm the sales seriously. When released in mid-January, the album was greeted with lavish praise, and immediately put into the pantheon of his best work of the 1960s. Some called it a sequel to the confessional *Another Side of Bob Dylan*, but Dylan still denied that *Blood on the Tracks* was drawn from his marital troubles. "A lot of people thought . . . that album, *Blood on the Tracks*, pertained to me," Dylan said. "'You're a Big Girl Now,' well, I read this was supposed to be about my wife . . . . I don't write confessional songs."[10]

Mary Travers (of Peter, Paul and Mary) had Dylan as a guest on her syndicated radio program ("Mary Travers and Friend") in March 1975, and complimented him on the album. She had enjoyed it, she said. Dylan responded that he wondered how anyone could "enjoy" something that was obviously the result of so much pain.[11] Though he had denied that the album was intensely personal, the fact remained that the Dylans' marital problems were matters of public discussion. Dylan had rarely been the subject of gossip columns since his marriage, and he had worked hard to keep his wife and family out of the limelight. Now, however, their movements were being tracked by reporters.

Sara did accompany her husband to San Francisco for a benefit concert, at the behest of Bill Graham. The city's public schools were losing extracurricular programs because of budget cuts and Graham organized a concert at Kezar Stadium for Students Need Athletics, Culture and Kicks (SNACK). There were several announced bands (Jefferson Starship, The Grateful Dead, Santana) and one that came as a surprise: a supergroup including Dylan, Neil Young and members of The Band.

After the 1974 tour with The Band and the triumph of *Blood on the Tracks*, Dylan was again on top of the rock 'n' roll world. By the beginning of 1975, he had re-established himself as a vital artist. Determined to control his work and his legacy now that he was back at Columbia, Dylan and Robbie Robertson began editing the hours of songs they had recorded during the summer of 1967. Bootleggers had been selling pirated versions of the songs for years, so Dylan and The Band sanctioned the official release of the set for the summer of 1975. *The Basement Tapes*, though already eight years old, was the freshest sounding record released that season. The Rolling Stones and the remnants of The Beatles seemed tired by comparison. Only a young artist, Bruce Springsteen, matched the vitality of Dylan's music with his new release, *Born to Run*.

After a vacation in France without his wife, Dylan again returned to New York and immersed himself in the Greenwich Village community. It was apparently not a true nostalgia that brought him back, because he did not want to relive the past with his old friends; rather, he wanted to make a new present with them. In so doing, Dylan pumped new life into careers that had gone fallow, reviving a form that had roots in vaudeville and mime.

Continually searching for new inspiration, Dylan decided to collaborate. He was introduced to Jacques Levy, a writer and theater producer who had worked with one of Dylan's associates in show business, Roger McGuinn. McGuinn was the founder and leader of The Byrds and had recorded several Dylan songs with the group, including "Mr. Tambourine Man" and "My Back Pages." In the late 1960s, McGuinn and Levy had collaborated on a musical called *Gene Trypp*, an update of the Scandanavian *Peer Gynt*. The show was never produced, though the McGuinn-Levy compositions appeared on the last several Byrds album before that band's breakup in 1972.

Working with Levy, who was a disciplined writer, forced Dylan to explore his subconscious as Raeben had taught him to do. Levy offered immediate, honest responses to Dylan's ideas and added some of his own. Almost before he realized it, Dylan again had on his hands an album full of material. One song, "Isis," was a complex tale of marriage, while another, "Joey," was an epic about a gangster. "Hurricane" was about boxer Rubin "Hurricane" Carter, who was imprisoned for a murder that Dylan believed the man did not commit. (Released as a single, "Hurricane" made it to No. 33 on the American charts.) These new pieces told stories and bore a distant resemblance to his old finger-pointing songs.

His jaunts through the Village and visits to the clubs had expanded his circle of musical acquaintances to include bassist Rob Stoner, drummer Howie

Wyeth and a violinist named Scarlet Rivera. Dylan and his new group recorded most of *Desire* in one nightlong session. The album was assembled quickly because Dylan was intent on fulfilling another vision. In October, he began rehearsing his new band, running the group through Hank Williams' "Kaw-Liga," The Impressions' "People Get Ready" and songs of his own that he had never played in concert, such as "Sad-Eyed Lady of the Lowlands." The revue concept included several other performers--McGuinn, Ramblin' Jack Elliott, Bob Neuwirth, and Ronee Blakely--who would have spots on the concert program. He also reconciled with Joan Baez, who became the Revue's costar.

This tour was to be the antithesis of the 1974 tour with The Band, which had been like a mammoth steamroller that plowed through stadiums. His new tour would be something intimate, involving visits to small concert halls and theaters by a traveling troupe of musicians. It was to be informal, involving no major egos.[12] That was the plan. Dylan said that he was inspired by the beginnings of a storm when he thought of the name for the tour: The Rolling Thunder Revue. (He might have also known *rolling thunder* was an Indian term for *truth*.)

Starting in New England in late October, the revue wound its way through the Northeast and Canada, culminating in a December 8 show at its largest venue, Madison Square Garden. This concert was dubbed the "Night of the Hurricane" and was Dylan's attempt to call attention to Carter's cause. By the time of the Madison Square Garden show, much of the revue's charm had been lost. It was intended for small halls, and its highly theatrical nature--Dylan appeared in whiteface, poets read from their work, backing musicians wore masks, and mimes performed--was out of place in a huge arena. In January 1976, Dylan and the revue performed three more dates, including "Night of the Hurricane II" in Houston's Astrodome. All attempts at intimacy were futile in that huge sports arena, though only one-fourth of the seats were occupied. The show lost $50,000, a good portion of which ($15,000) had come from Dylan's pocket. Nevertheless, Carter was pleased Dylan had made him his cause and within seven weeks of the concert, Carter was granted a retrial.[13] Eventually, Carter was cleared, although Dylan's song led to a libel suit (he had mentioned a witness by name and she accused him of misrepresenting her). Carter was grateful to his balladeer, saying "Bob Dylan . . . spent hundreds and thousands of hours and millions of dollars to get one man back what he never should have lost in the first place."[14]

The "Hurricane" controversy aside, the Rolling Thunder Revue was making news because of its unusual format, presenting a major artist in such small-scale settings, at least at the start of the tour. Musically, the shows had been richly satisfying. The early concerts had featured dramatic reinterpretations many of of Dylan's songs. For example, "The Lonesome Death of Hattie Carroll" was played on electric instruments, almost like a blues shuffle.

"Simple Twist of Fate," from *Blood on the Tracks*, was rewritten with Levy's help, and songs he had never played in concert, such as "I Dreamed I Saw St. Augustine," were debuted on stage. Dylan was also filming a number of the performances. Between shows, he urged the singers to improvise dramatic scenes with him. Working with Howard Alk and Jones Alk, who had assisted Pennebaker on *Don't Look Back*, he was crafting a film that he chose not to describe in detail to many of the people appearing in it. In between shows, in gas stations and hotel rooms, the cameras kept rolling.

The tour had created the best kind of publicity--word-of-mouth--for Dylan's new album, which was finally released in mid-January 1976. *Desire* became one of Dylan's biggest hits, reaching No. 1 on the American music charts. (This was to be the best sales performance of his career.)

Dylan began the second leg of his Rolling Thunder Revue tour in April in Florida and, by this time, it had become a stadium show. NBC's designated production company filmed a television special at the Belleview Biltmore Hotel in Clearwater, but Dylan rejected the program. The tour moved west, and Dylan not only performed in concert, he also filmed his fantasy feature movie, recorded a live album and made another attempt at making a television special.

In April 1976, near the end of the tour, Dylan learned that his longtime friend, singer Phil Ochs, had hanged himself. Dylan withdrew and the shows lost their joy for him. At the second-to-last concert of the tour, in Fort Collins, Colorado, Dylan finished the television special. An outdoor concert during a rainstorm seemed a fitting end to a tour that had begun with such promise yet had degenerated to an emotional trial. His relationship with Sara also was at its breaking point.

Since Dylan had rejected the NBC Television Network special filmed in Clearwater, he had to hire a documentary crew at his expense to shoot an alternate. Although the resulting program was acceptable to Dylan and was broadcast by NBC, to many viewers it seemed dreary. While rain fell on the football stadium crowd, a turbaned Dylan shouted his way through his songs. Nonetheless, Dylan's guitarist, Rob Stoner, thought that performance--which also formed the bulk of the album *Hard Rain*--was one of Dylan's best. To Stoner, it was an early punk record.[15] The album did fairly well when it was released in September 1976, but sales dropped off quickly, while the television special, which aired simultaneously, earned mostly negative reviews. Moreover, the omnipresent Bob Dylan was about to go back into hiding.

Going, Going, Gone

Dylan made only one major public appearance between April 1976 and February 1978. Most of his appearances were in court as he and his wife went through the painful process of divorce. However, on Thanksgiving Day 1976, he joined his old mates, The Band, for their final concert, at San Francisco's Winterland Palace. Bill Graham had helped The Band organize an elaborate farewell to the group's fans: a Thanksgiving dinner, followed by a concert by The Band and some of their friends: Dylan, Van Morrison, Joni Mitchell, Ronnie Hawkins, Muddy Waters, Neil Young and Neil Diamond. The inclusion of middle-of-the-road singer Neil Diamond might have seemed out of character, but Robbie Robertson had collaborated with Diamond on *Beautiful Noise*, a tribute to Tin Pan Alley songwriting. As Diamond left the stage after his set during The Band's farewell concert, he saw Dylan waiting for his cue. "You'll have to be pretty good to follow me," Diamond said. Dylan shrugged. "What do I have to do?" he asked. "Go on stage and fall sleep?"[16]

Dylan was the last of the guest stars, appearing briefly to play "Forever Young" and "Hazel" from *Planet Waves*, "I Don't Believe You (She Acts like We Never Have Met)" and two versions of "Baby, Let Me Follow You Down." He was apparently at ease, turning around to mug at The Band, and arching his eyebrows. Without having to fall asleep on stage, he stole the show from Diamond.

However, the real show was the battle in the courtroom in the case of *Dylan v. Dylan*. Sara Dylan had charged her husband with adultery and insisted he had threatened her physically, ordering her to leave their Malibu estate. Dylan, even when speaking with attorneys, sounded as elliptical as when he was parrying with reporters. The divorce proceedings took much of the year, and there was bitter fighting. Eventually, Sara Dylan was awarded a $13.5 million settlement and half the publishing money from the songs written during their 12-year marriage.[17] An even more acrimonious fight ensued over custodial rights to the children, although as the years passed the Dylans resolved most of these differences without further court battles.

Although he did not perform in concert or release any new albums, Dylan was active as an artist during 1977, editing his 100 hours of footage from the Rolling Thunder Revue. Beyond a mere concert film, he wanted to link the fantasy sequences into some sort of narrative. It was only mildly successful in that aspect, but the concert scenes were brilliant. Dylan and Howard Alk assembled a four-hour film that was released on a limited basis on January 25, 1978. *Renaldo and Clara* was roundly panned. The *Village Voice* sent seven critics to the film (Dylan called them a "firing squad") and all were unkind, to varying degrees, in their reviews. Richard Goldstein, however, was the kindest, finding the concert scenes with the revue to be "as moving as anything you're likely to experience in a rock-concert film."[18] Not all critics reviled the film, but Dylan was pilloried for vanity, among other vices. He had given himself enormous close-ups and centered much of the action on himself. "Dylan could love no one like he loves himself," wrote critic Karen Durbin.[19]

Whether to recoup the investment in the film or to settle his divorce payment with his ex-wife, Dylan launched an ambitious tour of the Orient and Australia in the spring. Again, he unveiled a new approach. Having witnessed a Neil Diamond concert in Las Vegas, he became Dylan the Entertainer, a la Diamond. He hired a big band--backup singers, brass, and woodwinds--and performed light, giddy, uptempo versions of some of his classics. New tunes were composed for old lyrics, and many of his best known songs were unrecognizable to old fans.

This "slicker" approach to performing may have owed itself, in part, to his new management. In 1977, Dylan signed with his first manager since his fissure with Albert Grossman at the beginning of the decade. Jerry Weintraub was one of the most successful managers in the business, handling the careers of Frank Sinatra, John Denver and Neil Diamond. He excelled at handling technical details and soon had hired Dylan a virtual army of assistants to help him carry off the huge tour.

After finishing with the Pacific basin, Dylan stopped in California to tape a new album with the big band. When he released the result, *Street-Legal*, in June 1978, Dylan was in the middle of a major European tour. He had played several shows in Los Angeles, but his drastic reinterpretations of his classic songs were not as well appreciated by U.S. audiences as they had been elsewhere. His new stage attire--shiny, three-piece suits--and his patter ("I'm just an entertainer," he frequently said) repelled those who had admired the less glitzy, unpretentious Dylan of earlier years. The European audiences were more welcoming of his experimentations with a new approach, and Dylan toured through the summer on the Continent.

Almost immediately on the heels of *Street-Legal* came another album, his third live record in four years. Intended as a souvenir of the Far East tour for the Japanese market, *Bob Dylan at Budokan* did so well that Columbia executives decided to release it in the United States. For those who had only heard about the accompanying flutes and saxophones, the album offered proof that Bob Dylan was changing his tunes ... literally. To those who criticized him for altering the music, Dylan said he was not subservient to the songs. Rather, he was trying to enhance that other part of his persona. Dylan said audiences that accepted him as a writer needed to learn to accept him as a performer. The writing of the songs was solitary, but the performance of them was not. The levels of energy involved in the two activities were also different. In order to maintain his equilibrium as a performer, he needed to remain a concert artist by reinventing his songs.[20]

He brought the show home to the states that fall and toured through mid-December. The reviews were decidedly mixed, but Dylan seemed ambivalent. "I'm just the postman," he said. "I deliver the songs. That's all I have in this world are those songs. That's what all the legend, all the myth is about--my songs .... Nobody else gives those songs life. It's up to me to do it."[21]

As the critics railed against the new stage performances--with some suggesting that he quit touring, move to Nevada, and officially declare himself the Las Vegas lounge act he had become, Dylan was growing discouraged. Things had not gone well. He had lost his wife and the closeness with his children. He also had lost money and reputation with *Renaldo and Clara* and his recent albums and concerts were being lampooned by the press. During a concert in San Diego, near the end of the tour, Dylan appeared deeply depressed, just going through the motions of performing. A fan sitting near the front tossed a silver cross on stage. Dylan recalled:

> I picked up the cross and put it in my pocket. I brought it with me to the next town, which was out in Arizona.... I was feeling even worse than I had in San Diego. I said, "Well, I need something tonight... that I didn't have before." And I looked in this pocket and I had this cross.[22]

A Satisfied Mind

It was nearly a full year before Dylan appeared on stage again, and he came to offer his audience a new controversy: his religion. Dylan has said that he experienced several profound moments of spirituality after finding the cross in his pocket in Arizona. At that moment, he said, he had felt a presence in the room that "couldn't have been anybody but Jesus." He felt Christ's hand on him, Dylan said, and his body trembled.[23] During the last few weeks of the tour, Dylan asked questions of the members of his band who were Christians. Helena Springs--a backup singer, sometime songwriting partner and one of his girlfriends--counseled him to pray and was shocked to learn that he rarely had.

Through another girlfriend, Mary Alice Artes, Dylan was led to a charismatic Christian group. Artes attended a meeting of the Vineyard Fellowship in Los Angeles and decided to rededicate herself to Christ. She asked the pastor of the group, Ken Gulliksen, if he could help her boyfriend, Bob Dylan. Dylan met with Gulliksen and was invited to go to Bible school. Dylan at first belittled the idea, suggesting that he could not take three months out of his busy schedule. Besides, he had always hated school. Nonetheless, one morning he woke up and drove to the Vineyard School of Discipleship and became a student. Gulliksen said he never missed a day of classes. Gradually, he came to accept Jesus as real, and his new belief imbued the music he was writing. He went to the heart of the Bible Belt to record the songs he felt coming out of his newly converted soul.

Muscle Shoals Sound Studio in Sheffield, Alabama, was home to the best soul and rhythm and blues session musicians in America. Working with keyboardist Barry Beckett and Atlantic executive Jerry Wexler as producers, Dylan recorded one of his most musically satisfying albums, *Slow Train Com-*

ing. He was backed by Mark Knopfler, the brilliant guitarist who led Dire Straits, and showed the sort of care in making this record that had been absent in the rushed *Street-Legal*. However, it was not the music that would attract the most attention. Dylan's embrace of Christianity led him, in the minds of some critics, to become too didactic. He croaked warnings of impending apocalypse and doom, these writers suggested, which threatened those who failed to follow his path.

The album was released to a stunned public, and Dylan played three of the tunes on NBC's "Saturday Night Live" in October. He began his gospel tours with 14 performances at San Francisco's Warfield Theater, starting November 1. He played a 17-song set, including all of *Slow Train Coming* and other new gospel songs. None of his older songs--"Like a Rolling Stone" or "Just Like a Woman" and not even "Blowin' in the Wind"--appeared in his shows, nor would they for a year.

Cynicism greeted Dylan's new music. Some wondered if it was yet another attempt to alienate the mass audience. Several members of the crowd apparently showed up at the concerts only to boo and heckle. Rather than ignoring them, Dylan lectured frequently. Once known for saying so little between songs, Dylan was now actually preaching to the audience. Some said they hoped that the new faith was just another one of his elaborate put-ons.

Helena Springs believed Dylan to be under the spell of the Vineyard Fellowship. Backstage at a show, Springs recalled, members of the fellowship would pressure Dylan not to drink wine. Some suggested the Vineyard group had barred Dylan from performing any secular songs. The group was aware of Dylan's stature, and there was speculation that evangelizing was the primary motive behind the tour.[24] It was difficult for the artist. Dylan recalled some of the tensions:

> College kids showed the most disrespect. I mean it was fierce. We'd play theaters in the mission and Times Square districts in some of the larger cities, in the inner cities where industry has moved out and people don't have work, some of the most beautiful theaters are there--the people that would come to those shows, you know, they'd be more or less from the neighborhood, prostitutes, pimps, whatever, shady looking characters .... They understood what I was doing and they let me know that. Then we'd play all the so-called colleges, where my so-called fans were. All hell would break loose. "Take off that dress," "We want rock 'n' roll," lots of other things I don't even want to repeat, just really filthy mouth stuff. This really surprised me, that these kids didn't know any better, all from good homes and liberal-minded to boot .... I was happier with the pimps and the hookers ... during the gospel tours.[25]

His 1980 tour was supporting an album whose cover served to alienate many record buyers, as it pictured the hand of God reaching down from heaven to musicians on stage. *Saved* included the spiritual "A Satisfied Mind" along with eight new Dylan gospel songs. Though immaculately played by his stage band, it was not a tremendous success in the United States (although it reached No. 3 on the English charts). The *Saved* tour did include selections from Dylan's back catalog during performances. (The shows were billed as "visual and musical retrospectives.") Often, after opening with two gospel songs, Dylan would play "Like a Rolling Stone," and he might perform "To Ramona," "Blowin' in the Wind" or "Love Minus Zero/No Limit" elsewhere in the set. However, the predominant theme was his new music.

What many of his long-term fans may have failed to appreciate was the effect Dylan was having on another musical genre. As he had with folk music and then rock 'n' roll, Dylan was altering yet another musical form. He was helping to revolutionize contemporary Christian music, which became a potent commercial force during the 1980s through artists such as Keith Green (with whom Dylan recorded), Terry Talbot and Amy Grant. Previously, spiritual songs did not *rock*, but Dylan changed that.

The touring continued, with the old audiences gradually warming to at least some of Dylan's new music. However, with his next recording (he was back to working at a mid-1960s pace), Dylan returned to more secular themes, though the influence of his Christianity was still felt. *Shot of Love*, which was recorded in April and May 1981, contained doses of rhythm and blues and rock 'n' roll, with songs that ranged from an elegy for comedian Lenny Bruce to a meditation on the relationship of life forms on earth. In the context of the two previous albums, it appeared religious (one song bore the title "Property of Jesus"), but in retrospect, it was an attempt to graft what he had learned from gospel music to his style--whatever that was. Dylan once claimed that this was his favorite album.

The gospel singers were retained, and the album had the looseness of his Christian shows. The songs were among his most interesting in years, particularly "Every Grain of Sand." This masterful work, apparently inspired by William Blake, finds Dylan admitting that he is troubled and in need of counsel and asking a higher spirit for guidance. It is a pure, heartfelt plea whose vulnerability has made it one of his most endearing compositions. Nonetheless, a significant number of his fans ignored the album, considering it only another chapter in his gospel works. Even the good press that the album received did not significantly help sales. When a song from the album, "Heart of Mine," was released as a single, Dylan put an outtake from the sessions on the flip side. The reviews of that song, "The Groom's Still Waiting at the Altar," were so good (some critics likened it to the best of his 1965 rock 'n' roll) that Columbia later restructured the album to include it.

During his American and European tours in the summer and fall of 1981, the shows included only a handful of *Shot of Love* songs and retained a healthy amount of gospel. The concerts increasingly evolved into greatest-hits sets, with the inclusion of "Maggie's Farm," "Mr. Tambourine Man," "Like a Rolling Stone" and "Blowin' in the Wind."

As the tour ended, Dylan entered 1982, which was to be a year of little professional activity. With backup singer and girlfriend Clydie King, he recorded an album of duets, which was not released. He dealt with legal problems (Albert Grossman was still suing him for royalties) and personal tragedies (his friend and filmmaking partner, Howard Alk, had committed suicide), but spent most of the year writing and taking stock of his work after its infusion with overtly Christian themes.

In March 1982, Dylan was asked to present the Gospel Song Award of the National Music Publishers Association. He declined, and there was speculation that the so-called "Christian period" had ended with Dylan back in the fold of Judaism. Indeed, when he appeared at the bar mitzvah of one of his sons that fall in Jerusalem, he wore a yarmulke and a prayer shawl. Though Dylan never renounced Christianity, he apparently remained a Jew throughout the gospel years, seemingly able to find some accommodation between the faiths.

Jokerman

Dylan began writing songs for a new album and considered hiring a real producer, an objective set of ears to help him create a more polished work that might reach a wider audience than *Shot of Love*, his lowest selling record in two decades. In December he showed up, unannounced, at the door of avant-garde musician Frank Zappa. "This is Bob Dylan," he said into the speaker phone at the front gate. "I want to play you my new songs." Zappa looked at the video screen to see if it was a joke. "There, in the freezing cold, was a figure with no coat and an open shirt. It was him."[26] Dylan came inside and played Zappa 11 new songs. Zappa was interested, but nothing came from the meeting.

Two other major artists, David Bowie and Elvis Costello, declined to produce Dylan's new recording sessions, but Mark Knopfler of Dire Straits, with whom he had worked on *Slow Train Coming*, signed on for sessions at New York's Power Station studio. For nearly a month, they ran through some of Dylan's most intriguing songs since the days of *Blood on the Tracks*, with the backing of a tight rhythm section assembled by Knopfler. Knopfler also introduced Dylan to more advanced recording techniques, giving the songs a bigger, fuller sound. Unfortunately, a tour with Dire Straits pulled Knopfler away from the project before the album was mixed and the song selection had been made. Knopfler later came to regret leaving early, as he felt that Dylan had made some poor choices on the final version. The rough takes of some of the songs were superior to the released versions, and Knopfler was only one of many to wonder why superb songs like "Foot of Pride" and "Blind Willie McTell" were left off of the album.

When *Infidels* was finally released in November 1983, it was received as one of Dylan's finest albums in years. Though it contained only eight songs, critics commented that there was a noticeable absence of filler. Most of the reviews noted what appeared to be Dylan's cranky conservatism in "Union Sundown" and what they saw as his defense of Zionism in "Neighborhood Bully." One of the ballads, "Sweetheart like You," received significant play as a single and a video, and "Jokerman," Dylan's second foray into video (not counting the "Subterranean Homesick Blues" clip from *Don't Look Back*), was acclaimed by *Rolling Stone* as a masterpiece of the form.

Only after the appearance of bootleg recordings of the material that had been left off of *Infidels* did critics revise their opinion of the album. Dylan's exclusion of "Blind Willie McTell" was particularly baffling. His ode to a blues singer was also a confession of his own unworthiness, a surprisingly modest statement from an artist of his stature, yet it was genuine in its self-deprecation.

Although he had produced a first-rate album, Dylan did not adhere to the standard industry practice of touring to promote the record. It was not until the following spring that he made a television appearance to boost the album's sales. With a punkish-sounding Los Angeles-based band called The Cruzados, Dylan performed three songs on "Late Night with David Letterman," NBC's post-"Tonight Show" gabfest, which did not exactly give his record prime-time exposure. Typically, Dylan opened his performance with a song that did not appear on *Infidels*. In fact, it was a song (Sonny Boy Williamson's "Don't Start Me to Talkin'") that The Cruzados had never even played before.[27] Clearly, Dylan was as perverse as ever.

He did not tour until the summer, and then it was in Europe, where his reputation had remained relatively intact, even during the gospel tours. Dylan's early 1980s performances, particularly those in London, were tremendous successes, while he often played to half-empty houses in his homeland. On several of the European dates, he appeared with Santana and Joan Baez. However, the media buzz about the third decade of Baez/Dylan collaboration overstated the fact. They sang together only a few times during the short tour and did not socialize offstage. Baez finally had to ask for an audience with her old friend, and even then she was unable to see him apart from the bodyguards that had become his constant companions. She found him increasingly isolated.

The shows of the 1984 tour featured a smaller band made up of English rock royalty (including Mick Taylor, formerly of The Rolling Stones, and Ian MacLagan of Small Faces) and was bereft of backup singers. The stripped-down sound worked particularly well on his new version of "Highway 61

Revisited," which Taylor infused with a Rolling Stone gut-level guitar, and "Masters of War," which Dylan had brought into the electric age, playing it the way he supposed Jimi Hendrix would have played the song. Several of the shows were recorded, and the by-now obligatory tour souvenir, *Real Live*, was released in time for Christmas 1984.

Dylan stayed off of the road for most of 1985, recording a new album, rehabilitating his career and making a few key live appearances. It was the year of rock 'n' roll commitment, as musicians gave their time and talents to social causes, just as Dylan and Baez had in the 1960s. The new generation, therefore, sought to honor their role models by including them in these festivities.

A BBC television report of Ethiopian famine moved two English musicians--Bob Geldof of The Boomtown Rats and Midge Ure of Ultravox--to write a song about children who were starving as the rest of the world celebrated Christmas. Gathering other musicians from England's top groups, this supergroup called Band-Aid recorded Geldof and Ure's "Do They Know It's Christmas?" with the proceeds used to send food and supplies to Africa.

Not to be outdone, the American music community rallied to the cause. Superstars Michael Jackson and Lionel Ritchie composed a much less distinctive song about the famine, "We Are the World," and attempted to form a similar American supergroup called USA for Africa. Managing so many conflicting schedules was difficult, but many artists had planned to attend the American Music Awards in Los Angeles on January 29, 1985, so an all-night session was scheduled following the ceremony. The cast of characters was impressive, including Harry Belafonte, Ray Charles, Michael Jackson and various Jackson siblings, Al Jarreau, Waylon Jennings, Billy Joel, Cyndi Lauper, Bette Midler, Willie Nelson, Smokey Robinson, Kenny Rogers, Paul Simon, Bruce Springsteen, Tina Turner and Stevie Wonder, among others. Bob Geldof was invited to attend and represent the British musical community.

With so many artists, several famous voices were relegated to the chorus, simply being assigned to repeat the banal title phrase. Dylan was, of course, granted a solo. He privately doubted the quality of the song, yet could not refuse to take part in a worthy cause.[28]

It was the first of the significant charity events that year. Geldof had organized simultaneous concerts called Live Aid in England and the United States for July 13, 1985. The English concerts included many younger performers but concluded with Paul McCartney and a superstar chorus singing The Beatles' swan song, "Let It Be." After a day of performances by a broad range of rock 'n' roll stars, the final solo spot at the American end of Live Aid was given to Dylan. Introduced by actor Jack Nicholson (" . . . it can only be *one* man: the transcendent Bob Dylan"), he brought along a couple of Rolling Stones, guitarists Keith Richards and Ron Wood. They were to play a short acoustic set, so they were stationed before the curtain as preparations were made a few feet behind them for the all-star finale. The backstage noise and the absence of monitors distracted Dylan, Wood and Richards. They were unable to hear what they were playing and, to the audience of the whole planet, sounded like three aging goofballs. Dylan was noticeably uncomfortable, sweating profusely, and appeared angry at his onstage treatment.

"They screwed around with us," Dylan said. Without the monitors, "we couldn't even hear our own voices, and when you can't hear, you can't play; you don't have any timing. It's like proceeding on radar."[29] He performed three old songs, two of which were startlingly appropriate: "Ballad of Hollis Brown," about a farmer driven mad by starvation, and "When the Ship Comes In," his song about the eventual triumph of good over evil. "Blowin' in the Wind" was obligatory. The audio track of the performance was good, minus the distraction of watching three uncomfortable rock 'n' roll stars dealing with technical difficulties.

An offhand comment made by Dylan during his performance led to yet another benefit. The increasing number of farm foreclosures in America had touched Dylan, and between songs he mentioned that perhaps "a few million" of the dollars raised for Live Aid could be used to help these people whose contributions, in turn, could feed the world. To many, the comment seemed inappropriate, as if the new cranky Dylan of *Infidels* was speaking a nationalistic line.

Country and western musician Willie Nelson, long a friend and admirer of Dylan, took the issue to heart. With Neil Young and John Mellencamp as partners, Nelson organized an American benefit for farmers called Farm Aid that fall. Of course, Bob Dylan was asked to appear in a prime spot during the evening. The Farm Aid concert mixed a number of musical styles, from traditional country to heavy metal. It also showcased a broad cross-section of the musical community. Mellencamp, in particular, emerged as a poet of the heartland and delivered a possessed performance (while wearing a Future Farmers of America jacket from his high school days in Indiana).

Dylan had a band this time: Tom Petty and The Heartbreakers, one of the best new groups to emerge during the 1970s and carry on the tradition of basic rock 'n' roll (along with Mellencamp's group and Bruce Springsteen's E Street Band). Dylan and The Heartbreakers played six songs at Farm Aid, and the mood was entirely different from the previous benefit. Dylan actually grinned during his performance, so pleased was he to be working with the superb musicians in his new backup group.

He also contributed to another cause, becoming another famous voice in the chorus for "Sun City," which was organized by guitarist Steve Van Zandt (known as Miami Steve during his days with Springsteen's E Street Band and as Little Steven as the leader of the Disciples of Soul) to call attention to South Africa's policies of apartheid.

Dylan took the year off from touring and, in addition to the benefits, confined his performances to court (the suit against Grossman was continuing) and the recording studio. He employed digital technology when he entered the studio in the spring of 1985 to make *Empire Burlesque*. The album featured synthesizer on some cuts and lavish strings on others. Although he did nothing embarrassing in his attempt to keep up with trends (The Beach Boys and The Rolling Stones had each recorded disco tunes in the 1970s; at least Dylan had not done *that*), he appeared to be making efforts to sound more contemporary, in short, to be more of a follower than the leader he once had been.

The album garnered a lot of attention, earning Dylan a prime spot on National Public Radio's "All Things Considered," whose reviewer raved about it, stopping just short of calling it a masterpiece. Dylan apparently felt strongly about the album and did a series of interviews to support it. With David A. Stewart, half of the English band Eurythmics, he made a video for one of the album's ballads, "Emotionally Yours." The opening track of the album, "Tight Connection to My Heart (Has Anybody Seen My Love?)" was also supported by a "concept" video that required Dylan to run around Tokyo with Oriental maidens, pursued by bad guys. After that experience, he bade goodbye to the video form for a while.

After *Infidels* and *Empire Burlesque*, Dylan had repaired his image which, some felt, had been tarnished by the preaching and admonishments that had characterized his work during the gospel years. What he did next allowed him to rehabilitate himself to the extent that he would be seen again as the undisputed leader of popular music. In part to capitalize on the shift in technology to compact discs, Columbia Records decided to issue a Dylan career retrospective. *Biograph* was released in November 1985 on five long-playing albums and three compact discs. The set contained his greatest hits, all digitally remastered and sounding like new recordings, along with some personal favorites and several songs that had never before been released. With a lavish packaging job, a booklet by music journalist Cameron Crowe and a song-by-song commentary by Dylan, the collection was irresistible, garnering extensive appreciations of the artist by the music press. The publisher Alfred A. Knopf simultaneously issued *Lyrics*, a collection of lyrics from Dylan's first album through *Empire Burlesque*, including many songs he had never released. It was basically an update of an earlier volume (*Writings and Drawings*) which was published during his dry period in the early 1970s.

He did not tour, technically, to support *Biograph*, but early in 1986, with the Farm Aid experience fresh in his mind, he joined Tom Petty and The Heartbreakers for a trip through the Far East. Working with this disciplined band, Dylan's appearances earned raves, and anticipation in America was high for a stateside tour. Since Dylan had an unusual work ethic, it was sometimes difficult for a tight unit like Petty's Heartbreakers to adapt. Drummer Stan Lynch said, "There's nothing tentative about Dylan onstage. I've seen gigs where the songs have ended in all the wrong places, where it's fallen apart, and it's almost as if, in some perverse way, he gets energy from that chaos."[30]

It was June before Dylan, Petty and company reached America, simultaneously with the broadcast of another television special. "Hard to Handle" was drawn from two Australian concerts which were filmed by director Gillian Armstrong. An immaculate long-form video, it employed a camera suspended over the stage and lovingly photographed Dylan and The Heartbreakers. It was first shown on the HBO cable network, and then was released to the market.

During the peak of this powerful concert tour, Dylan released a staggeringly weak album titled *Knocked Out Loaded*. The timing was right: Dylan was on the road and had a new record; this was how rock 'n' roll stars were supposed to do it. Unfortunately, the record was a collection of outtakes and songs that had not fit on other albums. He skipped superior material that was in the can ("Blind Willie McTell" and "Foot of Pride," for example) and instead offered cover versions of blues rambles and a tune by Kris Kristofferson. A collaboration with Tom Petty ("Got My Mind Made Up") did not approach the quality of their work on stage. Dylan even wrote a piece with Carole Bayer Sager, a middle-of-the-road songwriter whose previous partner was her husband, pop tunesmith Burt Bacharach.

The album was redeemed, however, by an 11-minute song that Dylan wrote with Pulitzer Prize winning playwright Sam Shepard. Shepard had accompanied Dylan on the Rolling Thunder Revue and had provided some dialogue and situations for *Renaldo and Clara*. "Brownsville Girl" was an epic that studied the relationship between an artist and his art, using the motion picture as a metaphor. Long in the works, and originally titled "New Danville Girl," the song stood out in the midst of the mediocre material that took up the remaining space on *Knocked Out Loaded*. After giving the world *Biograph*, the album was a huge letdown.

Dylan spent the summer on the road, then decided to make another foray into film. Joe Eszterhas, a former *Rolling Stone* writer, had crafted a screenplay about an older rock 'n' roll star who retires to the country after a near-fatal accident. A young woman in a local bar band excites the reclusive musician's interest and he reemerges to the public world in order to help her career. When he sees that she no longer needs him and has fallen in love with someone else, he again retreats.

The character of Billy Parker in *Hearts of Fire* had obvious similarities to Dylan. Richard Marquand, whose biggest success was the third volume of the "Star Wars" trilogy, *Return of the Jedi*, was signed as the director, and most of the shooting was done in the fall of 1986 in Canada and London. Fiona Flanagan played the young woman, and Rupert Everett played the rival rock star. Although the eventual film was a dud and was never released to American theaters, Dylan was magnetic. Even when he was not saying or doing anything, he was the major presence on film, overshadowing the professional actors. Although he was to provide original music, the song he played most often as the character's biggest hit was "The Usual," which was written by John Hiatt.

The experience with The Heartbreakers had been good and so, as Dylan contemplated his concert calendar in 1987, he attempted to repeat the success by sharing the bill again with The Heartbreakers and, on several dates, with The Grateful Dead. He toured throughout the year, though without the success of the previous summer. In an interview with Sam Shepard he seemed downright confused. "You always know who you are," Dylan said. "I just don't know what I'm gonna become."[31]

Dylan achieved a milestone in early 1988 when he was inducted into the Rock and Roll Hall of Fame by the reigning king of the form, Bruce Springsteen. Springsteen eloquently honored Dylan, who seemed truly moved. However, the evening was overshadowed by a speech made by Michael Love of The Beach Boys. Dylan, The Beatles, The Beach Boys and others were being inducted and Love, who was onstage and out of control, suggested that The Beach Boys of the 1980s were the best of all of the musicians assembled. Other members of the group (noticeably The Beach Boys' lead guitarist, Carl Wilson) grimaced during Love's remarks, which included wild and profane attacks on nearly all the members of the rock 'n' roll elite in attendance. Later in the evening, after accepting his award from Bruce Springsteen, Dylan said, "I want to thank Mike Love for not mentioning me." At the obligatory all-star jam after the ceremonies, Dylan performed "All along the Watchtower" (Hendrix style) and "Like a Rolling Stone," accompanied by George Harrison, Ringo Starr, Mick Jagger, Billy Joel, Ben E. King and various Beach Boys.[32]

Columbia Records congratulated Dylan on the honor in a series of trade magazine ads, which also promoted his imminent new album, *Down in the Groove*. However, the album's release was postponed a couple of times before it finally appeared in June. It was an even more disappointing effort than *Knocked Out Loaded*, lacking a "Brownsville Girl" to redeem it. Paradoxically, and perhaps even perversely, Dylan supported the *Down in the Groove* album with a tour that ranked as one of his best. Stripping down his supporting band to a three-piece unit led by the superb guitarist G. E. Smith, Dylan ripped through North America for the rest of the year with tight, frenetically performed 15-song sets that made the critics rave.

If Dylan lacked the conviction to make good Bob Dylan records, he was apparently able to make a good Lucky Wilbury record. With George Harrison, Roy Orbison, Tom Petty and Jeff Lynne, Dylan formed The Traveling Wilburys, a loose band that allowed them all to escape their celebrated personas and sink into anonymity as the fictional Wilbury brothers. "I'm only Bob Dylan when I want to be," he had told interviewers for years. Now he could be someone else. It was Dylan's first true band since The Golden Chords in Hibbing, and it came about as the result of an accident. Harrison had recently revived his recording career with a successful album, *Cloud Nine*, and was preparing the release of a single. The record company needed a song for the B-side. Harrison began writing with Lynne, who had produced *Cloud Nine*, and soon they had the outline of a tune. Harrison needed his guitar in order to record the song, and realized that he had left it at Tom Petty's house. When Lynne and Harrison dropped by Petty's home, they found Roy Orbison there. As the idea of a collaboration gelled, they brainstormed about possible studios they could use on short notice, since the record company was insistent on getting the new recording quickly. Petty suggested Dylan's garage studio.

Thus, the five artists met at Dylan's studio and worked through "Handle with Care." The five styles meshed perfectly, and the record executives, upon hearing the result, said that it was too good to waste as a secondary track on a single. Working around Dylan's active touring schedule, the artists agreed to make a whole album. Rather than have it appear as a superstar project, they all assumed different identities: they were the Wilbury brothers. Harrison called himself Nelson, Orbison was Lefty, Lynne was Otis and Petty was Charley, Jr. Dylan, of course, was just plain Lucky.

The album appeared that fall and was a tremendous success, reaching the No. 1 position in the United States and No. 2 in Britain. It also showed that Bob Dylan could still be a strong presence in the recording studio. Though he was surrounded with four artists of great stature, it was easy to judge which contributions were his. As Bob Dylan, he had a certain reputation to maintain. As Lucky Wilbury, however, he could be lewd and lascivious, as he was on "Dirty World," one of the standout tracks on The Traveling Wilburys album, which was called, teasingly, *Volume One*.

Dylan's success with G. E. Smith and the new band continued, so much so that he toured with the group well into the 1990s. Previous tours had had names: The Rolling Thunder Revue, the True Confessions tour with The Heartbreakers, and so on. Dylan dubbed his continuous road schedule "The Never-Ending Tour." He toured more than any other major artist, rarely taking a break of longer than a couple of months. Another Traveling Wilburys project (the second album, which was titled *Volume Three*) received even better reviews than the first, although the sales were not as good and the album lacked the piercing voice of Roy Orbison, who had died not long after the release of the Wilburys' first record.

During a tour stop in New Orleans in early 1989, Dylan dropped in on a session for The Neville Brothers' new album. The legendary rhythm and blues group was recording two of Dylan's old songs, "Ballad of Hollis Brown" and "With God on Our Side," to which they had added a new verse about Vietnam. Dylan sanctioned the new verse (and began using it when he performed the song) and said that it was one of the best covers of his work that he had ever heard. He particularly admired the session producer, Daniel Lanois.

Lanois had also produced Peter Gabriel's *So*, U2's *The Joshua Tree* and the first solo album of Dylan's old friend Robbie Robertson. Thinking it might be time for another career rehabilitation, Dylan approached Lanois about working together in New Orleans. Lanois had been planning to work on an album of his own, but could not pass up the opportunity to produce Dylan. That spring, Dylan and Lanois worked with The Neville Brothers, rhythm section on Dylan's new songs, which were stronger, more forceful tunes than anything he had written since *Infidels*, and perhaps since *Blood on the Tracks*. After two years of relative inactivity as a writer, the Wilburys sessions had loosened him up. Whereas the Wilburys' songs were frequently lighthearted, the new solo songs were dark, brooding, and almost menacing.

As Dylan toured Europe, Lanois mixed the album, *Oh Mercy*, for release in September. It was greeted with rave reviews by the critics, and *Rolling Stone* hailed it as one of the 100 best albums of the 1980s, the only true Dylan album to make the list (the first Wilburys album also appeared). Nonetheless, Dylan's supporting tour for *Oh Mercy*--again, employing the excellent G. E. Smith-led power trio--featured few songs from the new album. His tight greatest-hits sets probably boosted the sales of *Biograph* but did little for *Oh Mercy*, although that album did reach No. 6 on the American charts.

The Never-Ending Tour lived up to its name as Dylan entered his third decade as a performer, only taking time off of the road for recording. Working with producer Don Was, Dylan squeezed in sessions for another album, *Under the Red Sky*, in 1990. Returning to the simplicity of his earliest recordings, Dylan recorded an unadorned album of traditionals, *Good as I Been to You*, in 1992. These two albums might have each been termed comebacks had not *Oh Mercy* reminded listeners that Dylan never went away.

Forever Young

Dylan had decided to declare himself the victor in his continuing battle with the bootleggers. For 20 years, bootleggers had been releasing raw tapes of his performances and outtakes dubbed from studio masters. In order to both mark his 30 years as a recording artist and to finally make money from these recordings others had pirated, Dylan released a three-disc retrospective, *The Bootleg Series, Vols. 1-3* which prompted further reassessments of his career. The songs from the early days were expected to draw attention, but it was the material from the 1980s--"Blind Willie McTell," "Foot of Pride," "Angelina," and a new, hypnotic song completed in early 1991, "Series of Dreams"--that excited the most attention. Dylan had once again rehabilitated and reinvented himself.

The album's release was simultaneous with the media's career appraisals related to Dylan's 50th birthday. Dylan was the first rock 'n' roll artist of his generation to live to 50, and the media responded accordingly, with a slew of articles that brought out all the old cliches: "the voice of his generation," and similar laudatory statements. Dylan was only turning 50, but the press appeared ready to bury him, or at least write him off as an old man. His great work was in the past, at least a quarter-century ago, many of the articles stated, yet he was important because of what he had been. The articles had the feel of nostalgia and defensiveness, as if the writers had to justify to younger audiences why they were spending so much space on an aging rock 'n' roll star who had not had anything close to a hit in nearly two decades.

Taking the hint, the record industry decided to officially lionize Dylan on worldwide television. Remarkably, Dylan records had won only two Grammys: one for Johnny Cash's liner notes to *Nashville Skyline* and one for "Gotta Serve Somebody," as best male gospel performance. Therefore, it was determined that during the February 20, 1991 telecast of the Grammy Awards, the National Academy of Recording Arts and Sciences would honor Bob Dylan with a lifetime achievement award.

Actor Jack Nicholson eloquently introduced Dylan, sounding much like a eulogist. He said that trying to define Dylan was an exercise in futility. Though he had lived in the public eye, Nicholson said, Dylan remained an enigma. He noted that Dylan had often refused the honors and adulation bestowed upon him, as if to say to the audience, "Be grateful that he showed up tonight." Dylan, he said, had expanded the boundaries of popular music more than any other single figure in the culture, yet still maintained his exploration of the beauty of simplicity and rudimentary chords, frequently returning to the source of his inspiration. Quoting Dylan's writing about his work and himself, Nicholson drew heavily on the album notes from *Bringing It All Back Home* and then introduced a brief film of Dylan's career. While the soundtrack played a blend of some of his finest songs, the screen showed a montage of the young folksinger in transition from *Don't Look Back*; the rock 'n' roll star of *Eat the Document*; the prophet from *Concert from Bangladesh*; the fearless detective of the heart in *Renaldo and Clara*; the gypsy of "Hard Rain"; and finally, Dylan alone in a room, singing "Series of Dreams."

When the film had ended, Nicholson continued: "When I was a kid, growing up in Jersey, anybody who was a hoot or really funny or something, we'd call him a riot. Ladies and gents, this guy's a riot--in more ways than one." The curtain opened and there was Dylan, in a purple sports coat and a Fedora, backed by a tall, skinny band of similarly outfitted musical anarchists. The punk-style band crashed, wailed and boomed through a racuous song that flew in the face of Nicholson's eulogistic tone, but what Dylan was singing was at first unintelligible.

All through the evening, the Grammy award presenters and recipients had milked the audience for applause to honor the American troops in the Middle East, who were engaged in Operation Desert Storm against Iraqi leader Saddam Hussein. Flag-waving patriotism was at its peak; Whitney Houston's recording of "The Star-Spangled Banner" was in the top ten. Onstage, Dylan's words suddenly became clear. He was singing "Masters of War," and playing with the frenzy of a 20-year-old kid in a garage band. He sang urgently, as if the words were coming too fast for him. He leaned into the microphone, serving notice to all of those who glorify war and profit by it. His demonic-looking guitarist pinched out a solo and smiled with satanic glee. Dylan snarled, spat his words, and grinned at the ends of verses. It was a brutal performance, wild, crazed, and chaotic. It was essential rock 'n' roll.

The song crashed as if through a brick wall and suddenly ended. The audience was shocked by the performance. Cameras swept Radio City Music Hall and showed the clerisy of the rock 'n' roll establishment looking utterly bewildered by the three minutes of mayhem they had just witnessed. Nevertheless, the audience gave Dylan a standing ovation. He was being given a lifetime achievement award, after all. Placido Domingo and Diana Ross, with smiles plastered on, stood in the front row leading the applause. Others in the audience turned to talk to their partners, as if to confirm what they had just seen and heard.

Dylan stepped forward, shook Nicholson's hand, bowed gruffly, and joined in the applause, with his directed at the audience. Nicholson finished his remarks, ready for the presentation of the award itself. Standing behind Nicholson, Dylan made faces, grinned, and squinted. He was still a cut-up, a 50-year-old bad boy. Nicholson complimented Dylan for being a courageous artist and then, as shy as any other fan would be at such a moment, presented the award to the man he had introduced to the audience as "Uncle Bobby."

Dylan took the award and decided to speak. Nicholson and two hostesses tried to lead him away, but Dylan took control of the microphone. Nicholson shrugged; the hostesses smiled nervously, blinding the crowd with their rhinestones.

"Well, uh," Dylan said, fondling the award. "All right." Another pause. "Yeah."

The crowd laughed.

"Well, my daddy? He didn't leave me too much, you know. He was a very simple man, and he didn't leave me a lot, but what he did tell me was this, he did say, 'Sonnnnnn . . . ,' he said . . . . "

There followed a long pause. Dylan breathed heavily. It seemed an eternity on television. Millions watched. Dylan stared down at the award and scratched his chin. There were a few nervous snickers, and then giggles. Finally, laughter rose from the corners of the auditorium.

"He said so many things, you know," Dylan shrugged. The audience roared, again his. Then, quickly, Dylan added, "He said it is possible to become so defiled in this world that your own mother and father will abandon you and if that happens, God will always believe in your own ability to mend your own ways."

The audience was silent, stunned, thinking, "We've just been put on; he got us again."

"Thank you," Bob Dylan said, and walked away.[33]

Notes

1. Robert Shelton, *No Direction Home: The Life and Music of Bob Dylan* (New York: Ballantine Books, 1987), p. 496.
2. Ibid., p. 501.
3. Bill Yenne, in *One Foot on the Highway: Bob Dylan on Tour, 1974* (San Francisco: Klohne Books, 1974), has documented every word Dylan said to audiences during the tour.
4. Michael Krogsgaard, *Positively Bob Dylan: A Thirty Year Discography, Concert and Recording Session Guide* (Ann Arbor, Mich.: Popular Culture, Ink, 1991), p. 102.
5. Clinton Heylin, *Bob Dylan: Behind the Shades* (New York: Summit Books, 1991), p. 238.
6. Ibid., p. 239.
7. Ibid.
8. Ibid., p. 240.
9. Bob Spitz, *Dylan: A Biography* (New York: McGraw-Hill, 1989), p. 443.
10. Heylin, *Behind the Shades*, p. 241.
11. Shelton, *No Direction Home*, p. 513.
12. Ibid., p. 522.
13. Patrick Humphries and John Bauldie, *Absolutely Dylan* (New York: Viking Studio Books, 1991), p. 204.
14. Michael Blowen, "Ex-Boxer Struggles to Vanquish His Past," the *Orlando Sentinel*, 10 April 1992, p. E-1.
15. Heylin, *Behind the Shades*, p. 284.
16. Humphries and Bauldie, *Absolutely Dylan*, p. 204.
17. Ibid., p. 206.
18. *Village Voice*, 30 January 1978, cited in Shelton, *No Direction Home*, p. 546.
19. Ibid.
20. Shelton, *No Direction Home*, p. 557.
21. Ibid., p. 558.
22. Heylin, *Behind the Shades*, p. 315.
23. Ibid., p. 316.
24. Ibid., p. 335.
25. Cameron Crowe, Notes to *Biograph* [sound recording] (Columbia Records, 1985), side 10, song 4.
26. Humphries and Bauldie, *Absolutely Dylan*, p. 220.
27. Ibid., p. 222.
28. Heylin, *Behind the Shades*, p. 381.
29. Robert Hilburn, "Interview: Bob Dylan," the *Los Angeles Times*, 17 November 1985, cited in Humphries and Bauldie, *Absolutely Dylan*, p. 220.
30. Heylin, *Behind the Shades*, p. 385.
31. Sam Shepard, "True Dylan," *Esquire*, July 1987.
32. Krogsgaard, *Positively Bob Dylan*, p. 348.
33. "The Grammy Awards" [television special] CBS Television Network, 20 February 1991.

Part II

Bob Dylan's Songs and His Influence

Chapter 4

Writing on His Favorite Wall

BOB DYLAN ONCE WROTE A JOB DESCRIPTION for being Bob Dylan. It appeared as his prose poem on the jacket of *Bringing it All Back Home*. In the poem, he found himself tormented by people who blamed him for all the world's discontent, so he went to the country (Woodstock, we presume) and wrote "whaaat?" on his favorite wall. Then his recording engineer passed by in a jet and asked Dylan if he needed help. Thus began a long, delightful ramble through Dylan's mind as he questioned what he was and what he did. Describing a poem as a "naked person," Dylan acknowledged that some called him a poet. The meditation ended and Dylan told his recording engineer, "Well, yes, I could use some help getting this wall in the plane."[1]

That was his role: Writing *whaaat?* on his favorite wall. Dylan's songs changed so much over the years because the answer to that *"whaaat?"* question kept changing, as did the situation that prompted it. The times changed, and so did the answer. Dylan's career has traced three decades of response to that basic question. Sometimes his songs have been topical, related to events in society, sometimes they have been personal. Sometimes they have been pure flights of fancy. However, they were all, in one way or another, responses to that question. What listeners got from Dylan was whatever part of the wall he chose to share.

Dylan's songs have not been static. Each new concert tour included reconsidered versions of his classic songs. The melodies, the lyrics, and even the points of view of some of his greatest songs have varied wildly in performance. (Those aberrations are discussed in Chapter 9.) Our concern in this chapter is with the primary and standard Dylan work: his recordings.

Other works--books, films, and video--are discussed elsewhere. Technical details about his recordings, including release dates, producers, and song lists, are treated in Chapter 7.

Here we will discuss the work of Bob Dylan that has stood still. Unlike many other artists of his generation, we find Dylan's work readily available. Only one of his albums (the retributory selection of outtakes, *Dylan*, which was released by Columbia in 1973) is out of print in North America.

This chapter is devoted to a discussion of his albums, presented in chronological order. Many of the specific references are to the albums in their original format as long-playing (LP) records, hence references to "sides," a concept erased by compact discs (CDs), which became the dominant format in the late 1980s. Even "greatest hits" compilations are included because each has something of significance to add to Dylan's legacy. Several critics are noted who have devoted much of their work to Dylan. In his biography *No Direction Home*, Robert Shelton deals as much with Dylan's music as with his life, offering track-by-track assessments of his work. Other notable rock critics, including Jon Landau (later to be Bruce Springsteen's manager and producer), Greil Marcus, Dave Marsh and Robert Christgau, will also be cited, as will Alan Rinzler, who devoted a book to Dylan's first 22 albums.

Bob Dylan (1962): The eponymous debut album now appears to be but a rehearsal for greatness, although there was little on it to suggest Dylan's considerable abilities as a songwriter. Dylan recorded the album in two days, on November 20 and 22, 1961. John Hammond produced the sessions in Columbia's Studio A in New York. Dylan, accompanied by his girlfriend Suze Rotolo, performed live in the studio. Hammond was so impressed with Dylan's confident vocals that he invited Godard Lieberson, president of Columbia Records, into the engineering booth to listen to his protege sing. In *No Direction Home*, Robert Shelton comments that the schoolboy picture of Dylan on the cover does not match the old man's voice on the record.[2] Indeed, Dylan's weary blues performances are stand outs.

There were only two original songs, "Talkin' New York" and "Song to Woody." The first song fit naturally in the talking blues style of Dylan's hero, and its touches of humor were more subtle than might have been expected from such a young singer. The song addressed to Woody Guthrie was noteworthy for its panache. Dylan sang the song with pride and with a certain measure of defiance. Few would have the courage to address a song to one of the nation's great songwriters, and the fact that Dylan was willing to do so lifts his album above the norm.

Most of the album was made up of effective performances of borrowed songs. The best performance, perhaps, was of "Baby, Let Me Follow You Down." The label credits the song to Dylan's friend, folk singer Eric Von

Schmidt, yet a later performance of the song on The Band's *The Last Waltz* album lists the composer as the Reverend Gary Davis. The years have given the *Bob Dylan* performance more charm, owing largely to the quaint, tongue-in-cheek spoken introduction, in which Dylan recounts how he learned the song. It was chosen to represent *Bob Dylan* on his retrospective *Biograph*, nearly a quarter-century later.

Trying to judge *Bob Dylan* by the standard of the times is difficult. We know what followed, so assessing this album as just another entry in the folk-music boom of the early 1960s is difficult. We can safely assume that it fit the mold: a generous selection of traditional songs, many of which were performed by the scores of other artists who were part of that particular movement. Dylan sings "Man of Constant Sorrow," "Pretty Peggy-O" and "House of the Risin' Sun." This was fairly standard material.

More than the other artists who were classified as folk singers, Dylan relied on blues sources. His version of Blind Lemon Jefferson's "See That My Grave Is Kept Clean," the song he chose to close the album, was one of the highlights, and in "Freight Train Blues," an energetic Dylan holds a note for more than a minute in an imitation of a train whistle. The album shows Dylan's love for the blues, a constant throughout his career.

Dylan recorded several other songs at these sessions that he chose not to release. One of these, "Man in the Street," echoes "Tramp in the Street," a song by Hank Williams, Dylan's first hero. A smattering of other cover versions, including the traditional "He was a Friend of Mine," were also recorded but not used on the album.

The Freewheelin' Bob Dylan (1963): This album signaled Dylan's arrival as a major artist and lifted him above the heads of the other artists of the folk music movement. Although he was a couple of years away from his status as a major rock 'n' roll star, it was with his second album that Dylan's influence began to be felt. When The Beatles heard that album, their perspective began to change. As George Harrison recalled:

> The day Bob Dylan *really* turned us on was the day we heard his album, *The Freewheelin' Bob Dylan*. Right from that moment we recognized some vital energy, a voice crying out somewhere, toiling in the darkness. When we actually met him in '64 it had a certain effect on us, but I think the seed was sown by that album.[3]

John Hammond handed over the producing reins to Tom Wilson during this album. Wilson actually gave Dylan his electric sound for *Freewheelin'*, but for several reasons, these quasi-rock 'n' roll recordings were left off the album when it was finally released. Dylan had recorded "Mixed Up Confusion" in late 1962 and released it as a single. With its "Mystery Train" beat, it sounded an awful lot like Elvis Presley at a Woody Guthrie sound-alike contest. That folk-electric sound was heard again on "Rocks and Gravel," which appeared on the first 300 copies of *Freewheelin'* but was deleted for the well-known version of the album.

Songs were deleted for a number of reasons. After Dylan was told he could not sing "Talkin' John Birch Society Blues" on CBS Television's "Ed Sullivan Show," lawyers at CBS--the parent company of Columbia Records--insisted that the song be withdrawn from the album. Other songs were dropped in favor of new, stronger material: "Blowin' in the Wind," "Masters of War" and "Girl from the North Country."

"Blowin' in the Wind" led off the album in perhaps the best performance of one of Dylan's most famous songs. Sung thousands of times since, it is hard to imagine a better way to ask the series of questions that provides the song's theme. Peter, Paul and Mary had already made the song a hit by the time Dylan's version was released. Between them, Dylan and the trio made it a staple at civil rights demonstrations and rarely has Dylan performed a concert without including it, often as an encore. (The exception was during his early gospel tours in the 1980s.)

Another classic recording followed: "Girl from the North Country." Based on an old English melody ("Scarborough Fair," which would also inspire Simon and Garfunkel), this lovely lament evokes a love lost, tying her to a time and place that are also lost. Some have claimed this tune was inspired by Echo Helstrom; others say the "real girl" was Bonnie Beecher. Whatever the case, its seasoned wistfulness lends the song a poignance that the singer's mannered gruffness cannot deny.

A third classic, "Masters of War," was next. This song was perhaps the most relentless piece of music that Dylan ever recorded, yet it uses just his voice and guitar. The singer takes aim at those who profit from war by manufacturing the arms for mass annihilation. As Dylan hectors them with his charges, he builds a dossier of hate and finally states his hope that they will die soon. So emphatic is Dylan that he insists he will watch until the profiteers are buried and can no more visit hate on the earth. It was a blistering piece of music, and one of which Dylan was apparently fond. He ressurected it for concerts in the 1980s, performing it as savage rock 'n' roll. After "Masters of War," the album took a breather with "Down the Highway," a relaxing blues, and "Bob Dylan's Blues," which, despite its title, was actually quite amusing.

Those brief tunes prepared the way for "A Hard Rain's A-Gonna Fall," which was allegedly inspired by the Cuban Missile Crisis of 1962. It was an extremely detailed, visionary work that addressed life after the nuclear war. Dylan told critic Nat Hentoff, who wrote the album notes, that each line of the song was intended to be the first line of a complete song, but that, feeling he would not live long enough to write that many songs, he had used them all here. Whether that was true, and whether the missile crisis was truly the inspiration have been debated by Dylan fans since this song's release. What has not been debated, however, are the song's power and appeal. It is, in the end, a song of affirmation, as Dylan states that the human spirit will endure even the most hideous of man-made catastrophes.

"Don't Think Twice, It's All Right" was Dylan's first antilove song to be committed to record. It certainly followed no formula for love songs, as most of those were the products of song factory "assembly lines" in the fabled neighborhood of Tin Pan Alley. "Bob Dylan's Dream," which is based on an old English melody, was one of the prizes tucked away in the album--a superbly beautiful, bittersweet lyric and some of Dylan's best singing to that date. It had the same quality of reflection that graced "Girl from the North Country," and again called on images of home.

The one song based on an actual incident, "Oxford Town," was to become another civil rights standard. Dylan's brief tune chronicled James Meredith's controversial enrollment as the first black student at the University of Mississippi. It was straightforward, lacking the unusual angle that would highlight his other songs on racial themes, but still effective. The sprightly music masked a tight, sophisticated lyric. Rinzler noted the juxtaposition of "a cute ditty, whose musical flippancy contrasts sharply with the 'guns and clubs' of Oxford."[4]

Dylan came into the studio with "Talkin' World War III Blues" still unfinished, but he improvised much of the song during recording. It was a successful attempt at laughing through the apocalypse, the other side of "Hard Rain." The album slid downhill toward its conclusion, with the traditional "Corrina, Corrina," a blues number, "Honey, Just Allow Me One More Chance," and the comic-sounding "I Shall Be Free," which was downright silly. These songs allowed Dylan to showcase his humor.

The Times They Are A-Changin' (1964): The image of the working class hero dominated the cover of Dylan's third album. Marsh considered this album the "most dated" of Dylan's early work because of its political nature. The best material, he said, were those songs that were "more personal, less tied to issues."[5] Rinzler, on the other hand, considered the topical music the highlight.[6]

The title track, the anthem that began the album, was chilling in its directness, and years have not diminished the original recording. Never released as a single in the United States, it became a hit in Great Britain. "If ever a song crystallized the passions of a generation," Rinzler wrote, "it's this one. Out of the mouths of babes ... a young man warns his elders, and the message was loud and clear: shape up, fly right, make way or else."[7]

Dylan emerged as a near-journalist in some of the songs on this album. Three pieces on the record were drawn from headlines. "Ballad of Hollis

Brown" was about a poor South Dakota farmer who, in a moment of desperation, killed his family and took his life. Dylan resurrected this story of poverty amid plenty in 1985 for his performance at the Live Aid benefit which reached a global audience.

"Only a Pawn in Their Game" was known in an earlier incarnation as "The Ballad of Medger Evers." However, as Dylan toyed with the lyrics, he came up with a much better way to tell the story of the murdered civil rights leader. He presented the assassin sympathetically, as the product of a sick society. The Evers murder was merely a starting point for Dylan, whose song looked for cause rather than effect.

"The Lonesome Death of Hattie Carroll" was the strongest piece on the album. It told the story of Hattie Carroll, a 51-year-old black woman who bore ten children. While serving as a waitress at a society affair in Baltimore, she was recklessly struck by a cane twirled by a young society baron, William Zanzinger. Dylan's song asks us not to mourn her death or Zanzinger's indifference but rather a society that would not suitably punish this man for his deadly act. Dylan's singing was brilliant. At the moment when he delivered the key line, concerning Zanzinger's light sentence, he hesitated, stumbling over the words, as if he still could not believe them. "Hattie Carroll" was a brutal song, but Dylan could have been harsher. In life, William Zantzinger (Dylan dropped the "t") was at the Spinster's Ball, a charity affair in Baltimore in the spring of 1963. Dressed in tails and carrying a white cane, Zantzinger enjoyed playing "lord of the manor" that evening. Hattie Carroll and Ethel Hill were among the black women employed as servants for the affair. Zantzinger made frequent use of his cane, first on a bellman, then repeatedly on Hill, and then fatally on Carroll. When Carroll was slow to refill his drink, Zantzinger struck her between the neck and shoulder. She collapsed and died at a local hospital. The death appeared as a thoughtless accident in Dylan's song; in life, it appeared to have been more deliberate.[8]

The album built to "Hattie Carroll" as its climax, but there was strong material throughout. "With God on Our Side" was Dylan's bitter diatribe against war makers and popular myths that offer *right* as a defense in waging conflict. "North Country Blues" was a gritty, realistic look at a dead town and a land that had been exploited by developers until it was of no more use. Left behind was a raped countryside and people who were also used up. However, Dylan also had positive messages: "When the Ship Comes In" was a hopeful song that prophesied that good will eventually defeat evil.

Three songs of relationships (they are not really love songs) prefigured the direction Dylan would take with his next album. "One Too Many Mornings" deftly sums up the end of an affair. Apparently a Dylan favorite, he performed it regularly in concert decades later. "Boots of Spanish Leather" was a continuation of the theme, as it is addressed to a lover now long gone. It was notable for its touching vulnerability. "Restless Farewell" ended the album with the narrator again singing of lost love, but also of his capacity to endure the loss, and yet the song, which Shelton notes was based on an Irish drinking tune, may also be perceived as a farewell to the commitment demanded by the folk music community.[9]

Another Side of Bob Dylan (1964): This album forsook the social commentary that dominated Dylan's two previous records and instead examined personal relationships with the same precision that he had used for his analysis of society. The Dylan love song had made its debut on his second album, but it was fully realized on this album, with a number of pieces that reflected a cynicism heretofore unknown in popular songs. Dylan even had a hit in two genres with "It Ain't Me Babe." Johnny Cash took it up the country and western charts and The Turtles scored with it on the pop charts.

The opening track, "All I Really Want to Do," was a plea for a relationship to remain simple and uncomplicated, suggesting that to analyze something so fragile would be to destroy it. It was carried off with humor; Dylan even laughed while singing it. Recorded by The Byrds and by Cher, it became Cher's first major solo hit. "I Don't Believe You" told of a lover who literally turned the other cheek. He later revived the song as a rock 'n' roll set piece. "Ballad in Plain D" was an assault on the sister and mother of his former lover (in his anger, he called the sister a parasite), and "It Ain't Me Babe," which concluded the album, was an assertion of freedom and a statement of unwillingness to be owned by anyone.

The only song that fell into the protest category was "Chimes of Freedom," a surreal piling-on of words that led to a strong statement of affinity for the oppressed. One of Dylan's most admired lyrics, it was cited as an example of the growing influence of the poet Arthur Rimbaud on Dylan's writing.

There were a few experiments with humor, "Motorpsycho Nitemare" ("Nightmare" in the official lyrics), which would have easily fit on the rock 'n' roll albums, and "I Shall Be Free No. 10," a return to the form of the cleverly silly song that ended *The Freewheelin' Bob Dylan*. A couple of other curiosities, "Black Crow Blues" and a love paean to an exotic woman, "Spanish Harlem Incident," provided evidence of Dylan's unwillingness to stay put artistically.

Two songs stand out. The first was "To Ramona," which was full of tribute and instruction to a woman whom Dylan obviously loved and wished to save from a fate that he decried. The second, "My Back Pages" was the statement of a mature artist who is secure enough in his writing to realize that life was not as simple as he once imagined. Everything that was certain was lost, and the narrator resolved to go plunging into life with no more preconceptions. Rinzler called it "a fascinating and important piece of self-analysis," as the singer chided himself for thinking that he had answers to life's questions.[10]

Bringing it All Back Home (1965): Dylan's mid-1960s trilogy of rock 'n' roll albums may be one of the greatest achievements of popular music. Although *Bringing It All Back Home* was only half rock (the second side being primarily voice and acoustic guitar), there was nothing tentative about Dylan's step into electric music. Moreover, although he had outraged his former followers by no longer writing songs about specific incidents (the Medgar Evers shooting, the death of Emmett Till), the album left a lot between the lines. It had the feeling of protest--aimed against just about everything.

From the first bent note of "Subterranean Homesick Blues," which kicked off the album, Dylan sang with a confidence and swagger not often heard in the mainstream. The rat-a-tat-tat shower of words was unique in rock 'n' roll. Did you dance to this music, or did you take notes? It was a song of sufficient lyrical strength to encourage memorization. It was an amphetamine-hyped Chuck Berry song in its structure. Berry was the model songwriter when it came to the effective use of words. Nothing was out of place in one of Berry's opuses, and his tight writing style was an obvious influence on Dylan here.

Shelton cited "Motorpsycho Nitemare" and the first jacket poem on *Another Side* as the antecedents of this song, which ranked as one of Dylan's most played compositions.[11] Of course, the song's influence went far beyond popular radio. The radical faction of Students for a Democratic Society--a group called the Weathermen--took its name from a line in the song. Another oft-quoted passage involved Dylan's reduction of a lifetime of experience to eight lines, which denigrated the value of formal education and served as an attack on those who were "educated" but essentially ignorant.

Without pausing for breath after the first cut, Dylan confidently shifted into "She Belongs to Me," which moved at a nearly waltzlike pace. The soothing melody, Shelton noted, contrasted with the bitter tone of the lyrics.[12] Long seen as an attack on Baez, the reference to an Egyptian ring in the lyrics reflected a gift Dylan had given her. "Maggie's Farm" returned the album to a harder rock 'n' roll beat. (This wild tune was also to become part of Dylan's steady repertoire for decades.) In an outrageously nasal whine, Dylan listed a bill of particulars against Maggie and virtually all her relatives and firmly stated his dissatisfaction. Who was Maggie? Dylan hated to have his songs interpreted, and the conjecture about Maggie may be one reason why. One school of thought held that she was actually President Lyndon Johnson and the farm represented the United States. In Britain, Shelton noted, the song took on just such a meaning during the administration of Prime Minister Margaret Thatcher.[13] Others took the song to be another stab at the folk-music community.

"Love Minus Zero/No Limit" shifted the album back to love songs. Again, as in "She Belongs to Me," a lovely, nearly lilting melody, flowed with dark images: in this case, cloaks and daggers, a bridge at midnight, and a frightening storm. Nonetheless, the song was ultimately redemptive.

The remaining three songs of the first side (in the album's original LP configuration) were more exercises in hard rock that cannot meet the standard of the opening volley. "Outlaw Blues" and "On the Road Again" drove the same steam shovel beat as "Maggie's Farm," and "Bob Dylan's 115th Dream" was most notable for the inclusion of a studio breakdown at the beginning of the track, as, one line into the song, Dylan collapsed in laughter. The song itself was a tall tale.

Side two of the album was acoustic and therefore more listener-friendly to the fans who were distressed by the electric twang of side one. "Mr. Tambourine Man" would become a huge hit in an electrified version by The Byrds within months of the release of *Bringing It All Back Home*. Here, in Dylan's acoustic version with all the verses (The Byrds only had time for one), it was a communique from an artist who, in Shelton's words, was on a "search for transcendence," mulling the decision of whether to surrender to feeling or control it.[14] Because of the references to taking trips and smoke rings in the mind, this was widely regarded to have been talking about drugs as a means of escape, but Dylan always denied the drug reference. A more likely interpretation would be music as the escape, as exemplified by the obvious symbol of the tambourine. Writer Hunter S. Thompson dedicated his classic *Fear and Loathing in Las Vegas* to Dylan for his writing of "Mr. Tambourine Man."[15]

"Gates of Eden" had the feel of an epic. Apparently inspired by William Blake, it concerned the quest for salvation and the dread of what followed life. Shelton notes that the song was not really about Eden but rather what Eden was not.[16] It turned the message of "Subterranean Homesick Blues" on its head, but the point was the same: Do not look for salvation in things or other people.

"It's Alright Ma (I'm Only Bleeding)" was, to Shelton "the ultimate protest song" since it assaulted society on so many levels.[17] Rinzler said the song united the disparate themes on the album in a magnum opus and, although it was an excellent song, it was not enjoyable, as much of the rest of the album had been.[18] The song had a long life, surfacing at a key moment in the Dennis Hopper film, *Easy Rider*, though it was performed on the soundtrack by Roger McGuinn of The Byrds. (Dylan had refused to let his version be used.)

As had become tradition, the album ended with a song of farewell, although this one was not wistful. "It's All Over Now, Baby Blue" was a kiss-off, although whether to a woman, a political movement, a musical movement, only Dylan knew. Shelton called it Dylan's finest song about pain to be written before *Blood on the Tracks*.[19]

Highway 61 Revisited (1965): The album began with a clap of thunder: the smack of the drum that kicked off "Like a Rolling Stone." What followed was an hour of the most brilliantly sustained performance in rock 'n' roll history. Dylan was at the first of his peaks with this album, which is astounding at every turn. It was an album full of visions and ideas ... and it had a good beat. The insouciance of the cover photograph--there he was, motorcycle T-shirt, sneer in place--was carried through the album, from liner notes (which he wrote) and the nine blistering songs; from 6 minutes of "Like a Rolling Stone" to 11 minutes of "Desolation Row."

Tom Wilson produced "Like a Rolling Stone," and the rest of the songs were produced by Bob Johnston, with whom Dylan would work for the next five years. Wilson had guided Dylan through *Bringing It All Back Home* and had given Simon and Garfunkel their "folk rock" sound by overdubbing guitar, bass and drums to their acoustic track, "The Sounds of Silence," without the duo's knowledge. It became a hit. Though Wilson and Dylan made a brilliant record with "Like a Rolling Stone," it was the end of their association. Dylan had been feeling stifled by Wilson and was ready to move on.

For "Like a Rolling Stone," Dylan assembled a band that included Mike Bloomfield, a gifted guitarist and Al Kooper, a novice organist. The song succeeded on a number of levels. In a simple sense, it was the story of being judged by one's accomplishments, rather than the achievements or income of a parent. It was clearly about independence and self-worth. The song also appeared to be a denunciation, a suggestion that Dylan always refuted. Perhaps the narrator was singing to himself, he suggested.

The next song was the manic "Tombstone Blues," which dropped the album into a vat full of unusual imagery. The "mystery dwarf" had appeared in "Rolling Stone," but he was a lightweight character when compared to those in the next nine songs. An array of freaks, weirdos and historical characters awaited listeners in this manic, confident blues shout. Shelton suggested several allusions to Vietnam in the song, including President Lyndon Johnson as King of the Philistines. An early fragment of this tune, consisting of a one-minute ode to a transsexual, was eventually released as "Jet Pilot." From that simple starting point, "Tombstone Blues" grew into a spectacle of grotesqueries.

A hyped-up tune called "Phantom Engineer" was toyed with and slowed to eventually become "It Takes a Lot to Laugh, It Takes a Train to Cry," the album's third track. This song brought the album back to a normal speed, as Dylan shuffled through an oblique tale of a relationship that used the train metaphor with originality. If such a powerful album could have a throwaway tune, then "From a Buick 6" was probably it. Dylan confessed anxiety over some of the demands of his fame and sang testament to the woman who protected him from that world. It was a theme he would explore in other songs but with more seriousness than he used here. This tune was apparently just for fun, but it too showed careful attention paid to a clever lyric with memorable lines.

"Ballad of a Thin Man" was the most menacing piece on the album, with its sinister piano and ethereal organ notes wavering in the background. It was also one of Dylan's most analyzed songs and one he chose to record three more times: on *Before the Flood*, *Bob Dylan at Budokan* and *Real Live*. "Mr. Jones" was obviously clueless. He had no idea what was going on in the world and remained insulated from emotions, both his own and other people's. There were, of course, a lot of theories about who--or what--this character represented. Perhaps he was the older generation, the silent majority that was baffled by Dylan and the others of his generation. Perhaps it was a drug song, since *jones* was slang for addiction. Some suggested the song was aimed at Joan Baez, who could not follow Dylan's new path. Still other critics offered more specific suggestions: Horace Judson, the *Time* reporter with whom Dylan sparred with during his spring 1965 English tour (as later shown in *Don't Look Back*); former producer Tom Wilson, who was also baffled by Dylan's new direction; and Pete Seeger, who did not like Dylan's supposed betrayal of acoustic folk music. Shelton answered those who suggested that Dylan was turning on him, one of his earliest boosters, by noting that he had not been a thin man in years. Dylan's answers to those who ask the identity of Mr. Jones have been eliptical. If the character was based on a real person, Judson was a good candidate. The *Don't Look Back* sequence embodied Dylan's admonishment to Mr. Jones that he was out of touch.

"Queen Jane Approximately" was another song that some listeners thought was addressed to Joan Baez. Formerly the Queen of Folk (Dylan was the king who abdicated), the leap from Joan to Jane was not far. Though she was pictured on the back cover of the album and had accompanied Dylan on part of the spring tour of England, she and Dylan were estranged. In five verses, Dylan uses several variations on the theme of "grow up."

The title track of the album was announced by a police siren (credited on the cover to Dylan), and the lyrics piled up a list of attrocities, both real and mythical, that occurred on Highway 61. The highway held a significance for Dylan; it ran from Duluth to the Mississippi Delta, the home of the blues. Morevover, what better blues to be sung along this highway but Abraham's sacrifice of his son, told as a dialogue between the old man and God?

On its surface, "Just Like Tom Thumb's Blues" was the story of a disastrous, seamy trip to Ciudad Juarez. Of course, the surface story did not illuminate all the song's complexities. One critic suggested that Dylan was "calling on modern man to seek the spiritual values that are to be found by looking in the past."[20] The final track, "Desolation Row," was "an eleven-minute Kafkaesque parade of freaks," featuring only Dylan and Nashville session guitarist Charlie McCoy.[21] Many of the spectacular acoustic fills were of McCoy's invention. He was told to play whatever he felt like playing.[22]

Shelton has called the song a sequel to "A Hard Rain's A-Gonna Fall," describing the aftermath of a nuclear annihilation. Shelton was not alone in comparing it to T. S. Eliot's "The Waste Land" and similar visions of life after the apocalypse.

Blonde on Blonde (1966): The final part of Dylan's rock 'n' roll trilogy was the mammoth *Blonde on Blonde*. From the moment fans saw the cover, they knew (in the language of "Ballad of a Thin Man") something was happening here. The picture was sideways so that the album could be opened for a nearly full-body shot of Dylan. Neither his name nor the album title appeared on the front.[23]

From the opening notes--a martial drum, a drunken tambourine, a lascivious trombone--listeners knew that this would be a most remarkable album. *Blonde on Blonde* was the end of one trilogy and the beginning of new period for Dylan, being the first of four albums to be recorded in Nashville, the home of country music. However, there was no twang here. Marsh said the album was "rock 'n' roll at the farthest edge imaginable, instrumentalists and singer all peering into a deeper abyss than anyone had previously imagined existed."[24]

"Rainy Day Women # 12 & 35" was nearly a novelty song, yet it became one of Dylan's greatest hits. It sounded as if someone had slipped gin in the coffee mugs of a Salvation Army band. The constant references to getting stoned again implied that this was a drug song, which it was. Even if not *about* drugs, it may have been written with the aid of amphetamines. Dylan was having to stay up days at a time in order to meet his recording and concert schedule, and this song may match his mood. "Pledging My Time" carried that fatigued-high feeling into the realm of a love song sounding vaguely like an early rock 'n' roll tune that had been slowed down on the turntable. Indeed, the reference was explicit because the song distorts time.

"Visions of Johanna" was one of Dylan's most complex songs to date, and certainly contained one of the most involved lyrics of any song intended for popular consumption. Again, the singer sounded weary: Will he survive to the end of the song? Nonetheless, the way Dylan punched and emphasized the title phrase seemed to give him renewed strength to carry on into the next verse. The singer may not be able to realize his dream, but the quest for the dream still makes the exercise worthwhile. This is a love song, but it is a love song used as an excuse for depicting reflections on a larger scale. "One of Us Must Know (Sooner or Later)" was one of the first songs recorded for the album. A quick take on a conversation between a man and a woman, it served to end side one with urgency.

The second side was the album's most vigorous part, starting off with "I Want You," which became a hit single. It had the elements of a standard pop love song, yet contained references to undertakers, drunken politicians and weeping mothers, certainly not standard love song fare. "Stuck Inside of Mobile with the Memphis Blues Again" was another virtuoso performance, comparable in length to "Desolation Row." However, the mood was a mixture of despair and elation, and the studio band was superb. There were so many clever phrases, that several lines could have made wall samplers for homes of the incurably hip.

"Leopard-Skin Pillbox Hat" was the only song to identify a musician in the album notes: Bob Dylan on lead guitar. It was an infectuous, sloppy blues, and the album's main comic relief. "Just Like a Woman" brought Dylan much criticism over the years. A feminist critic suggested that the song defined "women's natural traits as greed, hypocrisy, whining and hysteria," with a male platitude for a title.[25] It was perhaps the meanest song Dylan ever wrote, as it casts away a lover in a shower of angry words. A beautiful melody and a sensitive acoustic guitar performance (apparently by Joe South, who was later to become a recording star in his own right) again mask bitter and angry lyrics.

The brass returned on side three for "Most Likely You Go Your Way and I'll Go Mine," a demented march tune that also dealt with the end of a relationship, though not as bitterly as in "Just Like a Woman." It became the signature song for his 1974 tour with The Band. "Temporary Like Achilles" was reminiscent of "Pledging My Love" in its slowed-down, South Chicago blues sound. Unlike most blues songs, however, it relied on Greek myths for inspiration. "Absolutely Sweet Marie," with Al Kooper again on organ, had a cheery, upbeat sound.

"Fourth Time Around" was taken to be a joke, a Dylan lampoon of John Lennon's "Norwegian Wood" on The Beatles' then-current album, *Rubber Soul*. Lennon confessed to paranoia about having been put on by the master. "Obviously Five Believers" showed more Nashville influence than the other tracks, though it was the Nashville of Hank Williams and the honky-tonks than the slick Nashville of the Grand Old Opry.

"Sad-Eyed Lady of the Lowlands" was unprecedented. The song took up all of side four of the double album with weary and worshipful tribute to a woman as a work of art. Later, in "Sara" on the *Desire* album, Dylan would recall for his wife that he wrote this song for her while they were staying in New York's Chelsea Hotel.

Bob Dylan's Greatest Hits (1967): This purported collection of hits was mostly made up of songs that others (Peter, Paul and Mary, The Turtles and The Byrds) had made popular, along with the few singles Dylan had managed to get onto the charts. It should have rather been labeled an anthology or a retrospective, since *greatest hits* was not a phrase generally associated with Dylan. The album was not his idea, either. It was assembled while he was recuperating from his motorcycle accident.

All these songs had appeared on albums before except for "Positively 4th Street," his nasty attack on former friends who were nice to his face but who, behind his back, wished he was paralyzed. In the aftermath of his motorcycle accident and the rumors of him living in a vegetative state in a mountain cabin, this line took on a cruel irony. It was difficult to argue with the song selection. Nothing could be deleted. However, frustrated fans might have wished for the inclusion of "Can You Please Crawl out Your Window?" which would remain uncollected on an album for 18 more years.

The album kept Dylan's name before the public, but the packaging did even more. Graphic designer Milton Glaser designed a poster that was slipped inside the original LP's sleeve. Unfolded, it was a silhouette of Dylan with rainbow-colored hair. The poster became one of the icons of the late 1960s and graced the walls of thousands of dormitory rooms when students returned to college that autumn.

John Wesley Harding (1967): After an 18-month layoff, Dylan quietly resumed his recording career with this album. Critics and fans hailed his return; what was quiet was the music itself. In the psychedelic world of 1967, this album was an exercise in understatement. Dylan and a trio of Nashville session musicians worked their way through 12 superb songs that were steeped in religious imagery and filled with riddles and puzzling allusions. It was not just the musical simplicity that made the album notable, although that was considerable. Marsh noted Dylan's lyrical "acceptance of bizarre phenomenon."[26] Strange things happened throughout the album, yet Dylan was nonplussed.

The title song created an outlaw hero, which was in fashion with the late 1960s. There really was a John Wesley Hardin, and Dylan was teased for adding a "g" to the name after dropping so many in "Blowin' in the Wind," "The Times They Are A-Changin'" and other songs.

"As I Went Out One Morning" mixed banalities with mutations of real and fictional characters. Tom Paine appeared in this song, but more as a place than a person. Dylan also turned conventions on their heads. Shelton noted that the "fair damsel" of the song was not in distress; she was the tormentor. Using the banal opening line (also the title) to enter into a world of remarkable occurrences was one clue that Dylan offers implying that things are not what they appear to be.

"All along the Watchtower" was the album's masterpiece. Rinzler wrote of it: "Understated, precise, economical, this important song reveals still more about the overtly moral message Dylan was expouding throughout the album."[27] Dylan said of the song, "it probably came to me during a thunder and lightning storm. I'm sure it did."[28]

After "Watchtower," Dylan wisely offered comedy: "The Ballad of Frankie Lee and Judas Priest." This tall tale and the album notes (also written by

Dylan) echo of western myth, and the sprightly, simple music punctuates the mood.

"Drifter's Escape" was another tale of a victim, but in this instance the persecuted character was victorious. Dylan merged the taste of the Old West present in many of the songs with biblical themes and allusions, stating that his reemergence as a recording artist found him "with his feet on the ground and the Bible in his hand."[29] "Dear Landlord," which appeared to be a simple, somewhat superficial plea from an indentured tenant, might have actually been the closest piece to a confessional on the album. Dylan was indebted: to Albert Grossman, to Macmillan Publishers, to ABC Television and others, and he was asking for a stay of execution, or, ideally, to be released from these obligations.

"I Am a Lonesome Hobo" showed the strong influence of Hank Williams, who had ignited Dylan's interest in writing and performance when he was still a teenager. This song and "I Pity the Poor Immigrant" were again archtypical American epics. "The Wicked Messenger" was rife with allusions to Shakespeare as well as the Bible. Was its reference to killing the messenger who brings bad news a reflection of Dylan's experience of casting off of his protest role? Artists, Dylan knew, were committed to truth, and this was an elliptical defense of that function.

The album's concluding songs did not match the mood of the rest of the work, but they were pleasant diversions. Both "Down along the Cove" and "I'll Be Your Baby Tonight" were romps, aided by the addition of Pete Drake's steel guitar. They were amiable, lighthearted and bereft of biblical images. Dylan's "new voice" (the smooth sound he would use on *Nashville Skyline*) appeared in the second verse of "Down along the Cove." The songs ended the album with a hopeful feeling, relieving the darkness.

Old West themes, country songs, and biblical allusions freckled through the album--and they baffled many listeners. Critics, however, saw something more to the album. Jon Landau, writing in *Crawdaddy* (the first serious rock magazine) said that there was a strong sense of political awareness in the album, which Dylan had concealed.[30] Writing in the *Village Voice*, Richard Goldstein said the album "not only eludes, but dares interpretation . . . . Dylan's major theme was human vulnerability . . . . [He] confronts a cliche the way a butcher eyes a chicken. His new songs abound with slaughtered platitudes . . . . Dylan is his own motif."[31]

Nashville Skyline (1969): Compare the cover photo of *Nashville Skyline* with the pictures on the covers of *Bringing It All Back Home* or *Blonde on Blonde*. Is this the same man? On this album, Dylan appeared as a smiling country gentleman, doffing his hat as if to say, "Howdy, Ma'am." Was this another put on from the master? Furthermore, Dylan's new voice, which he had tried out on *John Wesley Harding*, was smooth where it had been rough, tender where it had been coarse. Dylan suggested to *Rolling Stone* editor Jann Wenner that the new voice was a result of quitting cigarettes. Whatever the case, the album opened with a duet with Johnny Cash and listeners were puzzled: Which one was Dylan?

The first voice on the majestic rerecording of "Girl from the North Country" was Dylan. (Those unfamiliar with country music might have hoped that the second voice, the lumberjack voice, was him, but, of course, it was Cash. Despite stumbling over the lyrics (interestingly, when there was a misunderstanding over which verse was next, Cash bulled through and Dylan went along), the new version of "Girl from the North Country" was an outstanding recording. Before, the singer was still a child, now he was an older man, and the song took on a more bittersweet tone.

"Nashville Skyline Rag," the second tune, was an instrumental filler that allowed the session musicians--Charlie Daniels, Charlie McCoy, Peter Drake and the others--to take solos and show off. It solidified the country tone of the album. The third song--and the third *start* to the album--was "To Be Alone with You." So casual were the sessions that Dylan's question to producer Bob Johnston at the beginning of the tape ("Is it rolling, Bob?") was retained. The first new real song on the album was "I Threw It All Away," a straight-faced "lost-my-woman" song that employed salacious metaphors that were too obvious to have been accidental. "Peggy Day" was pure wordplay.

"Lay Lady Lay," a moving plea from a desperate man, was Dylan's first hit since the *Blonde on Blonde* days. The charming "One More Night," which showcased Norman Blake's superb dobro playing, was one of the overlooked gems of Dylan's career. His attempt at a straight-ahead country ballad, "Tell Me That It Isn't True," was surprisingly successful, and sounded like a rewrite of "All I Really Want to Do." "Country Pie" was another throwaway, as Dylan veritably licked his lips in contemplation of dessert. He did not seem to resemble the same man who wrote "Gates of Eden." (Marsh called "Country Pie" mere babble.)

The final track, "Tonight I'll Be Staying Here with You," was the sort of histrionic showstopper that Loretta Lynn would have enjoyed belting out at the Grand Old Opry. The simpleminded songs stuck in the craw of many critics. Marsh concluded that the album "painted a picture of a blissfully romantic, decidedly uninteresting fool."[32]

Self Portrait (1970): Greil Marcus's review of this album in *Rolling Stone* began, "What is this shit?"[33] It was not hard to understand his confusion. The album started with "All the Tired Horses," on which Dylan did not sing. The lyrics consisted of one line--an implied confession that he had been unable to write anything recently--repeated for three minutes by a female chorus while an orchestra sailed heavenward. It was odd: A longtime Dylan listener would find no relationship between "Masters of War" and "All the Tired Horses."

When Dylan did begin singing, on the second song, things were not cleared up. The album was called *Self Portrait*, but there were few original compositions. Moreover, those that bore a "B. Dylan" credit on the label were often rearrangements of traditional tunes, which had now been claimed by Dylan and his publishing company.

As a double album, *Self Portrait* was naturally compared to *Blonde on Blonde* and, therefore, did not fare well. The earlier album had a unified sound, the "wild mercury" with which Dylan was so pleased. There was no unification on *Self Portrait*. There were songs in the *Nashville Skyline* style, songs that sounded like outtakes from his early 1960s albums, feeble efforts to cover pop tunes and some ragged live recordings with The Band from the Isle of Wight Festival in 1969.

As Marcus' opening salvo suggested, critics were confused by the album. Christgau, in the *Village Voice*, considered it a brilliant concept: defining the self through the works of others. However, the execution was poor, Christgau wrote, though he gave most of the blame to Bob Johnston.[34] (Johnston was to produce only one more album with Dylan.) Several critics suggested that it would have been acceptable as a single album. An old folk song of the gold rush, "Days of '49" was one of the album's most sustained performances. The traditional "Copper Kettle" was sung movingly, and an instrumental called "Wigwam" was also cited by most critics. Two versions of "Alberta" were offered, both credited to Dylan though they were actually the work of Leadbelly.

There were also some oddities. Dylan double-tracked a vocal on Simon and Garfunkel's "The Boxer," making a joke that was funny on the first hearing but not afterward. He sang two Everly Brothers songs, "Let It Be Me" (in a honey-coated voice) and "Take a Message to Mary" (without enough conviction to pull off the Old West tale.) His version of Gordon Lightfoot's "Early Mornin' Rain" was affecting but innocuous. The cover version of Rodgers and Hart's "Blue Moon" outraged Marcus. The live recordings from the Isle of Wight angered critics the most. "Like a Rolling Stone" was extremely sloppy, and some called it a desecration of rock's greatest song. Perhaps it was intentional, a way of dealing with a legacy that was impossible to maintain. "The Mighty Quinn (Quinn the Eskimo)" was similarly slipshod.

Put together, *Self Portrait* was one of the strangest albums ever released by a major artist. Packaged grandiosely--with script lettering, soft-focus color photos, and Dylan's primitive painting on the front, it reeked of a commercial product. In the vernacular of the time, it was called a shuck.

Marcus said in his *Rolling Stone* assault, "I once said I'd buy an album of Bob Dylan breathing hard, but I never said I'd buy an album of Dylan breathing softly."[35] Nonetheless, Dylan revisionists find a great deal to like about the album. Far from being just a misstep in a heretofore brilliant career, it provided further background on a perplexing artist.

New Morning (1970): Ralph J. Gleason, the revered music columnist for *Rolling Stone*, cheered when *New Morning* was released. "We've got Dylan back again!" he headlined his "Perspectives" column in the issue announcing the album. For many, this album marked Dylan's return after stumbling through the wilderness with *Self Portrait*.

The sound was rougher, definitely more rock 'n' roll than the previous album. Al Kooper led the studio band, and the recording was done in New York. With those two ties to the *Highway 61* era, the album was set up for a tough comparison. It fared better than *Self Portrait*. Writing in the Sunday edition of the *New York Times*, Marcus said the album was Dylan's best in years and called it "an act of vitality," while Ed Ward of *Rolling Stone* said he thought it might be Dylan's best album.[36]

Some of the songs were intended for a Broadway production of Archibald MacLeish's play *Scratch*. It was unclear whether the piece was supposed to be a musical, which was what Dylan apparently had in mind, or a play featuring some of Dylan's songs, which was apparently what MacLeish wanted. Whatever the case, as Dylan noted, he and the poet "didn't see eye-to-eye" on one of the songs, and that ended the collaboration.[37]

The album began with one of Dylan's simplest love songs, "If Not for You," followed quickly by "Day of the Locusts," a tale about picking up an honorary doctorate from Princeton and heading off for a family vacation. "If Not for You" had a simple, guitar-based arrangement, but the second song featured Dylan's strong piano playing, which dominated the album.

He extolled the pastoral life of Woodstock in "Time Passes Slowly," whose melody masked a simplistic lyric. "Went to See the Gypsy," may have had its genesis in Dylan's trip to see Elvis Presley perform in Las Vegas. There was a ribald bit of rock 'n' roll, "One More Weekend," and then the album headed toward a spiritual conclusion with the monologue "Three Angels" (which sounds a lot like the Flying Burrito Brothers' tongue-in-cheek "Hippie Boy," a song Dylan told critics he loved)[38] and a quick piano turn, "Father of Night." However, in the wake of *Nashville Skyline* and *Self Portrait*, anything with Dylan's characteristic bite was bound to be noticed by listeners.

Bob Dylan's Greatest Hits, Vol. II (1971): This time, Columbia Records included some new recordings and rarities in a greatest-hits package. Still, few of the songs on this double album had truly been hits for Dylan. Several were included because they had been hits for others: "My Back Pages" for The Byrds, "All I Really Want to Do" for Cher, "She Belongs to Me" for Rick Nelson, "If Not for You" for Olivia Newton-John and "The Mighty Quinn" for Manfred Mann. Some songs had not been huge hits but had been superbly covered by other artists and become staples of FM radio in the early 1970s. Jimi Hendrix's blistering cover of "All along the Watchtower" may have been a factor in the decision to include Dylan's version in this set. The Band had not released "When I Paint My Masterpiece" as a single and Dylan did not record it until preparing this anthology. How it could be called a "greatest hit" was a question that only someone in Columbia's marketing department could answer.

Some of his songs had become hits yet he had never recorded them himself, at least not outside the basement of Big Pink. Dylan and Happy Traum rerecorded three Big Pink tunes for *Greatest Hits, Vol. II*: "You Ain't Goin' Nowhere," "I Shall Be Released" and "Down in the Flood." A few songs were included because they were bona fide Dylan hits, including "Watching the River Flow," which he had recorded earlier in the year with Leon Russell producing.

There was a legitimate rarity on the disc: Dylan's performance of "Tomorrow Is a Long Time," from his Town Hall concert in New York City on April 12, 1963. There was no apparent logic to the sequence of the songs, and Dylan's many styles and voices were mixed on each of the four sides of the original album. The album was compiled with Dylan's cooperation, unlike the first volume, and Marsh called it the ideal greatest-hits album.[39]

Pat Garrett and Billy the Kid (1973): This collection of mostly instrumental music from the film was distinguished by "Knockin' on Heaven's Door," a bit of mood music created for a death scene, which ended up as one of the biggest hit singles of his career. The rest of the album served as an audio documentary of an artist at work. Dylan made three attempts at "Billy," his main theme, changing the song significantly each time. However, later recordings and outtakes (on *Biograph* and *The Bootleg Series*) would better satisfy fans craving insight to Dylan's creative process.

Nevertheless, the album had its admirers. Of "Final Theme," critic Paul Nelson wrote: "Instrumental music so mythic that it's perfectly suitable for both weddings and funerals, births and rebirths, or whatever the essences are."[40] Marsh rated it as better than *New Morning*. To him, "Knockin' on Heaven's Door" and "Final Theme" had "an epic grandeur reminiscent of Dylan's best electric work."[41]

Dylan (1973): This was Bob Dylan's punishment for leaving Columbia, and most critics said it was only good for perverse pleasure. When Dylan did not re-sign with the label, this album was hastily assembled, mostly from outtakes of *Self Portrait*. If these recordings were not considered good enough for that album, that was a damaging statement about their quality. These songs were often done as warm-ups before the "real" recording session began and were not intended for issue. Columbia's release of the recording made it, in Rinzler's words, a "corporate bootleg."[42] However, the album was not without worth. One of the strongest cuts was Dylan's version of Peter

LaFarge's "Ballad of Ira Hayes," the story of the Native American soldier who raised the flag on Iwo Jima but who was forgotten upon his return home.

Dylan's take of Jerry Jeff Walker's "Mr. Bojangles" escaped show-biz schmaltz. "A Fool Such As I," his tribute to Elvis Presley, "cooked" according to Rinzler. A version of the traditional "Spanish Is the Loving Tongue," a story of a cowboy's romance with a Mexican woman, had been issued two years before as the flip side of the "Watching the River Flow" single. The version on *Dylan* was an alternate take.

Most of the album was disposable. It was an interesting song selection for Columbia to make: With so much rich Dylan material in the vault--enough to later enrich *Biograph* and *The Bootleg Series*--why were these inferior outtakes used? Why did the company not collect the rare singles? Copies of "Can You Please Crawl out Your Window?" and "George Jackson" were in great demand. If Columbia wanted to punish Dylan, why did they not release that sort of material and create an album that would have been devoured by his fans, rather than outtakes that merely depressed them?

Planet Waves (1974): Recorded largely in just three days with The Band at their Shangla-La studio in Malibu, *Planet Waves* was intended to be ready before the Dylan/Band tour began on January 3, 1974. However, last-minute tinkering with the song sequence and a title change delayed the album's release, frustrating Asylum Records president David Geffen, who had a great deal invested in Bob Dylan. Dylan's album notes indicated that he was at the beginning of a new cycle. "Back to the starting point!" he proclaimed.[43] Whether *Planet Waves* was the true beginning of a new cycle was yet to be seen: More critics came to regard it as a warm-up for the tour with The Band. Marsh said that the songs were insubstantial and barely filled the album. An artist of Dylan's reputation needed to produce more and better material.[44]

"On a Night Like This" was an innocuous song of friendship fueled by the superb musicianship of The Band. Garth Hudson's accordian pushed the song along, over the simple "be-my-friend" lyrics of Dylan. Robbie Robertson's abilities as a blues guitarist nearly overshadowed Dylan on "Going Going Gone," a song that could be referring to death or simple departure. Like many of the songs on the album, the lyrics were vague. However, its vagueness was more superficial, not as dense as *John Wesley Harding*.

"Tough Mama" was a bow to the times, the song of tribute to the "old lady," a form that, thankfully, feminism has helped to eradicate. Dylan's song was far from the most vile example of that particular genre and it had a strength to it that echoed the album's subtitle: "Cast Iron Songs and Torch Ballads." Shelton found traces of Echo Helstrom in "Hazel," a song of praise for a woman from the poor side of town. The theme of reminiscence was carried through on the following track, "Something There Is about You." Unfortunately, Dylan seemed to have piled too many syllables into the lines for him to sing this song comfortably.

Two recordings of "Forever Young" provided the centerpiece of the album; one was slow, the other fast. Dylan had written a prayer before ("Father of Night" on *New Morning*), but the touching nature of this song lifted it above the rest of the material on *Planet Waves*. Dylan had also made references to his children before, but this was the first song he had released that was addressed to a child. "I wrote it thinking about one of my boys and not wanting to be too sentimental," he said.[45]

"Dirge" may have been another farewell to the 1960s, in which Dylan sang of all the things that he used to require that are inconsequential to him now. In theme at least, the song echoed "My Back Pages." "You Angel You" was pleasant, an antecedent of "Precious Angel," which was to follow at decade's end, and "Never Say Goodbye" sounded hastily written and recorded. "Wedding Song" was the album's major work, which was a high compliment, since the album also contained "Forever Young." It was a pure testament of love, of the singer's willingness to give up everything for the love of another. Some also saw this song as being intensely personal, perhaps as Dylan's apology to his wife for returning to public life. He was about to embark on his tour with The Band and become professionally active again. Consequently, his privacy and much of his time with her and their children would be sacrificed. Thus, he asked her to understand his commitment as an artist. Critics were happy to have any reasonable sort of album from Dylan, and they could confidently rank "Forever Young" and "Wedding Song" with some of his best work.

Before the Flood (1974): This album exists primarily as a document of Dylan's tour with The Band. It was also released to fulfill a moral obligation Dylan felt to David Geffen, the president of Asylum Records. Geffen had been supportive and Dylan felt he was owed such an album, so he got one. None of Dylan's new songs were featured, though he played three or four from the Malibu sessions at most of the shows. Instead, it was a greatest-hits set with few surprises. Two recordings, however, stood out. The new version of "Most Likely You Go Your Way (and I'll Go Mine)" opened and closed most of the concerts. Its powerful kick was perfect to start the live album. The reworking of "All along the Watchtower," with Robertson's stinging guitar solos, was another highlight. The recording did not eclipse the power of the original but rather remade it into a rock 'n' roll song.

Dylan played piano on "Ballad of a Thin Man," which took on a nearly fun-house tone with Garth Hudson's organ percolating behind Dylan. The Band also performed several songs on its own, including "The Weight," "The Night They Drove Old Dixie Down" and "Stage Fright." The criticism of Dylan's singing on that tour might be carried over to this album. He shouted many of his songs, quickly running through the tunes as if in a hurry. Some took that to mean he was impatient to finish, while others took it to be a concession to the large-scale nature of the show and the stadium crowds. Marsh was among those who were disappointed. He suggested that the songs that meant so much to the audience meant little to Dylan, judging from the new performances. This made Marsh reexamine just what the lyrics had meant to him.[46] Despite these complaints, Marsh said the new versions were "at least interesting" and that some of the reinterpretations were downright fascinating.

Blood on the Tracks (1975): Some call this album Bob Dylan's masterpiece. That was high praise, considering his rock 'n' roll trilogy of the mid-1960s, *John Wesley Harding* and the two vital protest albums. These tales of unraveling relationships began a major period of artistic activity for Dylan and marked his return to the marketplace as a potent recording artist. Recorded first in New York, and then substantially re-recorded in Minneapolis, *Blood on the Tracks* was the result of Dylan's schooling with art teacher Norman Raeben, who helped him redirect his approach to writing.

"Tangled Up in Blue," the opening song, was the story of a relationship over the course of years. However, Dylan shifted between the time periods so blithely that it was hard to keep up. (This is much like what William Faulkner accomplished in *The Sound and the Fury*.) Some have suggested that the song was not about one woman but several, and each verse addressed a different figure in a different time. Dylan originally wrote the song in the third person. He recorded here in the first, but then performed it in concert in the third person again. This was one of the five songs to be rerecorded in Minneapolis. (The original version appeared on *The Bootleg Series, Vols. 1-3*.)

"Simple Twist of Fate" recounted another breakup, but did so through the guise of an artist who must relive the pain constantly, unlike someone who does not carry the curse of creativity that demands a reexamination of the pain. Joan Baez admired this song and recorded it soon after Dylan. "You're a Big Girl Now" has been called by Shelton a sequel to "Just Like a Woman" and has been cited for being some of Dylan's most emotional singing. When he sang of the pain in his heart, his voice shuddered. Dylan had often played the part of a lover who cannot be hurt further. This song made it clear that he was still vulnerable.

"Idiot Wind" was rerecorded in Minneapolis with a big band after Dylan grew dissatisfied with the simple New York version. It concerned chaos and demanded a sound that Dylan was only able to achieve with a band. It was one of Dylan's classic truth attacks, a finger-pointing song, and a catharsis. "You're Gonna Make Me Lonesome When You Go" punctuated the heavy mood of "Idiot Wind." Though also a song of loss, it was quick, and brightly played, with a reference to poet Arthur Rimbaud, who was one of Dylan's major influences.

"Meet Me in the Morning" was the album's blues number. It was musically identical to "Call Letter Blues," which Dylan rejected for inclusion. "Lily, Rosemary and the Jack of Hearts," another western tall tale, was performed frenetically by the Minneapolis band. It was like *John Wesley Harding*'s "Ballad of Frankie Lee and Judas Priest" playing at a faster speed. Marsh was not happy with the revised versions of the songs, calling the Minneapolis group amateurish.[47]

"If You See Her, Say Hello" has also been called a sequel: This time, to "Girl from the North Country." It echoed a line from the earlier song and also had the same aura of toughness in the face of heartbreak. "Shelter from the Storm" was a recollection of the beginning of a relationship that had also ended. In it, Dylan strongly stated his case that love was the salvation that he sought. He punctuated the album perfectly with the playful "Buckets of Rain," a statement of his resolution to carry on. Some critics found the album to be ultimately inspirational, sending a message to endure.[48]

Christgau was among the score of critics to consider *Blood on the Tracks* among Dylan's finest work. "Dylan's new stance was as disconcerting as all the previous ones, but the quickest and deepest surprise was the music.... On the whole, this was the leader's most mature and assured record."[49]

The Basement Tapes (1975): Dylan and The Band finally sanctioned the release of these songs eight years after they had been recorded. Dylan may have wanted to undercut the bootleggers, or The Band may have needed money. Whatever the reason, their release in the wake of *Blood on the Tracks* meant that critics could not point to the old recordings and say "See how good he used to be," when Dylan had just produced a superb album showing his creative faculties to be in good working order.

Dylan's sense of humor stood out on *The Basement Tapes*. The album began with "Odds and Ends," the first of several nonsense songs. "Apple Sucking Tree," "Please Mrs. Henry," "Tiny Montgomery" and several others showed Dylan being as wickedly funny as he had ever been and, at some points, laughing too hard to finish a line. "Clothes Line Saga" may have been a parody of a talking blues or it may have been a barb thrown in the direction of popular music in 1967, a world that put Bobbie Gentry's mashed-potato opus "Ode to Billy Joe" at the top of the charts. In Dylan's song, the virtues of laundry, a hot lunch and being a good boy are delineated.

"Tears of Rage" (written with Richard Manuel) was one of the most effective new songs, dealing as it did with the rift between generations. Whereas three years before Dylan had pointed a finger at his elders and told them to move, he now spoke from their point of view, with great compassion and understanding. "This Wheel's on Fire" (written with Rick Danko) was menacing, drawn as it was from references to *King Lear*. Dylan was evidently doing a lot of reading up in the mountains.

The release of these songs was greeted with exultation by most critics. Greil Marcus's album notes nearly declare the album's release a cause for national holiday. However, Marsh and others lamented that many songs were still being withheld. Dylan's version of "I Shall Be Released," for example, had been bootlegged. "I'm Not There (1956)" was also left off. Despite its incomplete nature, Marsh pronounced the album "brilliant."[50]

Desire (1976): Within the space of 12 months, Dylan released three albums: *Blood on the Tracks*, *The Basement Tapes* and *Desire*. This third album became his best-selling record to that date. Recorded mostly in one night with the musicians who would become the core of the Rolling Thunder Revue, *Desire* had a unity of sound resulting from the crisp recording of the acoustic guitars, the violin of Scarlet Rivera and the harmonies of Emmylou Harris. Harris had trouble keeping up with Dylan, whose every performance of a song was different, yet her voice was one of the most endearing things about *Desire*.[51]

"Hurricane," the album's first track, was Dylan's story-song about boxer Rubin "Hurricane" Carter, who was convicted of a murder Dylan believed he did not commit. Dylan sang the song furiously and Rivera's violin swirled around his voice. The song was effective, even when shortened for radio airplay. "Isis" was the first song that Dylan wrote with Jacques Levy, with whom he collaborated for most of *Desire*. A song that evoked both mythology and modern marriage, it dealt with love as torment and became a signature for Dylan's performances with the Rolling Thunder Revue.

"Mozambique" and "One More Cup of Coffee" were showpieces that allowed the band to impersonate gypsies. Indeed, "One More Cup of Coffee" made overt references to these people, and was apparently drawn from a meeting between Dylan and a gypsy king in France. However, the song also had a quasi-religious tone. Rinzler said that Dylan sounded like a cantor.[52] (Incidentally, a young Australian named Richard Dickinson was so infatuated with this song that when his mother complained once too often about his repeated playing of *Desire*, he stomped her to death. The man then sprinkled instant coffee grounds on her body. Dickinson has been institutionalized ever since the killing in 1987, but was released in the company of guards for one night--to see Bob Dylan in concert.)[53]

"Oh, Sister," which is sung with Harris, was one of Dylan's most beautiful compositions, and it was superbly performed. A song of love and duty, the violin cut into Dylan's vocal, rendering the song all the more effective a plea. Harris also sang with Dylan on "Joey," an 11-minute song about gangster Joey Gallo. The story was apparently derived from Gallo's friends, as he came off as a near-saint. Dylan was taken to task for making this particular outlaw a hero. "Romance in Durango" and "Black Diamond Bay" were linked tracks on the album and were similar in theme. Though not disposable, the songs did not fit with the powerful declarations found elswehere on the disc.

"Sara," the closing piece, was the other half of "Wedding Song." It was the plea of a desperate man to his wife, as he serenades her, celebrates her, and circles her with his words. He would do whatever he could to be with her--whether it meant being a minstrel or a fool. Dylan often said that he did not write strongly personal songs, but perhaps that statement was not meant to apply to "Sara."

Marsh said that *Desire* was nearly a masterpiece because of its scope, yet in his view it lacked a good band.[54] Rinzler unabashedly called it his favorite album. To Rinzler, *Planet Waves*, *Blood on the Tracks* and *Desire* "represent the most fully realized expressions of a great artist in his maturity.... [Dylan was] at the height of his powers."[55]

Hard Rain (1976): This was another tour document, but from the wrong end of the tour. The early shows of the Rolling Thunder Revue, during its opening swing through New England, were superb performances. Those shows were recorded. The music on *Hard Rain* was taped nearly eight months later, at shows in Fort Worth, Texas, and Fort Collins, Colorado. By then, the sets had become routine, the sound bloated, the spontaneity reduced to formula.

Nonetheless, there are high moments on *Hard Rain*. Dylan's stop-and-start version of "Maggie's Farm" nearly matched the original. "Lay Lady Lay" was rerecorded as more of a demand than a plea. A march-like, drum-driven "Shelter From the Storm" alone justified the album. Mick Ronson of Dylan's stage band referred to the record as a progenitor of punk, and it does have a rough edge to it. Marsh, however, disagreed. He considered it insignificant.[56]

Street-Legal (1978): There was a gap of over two years between studio albums, and when Dylan returned, with *Street-Legal*, his sound was utterly different. He had hired a big band, including several session pros who had worked with Elvis Presley. Dylan had spent much of the previous year in court, getting a divorce and settling child custody disputes. The album seemed, in that context, to be one of his most autobiographical works. Shelton cited its tales of "loss, searching, estrangement and exile" and saw a foreshadowing of Dylan's Christian conversion, which was to happen within a year.[57] Shelton, who had known Dylan well for 20 twenty years by the time of the album's release, still found the references difficult.

"Changing of the Guards" was about estrangement, but was it from a woman, a movement, some friends or a rock 'n' roll band? Shelton could not be sure. "New Pony" could be one of Dylan's most overtly sexual songs, when read on one level. His new band included gospel-type singers, and the interplay between Dylan and the chorus created sexual tension that reinforce that primal interpretation. "No Time to Think" seemed directly drawn from the turmoil in Dylan's life. "I almost didn't have a friend in the world," Dylan said of that period. "I was being thrown out of my house, I was under a lot of pressure...."[58]

"Baby, Stop Crying" could have easily fit on the gospel albums in terms of its performance, but its threat of violence (the narrator asks for a gun in the opening verse) set it apart. The song had a hook, in the classic commercial sense, and it showed that when he wanted to, Bob Dylan could write a pop song. "Is Your Love in Vain?" echoed Robert Johnson's classic blues ("Love in Vain") and was the best-sounding big-band song on the record. It also was one of the few new songs Dylan performed on his tours in the era.

"Senor (Tales of Yankee Power)" carried on Dylan's fascination with Latin culture (as in "Cantina Theme," "Romance in Durango"), or, as he put it, "sort of like lost yankee on a gloomy Sunday-carnival-embassy-type thing, the unforgettable wench, not a friend in the world, all messed up for something like say a murder charge, having to pay for sins that you didn't commit when all the while you were getting away with murder.... So it all evens out in the end."[59] "True Love Tends to Forget" was a great pop song. It could have been a hit for Dylan or for Neil Diamond. The guitar style was reminiscent of David Lindley, known for his work with Jackson Browne.

The gospel singers had apparently inspired Dylan to explore more musical themes, and he even tasted a little rhythm and blues in "No Time to Think." He apparently thought highly of "We Better Talk This Over," another quasi-confessional tune, for he included it on the flip side of a single nearly five years later. The album's final track, "Where Are You Tonight? (Journey through Dark Heat)" explicitly stated Dylan's desire to take a new journey. The journey, of course, turned out to be more spiritual than geographical.

In the end, despite the experiments with a new musical style, Marsh felt the album "didn't add up to much.... [Dylan] failed to communicate anything of importance to even the most ardent listener."[60] The unusual sound of the album--nothing else in Dylan's catalog sounded quite like it--puzzled listeners. The band bloated the arrangements and the songs were even more obscure than they had been in the mid-1960s.

Bob Dylan at Budokan (1978): Yet another tour document, this album was created for the Japanese market as a souvenir of Dylan's shows there. Seeing its success overseas, Columbia executives quickly issued it in the United States. Accompanied by the *Street-Legal* band, Dylan offered a selection of greatest hits over the course of the double album. Only a couple of new songs were recorded (including "Oh, Sister," which had appeared on three of the last four albums), and the old songs were drastically reworked: "Mr. Tambourine Man" was given flute accompaniment, "All I Really Want to Do" got the march treatment and "The Times They Are A-Changin'" became the syrupy, pull-out-all-the-stops big-band show closer. Dylan, who was often taciturn during concerts (he barely spoke from the stage during the tour with The Band) was verbose while talking to his Japanese fans.

Slow Train Coming (1979): Aside from revealing Dylan's conversion to Christianity, this was one of his best-sounding albums. He had worked with three great producers--John Hammond, Tom Wilson and Bob Johnston--in the first decade of his career, and then he had drifted. Hooking up with Barry Beckett of the Muscle Shoals Sound Studio and Jerry Wexler of Atlantic Records was an inspired move, and the gospel albums profited greatly from their collaboration.

The opening track was also the album's first single. "Gotta Serve Somebody," which became Dylan's show opener for a full two years of touring. Ironically, when Beckett and Wexler were sequencing the album, it did not appear. "I had to fight to get it on the album," Dylan said.[61] With interchangable lyrics (by the time he performed it on "Saturday Night Live" two months after the album's release, he had added three new verses), it was the perfect statement of Dylan's new faith, which he did with some humor (calling himself "Zimmy"). "I Believe in You" was another concert stalwart that outlasted the gospel years. In the album's context, the song was about God, but it could also be about a woman or a child.

"Precious Angel" was another song of love, presumably about a Jew and a black woman, judging by the reference to the ancestors of both as having been slaves. "Gonna Change My Way of Thinking" and "Do Right to Me Baby" were pop songs that Dylan might conceivably have included on *Street-Legal*. Dylan's gospel tours were often criticized for his frequent preaching from the stage, and "When You Gonna Wake Up?" was the most didactic on this album. "Man Gave Names to All the Animals" was either nonsense or intended as a children's song.

"Slow Train," the album's theme song, had begun to evolve as an instrumental used to open concerts during the *Street-Legal* tour. "Slow Train" and "When He Returns" both foretold judgment day, the first in near-apocalyptic terms, and the second in serene and peaceful language. Many critics commented on the superior musicianship on the album, which featured half of Dire Straits, a new English band whose singer and lead guitarist, Mark Knopfler, sometimes sounded more like Bob Dylan than Dylan himself. Marsh, however, did not find the album endearing. He felt that Dylan was babbling.[62]

Saved (1980): This was another gospel album, and was superbly played and produced. However, the heavy-handed album graphics (a hand reaching down from heaven, it would have looked more suitable painted on black velvet) and the admonishing tone put off a lot of listeners. The stongest material on *Saved* seemed familiar. "In the Garden" was basically a rewrite of the story of Jesus at Gethsemene. "Saved," which was written with Dylan's bassist Tim Drummond, was the story of an individual's salvation told in the usual phraseology of the recently converted. "Covenant Woman" was a new sort of love song for Dylan, in which he regarded a woman as an extension of a larger spirit. "Solid Rock" was what its title implied, yet the rock was the rock of the church. What was unusual about the album was its lack of clever lyrics. Even the weakest Dylan albums before had had some sort of unusual vision, but here Dylan seemed to be merely serving as a messenger.

Marsh thought that *Saved* was worse than *Slow Train Coming*. It was "a caricature of fundamentalist cant [that] prevents anyone else ever from doing an effective satire of the Christian Dylan, because he's satirized himself."[63] Christgau was driven to pray, "May Bobby never indenture soul sisters again."[64]

Shot of Love (1981): This was a superb yet ultimately overlooked album. Dylan has called it his favorite, which may be because he was able to take what he had learned during his two-year apprenticeship in gospel and bring it to his secular music. The title track was produced with Bumps Blackwell and sounded like one of the simple litanies of the gospel albums. However, it indicated that Dylan expected to explore urban blues on this album, and he did so, with "Trouble" (on which he was joined by Ron Wood of The Rolling Stones) and "Dead Man, Dead Man."

"Heart of Mine" was a simple but beautiful love song from a man who feels that his heart has been broken too many times for him to risk falling in love again. "Lenny Bruce" was a memoir (they once shared a cab ride) and a lament for the innovative comedian, who died of a drug overdose. Dylan did not paint Bruce as a martyr (as many others had) for the persecution he received for being different. Instead, he merely noted Bruce's loss and the fact that he had an unusual outlook on the world.

Later versions of the album included "The Groom's Still Waiting at the Altar," one of Dylan's strongest rock 'n' roll songs of the 1980s. It was compared to his mid-1960s work because of its hard edge (like "Tombstone Blues"), but it was more of a look forward to his new style. The song might have been referring to the fact that Dylan contemplated getting married again around the time of *Shot of Love*. The final song on the album, "Every Grain of Sand," was one of Dylan's best. Critics commented on the vulnerable lyrics, in which the narrator, who is in need of guidance, finds evidence of God everywhere. Dylan had said before, "I can see God in a daisy," echoing William Blake, who was the direct inspiration for this song.[65]

Critics began to sense that Dylan was returning to form. Marsh said *Shot of Love* "is close to the rock 'n' roll of vintage Sixties Dylan . . . . For the first time, one begins to sense the strength Dylan draws from Christianity--and the deep need he felt for some humility to balance his life." Marsh called "Every

Grain of Sand" an undeniably superior piece of music.[66] He also admitted that he was ready to consider Dylan a great artist again.

Infidels (1983): This album's reputation has grown with the years. It was one of his most sharply produced albums, largely because of his renewed collaboration with Knopfler, who was as brilliant a producer as he was a musician. There were only eight songs on the album, yet it seemed full of ideas. "Jokerman" was like an old Dylan riddle to be searched for clues. It was a journey through both art and literature.

"Sweetheart Like You" was ostensibly a love song, yet it contained some of Dylan's most devastating political one liners, suggesting, as Balzac had, that "behind every great fortune there was a crime." "Neighborhood Bully" was considered a defense of Zionism, which was an easy interpretation to make. However, it was most notable as one of the album's two rock 'n' roll showpieces. The second, "Union Sundown," used the blues motif to convey what many saw as an essentially conservative message about labor unions.

"Man of Peace" was somewhat superficial in comparison to the rest of the album, an incantation of the story of the sheep in wolf's clothing. "License to Kill" carried an environmental theme, and "I and I," which was rife with biblical allusions, was a secular sermon, if such a thing exists. "Don't Fall Apart on Me Tonight" was a confession of self-doubt couched as a love song. It was not as powerful as "Every Grain of Sand," yet it conveyed Dylan's confusion about his role in the world and his use of his time on earth.

Dylan produced the album with Knopfler and employed a former Rolling Stone, Mick Taylor, to play guitar. The rhythm section included Sly Dunbar and Robbie Shakespeare, two brilliant reggae musicians. The digital sound and Knopfler's precision earned the album good reviews. Christgau said that all the work and care that had been put into the album showed, but that Dylan "has turned into a hateful crackpot."[67] Nonetheless, he ranked it as one of Dylan's best records.

Real Live (1984): Dylan released yet another tour document. The ten tracks on this album were recorded during Dylan's 1984 trek through Europe, with Taylor on guitar. Taylor, therefore, gave many of Dylan's songs a Rolling Stones feel. The opening track, "Highway 61 Revisted," was tougher and more ominous because of the band's low register. Christgau wrote, "Hitch Mick Taylor to a locomotive, make sure the songs are twenty years old, and you could get shit. But you could also get a decent live album if the auteur happened to be interested that night."[68]

Dylan recorded his new version of "Masters of War," in the same way that he figured Jimi Hendrix would have cut it.[69] He also performed the third-person "Tangled Up in Blue" and "Girl from the North Country," which was rendered even more touching with the vantage of a quarter-century. Of

Dylan's many live albums, *Real Live* will probably stand as the best until he releases recordings from the first leg of the Rolling Thunder Revue, or an album drawn from the 1966 English tour (source of the celebrated *Royal Albert Hall* bootleg).

Empire Burlesque (1985): Christgau considered this Dylan's best record since *Blood on the Tracks*. "I wish that was a bigger compliment," he wrote. The songs on the album were strong, but Dylan's use of synthesizers and other up-to-date recording techniques bothered some critics. (Ironically, critics had been pleading with him for years to modernize his approach and use outside producers.) Sometimes the sound worked. The opening track, "Tight Connection to My Heart (Has Anybody Seen My Love?)" beautifully blended horn, soul singers and Dylan's vocal.

"Seeing the Real You at Last" was a song of accusation, but it showed that Dylan had mellowed with the years. In terms of nastiness, it in no way approached "Positively 4th Street." "I'll Remember You" and "Emotionally Yours," the two ballads, were charming to various degrees. The first was simpler than the second, which risked suffocation by the string accompaniment.

"Clean Cut Kid" contained Dylan's first reference to Vietnam in a song and was, to Christgau, "the toughest Vietnam vet song yet."[70] Dylan had been working on the song for some time and finally gave it to a group called The Textones. That group polished the lyrics and Dylan finally recorded it. "Clean Cut Kid," like "Trust Yourself," was a hard rocking song that showed off the superstar players on the album: Taylor, Keith Richards, and several members of Tom Petty's Heartbreakers.

The album's major piece was "When the Night Comes Falling from the Sky." Dylan had attempted to record this song for a couple of years and employed the album's most obvious synthesizer on this apocalyptic tune. The song was somewhat marred by these intrusions and an earlier version (available on *The Bootleg Series*) better showcased the lyrics. Christgau and other critics bemoaned Dylan's apparent need to follow trends and he derisively passed on a phrase he had heard used to describe the album: "Disco Dylan."[71]

Biograph (1985): Dylan was the first major rock 'n' roll artist to produce a boxed set retrospective, a form that became increasingly popular as the compact disc (CD) market began to take hold. Eric Clapton, Chuck Berry, The Byrds and other artists followed Dylan's lead, producing multiple-disc sets that survey an artist's career and offer insight to the creative process by including working takes of songs and songs withheld from release.

Biograph took up five LPs and three CDs. It was also issued as three cassettes. It came with a booklet, which was superbly written by music journalist/filmmaker Cameron Crowe, and offered Dylan comments on several of his songs.

Virtually anything that could conceivably be called a hit was on the album. All his greatest protest songs were together on one side and the famous rock 'n' roll tracks were similarly grouped. There were a number of outtakes and live performances that made the set attractive for fans who already owned all of his albums: "Visions of Johanna" was featured in a live version from the 1966 tour; "Isis," from a great performance with the Rolling Thunder Revue; and a much-improved "Heart of Mine" from a 1981 show.

Some songs, like "The Groom's Still Waiting at the Altar" and "Mixed Up Confusion," were given their first wide release. Several songs that were previously left off albums were presented. Perhaps the best was "Abandoned Love," an uptempo lament that had not fit on *Desire*, and "Carribbean Wind," which suffered a similar fate during the *Shot of Love* sessions.

Knocked Out Loaded (1986): This album was one of Dylan's weakest efforts. Drawn as it was from several sessions, it cannot really be considered an album in the usual sense. It had one standout track, "Brownsville Girl," a collaboration with playwright Sam Shepard, which was a meditation on the meaning of art while standing in line to see a movie. Dylan had attempted this song for a couple of years before finally putting it on an album.[72] Christgau called it "one of the greatest and most ridiculous of his ridiculous epics."[73]

Other songs did not show such care or precision. Most songs were cover versions or collaborations, and one of the best of these was the blues track "You Wanna Ramble," which opened the album. To Christgau, Dylan was only going through the motions, compiling an album that sounded "like something he threw together in a week and away forever. But throwing it away was how he gets that off-the-cuff feel and side two was great fun."[74]

Down in the Groove (1988): This was an embarrassing album that reeked of being thrown together. Barely a half-hour long, the album contained only two original solo compositions and two collaborations. The bulk of the album was cover material, ranging widely from "Let's Stick Together," Wilbert Harrison's 1969 hit (Harrison was not really a one-hit wonder; his other hit was "Kansas City") to a gospel-tinged reworking of the traditional "Shenandoah." Dylan cowrote two songs with Grateful Dead lyricist Robert Hunter (one of these, "Silvio," earned some airplay) and threw in a leftover from the *Infidels* sessions, "Death is Not the End." Dylan took "Had a Dream about You, Baby" from the *Hearts of Fire* soundtrack and remixed it for this album, but he dropped a superior film cut, John Hiatt's "The Usual," from the original running order of *Down in the Groove*. ("The Usual" and a cover of "Got Love if You Want It" appeared on the Argentinian version of *Down in the Groove*.)

Even in the midst of the disappointing chaos of the album, there was something to like. Christgau was fond of "The Ugliest Girl in the World," which was "guaranteed to remind the faithful how much fun the one-take ethos used to be."[75] Several critics have called this album the low point of Dylan's career, an indication that he no longer cared about his music, his fans or perhaps even himself.

Dylan and the Dead (1989): This album was an uneccessary tour document. The combination of Dylan and The Grateful Dead was irresistible for concert promoters and had a lot of wisdom behind it. Both Dylan and the band were known for rarely performing songs alike in succeeding concerts. The Dead's musicianship could shore up Dylan's reputation as a live act, and Dylan's powerful material could help speed the pace of the typically long, rambling Dead show. The joint-billed tour lasted for six dates in July 1987, but the decision to release the album came much later, after the release of *Down in the Groove*. Dylan asked Dead guitarist Jerry Garcia and Dead manager John Cutler to go through the tapes and cull enough performances for an album.

Dylan and the Dead, featuring a Rick Griffin cover portrait of mid-1960s Dylan, had only seven tracks and the song selection itself was perverse. Few would deny the inclusion of concert staples "Knockin' on Heaven's Door" and "All along the Watchtower," but "Joey," even when shortened from its 11-minute *Desire* length, was a test for some listeners. Two songs from the gospel period, "Gotta Serve Somebody" and "Slow Train," were revisited, and one *Highway 61* tune, "Queen Jane Approximately," was given the Dead treatment. Reaction to the album seemed to depend on the critic's feelings about The Grateful Dead. Christgau said that the Dead were grateful to be rich men, "and they sound like it."[76] Dylan, on the other hand, sounded just plain terrible.

Oh Mercy (1989): For the first time since *Infidels*, Dylan worked with a real producer. Daniel Lanois had produced albums for Peter Gabriel and U2 by the time he went to New Orleans to work with The Neville Brothers. Dylan visited the sessions and was impressed with Lanois's work. Lanois had interrupted work an his album, *Acadie*, to produce *Yellow Moon* for the Nevilles, and Dylan asked him to put off finishing his album again to help produce a new Dylan album. *Oh Mercy*, which he also recorded in New Orleans, was the result. Lanois earned much of the praise when the album was released and several writers congratulated him for getting such disciplined work out of a somewhat undisciplined artist. Christgau wrote, "Daniel Lanois' understated care and easy beat suit his casual ways, and three or four songs might sound like something late at night on the radio or after the great flood."[77]

The tracks were recorded live, and Dylan showed up at the sessions with his songs more or less completed. Dylan had his lyrics on a music stand before him and seemed "extremely focused on his writing," one of the musicians said.[78] The sound of the album was sharp and full, immediately placing it above *Knocked Out Loaded* and *Down in the Groove* on a technical level. However, the songs were also clearer and more focused, and Dylan's singing, though not far removed from a growl, was his most forceful and confident since *Infidels*. Critics agreed that *Oh Mercy* was a superb album.

Writing in *Rolling Stone*, Anthony DeCurtis called the songs "evocative, atmospheric soundscapes." DeCurtis also admired Dylan's lyric style, "a plain-spoken directness with rich folkloric and Biblical shadings."[79] The magazine later named it as one of the top hundred albums of the decade. The album focused on the middle-aged Dylan's reactions to the still troubled world that he had savaged mercilessly in his mid-1960s rock 'n' roll trilogy. Several of *Oh Mercy*'s songs were powerful rockers in an updated *Highway 61* vein. The album kicked off with the swirling "Political World" and "Everything Is Broken." (The support band included Lanois and the rhythm section for The Neville Brothers.)

"Most of the Time" was one of Dylan's most beautiful ballads. Like the classic "I Get Along without You Very Well," it is a statement of mock-independence. The narrator sings of his former lover, protecting himself by saying that he never thinks of her and cannot even remember what it felt like to kiss her. It is all, of course, a self-deceiving lie. The most hypnotic piece on the album was "Man in a Long Black Coat," an ominous tale that hinted at the evil that is characteristic in some of Mark Twain's last writings ("The Man That Corrupted Hadleyburg" and "The Mysterious Stranger," for example). There was a timelessness to the story, which concerned greed, betrayal and torment. Lanois' production was hushed: crickets opened and closed the track, and Dylan's croaked vocal was frightening; it was like hearing a ghost story around a campfire.

The album closed with two reflective pieces. In "What Was It You Wanted?" the artist may be addressing his fans, berating them for asking too much from him in order to escape responsibility for their own lives. If Dylan was a disappointment, he told his audience, perhaps it was because the audience had unrealistic expectations. In "Shooting Star," the album's final track, Dylan may have been wrestling with the memory of a former lover. (It could be Joan Baez, who helped and adored Dylan when they both were young.) Now Dylan questioned if he had become what the lover had wanted him to become. It was a vulnerable moment in a confidently performed song.

Oh Mercy was not a huge commercial success, but it did focus a lot of attention on Dylan. As DeCurtis noted, "While it would be unfair to compare *Oh Mercy* to Dylan's landmark Sixties recordings, it sits well alongside his impressive body of work. It was also an encouraging sign that Dylan's creativity will continue to flourish in the coming decade."[80]

Under the Red Sky (1990): Dylan moved further in the direction of blues singing with this excellent album, which suffered the misfortune of following *Oh Mercy* and, therefore, was overshadowed by it. With a style that appeared deliberately simple, Dylan and various superstar guitarists blared through several original blues numbers, ranging from the deliberately simplistic "Wiggle Wiggle" to the hypnotic "Cat's in the Well." Jimmie and Stevie Ray Vaughan, Slash (of Guns n' Roses) and others contributed the guitar lines, and Dylan growled out his lyrics. His voice was a mere croak on the album, and he sounded like a club singer from Chicago's South Side.

Dylan also resurrected a talking blues for the album and as well as a pretty ballad (the title tune). However, the predominant feel was of the blues on an large scale. The production by Don Was and David Was of the studio band Was (Not Was) paled next to Lanois's more pristine sound but was perfectly suited to the rough-hewn style that Dylan obviously wanted for this recording. This album made a perfect companion to the acoustic blues of his debut album.

The Bootleg Series, Volumes 1-3 (1991): This declaration of victory against the bootleggers (Dylan would now undercut their sales) was another opportunity to reassess the musical legacy of Bob Dylan. The critics agreed, once again, that he was not only a major artist, but perhaps the most important writer and performer in the history of American popular music. Moreover, they based those assessments on this collection of songs that he had left *off* of his albums.

The first third of the collection was comprised of solo performances from the folk years. Dylan had been so prolific that recording engineers could not keep up with him. This set offered the first official releases of countless Dylan songs, including "Talkin' Bear Mountain Picnic Massacre Blues," "Paths of Victory," "Walkin' Down the Line," "Talkin' John Birch Paranoid Blues" and "Who Killed Davey Moore?" Some of the songs that had been removed from *The Freewheelin' Bob Dylan* were released as were demo recordings (on piano) of "When the Ship Comes In" and "The Times They Are A-Changin'."

Outtakes and rehearsals from the electric era were equally fascinating: an acoustic "Subterranean Homesick Blues" lacked the bite of the rock 'n' roll version; a rehearsal for "Like a Rolling Stone" showed it to have waltz structure; and an early, uptempo "It Takes a Lot to Laugh, It Takes a Train to Cry" rendered it an entirely new song. Dylan's long spoken poem, "Last Thoughts on Woody Guthrie," was as riveting as any of the songs, and the alternate takes of the *Blood on the Tracks* songs were, in some cases, more heartbreaking than the familiar verions.

However, most of the critical assessments of *The Bootleg Series* focused on Dylan's writing in the 1980s. The songs left off *Shot of Love*, *Infidels* and *Oh Mercy* garnered the most notice. In "Blind Willie McTell," from *Infidels*, Dylan sang of an old blues singer in whose voice he could feel all the horrors of slavery and of human experience. Dylan maintained in his tribute that he would never be an artist of that stature. In so confessing, of course, he became such an artist. The other outtake that earned the most acclaim was "Series of Dreams," used as the closing track on *The Bootleg Series*. Lanois recorded it for *Oh Mercy* and it was one of the most relentless and powerful recordings that Dylan had ever made. A hypnotic lyric about the confusions of dreams and reality was framed by inescapable percussion. It was pure lyricism amid frenzy, thus creating a triumphant metaphor for Dylan's songs and his life.

Good as I Been to You (1992): This all-acoustic album, Dylan's first since *Another Side of Bob Dylan*, was widely hailed, with *Time* magazine calling it "one of the best things he has ever done."[81] That was a difficult accolade for some critics to swallow, although most of them ranked the album as one of Dylan's most endearing.

One critic termed the record "inessential but fun," and noted that Dylan's "battered squeeze box of a voice" was "even more its own instrument now."[82] The album gave an arc to his career, as Dylan again returned to the simplicity with which he started, and to some of the same material. Many of these songs were in young Dylan's repertoire and as his voice aged, he became tinged with the hard edge he had affected as a young man.

The album was a simple counterpart to the machine-driven pop music of megastars Madonna and Prince, whose new records dominated the charts while Dylan's record commanded the attention of his usual fans. Much as *John Wesley Harding* had flown in the face of convention, this album, too, seemed a deliberately perverse boat against the current.

Dylan highlighted the pop overtones in "Tomorrow Night," and his bluesy cover of Skip James's "Sittin' on Top of the World" proved that Dylan had been a blues singer all along. The most delightful moment was his version of "Froggy Went A-Courtin'," an extension of his contribution to a Pediatric AIDS Foundation album, *For Our Childen*. (See Chapter 7, Section III.) It gave his audience a glimpse of Dylan, the father of five, singing a children's song.

Recording "Frankie and Albert," "Canadee-I-O" and Stephen Foster's "Hard Times" made abundantly clear what Dylan was up to. These recordings again reminded listeners of his distinguished place in the American musical tradition. Dylan's contribution to the nation's musical heritage has been large and his place alongside Foster, Guthrie, Scott Joplin and Leadbelly is secure.

Notes

1. Bob Dylan, Notes on *Bringing It All Back Home* [sound recording] (Columbia Records, 1965).
2. Robert Shelton, *No Direction Home: The Life and Music of Bob Dylan* (New York: Ballantine Books, 1985), p. 117.
3. Derek Taylor, *It Was Twenty Years Ago Today* (New York: Simon and Schuster, 1987), p. 86.
4. Alan Rinzler, *Bob Dylan: The Illustrated Record* (New York: Harmony Books, 1978), p. 17.
5. Dave Marsh, *The New Rolling Stone Record Guide* (New York: Random House, 1984), p. 154.
6. Rinzler, *Illustrated Record*, p. 23.
7. Ibid., p. 7.
8. Maria Vespiri, "Maryland Poor Hear Echo of '63 Killing," the *St. Petersburg Times*, 9 June 1991, p. 8A.
9. Shelton, *No Direction Home*, p. 240.
10. Rinzler, *Illustrated Record*, p. 33.
11. Shelton, *No Direction Home*, p. 272.
12. Ibid., p. 310.
13. Ibid., 311.
14. Ibid., p. 313.
15. Hunter S. Thompson, *Fear and Loathing in Las Vegas* (New York: Random House, 1971).
16. Shelton, *No Direction Home*, p. 314.
17. Ibid., p. 316.
18. Rinzler, *Illustrated Record*, p. 45.
19. Shelton, *No Direction Home*, p. 317.
20. The critic, David M. Monaghan, in cited in Shelton, *No Direction Home*, p. 282.
21. Clinton Heylin, *Bob Dylan: Behind the Shades* (New York: Summit Books, 1991), p. 145.
22. Ibid., p. 146.
23. The absence of track-by-track credits for *Blonde on Blonde* frustrated Dylan listeners for years. Fortunately, Michael Krogsgaard's *Positively Bob Dylan* (Ann Arbor, Mich.: Popular Culture Ink, 1991), rectifies the situation.
24. Marsh, *Record Guide*, p. 155.
25. Marion Meade, the *New York Times*, 14 March 1971, cited in Shelton, *No Direction Home*, p. 373.
26. Marsh, *Record Guide*, p. 155.
27. Rinzler, *Illustrated Record*, p. 60.
28. Bob Dylan, Notes to *Biograph* [sound recording] (Columbia Records, 1985).
29. Rinzler, *Illustrated Record*, p. 57.
30. Cited in Shelton, *No Direction Home*, p. 447.
31. Ibid.
32. Marsh, *Record Guide*, p. 155.
33. Cited in Heylin, *Behind the Shades*, p. 204.
34. Robert Christgau, "Consumer Guide," in Craig McGregor, editor, *Bob Dylan: The Early Years* (New York: DaCapo Press, 1990), p. 359.
35. Greil Marcus, "Self Portrait," *Rolling Stone*, June 1970, cited in Bob Spitz, *Dylan: A Biography* (New York: McGraw-Hill, 1989), p. 378.
36. Cited in Shelton, *No Direction Home*, p. 419.
37. Bob Dylan, *Biograph*.
38. Jann Wenner, "The Rolling Stone Interview: Bob Dylan," in McGregor, *Early Years*, p. 341.
39. Marsh, *Record Guide*, p. 157.
40. Paul Nelson, "The Songs That Still Remain," *Rolling Stone*, 15 December 1977, p. 155.
41. Marsh, *Record Guide*, p. 156.
42. Rinzler, *Illustrated Record*, p. 85.
43. Bob Dylan, Notes to *Planet Waves* [sound recording] (Asylum Records, 1974).
44. Marsh, *Record Guide*, p. 156.
45. Cameron Crowe, Notes to *Biograph* [sound recording] (Columbia Records, 1985).

46. Marsh, *Record Guide*, p. 156.
47. Ibid.
48. Rinzler, *Illustrated Record*, p. 103.
49. Robert Christgau, "Blood on the Tracks," the *Village Voice*, 27 January 1975, cited in Shelton, *No Direction Home*, p. 514.
50. Marsh, *Record Guide*, p. 155.
51. Shelton, *No Direction Home*, p. 542.
52. Rinzler, *Illustrated Record*, p. 110.
53. "Closing Out," *Spin*, July 1992, p. 96.
54. Marsh, *Record Guide*, p. 156.
55. Rinzler, *Illustrated Record*, pp. 107-113.
56. Marsh, *Record Guide*, p. 156.
57. Shelton, *No Direction Home*, p. 555.
58. Ibid., p. 554.
59. Crowe, Notes to *Biograph* (side nine).
60. Marsh, *Record Guide*, p. 156.
61. Crowe, Notes to *Biograph* (side nine).
62. Marsh, *Record Guide*, p. 157.
63. Ibid., p. 130.
64. Robert Christgau, *Christgau's Record Guide: The 80s* (New York: Pantheon Books, 1990), p. 130.
65. Neil Hickey, "Interview: Bob Dylan," *TV Guide*, 11 September 1976, cited in Shelton, *No Direction Home*, p. 476.
66. Marsh, *Record Guide*, p. 157.
67. Christgau, *The 80s*, p. 130.
68. Ibid.
69. Bob Dylan, Notes to *Biograph*.
70. Christgau, *The 80s*, p. 131.
71. Ibid.
72. Krogsgaard, *Positively Bob Dylan*, p. 285.
73. Christgau, *The 80s*, p. 131.
74. Ibid.
75. Ibid.
76. Ibid.
77. Ibid.
78. "The Best 100 Albums of the Eighties," *Rolling Stone*, 16 November 1989, p. 102.
79. Anthony DeCurtis, "Shock of the New," *Rolling Stone*, 21 September 1989, p. 116.
80. "100 Best Albums," p. 102.
81. Jay Cocks, "Bringing the Folk Back Home," *Time*, 26 October 1992, p. 73.
82. Chris Willman, "Record Rack," the Los Angeles Times/Washington Post News Service, 1 November 1992.

Chapter 5

Something Is Happening Here

BOB DYLAN MAY BE THE MOST INFLUENTIAL popular musician of the twentieth century. He did not launch a thousand hips, as Elvis did. He did not want to hold our hands, as The Beatles did. He had no interest in inciting sympathy for the devil, as The Rolling Stones did. (Showman Bill Graham once said, "When the Stones performed, every man felt like a man and every woman felt like a woman. And they all wanted to take the Stones home. I think with Dylan they wanted to give him a bowl of soup."[1])

Elvis Presley, The Beatles and The Rolling Stones sold more records than Bob Dylan, as did The Beach Boys, The Jacksons and Led Zeppelin, and Madonna as well. However, Dylan's influence is greater than that of those artists, because he was the catalyst for more cultural change than any of them.

Presley was not a creative artist; he was an interpreter. He fused musical styles and helped launch a new synthesis that came to be known as rock 'n' roll. As a creative artist, Bob Dylan showed the possibility of the form that Presley had popularized. The Beatles were talented, charming personalities, but their songs were innocuous until they heard the music of Bob Dylan. First they mimicked his sound. Then they tried to match the depth of meaning in his lyrics, and they did so, often with spectacular results. However, had The Beatles never heard of Dylan, perhaps they would today be considered cultural oddities like their contemporaries, Gerry and The Pacemakers and The Dave Clark Five.

The Rolling Stones have been for more than three decades a superior group, perhaps, as they proclaim themselves, "the world's greatest rock 'n' roll band." They have entertained millions around the world, but they have merely been very good at doing a job. There have been a number of popular artists--Bruce Springsteen, Paul Simon, Madonna, Paula Abdul and the like--who have been extremely successful as entertainers, but it is wrong to confuse popularity with influence.

Dylan was extremely popular for a brief period. In 1965-1966, his records sold exceedingly well. At other points in his career, he also had hit singles and albums at the top of the charts. His sales performance was sometimes lackluster, yet he remained the most important and influential artist in rock 'n' roll. To understand Bob Dylan's influence on popular culture, it is necessary to understand what went before.

The Coming of Rock 'n' Roll

The American popular song has a long and glorious history in the twentieth century. Dylan certainly did not invent witty writing and clever lyrics, which are very in evidence in the work of the best of the songwriting breed. Artists such as Cole Porter, Hoagy Carmichael, the Gershwin brothers and the teams of Rodgers and Hart and of Lerner and Lowe wrote some of the best songs of the century.

This form is an amalgamation of a number of styles, with each new style grafted onto the music of a changing culture. Certain musics develop as products of subcultures and are then assimilated into the whole.

Jazz, for example, has retained its separate identity, yet elements of that form joined the nucleus of popular culture through being grafted onto the veneer of mainstream music. This early twentieth century development preceded the similar absorption of other subculture music (rhythm and blues and also country and western) into the music of the masses. Topical songs, which is to say, songs about real events or people, are ancient. The ballad is one of the oldest forms of literature in human culture. Often, ballads have been adapted and fictionalized, but the narrative form has been a staple. In the twentieth century, however, the topical song has been most closely associated with folk music, which, by definition, is a modern culture's link to its past. Much of popular music had dealt with the present, with the exaltation of self and the immediate emotions. Folk musicians were thus historians who preserved a rich cultural heritage.

This is not to state that the folk music community held dominion over topical themes. Jazz musicians also occasionally experimented with the form. For example, singer Billie Holliday set to music Lewis Allan's poem about a lynching and the result was "Strange Fruit," a 1939 song that ranks among the most hypnotic and disturbing recordings of the century. That was out of the norm, however. The banter of a Cole Porter lyric or the poetry of Oscar Hammerstein's words dealt more often with love than war, hate or any other theme not considered commercial. (To their great credit, Rodgers and Hammerstein made an interracial relationship central to their musical *South Pacific*.) Generally, music was music: It was for entertainment. Songs of mine disasters, union troubles and starving families were confined to the music of the American subcultures and were not for mass consumption.

However, it was during the rock 'n' roll era, whose beginning can be set as 1954, that we begin to see a flowering of popular music as more than just music. The very coming of rock 'n' roll was a political statement. It was, after all, the mass recognition of black America. The music came the same year as *Brown v. Board of Education*, the Supreme Court decision outlawing segregated schools. It came after the integration of Major League Baseball, and was beginning to dominate the airwaves the year before the Montgomery bus boycott and the emergence of the Rev. Martin Luther King, Jr. as the leader of a social revolution.

The music called rock 'n' roll was, of course, a hybrid of styles. One of its sources was country and western music. In the earliest recordings of Jimmie Rodgers (the "singing brakeman"), the Carter Family, and Hank Williams we hear the pure components of this music. The other major source of rock 'n' roll was rhythm and blues, which in the 1950s was still underground. Robert Johnson, Muddy Waters, Howlin' Wolf and others exemplified this music in its rawest form. Rhythm and blues was, largely, the music of black America. It was not played on the largest and most profitable radio stations but rather on stations aimed at the black community. A few powerful rhythm and blues stations reached out to white America, and adventurous listeners who were willing to spin the dials might find Nashville's legendary WLAC-AM. Bob Zimmerman found a disk jockey closer than Nashville (Jim Dandy in Virginia, Minnesota) to introduce him to the music and to another part of his nation's culture. Country and western and rhythm and blues are two distinct forms of music, with little apparently in common. However, they share their status: they were both products of subcultures. Neither form could be considered part of the popular music that reached the mass audience through "Your Hit Parade" and network radio broadcasts.

The radio networks were dominated by pop music derived from the show business traditions of Tin Pan Alley (a catch phrase coined to describe the songwriting factories of New York), and from the world of theater. Big hits of the pre-rock 'n' roll era were "I've Got a Lovely Bunch of Coconuts" and "Come on-a My House." These were pleasant songs, perhaps, but they were inconsequential.

It appeared that the music of the white (country and western) and black (rhythm and blues) subcultures would not meet, but then came Elvis. It is hard for many observers today to take Elvis Presley seriously as an important cultural figure. In part, it is because we know how the story ended: Presley became a bloated, paranoid, right-wing drug addict who keeled over in his bathroom at the age of 42. He had made only a handful of passable recordings during his last 20 years as a performer. Nonetheless, he was a vital character in the development of American music. Between 1954 and 1956, Elvis Presley not only made music, he made history. He was not known as a songwriter. He was not a musician of any worth, and wore a guitar mainly as a prop. His voice was crude and untrained. However, quite by accident, he merged the forms of country and western and rhythm and blues. He went to the studios of Sun Records in Memphis in 1954 as a 19-year-old who hoped to become a country singer. With a couple of musicians backing him and the owner of the studio, Sam Phillips, in the booth, he made some attempts to record ballads. Presley's idea of a great singer was crooner Dean Martin.

During a break in recording, Presley began fooling around with Scotty Moore and Bill Black, the two supporting musicians. He began playing a blues song he had heard on WLAC: "That's All Right (Mama)," by Arthur "Big Boy" Crudup. Elvis was not a blues singer, so he sang it with the inflections of a country singer. Phillips overheard the improvisation and made Elvis, Scotty and Bill (this would be their billing on the eventual record) go back into the studio and record the performance. Phillips had long wanted to find a white singer who could sing black music. He knew that if tradition held, whites would not buy black music (called "race music" in the industry publications), but if a white artist could sing *those* songs in *that* style, Phillips believed that breakthrough would come.

When Phillips heard Elvis Presley, he thought he had found the voice. After recording "That's All Right (Mama)," Presley needed a flip side for the record. He chose the classic bluegrass song by Bill Monroe, "Blue Moon of Kentucky." On that seven-inch Sun Records single, Presley, Phillips and company had combined the musics of black and white America; a rhythm and blues song was paired with a country and western song. Without making an overt statement, the record was political. Although the songs were sung by a white artist, the political impact was not lessened. It lay in the recognition of these musical forms. Moreover, the recognition continued as Presley and Phillips continued making records for the next two years, until Presley went to a larger record label, RCA, and began his domination of the record charts.

Presley was a popularizer. He gave the nation the appetite for new music. White Americans, in particular, had been denied rhythm and blues. It was not largely available for their consumption. Even screened through the filter of a white performer, the music was powerful enough to make the audience demand more. Soon the audience was getting its music from the source. The first great black rock 'n' roll star, the man who probably deserved the title of king which was granted to Presley, was Chuck Berry. Berry was an artist while Presley was just a singer (a singer with a good ear and brilliant instincts, but merely a singer nonetheless).

Berry was a songwriter. His songs were essentially country and western in their approach, but he was black, and there was no market for black country singers in the 1950s. Berry also had a love for the blues. He became a rock 'n' roll singer when he figured out how to combine the forms. In 1955, Berry wrote a country and western song called "Ida Red," which was a comical narrative tale. Recording it at the studios of Chess Records in Chicago, he "goosed" the melody a bit at the insistence of record company president Leonard Chess and changed the woman's name--and the name of the song--to "Maybelline." The record was released and Berry gave up his day job as a hair stylist. At age 29, he became rock 'n' roll's first poet.

Berry has said that he consciously tried to bridge the gap between the races by writing songs about things that were generic, and not confined to experiences of the black community. He wanted to write songs that young white listeners could understand, so many of his early tunes celebrate schools, malt shops and teenage frustrations: "School Day," "Sweet Little Sixteen" and "Almost Grown." However, he also made subtle statements with his songs: "Brown-Eyed Handsome Man" was a statement of black pride ten years before the black-is-beautiful movement, "Too Much Monkey Business" spoke of the shabby treatment given war veterans, and "Memphis" saw divorce from the perspective of a six-year-old.

Berry's popularity paved the way for other black artists: as Little Richard, Richard Penniman wrote and sang nonsense songs, largely about sex; as Bo Diddley, Elias McDaniel offered strong rhythmic hooks and menacing guitar lines; and as Fats Domino, Antoine Domino injected bluesy, New Orleans-tinged music into the mix. These three artists found that white artists rerecorded their songs ("covering" was the industry term) and made more money with these sanitized versions. Still, they reasoned, some success in the mass market was better than being shut out entirely.

Aside from Berry, there were a few artists in the late 1950s who used the new medium of rock 'n' roll to make political statements, although they were usually couched in humor. The classic example was "Summertime Blues," which was written and performed by a white artist, Eddie Cochran. Cochran came to rock 'n' roll from the country perspective, as had Presley, yet he was a creative artist, writing most of his hits. In "Summertime Blues," Cochran showed the alienation that many young Americans felt. He sang of a teenager's frustrations, and then, lowering his voice, answered with the "voice of authority." Unable to borrow a car, get a job or find a date, he went to his congressman to help. Alas, the lawmaker refuses because the narrator was too young to vote. The song was funny, but it was also political.

Dylan's Role

Consequently, alienation was not exactly new to rock 'n' roll. Clever songs with poetic lyrics had also appeared. Story-songs were part of the American tradition, and master songwriters like Berry learned the power of brevity in writing, pumping a lot of experience into a three-minute narrative.

Dylan approached the landscape of popular music from yet another subculture: folk music. Folk music was as old as history, yet a sanitized, well-scrubbed form of it had become commercially popular in the late 1950s. The Kingston Trio and other so-called folk acts were recording folk songs and topical songs, many of them written by Woody Guthrie. By that time, Guthrie was seriously ill with Huntington's chorea, and was unable to perform himself. In the early 1960s, however, he might not have fit in. Most of the tremendously popular folk acts resembled The Kingston Trio, who wore striped shirts, told jokes between songs and chirped happy harmonies. They were good entertainers, but it was not authentic folk music.

A true folk song has no known composer. Writers like Guthrie often appropriated folk tunes, some of which were hundreds of years old, and laid their tales on top of them. Many of Guthrie's tales were songs of union struggles. One of his most famous, "Deportees," was inspired by a radio news report of a plane crash. The announcer told listeners that the crash was of little consequence because only migrant workers were killed. Guthrie was an authentic folk singer, but he was also a creative artist, writing hundreds of songs during his lifetime. By the early 1960s, as he was dying in the New Jersey hospital where Dylan visited him, Guthrie was a near god to folk musicians. No one had approached what he had done with the form of the topical song.

Then Dylan came along. Dylan brought with him his childhood as Robert Zimmerman, a fan of rhythm and blues and rock 'n' roll, who wanted to be a star, like Elvis. Dylan's infatuation with Guthrie's life and music was genuine, but it was just another stage in his long career. Often, appreciations of Bob Dylan focus on this narrow strip of his career in the early 1960s when he was lumped with other folk singers and wrote some of his most enduring songs, often about the social upheaval of that decade. His style dissuaded a lot of people, but it was in homage to Guthrie. He adopted Guthrie's Okie accent, his manner of dress, and his way of playing guitar. He borrowed from a number of artists, and almost any blues or folk performer he ever saw had something to offer him. Borrowing was the tradition of folk music; the music belonged to no one. However, Dylan, in particular, was a sponge. He absorbed and distilled it all.

His importance rests in the fact that he mastered the style of traditional music. He was a brilliant singer of folk songs and rural blues. As he evolved, he went far beyond being a mere interpreter of songs and became a writer. Dylan's writing soon rivaled Guthrie's in quality and subject matter, and the young man then eclipsed his idol. Others were content to merely repeat Guthrie's words, since he could no longer sing them, but few writers were able to carry on the traditions of the form.

Many of Dylan's songs dealt with specific incidents. Perhaps the greatest is "The Lonesome Death of Hattie Carroll," his tale of the black maid who was killed by the wealthy young white man. "The Death of Emmett Till" was the true story of a 1955 racial murder, and "Only a Pawn in Their Game" saw white and black victims in the murder of civil rights leader Medgar Evers. The songs were both music and journalism. Dylan was also tremendously skilled in crystallizing moments and feelings in his anthems, like "Blowin' in the Wind" and "The Times They Are A-Changin'." In another sense, and in a way apparently unappreciated by his followers in folk music, he did the same with love songs. His songs offered no happy endings, they were not empty tributes to impossibly perfect women. Rather, they explored the honesty of relationships and the uncharted depths of emotional pain. Dylan celebrated the romance of independence. His were not really love songs: They were antilove songs.

No one since Guthrie's time had excelled in the ability to write such powerful material. Then Dylan--who was revered, honored, admired, nearly deified by the folk music establishment--turned his back on that audience. He wanted to move on, but the audience refused to let him change. He turned to one of the original sources of his inspiration: rock 'n' roll. He did it because he was backed into a corner by those who had selected a role for him that he did not want. He did it because he did not want other people setting his agenda. Finally, in part, he did it because he heard The Beatles.

The Beatles were a delayed response to what had happened in America ten years before. They were a British distillation of the rock 'n' roll experience, which evolved as racial barriers began to crumble. Their sound, coming as it did when Dylan was trying to break away from the confines of the role to which his musical subculture had assigned him, was liberating. Dylan went back to the starting point, bringing it all "back home," reclaiming American music for his homeland. He would become a rock 'n' roll star. Naturally, he was denigrated for his change. During 1965-1966, as he debuted his new rock 'n' roll songs, he was greeted with derision. Audiences booed. In England, one night in May 1966, a famous cry came from the audience: "Judas!"

He may have been Judas to that narrow musical community, but what Bob Dylan had done was to take his sensibilities and his concept of social justice, which had largely been honed in the world of folk music, into the mainstream. He also brought with him the topical song, the antilove song and lyrical elements that before would have been considered uncommercial. Dylan upped the ante. His songs spoke with a brutal honesty heretofore unknown in popular music. Earlier, the mainstream would have relegated his "truth attacks" like "Positively 4th Street" or "Just Like a Woman" to mere sideshow attractions. A six-minute rant, "Like a Rolling Stone," became a huge hit. It could not be ignored and was, of course, soon imitated by scores of artists.

Commercial songwriters for decades had looked down on the audience and insulted their intelligence. Even brilliant songwriters like Porter and Gershwin had worked within the straitjacket of commercialism. Dylan, however, expanded those boundaries. Even the most successful of popular musicians, The Beatles, were under Dylan's influence. Before Dylan, they wrote pleasant but mindless ditties that incorporated record numbers of first and second person references. After hearing Dylan, they learned to look inward to honestly study themselves, and outward, to understand their society.

The new levels of pain which Dylan excavated in *Blood on the Tracks* were unprecedented in popular music. He maintained an unflinching sense of integrity throughout the duration of his career, with only short (and, in retrospect, relatively minor) lapses. His influence on other artists was perhaps greater than his influence on the mass, if measured through sales. Much of his work dealt with the nature of art and of self (he often quoted Rimbaud: "I is another") and he constantly toyed with the concept of identity throughout the *Blood on the Tracks/Renaldo and Clara* period of the mid-1970s.

Dylan's songs spoke with a bitterness and honesty that were previously unknown in mainstream music. In the 30 years since he emerged as a performing artist, he has provided the standard by which popular songwriting is judged. He liberated writers and performers of popular music from the bounds of commercialism and showed that an intelligent public could (and would) value an artist speaking honestly. Although he worked in other media, it was not as an author or filmmaker that Dylan made his most important contribution. His greatest influence has clearly been on the course of popular music. He created a legacy more intimidating than that of any other active artist.

Dylan reinvented the popular song and opened its narrow boundaries wide enough to include messages from an often cruel and imperfect world. The commercial instincts of the music industry led in the other direction, yet he challenged them, demanding that his songs be true reflections of his times and of himself. In so doing, he may have saved popular music from itself.

A Note of Thanks

There is a debt that has been widely acknowledged by the many musicians Dylan influenced. Inducting Bob Dylan into the Rock and Roll Hall of Fame in 1988, Bruce Springsteen eloquently outlined what was owed to Dylan:

> When I was a kid, Bob's voice somehow thrilled and scared me . . . . Dylan was a revolutionary. Bob freed your mind the way Elvis freed your body. He showed us that just because the music was innately physical did not mean that it was anti-intellectual. He had the vision and the talent to make a pop song that contained the whole world. He invented a new way a pop singer could sound, broke through the

limitations of what a recording artist could achieve and changed the face of rock 'n' roll forever.

Without Bob, The Beatles wouldn't have made *Sgt. Pepper*, The Beach Boys wouldn't have made *Pet Sounds*, The Sex Pistols wouldn't have made "God Save the Queen," U2 wouldn't have done "Pride (In the Name of Love)," [and] Marvin Gaye wouldn't have done *What's Goin' On?* . . . . To this day, wherever great rock music is being made, there is the shadow of Bob Dylan. Bob's own modern work has gone under-appreciated because it's hard to stand in that shadow. If there was a young guy out there writing the *Empire Burlesque* album, writing "Every Grain of Sand," they'd be calling him the new Bob Dylan.

About three months ago, I was watching *The Rolling Stone Special* on TV. Bob came on and he was in a real cranky mood. He was kind of bitching and moaning about how his fans come up to him on the street and treat him like a long lost brother or something, even though they don't know him. Now, speaking as a fan, when I was fifteen and I heard "Like a Rolling Stone," I heard a guy who had the guts to take on the whole world and who made me feel like I had to too. Maybe some people misunderstood that voice as saying that somehow Bob was going to do the job for them, but, as we grow older, we learn that there isn't anybody out there who can do that job for anybody else. So I'm just here tonight to say thanks, to say that I wouldn't be here without you, to say that there isn't a soul in this room who does not owe you his thanks, and to steal a line from one of your songs--whether you like it or not--"You was the brother I never had."[2]

The honors continued. After the Rock and Roll Hall of Fame, Dylan was feted at the 1991 Grammy Awards ceremony for his lifetime achievement. To mark his 30th year as a recording artist, Columbia Records sponsored a star-studded celebration of "the Music of Bob Dylan" at Madison Square Garden in October 1992. The concert drew enormous media attention and was, by most accounts, an event worthy of its subject.

The royalty of rock 'n' roll took four hours to say what Springsteen had said in his brief speech. Without you, they seemed to be telling Dylan, we would not be here. John Mellencamp courageously opened the show with "Like a Rolling Stone," featuring Al Kooper on organ, repeating the distinctive chording he had stumbled upon during the original sessions with Dylan. The evening began with that peak and went higher.

It was a concert full of high points. Surprise guest Stevie Wonder played "Blowin' in the Wind," which he had turned into a soul hit when he was 15. Journeyman rocker George Thorogood sang "Wanted Man," sounding more like Johnny Cash than Johnny Cash. Cash and his wife, country singer June Carter, performed a rather ragged "It Ain't Me Babe" and other country performers showed Dylan's adaptability to that style: Kris Kristofferson sang "I'll Be Your Baby Tonight," Willie Nelson performed "What Was it You Wanted?" and a one-night-only trio of Shawn Colvin, Mary-Chapin Carpenter and Rosanne Cash joined voices on "You Ain't Goin' Nowhere."

The concert made headlines because of the appearance of Irish singer Sinead O'Connor, who was to perform Dylan's emotional confessional "I Believe in You." Boos from the audience, presumably in response to O'Connor's ripping up a photograph of Pope John Paul II on television two weeks before, kept her from singing. She performed a Bob Marley rant called "War" (based on a speech by Ethiopian emperor Haile Selassie), then stalked from the stage.[3]

None of the performers chose to lecture the audience about its treatment of O'Connor and note the irony that the concert was to honor Bob Dylan, whose work was dedicated to the concept of free expression. Instead, the performers went on with the show. Neil Young, whose career owed much to Dylan (the older man having paved the way for "non-singers" such as Young), played a blistering "All along the Watchtower" that was as much a tribute to Jimi Hendrix's celebrated cover version. (Young, by the way, dubbed the evening "Bobfest."[4]) Rolling Stone Ron Wood, who appeared not to have combed his hair since the 1970s, sang "Seven Days," then introduced Eric Clapton, whose blues guitar turned the formerly acoustic "Don't Think Twice, It's All Right" into a stinging testament worthy of Robert Johnson. George Harrison, appearing as an elder statesman, sang "If Not for You," then surprised the crowd with "Absolutely Sweet Marie." Tom Petty and the Heartbreakers romped through "Rainy Day Women # 12 & 35," then were joined by Roger McGuinn for "Mr. Tambourine Man."

Harrison introduced Dylan. "Some of you may call him Bobby," he said. "Some of you may call him Zimmy. I just call him Lucky." Dylan strode onstage stiffly, fiddled with his microphone then briskly stepped to the microphone and began "Song to Woody." In a night of musicians paying homage to their hero, Dylan chose to do the same. His voice was its middle-aged growl, making the young man's song of tribute even more touching. Then, as if to demonstrate his virtuosity, he sang the complicated "It's Alright Ma (I'm Only Bleeding)."

The most moving moment of the evening came when the cast assembled for "My Back Pages." Petty, Clapton, Harrison and Dylan took turns with the verses, then Neil Young pinched out a guitar solo and, rushing to the microphone, looked toward Dylan, grinning beatifically. He sang the chorus to its author, offering his thanks for being the paradigm for a modern musical artist. As eloquent as Dylan's words were, in this instance they paled before the expression on Young's face. Dylan nodded in acknowledgment.

The concert was another major media event in Dylan's career, a mid-life celebration of his body of work. Despite the summing-up tone, Dylan was in no mood to close a chapter in his life. A week later, he was on the road again.

Notes

1. Joe Smith, *Off the Record: An Oral History of Popular Music* (New York: Warner Books, 1988), p. 233.
2. Bruce Springsteen, "Speech Delivered at the Annual Rock-and-Roll Hall of Fame Induction Dinner," in Elizabeth Thomson, and David Gutman, editors, *The Dylan Companion* (New York: Delta Books, 1991), pp. 286-288.
3. Jon Pareles, "The Man Who Moved Rock into a New Era," the *New York Times*, 19 October 1992, p. B1.
4. Ibid.

Part III

Bibliography

Chapter 6

Words and Music

BOB DYLAN IS THE MOST IMPORTANT WRITER in rock 'n' roll history--more important than Elvis Presley, more important than John Lennon and Paul McCartney, more important than the great non-performing teams of Jerry Leiber and Mike Stoller, Doc Pomus and Mort Schuman, Gerry Goffin and Carole King, and the like.

Elvis Presley may have been a more influential performer than Dylan. Certainly he was responsible for launching the careers of the hundreds of entertainers he inspired. The Beatles may have written some classic songs and also served as arbiters of style for a generation. However, clearly, no other performer has had an impact as a writer than Bob Dylan. Few artists have attempted to range over the media as successfully as Dylan, who has published a free-form novel as well as two large collections of lyrics. In addition, he has ventured into film as a director, writer and actor. Primarily, though, Dylan has made his greatest impact through his words.

Dylan's songs have inspired the works of others. As important as the songs have been in providing the catalyst for hundreds of other writers, perhaps the songs are most important to their creator. In 1978, after his devastating divorce had uprooted him from his home, he went on the road for a major tour. He said of his songs: "That's all I have in the world .... That's what the legend, all the myth is about--my songs.... Nobody else gives those songs life. It's up to me to do it."[1] The singer and his songs attracted a following unlike any other in rock 'n' roll. His fans were not fans in the sense of the devoted legions that followed Elvis Presley and The Beatles. Certainly, there have been important works about those latter artists and their contributions to popular culture, but the bulk of writing about them has been from the fan's perspective. On the other hand, there has been a significant amount of writing about Dylan that qualifies as genuine scholarship. His work has been treated more seriously than the work of any other popular rock 'n' roll star. This chapter will briefly discuss works by and about Dylan. The bibliography that follows in similarly divided: works by Dylan (primarily his books and his songs) and works about Dylan.

Dylan the Writer

Dylan's songs are his primary works and have been dealt with elsewhere. In this chapter, most of his songs are simply catalogued. He has published the music and lyrics over the years in songbooks. His attempt to publish a novel has been discussed in Chapters 2 and 3. He was approached to write a novel in 1965, as he was becoming a powerful new voice in rock 'n' roll. Macmillan was envied by other publishers, who assumed that anything by Bob Dylan would probably sell truckloads of books.

Dylan worked on the novel during his hellish concert tours of 1965 and 1966 and was involved in editing the typescript during his long period of recuperation following the July 1966 motorcycle accident. He was apparently dissatisfied with the work and wanted to scrap it, but the typescript had been bootlegged and these contraband copies were being widely circulated by the early 1970s. When *Tarantula* (New York: Macmillan, 1971) was finally published, it was not in an effort to make an impact on the literary world: It was merely to thwart bootleggers.

Tarantula read like an extended version of Dylan's album notes for *Bringing It All Back Home* and *Highway 61 Revisited*, which together were his most satisfying prose writings. *Tarantula* was called a novel, but its plot was so difficult to locate that it can only be called so with tongue in cheek. It baffled critics, some of whom made comparisons with James Joyce's *Ulysses* and *Finnegans Wake*. The book could not easily be read for any narrative satisfaction; it *could* be read as mere wordplay, as an exercise by a writer who was well tuned to the sound of words and their relationships. Some found a plot in the book; others found it to be a telling antiwar testament. Whatever the case, it was not a major work, and it neither enhanced nor diminished Dylan's reputation.

His two other books (other than songbooks) were *Writings and Drawings* (New York: Knopf, 1973) and *Lyrics* (New York: Knopf, 1985), two collections of song lyrics and collected writings. The second book contains all the material in the first. *Writings and Drawings* was published during Dylan's slow period in the early 1970s, immediately before his reemergence with *Planet Waves* and the tour with The Band in early 1974. He had never published lyrics on an album jacket, since that was not the industry practice. The Beatles, with *Sgt. Pepper's Lonely Hearts Club Band* in 1967, established a precedent, but Dylan still refrained from publishing lyrics with his albums until 1985, with *Empire Burlesque*. He did it only one other time, with *Under the Red Sky* in 1990.

Consequently, *Writings and Drawings* was a revelation because it allowed readers to study the lyrics from his revered albums of the 1960s. Dylan had no introduction to offer, and he organized the songs in the order of the albums, with each heading bearing the album title. The lyrics of songs that had never appeared on an album were in sections associated with the contemporary recordings. The end papers were typescripts of Dylan works in progress and in the *Bringing It All Back Home* section, he offered a page of typed attempts at lyrics for "Subterranean Homesick Blues," complete with coffee rings staining the paper. It was a fascinating and tantalizing glimpse of his working methods.

Other miscellaneous writings also appeared. Dylan's program notes for his 1963 Carnegie Hall concert, "My Life in a Stolen Moment," were given their first wide audience. His long poem for the album *Joan Baez in Concert, Part 2* was a revelation to Dylan fans who had never investigated his benefactor's work. All Dylan's notes for his own albums, appeared: "Some Other Kinds of Songs," "11 Outlined Epitaphs," and the brilliant, previously untitled pieces for *Bringing It All Back Home*, *Highway 61 Revisited* and *John Wesley Harding* (which he titled "Three Kings" for the book).

It was a wealth of material, and critics applauded the collection and began carping about all the unreleased material in Dylan's vaults. The song lyrics from the basement tapes period appeared in a section called "From *Blonde on Blonde* to *John Wesley Harding*." Some of these songs were still unreleased two years later when Dylan sanctioned an album from those sessions called *The Basement Tapes*.

The 1985 update of the book, simply called *Lyrics*, toyed with the order of some of the *Writings and Drawings* material and supplemented it with all the lyrics from the songs up through *Empire Burlesque*. Interestingly, Dylan placed the "basement tapes" songs in the chronology, not in the period during which they were written, nor in the period during which they were released. Rather, they were dropped in at the time of their appearance as bootleg records. There were some omissions, principally his notes to *Planet Waves*, which were also deleted from subsequent rereleases of that album (the notes contained a few vulgarities). The dedication for the first volume was poetry itself, as Dylan honored the outcasts of the world and, more specifically, the women who had assisted him in assembling the volume, Woody Guthrie and Robert Johnson (he misspelled Guthrie's first name), and to "Sara, who made it all complete." *Lyrics* is dedicated simply "to Narette," leaving readers to speculate on her identity.

Dylan has not actively pursued other sorts of writing during his career, instead focusing on songwriting. A detailed--though not necessarily complete--

listing of his songs appears later in this chapter. It is not complete because Dylan has not copyrighted all his compositions, but it is as complete as can be determined.

Dylan the Subject

Books

Writing about Dylan is generally about Dylan's work. He has not inspired the sorts of scandalous books about the private lives of public performers exemplified by Albert Goldman's tell-all books *Elvis* (New York: McGraw-Hill, 1981), and *The Lives of John Lennon* (New York: Morrow, 1988). He is to be congratulated for managing to maintain at least some privacy while keeping a high public profile as an artist and entertainer.

Some authors have attempted biographies of this difficult, sometimes reclusive subject, but many Dylan books fall into the realm of scholarship and are apparently intended for a market that takes music seriously. The first Dylan biographer, Anthony Scaduto, had some cooperation from his subject. *Bob Dylan: An Intimate Biography* (New York: Grosset and Dunlap, 1971; rev. ed., Signet/New American Library, 1979) appeared when Dylan's seclusion had rendered him one of the most mysterious figures in popular music. Since he had gone from his ubiquitous stage in 1966 to his utter departure from public life within a year, stories and myths circulated about him.

Scaduto, a journalist, pieced together a relatively coherent narrative of Dylan's life using the standard reporter's techniques. He journeyed to Minnesota, met Bonnie Beecher and Echo Helstrom, and constructed a reliable version of Bobby Zimmerman's childhood. By far the largest section of the book was Scaduto's retelling of Dylan's first years in New York. He found many of Dylan's former friends willing to tell stories on him. Finally, by the end of his research, Scaduto managed to talk to Dylan and earned a sanction. As Dylan said, "The weird thing is, I kind of like your book."[2]

Scaduto's book ended its narrative after only a decade of Dylan's professional career. The second large-scale biography of Dylan was by his friend, journalist Robert Shelton. Shelton wrote the *New York Times* review of Dylan that earned the singer his first attention from John Hammond and Columbia Records. He was supposedly working on a book about Dylan as far back as the mid-1960s, yet it was not published until 1986. The eventual book, *No Direction Home: The Life and Music of Bob Dylan* (New York: Beech Tree Books/Morrow, 1986) benefited from its author's close association with Dylan. Although it had more insights and details than Scaduto's book (or almost any other book about Dylan), Shelton's closeness to his subject and occasional protectiveness on his behalf marred the book somewhat. We learn, however, that Dylan could be temperamental, even with a longtime friend like Shelton. He has had a career full of spats with the press, Shelton included.

The Shelton book was not entirely linear, and a reader seeking a methodical chronology of Dylan's life might be advised to look elsewhere. Shelton followed a rough chronology, but when he introduced a theme he followed it through with examples from later in Dylan's life. His forays into the first person were sometimes startling in a biography of this scope, whose aspirations reached far beyond mere memoir. Nonetheless, they were valuable side trips. One of the strongest scenes of the book is Shelton's trip with Dylan and The Hawks during the hellish spring of 1966. Dylan had been up for days, was unable to sleep, and stayed up during a red-eye flight, talking to Shelton while the other musicians collapsed, exhausted. It was a long, rambling monologue, but it provides evidence of the dangerous course that Dylan was traveling and explains how, indeed, the motorcycle accident may have saved his life. Two of the most valuable features of the book were Shelton's song-by-song discussion of Dylan's albums and the extensive discography and bibliography.

The Shelton book was followed in a couple of years by an unauthorized biography by Bob Spitz. *Dylan: A Biography* (New York: McGraw-Hill, 1989) was, in a sense, an update of the Scaduto book, with a heavy dose of sensationalism thrown in. Spitz, whose previous book, *Barefoot in Babylon*, was about the Woodstock festival, dwelled on Dylan's various love affairs. For example, Spitz wrote of a casual encounter in which Dylan met a woman, went home with her and rode around her apartment on a bicycle. Then, he huddled on the couch beside the woman and wept. Spitz offered no explanation for Dylan's behavior.

Reporting such incidents seems an invasion of privacy, and irrelevant. However, the writing was not entirely scandalous and when Spitz discussed Dylan's work, the prose contained a plethora of details, and Spitz probed deeper into events that Scaduto only summarized. Spitz's book featured a combination chronology and discography that was its greatest contribution. However, Spitz and Shelton discounted nearly all Dylan's albums since the Rolling Thunder Revue. Spitz particularly ignored the gospel era, which Shelton did attempt to analyze. (Shelton also offered glimpses of Dylan's conversion, through conversations not only with the artist, but also with the fellowship that converted him.)

Most of the books about Dylan were top-heavy with the 1960s. Since it went against that particular grain, Clinton Heylin's *Bob Dylan: Behind the Shades* (New York: Summit Books, 1991) stood out. Heylin, a codirector of Wanted Man, England's "Dylan Information Office," assembled a biography of Dylan from 30 years' worth of quoted material. The narrative was loose, connected by quote blocks from other sources. Unfortunately, Heylin did not document these quotes thoroughly. In the chapter notes, he merely listed the sources by year and not individually.

However, *Behind the Shades* treated all Dylan's career and was particularly generous in its discussion of the 1980s. The myopic authors who focused only on the 1960s missed some of Dylan's most vital work, while Heylin's book reached through *The Bootleg Series* and, therefore, offered a 30-year perspective on his subject. Since Heylin and his Wanted Man partner, John Bauldie, are Dylan scholars, *Behind the Shades* corrected the errors of earlier works. Heylin cited a number of errors made by Scaduto, Shelton and Spitz. Those three authors had differed on a number of things, including the spelling of some vital names. Heylin was willing to recognize Dylan's flaws, but his book was written obviously out of great affection for the man's work. The oral history approach gets in the way of a narrative flow, but it also made the book accessible at nearly any point.

Heylin's partner, John Bauldie, collaborated with Patrick Humphries on *Absolutely Dylan* (New York: Viking Studio Books, 1991), a biography that was most notable for its inclusion of much graphic material. The authors assembled a number of picture sleeves, promotional advertisements and rare photographs for the large-size volume. Bauldie's major contribution was a year-by-year bibliography, discography, chronology and performance schedule. The day-by-day calendar also included relevant quotes. Like Heylin's book, the wealth of information was considerable. Also like Heylin's book, much of the material was documented only informally.

Bob Dylan has not written an autobiography, but as a substitute, Barry Miles assembled several years worth of quotes from the artist. *Bob Dylan: In His Own Words* (New York: Quick Fox Press, 1978) was part of a series Miles did that also included Paul McCartney, John Lennon and David Bowie.

Two works have focused on Dylan as a concert performer. Paul Williams's *Performing Artist: The Music of Bob Dylan, Volume 1, 1960-1973* (Novato, Calif.: Underwood-Miller, 1990) and Betsy Bowden's *Performed Literature: Words and Music by Bob Dylan* (Bloomington: Indiana University Press, 1982). These are referred to in Chapter 9, which concerns Dylan's concerts. Williams's excellent book allows the author, long recognized as the first rock music critic, to analyze the first several years of Dylan's performing career. Bowden's book (which is based on her doctoral dissertation) examines the evolution of Dylan's songs through his constant reinterpretations in performance.

Of the bibliographic works, Michael Krogsgaard's *Positively Bob Dylan: A Thirty-Year Discography, Concert and Recording Session Guide* (Ann Arbor, Mich.: Popular Culture, Ink, 1991) is the touchstone. This massive work noted nearly every public appearance by Dylan (and several private ones as well). It offered detail of every recording session but also included listings of coffeehouse and night club performances in his early years, offering set lists of songs and information about changing instrumentation. Dylan's performances at parties, early in his career, were also noted. From the 1974 tour with The Band until 1991, Krogsgaard's book listed every song played at every Dylan concert. Krogsgaard went beyond set lists and recording sessions, listing every snatch of music played in any of Dylan's films and television appearances. *Positively Bob Dylan* is the most valuable work available for any Dylan researcher. It is an update of two earlier books by Krogsgaard which are available in Europe but not the United States: *Twenty Years of Recording: The Bob Dylan Reference Book* (Copenhagen: Scandanavian Society of Rock Research, 1980) and *Master of the Tracks: The Bob Dylan Reference Book of Recording* (Copenhagen: Scandanavian Society of Rock Research, 1988). Indispensable to scholars and fascinating to fans, these books were apparently unappreciated by the artist himself. When journalist Robert Hilburn presented Dylan with a copy of *Master of the Tracks* during a 1992 interview, Dylan quickly thumbed through it, and then said that he was not interested in its contents. "I've already been those places and done all those things," he told Hilburn. "Now if you ever find a book out there that's going to tell me where I'm *going*, I might be interested."[3]

Other bibliographers have sought to categorize and analyze Dylan's work, though none on such a large scale as Krogsgaard. Paul Cable's *Bob Dylan: His Unreleased Recordings* (New York: Schirmer Books, 1980) listed much of the material that Dylan later released commercially on his boxed set retrospectives of bootlegged songs. However, Cable's book was far from outdated, since Dylan still has much in the vaults at Columbia Records. Similarly, Glen Dundas's *Tangled Up in Tapes: A Collector's Guide to Tape Recordings of Bob Dylan* (Thunder Bay, Ontario: SMA Services, 1987) was a reference primarily for what Clinton Heylin and John Bauldie like to call the "Dylan collecting fraternity," a significant network of fans and admirers that tapes Dylan concerts and duplicates them for friends and acquaintances.[4] Dundas's book listed all the performances that had been recorded to that date, with highlights: unusual cover versions, noteworthy backup musicians and so forth. James Dorman's *Recorded Dylan* (San Francisco: Soma Press, 1982) touched on the area of collector recordings but was primarily concerned with Dylan's commercial releases. Similarly focused was Alan Rinzler's *Bob Dylan: The Illustrated Record* (New York: Harmony Books, 1978), a combination loose biography, discography and picture book. It was part of a series that included similar books on The Beatles and The Rolling Stones.

A career as literate and carefully constructed as Bob Dylan's would not seem to lend itself to the publication of coffee-table books, yet there have been a few large-size, heavily illustrated works focusing on the singer. The first of these was Daniel Kramer's *Bob Dylan* (New York: Citadel Press, 1967; rev. ed., Citadel, 1991). Kramer was a photographic James Boswell of Dylan during the *Bringing It All Back Home/Highway 61 Revisited* period, and his pictures adorned those album covers. This picture book with text was about to be published in early 1967 when Dylan, through manager Albert Grossman, sought to stop Kramer. A court ruling found no basis for Dylan trying to squelch the book since it was an entirely flattering work. Perhaps Dylan feared that Kramer's photos of him in 1965 would endure and overshadow who he chose to become later. Whatever the case, the black-and-white images in that book were among the most memorable photographs taken of Dylan. The book was republished in 1991 to coincide with the artist's 50th birthday, bearing a logo on its cover that said "50: Forever Young."

Michael Gross's *Bob Dylan: An Illustrated History* (New York: Grosset and Dunlap, 1978; rev. ed., Tempo Books, 1980) did not have the gloss of Kramer's book but did add a decade more to the pictorial record of Dylan. Gross credited himself as the book's producer, and the text, which was drawn from the familiar sources, was by Robert Alexander.

Rolling Stone magazine, through its book division, produced several books devoted to major rock 'n' roll artists. Several of these were splashy, lavishly produced and large. The series included *The Beatles* by Geoffrey Stokes (New York: Rolling Stone Press/Times Books, 1980), which offered an inside cover, an Andy Warhol print of the Fab Four. Elvis was part of the series, as were The Rolling Stones and Bruce Springsteen. The Dylan volume, Jonathan Cott's *Dylan* (New York: Rolling Stone Press/Summit Books, 1984) was perhaps less successful than the other books in the series because Cott's dense, intellectual text was not as easily accessible as the more generic biography that writers had provided for the other artists. The cover picture also showed a scowling Dylan: perhaps typical of the man, but not the sort of picture that readers would be drawn to place on coffee tables. A similarly lavish volume, *Dylan: A Man Called Alias* (New York: Henry Holt, 1992), was more reader-friendly, thanks to the text by British journalist Richard Williams. The author relied on a straight-forward account of Dylan's life and career, leaving the rumination on the meanings of the songs to the reader.

Three anthologies provide background and illuminate Dylan's career. Craig McGregor edited *Bob Dylan: A Retrospective* (New York: Morrow, 1972), which was republished nearly two decades later as *Bob Dylan: The Early Years* (New York: DaCapo Press, 1990). All the vital Dylan articles from the first ten years of his career are presented: the original Robert Shelton article from the *New York Times*; the *Playboy* interview with Nat Hentoff; Jules Siegel's 1966 *Saturday Evening Post* profile; Jann Wenner's *Rolling Stone* interview; and A. J. Weberman's account of his hostile confrontation with his idol.

Elizabeth Thomson and David Gutman's collection, *The Dylan Companion* (New York: Delta Books, 1990), adapted McGregor's approach for a survey of the artist's entire career. Their earlier articles did not repeat McGregor's selections for his anthology, and the *Companion* contained more critical assessments of Dylan's work. A thorough treatment is given to the gospel period, an era ignored or belittled by most other Dylan works.

John Bauldie's collection, *Wanted Man: In Search of Bob Dylan* (New York: Citadel Underground Press, 1991) has a 30-year focus and is primarily composed of interviews from the pages of the *Telegraph*, the superb magazine published by Wanted Man, the so-called "Dylan Information Office." Almost anyone who touched Dylan's career and would sit for an interview was interviewed. Bauldie's book included conversations with Christopher Parker, Dylan's bassist in the late 1980s; Daniel Lanois, producer of *Oh Mercy*; Richard Marquand, director of *Hearts of Fire*; and Terry Ellis, the "science student" who was ridiculed so mercilessly by Dylan in *Don't Look Back*. The works of Bauldie and Heylin were notable for their concern for all of Dylan's career, not just the 1960s.

Bauldie and Heylin deserve special mention. Their Wanted Man Press in Romford, England, has published several books that are unavailable in the United States. Bauldie's *Bob Dylan and Desire* (Romford, England: Wanted Man Press, 1982) and Heylin's *Rain-Unravelled Tales: A Rumourography* (Romford, England: Wanted Man Press, 1982), *Bob Dylan: Stolen Moments* (Romford, England: Wanted Man Press, 1988), and *To Live Outside the Law* (London: Labour of Love Productions, 1989) are four of the editors' entries into the Dylan market. *Stolen Moments* is notable as Heylin's first attempt to do what he later accomplished with *Bob Dylan Behind the Shades*: present an oral history of the artist. *To Live Outside the Law* was a consumer guide to bootlegs of Dylan. Heylin and Bauldie have also supervised other England-only books, including Bert Cartwright's *The Bible in the Lyrics of Bob Dylan* (Romford, England: Wanted Man Press, 1985) and John Hinchey's *Bob Dylan's Slow Train* (Romford, England: Wanted Man Press, 1982).

The editors of *Rolling Stone* assembled a reader on Dylan's 1974 tour with The Band called *Knockin' on Dylan's Door: On the Road in '74* (New York: Pocket Books, 1974), which was culled entirely from its exhaustive coverage of the two-month trek across North America. Other anthologies have included sections on Dylan, although they attempt to cover the whole scope of popular music. Ben Fong-Torres, one of the best music writers ever employed by *Rolling Stone*, assembled a collection called *What's That Sound? Readings in Contemporary Music* (New York: Anchor Books, 1976). Fong-Torres had covered Dylan's 1974 tour for the magazine, and his insights into the singer were interesting. R. Serge Denisoff and Richard Peterson edited a reader called *The Sounds of Social Change: Studies in Popular Culture* (Chicago: Rand McNally, 1972), which concerned the effects of topical songs on society. Dylan was the main subject of three of the book's essays and was frequently mentioned in others. The cover included, among other illustrations, a rendering of Dylan with the cloud of hair that he sported on the *Blonde on*

Blonde cover.

Several books have examined folk and folk-rock music and used Dylan as a centerpiece. Many of these works were published as those forms were experiencing their booms in the early and mid-1960s. The most prescient of these was *Folk-Rock: The Bob Dylan Story* (New York: Dell, 1966), by Sy Ribakove and Barbara Ribakove. Despite its subtitle, the book did not concern itself only with Dylan. It examined the rock 'n' roll bands that mined the form--The Byrds, The Turtles, and many long-forgotten musicians. The same publisher mined this terrain the following year with David A. DeTurk and A. Poulin, Jr.'s *The American Folk Scene* (New York: Dell, 1967), a post-boom book that attempted to cash in on the form in the wake of psychedelia.

A school of books focused on Dylan (and folk rock) as a vehicle for social protest, making him a political character. R. Serge Denisoff, of Bowling Green State University (home of the Center for Studies in Popular Culture), wrote two books that emphasized the role of the topical songwriter. *Great Day Coming: Folk Music and the American Left* (Urbana: University of Illinois Press, 1972), and *Sing a Song of Social Significance* (Bowling Green, Ohio: Bowling Green Popular Press, 1972) used Dylan as a central character. Morris Dickstein's *Gates of Eden: American Culture in the Sixties* (New York: Basic Books, 1977) attracted a lot of attention in the mainstream press upon its publication, as it was the first major attempt to provide a scholarly assessment of the 1960s. Dickstein used Dylan's music as a window on that decade, borrowing the title of the *Highway 61 Revisited* tune for the name of his book.

Michael Gray's *Song and Dance Man: The Art of Bob Dylan* (New York: Dutton, 1973) was a ten-year assessment of Dylan's influence on popular music and reached a wide, popular audience. Although it contained elements of biography, it was largely about Dylan's work. (Its title was drawn from Dylan's response to a reporter's question, asking the artist to define himself. It appeared to be a jocular answer, but time has proven it more apt than perhaps even Dylan realized.) A book with the same mission, Wilfred Mellers' *A Darker Shade of Pale* (New York: Oxford University Press, 1985) examined Dylan's songs from a technical and musicological point of view as well as from a social perspective. Mellers wrote a book with similar ambitions about The Beatles, *Twilight of the Gods* (New York: Viking Press, 1974). Whereas he was hugely successful in his analyses of his four fellow Englishmen, a lucid interpretation of Dylan eluded him. Tim Riley, a commentator on National Public Radio, also wrote books about the music of The Beatles and Dylan. Whereas *Tell Me Why: A Beatles Commentary* (New York: Knopf, 1988) was nearly apostolic in its approach to the subject, Riley was more critical in *Hard Rain: A Dylan Commentary* (New York: Knopf, 1992). Riley's book contained several factual errors, but his analysis of Dylan's lyrics were, at the least, unusual. Unfortunately, Riley shrugged off most of Dylan's post-*Desire* work.

Wayne Hampton's *Guerrilla Minstrels* (Knoxville: University of Tennessee

Press, 1987) was one of the most lucid discussions of Dylan's career, from his beginnings as a coffeehouse singer of folk songs to his overlooked work in the 1980s. Hampton forcefully stated that Dylan's gospel era was another mutation of his role as a protest singer. Readers may want more of Hampton's interpretations, but he was limited by the book's scope. *Guerrilla Minstrels* was not only about Dylan; it gave equal space to Woody Guthrie, Joe Hill and John Lennon. Tim Dowley and Barry Dunnage also used the natural bookends of "protest Bob" and "gospel Bob" for their book, *Bob Dylan: From a Hard Rain to a Slow Train* (New York: Hippocrene Books, 1982). Their interpretation--and Hampton's--was rather unusual in the wake of the complete dismissal of Dylan's gospel years as an abberation by several of his biographers and other chroniclers of his career.

A book intended for a more popular audience, Jerome L. Rodnitzky's *Minstrels of the Dawn* (Chicago: Nelson-Hall, 1976) was timed to coincide with Dylan's mid-1970s burst of creativity and went beyond Dylan to examine not only folk singers but the whole school of confessional songwriters that had come into prominence in that decade. Rodnitsky classified such singers as "truly heroic," even when they were dealing with personal as opposed to political themes.

Another series of books focused not only on the character of Dylan as a protest singer--and as social force--but also on his words and his redefinition of popular music. Several of these were quite serious, scholarly tomes. Others were part of the late 1960s attempts to earn recognition for rock 'n' roll as an art form. Nathan Aaseng's *Bob Dylan: Spellbinding Songwriter* (Minneapolis: Lerner Press, 1987) tried to carve a place for Dylan within the traditions of the American popular song. The book was aimed at a teenage audience. Richard Goldstein's *The Poetry of Rock* (New York: Bantam Books, 1969) naturally included prolific references to and quotes from Dylan, but he was only one of several songwriters profiled. John Herdman's *Voice without Restraint: Bob Dylan's Lyrics and Their Background* (New York: Delilah Books, 1982) focused entirely on Dylan's lyrics, annotating them where appropriate. Delilah Books was responsible for several of the finest books about popular music, and this work was presented with sophistication and great care.

As some writers attempted to interpret the meaning in Dylan's song lyrics (certainly no easy task), one writer devoted a book to interpretations of Dylan's novel, *Tarantula* (New York: Macmillan, 1971). Many critics had compared Dylan's wordplay to the writing of James Joyce. The prose of Joyce's *Finnegans Wake* (New York: The Viking Press, 1939) was so dense that a guide book and been published for puzzled readers. Similarly, Craig Karpel published *The Tarantula in Me: Behind Bob Dylan's Novel* (San Francisco: Klohn, 1973), as an attempt to make the book accessible to readers.

Dylan's gospel period offended some, including Paul Williams, who wrote

Dylan: What Happened? (San Francisco: Entwhistle Books, 1979) in reaction. (The title was a reference to *Elvis: What Happened?*, an account by three of Elvis Presley's bodyguards of that singer's decline into drug use and sloth. Apparently, Williams intended to draw a parallel.) After the release of *Saved*, Williams offered an amendment, *Dylan: One Year Later*, which he printed privately (San Francisco, 1980). However, Dylan's Christian lyrics were also greeted with praise by at least one author whose work was released by a faith/inspirational publishing house. Don Williams' *Bob Dylan: The Man, the Music, the Message* (Englewood Cliffs, N. J.: Fleming-Revell, 1985) embraced his gospel songs with the same fervor with which other writers had greeted Dylan's protest work.

Several memoirs touch on Dylan, including those of John Hammond, which were written with Irving Townsend, *John Hammond on Record* (New York: Ridge Press/Summit Books, 1977). A career as long and distinguished as Hammond's was worth such a book and in it he detailed his involvements in the careers of Benny Goodman, Billie Holiday, Robert Johnson and Bruce Springsteen. The passages devoted to Dylan were obviously written with great affection and pride and seemed intent on righting some false impressions that were offered by other books, primarily through Hammond's assertion that he did not sign Dylan to Columbia Records until he had heard him sing. (Some books had stated that Hammond put him under contract on sight.)

Eric von Schmidt was a friend of Dylan during the early years. His *Baby Let Me Follow You Down: The Illustrated Story of the Cambridge Folk Years* (New York: Anchor Books, 1979), which was written with Jim Rooney, was a heavily illustrated account of those years, focusing on the northern bastion of the folk society, Cambridge, Massachusetts. The title was drawn from the song of the same name, and Dylan's version on his debut album acknowledged von Schmidt (who performed as *Ric* von Schmidt) and the "green pastures of Harvard University" in the impromptu spoken introduction.

Sam Shepard's *Rolling Thunder Logbook* (New York: Viking, 1977), was a chronicle of that tour and an account of Shepard's adventures as a collaborator on *Renaldo and Clara*. Larry Sloman's *On the Road with Bob Dylan: Rolling with the Thunder* (New York: Bantam Books, 1978) was a paperback memoir of the tour that was intended as a tie-in with *Renaldo and Clara*.

Joan Baez's first volume of autobiography and reflection, *Daybreak* (New York: Dial Press, 1968) did not include any references to Dylan in the first draft. After the publisher insisted that she write about Dylan--assuming that people would expect some reference to her former lover in such a volume, she produced a two-page episode called "The Dada King," which did not invoke his name. The publisher has to make due with that. A later volume, *And a Voice to Sing With* (New York: Summit Books, 1987), included more reminiscences, since Baez had had two more decades to reflect on her relationship with Dylan as well as two more decades of encounters with the man. She had worked closely with him in the mid-1970s, during the Rolling Thunder Revue period, and also toured Europe with him in 1984, although that was hardly a time of intimacy. As would be expected of Baez, her writing was always excruciatingly honest on every point, and bluntly so in the passages about Dylan.

Clive Davis wrote about his years as president of Columbia Records in *Clive: Inside the Record Business* (with James Wilwerth; New York: Morrow, 1975). Davis had left Columbia under a cloud of payola charges, yet he was later exonerated and built Arista Records into a major company. This memoir included his stories of dealings with Dylan. Davis was the CBS lawyer who insisted that the controversial "Talkin' John Birch Paranoid Blues" be left off *The Freewheelin' Bob Dylan*. Dylan did not much like him then, Davis figured, but they had an excellent relationship during Davis's tenure as president of the company. Davis had a good ear for singles, plucking "Lay Lady Lay" and "Knockin' on Heaven's Door" off albums and making them into hits, and in both cases overruling Dylan, who did not think the songs had mass appeal.

Another record company president, Joe Smith (who was with Warner Bros. and Elektra during his long career) went beyond a mere memoir with *Off the Record: An Oral History of Popular Music* (New York: Warner Books, 1988). Smith wanted to bring together comments by participants in popular music from the big-band period to the late 1980s, and to have the artists speak in their own words, in the Studs Terkel approach to oral history. Dylan appeared only briefly, but was referred to frequently by other artists.

Al Kooper was one of the most talented musicians of the rock 'n' roll era, as well as one of its liveliest writers. Kooper wrote several record reviews in early issues of *Rolling Stone*, which were noteworthy for their humor and skill. Consequently, it was no surprise that his memoirs of his musical career, *Backstage Passes: Rock 'n' Roll Life in the Sixties* (New York: Stein and Day, 1977), were so entertaining. If "Like a Rolling Stone" is, as some critics claim, the greatest rock 'n' roll song of all time, then Kooper's hilarious account of its recording amounts to pop-music gospel. The book ranged over all Kooper's work, including his legendary recordings with Michael Bloomfield and his creation of Blood, Sweat and Tears, but the book was at its best where it concerned the enigmatic Dylan.

Finally, the strangest of the memoirs is A. J. Weberman's *My Life in Garbology* (New York: Stonehill Press, 1980), a no-holds-barred account, if anyone wanted such a thing, by the man who made a career out of rooting through Bob Dylan's trash cans.

Articles

Dylan has parried with journalists throughout his career, and a journey through magazine articles about the musician shows him as the master put-on artist. After his early bad experience with *Newsweek* ("I Am My Words," 4 November 1963), in which the magazine suggested he had plagiarized "Blowin' in the Wind," Dylan grew increasingly wary and hostile toward the press. His skewering of *Time* magazine's Horace Judson in *Don't Look Back* may have been the inspiration for Dylan's diatribe against the unhip, "Ballad of a Thin Man."

A guide to vital Dylan articles would begin, of course, with *Broadside* and *Sing Out!* magazines. In addition to the appearances of his work in those publications, he became the focal point for many of the articles and letters. When *Sing Out!* editor Irwin Silber attacked Dylan in his publication for his betrayal of the protest movement (no. 5, 1964), Johnny Cash wrote a piece in *Broadside* (no. 41, 1964) defending Dylan's emotional honesty in the songs on *Another Side of Bob Dylan*. When singer Tom Paxton criticized Dylan and others in his famous "Folk Rot" article about the blending of two musical forms (*Sing Out!* no. 6, 1966), the letter columns were filled with further attacks and occasional defenses of Dylan. Those publications chronicled much of Dylan's early career. They also took music seriously. *Variety* and *Billboard*, the entertainment trade publications, also treated musicians with some semblance of respect, despite viewing them largely as commodities. Whenever mass magazines took note of changes in rock 'n' roll, however, it was usually to announce some new fad, often couching the report in howls of derision. Dylan, naturally, changed the way in which mainstream journalists regarded pop heroes because they could not deny his gifted lyricism. He did not sing about squirming adolescents, though they often filled concert halls to see him. Dylan's mid-1960s popularity mystified the press, largely because of his unwillingness to pander to a mass audience.

Perhaps a watershed magazine article in tracing this development was Jules Siegel's "Well, What Have We Here?" in the *Saturday Evening Post* (30 July 1966). Siegel was the hippest writer at the *Post* and turned out what later came to be regarded as vital works about rock 'n' roll. Prior to the founding of *Rolling Stone* in 1967, there was no home for journalism that dealt seriously with the new music. Siegel's articles showed artists in the process of creating. He wrote a legendary piece called "Goodbye Surfing, Hello God," for the *Post*, which was the story of Brian Wilson's efforts to record an album called *Smile* with his group, The Beach Boys. The album was too avant garde for release and Siegel's descriptions of the songs were as legendary in the literature of rock 'n' roll as the songs would have been. (Siegel, by the way, hated the titles the *Post* editors stuck on his stories about Dylan and Wilson.) Siegel's article on Dylan was hilarious, in part because of the writer's ear for dialogue. Dylan, he noted, spoke in italics, and he used this device to convey Dylan's characteristic speech, breaking the singer's evocation of his manager's name into halves (Al-*bert*) to match his midwestern nasal twang. Siegel's piece managed to explain Dylan to a mass (and, therefore, "unhip") audience while not condescending to Dylan's admirers.

Early attempts at rock magazines that reached beyond the fanzine form (*16, Teen Beat, Tiger Beat* and so on) were not successful. Although *Cheetah* produced excellent reportage about music during its short life (including Ellen Willis' tribute, "Dylan"), it operated in the red from the start. The Hearst Corporation launched *Eye*, another rock magazine that contained excellent writing--and it, too, failed, as did *GQ Scene*, an offshoot of *Gentleman's Quarterly*.

The successful rock 'n' roll magazines were created by media outsiders who knew little of publishing. The earliest of these was Paul Williams, who founded *Crawdaddy* in 1966, often cited as the first serious magazine about rock 'n' roll. Williams's well-crafted essays (including "Understanding Dylan," August 1966) made the case for taking the music seriously. Williams became a near-god to a generation of rock critics, but he did not run *Crawdaddy* for long. The first hugely successful publication was *Rolling Stone*, which was established by Jann Wenner in 1967.

From the start, *Rolling Stone* was linked to Dylan. His song was cited as one of the inspiration for the magazine's name and, as soon as he would agree to sit for one, Dylan was the subject of a series of *Rolling Stone* interviews. The first was with Wenner himself, who tried to draw the reclusive Dylan from his shell during a talk that coincided with the Nashville period (*Rolling Stone*, 29 November 1969). Dylan may have been putting on Wenner. Wenner quoted Dylan's lyrics frequently, and the musician pretended to be unfamiliar with the words. He played the role of family man and country squire.

Nevertheless, the magazine remained faithful in its mission to chronicle Dylan's every move and to review every album and film. The magazine produced a book of interviews and articles dealing with the 1974 tour (*Knockin' on Dylan's Door: On the Road in '74*) and later a coffee table book (*Dylan*, largely assmbled from Jonathan Cott's talks with the artist). *Rolling Stone* put Dylan on the cover to promote *Renaldo and Clara* in 1978, but Cott's conversation with Dylan in the magazine (carried over two issues) was baffling to many readers, although it made it clear that Dylan was not a back-country accidental genius like Elvis Presley, but was indeed a literate, creative artist.

All Dylan's albums from *John Wesley Harding* on, have been reviewed in *Rolling Stone*, some rather viciously. Greil Marcus and a chorus of critics ganged up on Dylan to trash *Self Portrait* on its release (23 July 1970) and their condemnation was so harsh that editor Wenner wrote a personal review a few issues later in order to restore good relations with Dylan. When Dylan followed that album with *New Morning* in the fall, the magazine proclaimed "We've Got Dylan Back Again!" over a glowing review by Wenner's partner, Ralph J. Gleason (26 November 1970).

Reviews in the vein of Greil Marcus's attack on *Self Portrait* tended to assume legendary status in the bibliography of Dylan critiques. Lester Bangs reviewed *Desire* in *Creem* (April 1976), taking Dylan to task for glorifying the Mafia in "Joey," which was drawn from the life of a gangster. He accused Dylan of playing fast and loose with the facts on that song and on "Hurricane," his account of boxer Rubin "Hurricane" Carter's false conviction for murder. In her brutalization of *Renaldo and Clara*, film critic Pauline Kael nearly crucified Dylan in the appropriately titled "The Calvary Gig" (*New Yorker*, February 13, 1978). The review was anthologized, perhaps as a how-to piece for vicious critics-in-training.

Esquire magazine had been the most effective chronicler of American popular culture in the 1960s, yet it was strangely silent on the subject of Bob Dylan until Sam Shepard's "True Dylan" (July 1987), which may be fact or fiction. It could be an interview or a meta-interview, along the lines of an Andy Warhol piece. Whatever the case, the mingling of Shepard and Dylan was intriguing, all the more so because they were simultaneously crafting their joint epic, "Brownsville Girl."

If Dylan had died in that 1966 motorcycle accident or in the late 1970s, or at some other time prior to his 50th birthday, perhaps today he would be more recognized for his achievements. His legacy is somewhat dusty, and his astonishing contributions to popular music are largely overlooked. In part, Dylan may be to blame because he chooses to be an active artist, performing more concerts each year than any other rock 'n' roll artist of his stature.[5] The mainstream press has, therefore, largely ignored or downplayed Dylan since the mid-1970s, although music magazines still recognize his influence. Only occasionally (lifetime achievement awards generally being granted but once a lifetime) do the major magazines assign pieces on Dylan. His 50th birthday would have been an appropriate occasion, but Dylan granted only one "interview": a taped telephone call with a staff member of *Spy*.

The most moving portrayal of this artist in repose was written a year later, while the mainstream press again ignored Dylan. Robert Hilburn, who had been writing about the singer for a quarter-century, followed him through a few stops during a Midwestern winter on the Never-Ending Tour. The after-hours visits to the coffee shops, the encounters with the old high-school buddies, and the monotonous hours on the bus were vividly described in "Dylan Now" (*Los Angeles Times Magazine*, February 9, 1992). Although Hilburn and Dylan did not sit for a formal interview, the writer's tracking of the artist through three days on the road is one of the most revealing pieces ever written on the man. Dylan frankly discussed his legacy, his concert performances (he was harshly critical of his work when it did not meet his standard) and his periods of inactivity. There were times, he said, when he could not write. He feared that he had peaked too soon, that writing would never be as easy for him as it had been in the 1960s, or in the 1970s, when he needed lessons from Norman Raeben to consciously do what he had previously done unconsciously. Nonetheless, even if these moments of self-criticism, Dylan refused to write himself off as a creative artist. "Once in a while," he told Hilburn, "the odd song will come to me like a bulldog at the garden gate and demand to be written."[6]

What follows is a bibliography of works by and about Bob Dylan. The first section deals with Dylan's works--his books and his songs. The second section is a standard bibliography of works about Dylan.

Section I: Works by Bob Dylan

Books

Tarantula. New York: Macmillan, 1971.
Writings and Drawings. New York: Knopf, 1973.
Lyrics, 1962-1985. New York: Knopf, 1985.

Songbooks

The Freewheelin' Bob Dylan. New York: Warner Bros. Inc., 1963
The Times They Are A-Changin'. New York: Warner Bros. Inc., 1964.
Bringing It All Back Home. New York: Warner Bros. Inc., 1965.
Highway 61 Revisited. New York: Warner Bros. Inc. 1965.
Bob Dylan Songbook. New York: Warner Bros. Inc., 1965.
Blonde on Blonde. New York: Music Sales Corp., 1966.
Bob Dylan's Greatest Hits. New York: Warner Bros. Inc., 1967.
John Wesley Harding. New York: Music Sales Corp., 1967.
Bob Dylan: A Collection. New York: Warner Bros. Publications, 1967.
Bob Dylan: A Retrospective. New York: Warner Bros. Publications, 1968.
Nashville Skyline. New York: Music Sales Corp., 1969.
Song Book. New York: Warner Bros. Inc., 1970.
Self Portrait. New York: Music Sales Corp., 1970.
New Morning. New York: Music Sales Corp., 1970.
Pat Garrett and Billy the Kid. Berlin: Rolfe Budde Musikverlag, 1973.
Planet Waves. New York: Music Sales Corp., 1974.
Blood on the Tracks. New York: Music Sales Corp., 1975.
The Basement Tapes. New York: Music Sales Corp., 1975.
Desire. New York: Music Sales Corp., 1976.
The Songs of Bob Dylan, 1966 through 1975. New York: Knopf, 1976.

Street Legal. New York: Music Sales Corp., 1978.
Slow Train Coming. New York: Music Sales Corp., 1979.
Saved. New York: Music Sales Corp., 1980.
Shot of Love. New York: Music Sales Corp., 1981.
Infidels. New York: Music Sales Corp., 1983.
Empire Burlesque. New York: Music Sales Corp., 1985.
Knocked Out Loaded. New York: Music Sales Copr., 1986.
Down in the Groove. New York: Music Sales Corp., 1988
Oh Mercy. New York: Music Sales Corp., 1989
Bob Dylan: Anthology. New York: Music Sales Corp., 1990
Rock Score. New York: Music Sales Corp., 1990
Under the Red Sky. New York: Music Sales Corp., 1990
Good As I Been to You. New York: Music Sales Corp., 1992

Songs

Song titles are followed by copyright and publishing information. Recording information pertains to Bob Dylan recordings, not recordings by other artists.

For the song listing for each Dylan album, see Chapter 7, where significant cover versions of Dylan songs and songs he wrote for other artists are also discussed.

The initial appearance of a recording is noted, as are subsequent appearances of that recording on anthologies as well as concert performances of the song.

"Abandoned Love." Copyright 1975, Ram's Horn Music. Appears on *Biograph*.
"Absolutely Sweet Marie." Copyright 1966, Dwarf Music. Appears on *Blonde on Blonde*.
"Ain't Gonna Go to Hell for Anybody." Copyright 1980, Special Rider Music. Has not appeared on an album, though it was performed in concert during his gospel tours.
"Ain't Gonna Grieve." Copyright 1963, 1968, Warner Bros. Inc.
"Ain't No Man Righteous, Not One." Copyright 1981, Special Rider Music. Has not appeared on an album, though it was performed in concert during the gospel tours.
"Alberta # 1." Copyright 1970, Big Sky Music. Appears on *Self Portrait*.
"Alberta # 2." Copyright 1970, Big Sky Music. Appears on *Self Portrait*.
"All along the Watchtower." Copyright 1968, Dwarf Music. Appears on *John Wesley Harding*. This recording also appears on *Bob Dylan's Greatest Hits, Vol. II*. Live recordings of the song appear on *Before the Flood*, *Bob Dylan at Budokan*, *Dylan and The Dead* and *Biograph* (a reprise of the *Before the Flood* version).
"All I Really Want to Do." Copyright 1964, Warner Bros. Inc. Appears on *Another Side of Bob Dylan*. This recording also appeared on *Bob Dylan's Greatest Hits, Vol. II*. A live recording appeared on *Bob Dylan at Budokan*.
"All over You." Copyright 1968, 1970, Warner Bros. Inc. Also known as "If I Had to Do it

Again (All over You)." Has not appeared on an album, though it was performed in concert in 1963.

"All the Tired Horses." Copyright 1970, Big Sky Music. Appears on *Self Portrait*.

"Angelina." Copyright 1981, Special Rider Music. Appears on *The Bootleg Series, Vols. 1-3*.

"Angel of Rain." Copyright 1984, Special Rider Music.

"Are You Ready." Copyright 1980, Special Rider Music. Appears on *Saved*.

"As I Went Out One Morning." Copyright 1968, Dwarf Music. Appears on *John Wesley Harding*.

"Baby, Give it Up." Written with Helena Springs. Copyright 1979, Special Rider Music.

"Baby, I'm in the Mood for You." Copyright 1963, 1966, Warner Bros. Inc. Appears on *Biograph*.

"Baby Stop Crying." Copyright 1978, Special Rider Music. Appears on *Street-Legal*.

"Ballad for a Friend." Copyright 1962, 1965, Duchess Music Corp.

"Ballad in Plain D." Copyright 1964, Warner Bros. Inc. Appears on *Another Side of Bob Dylan*.

"Ballad of a Thin Man." Copyright 1965, Warner Bros. Inc. Appears on *Highway 61 Revisited*. Live recordings appear on *Before the Flood*, *Bob Dylan at Budokan* and *Real Live*.

"Ballad of Donald White." Copyright 1962, Special Rider Music. Appears on *Broadside Reunion*.

"The Ballad of Frankie Lee and Judas Priest." Copyright 1968, Dwarf Music. Appears on *John Wesley Harding*.

"Ballad of Hollis Brown." Copyright 1963, Warner Bros. Inc. Appears on *The Times They Are A-Changin'*.

"Band of the Hand." Copyright 1986, Special Rider Music. Appears on *Band of the Hand: Original Soundtrack*.

"Belle Isle." Copyright 1970, Big Sky Music. Appears on *Self Portrait*.

"Billy." Copyright 1972, 1973, Ram's Horn Music. Three versions of the song ("Billy 1," "Billy 4," and "Billy 7") appear on *Pat Garrett and Billy the Kid*.

"Billy's Surrender." Copyright 1973, Ram's Horn Music. Appears in the film *Pat Garrett and Billy the Kid*, but not on the soundtrack album.

"Black Crow Blues." Copyright 1964, Warner Bros. Inc. Appears on *Another Side of Bob Dylan*.

"Black Diamond Bay." Written with Jacques Levy. Copyright 1975, 1976, Ram's Horn Music. Appears on *Desire*.

"Blessed Is the Name." Copyright 1979, Special Rider Music. Has not appeared on an album, though it was performed in concert in 1979 and 1980.

"Blind Willie McTell." Copyright 1983, Special Rider Music. Appears on *The Bootleg Series, Vols. 1-3*.

"Blowin' in the Wind." Copyright 1962, Warner Bros. Inc. Appears on *The Freewheelin' Bob Dylan*. This recording also appears on *Bob Dylan's Greatest Hits* and *Biograph*. Live recordings appear on *The Concert for Bangladesh*, *Before the Flood* and *Bob Dylan at Budokan*.

"Bob Dylan's Blues." Copyright 1963, 1966, Warner Bros. Inc. Appears on *The Freewheelin' Bob Dylan*.

"Bob Dylan's Dream." Copyright 1963, 1964, Warner Bros. Inc. Appears on *The Freewheelin' Bob Dylan*.

"Bob Dylan's New Orleans Rag." Copyright 1970, Warner Bros. Inc. Has not appeared on an album, though it was performed in concert in 1963.

"Bob Dylan's 115th Dream." Copyright 1965, Warner Bros. Inc. Appears on *Bringing It All Back Home*.

"Boots of Spanish Leather." Copyright 1963, 1964, Warner Bros. Inc. Appears on *The Times They Are A-Changin'*.

"Born in Time." Copyright 1990, Special Rider Music. Appears on *Under the Red Sky*.

"Brownsville Girl." Written with Sam Shepard. Copyright 1986, Special Rider Music. Appears on *Knocked Out Loaded*.

"Buckets of Rain." Copyright 1974, 1975, Ram's Horn Music. Appears on *Blood on the Tracks*.

"Bunkhouse Theme." Copyright 1973, Ram's Horn Music. Appears on *Pat Garrett and Billy the Kid*.

"California." Copyright 1972, 1985, Warner Bros. Inc.

"Call Letter Blues." Copyright 1974, Ram's Horn Music. Appears on *The Bootleg Series, Vols. 1-3*.

"Cantina Theme (Workin' for the Law)." Copyright 1973, Ram's Horn Music. Appears on *Pat Garrett and Billy the Kid*.

"Can You Please Crawl out Your Window?" Copyright 1965, 1966, Warner Bros. Inc. Released as a single in 1965, it did not appear on an album until 20 years later, with the release of *Biograph*.

"Caribbean Wind." Copyright 1985, Special Rider Music. Appears on *Biograph*.

"Catfish." Written with Jacques Levy. Copyright 1975, 1976, Ram's Horn Music. Appears on *The Bootleg Series, Vols. 1-3*.

"Cat's in the Well." Copyright 1990, Special Rider Music. Appears on *Under the Red Sky*.

"Champaign, Illinois." Copyright 1969, Cedarwood Publishing Company.

"Changing of the Guards." Copyright 1978, Special Rider Music. Appears on *Street-Legal*.

"Chimes of Freedom." Copyright 1964, Warner Bros. Inc. Appears on *Another Side of Bob Dylan*.

"City of Gold." Copyright 1980, Special Rider Music. Has not appeared on an album, though it was performed in concert in 1980 and 1981.

"Clean Cut Kid." Copyright 1984, Special Rider Music. Appears on *Empire Burlesque*.

"Clothes Line." Copyright 1969, 1975, Dwarf Music. Appears on *The Basement Tapes* under the title "Clothes Line Saga."

"Coming from the Heart (The Road Is Long)." Written with Helena Springs. Copyright 1979, Special Rider Music. Has not appeared on an album, though it was performed in concert in 1978.

"Congratulations." Written with George Harrison, Jeff Lynne, Roy Orbison and Tom Petty. Copyright 1988, Special Rider Music, Ganga Publishing B.V., SBK-Blackwood Music, Orbisongs Music and Gone Gator Music. Appears on The Traveling Wilburys' *Volume One*.

"Cool, Dry Place." Written with George Harrison, Jeff Lynne and Tom Petty. Copyright 1990, Special Rider Music, Ganga Publishing B.V., SBK-Blackwood Music and Gone Gator

Music. Appears on The Traveling Wilburys' *Volume Three*.

"Country Pie." Copyright 1969, Big Sky Music. Appears on *Nashville Skyline*.

"Covenant Woman." Copyright 1980, Special Rider Music. Appears on *Saved*.

"Cover Down, Break Through." Copyright 1980, Special Rider Music. Has not appeared on an album, though it was performed in concert in 1980.

"Dark Eyes." Copyright 1985, Special Rider Music. Appears on *Empire Burlesque*.

"Day of the Locusts." Copyright 1970, Big Sky Music. Appears on *New Morning*.

"Dead Man, Dead Man." Copyright 1981, Special Rider Music. Appears on *Shot of Love*.

"Dear Landlord." Copyright 1968, Dwarf Music. Appears on *John Wesley Harding*. This recording also appears on *Biograph*.

"Death Is Not the End." Copyright 1988, Special Rider Music. Appears on *Down in the Groove*.

"The Death of Emmitt Till." Copyright 1963, 1968, Warner Bros. Inc. Appears on *Broadside Reunion*.

"Denise." Copyright 1970, Warner Bros. Inc.

"Desolation Row." Copyright 1965, Warner Bros. Inc. Appears on *Highway 61 Revisited*.

"The Devil's Been Busy." Written with George Harrison, Jeff Lynne and Tom Petty. Copyright 1988, Special Rider Music, Ganga Publishing B.V., SBK-Blackwood Music and Gone Gator Music. Appears on The Traveling Wilburys' *Volume Three*.

"Dirge." Copyright 1973, 1974, Ram's Horn Music. Appears on *Planet Waves*.

"Dirty Lies." Copyright 1984, Special Rider Music.

"Dirty World." Written with George Harrison, Jeff Lynne, Roy Orbison and Tom Petty. Copyright 1988, Special Rider Music, Ganga Publishing B.V., SBK-Blackwood Music, Orbisongs Music and Gone Gator Music. Appears on The Traveling Wilburys' *Volume One*.

"Disease of Conceit." Copyright 1989, Special Rider Music. Appears on *Oh Mercy*.

"Don't Ever Take Yourself Away." Copyright 1982, Special Rider Music.

"Don't Fall Apart on Me Tonight." Copyright 1983, Special Rider Music. Appears on *Infidels*.

"Don't Think Twice, It's All Right." Copyright 1963, Warner Bros. Inc. Appears on *The Freewheelin' Bob Dylan*. This recording also appears on *Bob Dylan's Greatest Hits, Vol. II*. Live recordings appear on *Before the Flood* and *Bob Dylan at Budokan*. First published under the title "It's All Right."

"Don't Ya Tell Henry." Copyright 1971, 1975, Dwarf Music. Appears on *The Basement Tapes*.

"Do Right to Me Baby (Do Unto Others)." Copyright 1979, Special Rider Music. Appears on *Slow Train Coming*.

"Down Along the Cove." Copyright 1968, Dwarf Music. Appears on *John Wesley Harding*.

"Down in the Flood." Copyright 1967, 1975, Dwarf Music. Appears on *Bob Dylan's Greatest Hits, Vol. II*, and *The Basement Tapes*. Also known by the title "Crash on the Levee." The song carries a different variation on the title on each album.

"Down the Highway." Copyright 1963, 1967, Warner Bros. Inc. Appears on *The Freewheelin' Bob Dylan*.

"Drifter's Escape." Copyright 1968, Dwarf Music. Appears on *John Wesley Harding*.

"Driftin' Too Far from Shore." Copyright 1986, Special Rider Music. Appears on *Knocked Out Loaded*.

"Dusty Old Fairgrounds." Copyright 1973, 1985, Warner Bros. Inc. Has not appeared on an album, though it was performed in concert in 1963.

"Emotionally Yours." Copyright 1985, Special Rider Music. Appears on *Empire Burlesque*.

"End of the Line." Written with George Harrison, Jeff Lynne, Roy Orbison and Tom Petty. Copyright 1988, Special Rider Music, Ganga Publishing B.V., SBK-Blackwood Music, Orbisongs Music and Gone Gator Music. Appears on The Traveling Wilburys' *Volume One*.

"Enough Is Enough." Copyright 1984, Special Rider Music. Has not appeared on an album, though it was performed in concert in 1984.

"Eternal Circle." Copyright 1963, 1964, Warner Bros. Inc. Appears on *The Bootleg Series, Vols. 1-3*.

"Every Grain of Sand." Copyright 1981, Special Rider Music. Appears on *Shot of Love*. This recording also appears on *Biograph*. A demonstration recording appears on *The Bootleg Series, Vols. 1-3*.

"Everything Is Broken." Copyright 1989, Special Rider Music. Appears on *Oh Mercy*.

"Every Time Somebody Comes to Town." Written with George Harrison. Copyright 1970, Big Sky Music and Harrisongs Music Ltd.

"Farewell." Copyright 1963, 1973, Warner Bros. Inc. First published under the title, "Fare-Thee-Well."

"Farewell Angelina." Copyright 1965, 1966, Warner Bros. Inc. Appears on *The Bootleg Series, Vols. 1-3*.

"Father of Night." Copyright 1970, Big Sky Music. Appears on *New Morning*.

"Final Theme." Copyright 1973, Ram's Horn Music. Appears on *Pat Garrett and Billy the Kid*.

"Foot of Pride." Copyright 1983, Special Rider Music. Appears on *The Bootleg Series, Vols. 1-3*.

"Forever Young." Copyright 1973, 1974, Ram's Horn Music. Two versions appear on *Planet Waves*. Live versions appear on The Band's *The Last Waltz* and *Bob Dylan at Budokan*. A demonstration recording of the song appears on *Biograph*.

"Fourth Time Around." Copyright 1966, Dwarf Music. Appears on *Blonde on Blonde*, with the title reading "4th Time Around."

"From a Buick 6." Copyright 1965, Warner Bros. Inc. Appears on *Highway 61 Revisited*.

"Fur Slippers." Copyright 1982, Special Rider Music.

"Gates of Eden." Copyright 1965, Warner Bros. Inc. Appears on *Bringing It All Back Home*.

"George Jackson." Copyright 1971, Ram's Horn Music. Two versions were released back-to-back on a single.

"Get Your Rocks Off!" Copyright 1968, 1973, Dwarf Music. Has not been on an album, though recorded during the sessions for *The Basement Tapes*.

"Girl from the North Country." Copyright 1963, Warner Bros. Inc. Appears on *The Freewheelin' Bob Dylan*. The song was recorded as a duet with Johnny Cash for *Nashville Skyline*. A concert recording appears on *Real Live*. Sometimes appears under the title "Girl of the North Country."

"God Knows." Copyright 1990, Special Rider Music. Appears on *Under the Red Sky*.

"Going, Going, Gone." Copyright 1973, 1974, Ram's Horn Music. Appears on *Planet Waves*. A live recording appears on *Bob Dylan at Budokan*.

"Goin' to Acapulco." Copyright 1975, Dwarf Music. Appears on *The Basement Tapes*.

"Golden Loom." Copyright 1975, 1976, Ram's Horn Music. Appears on *The Bootleg Series, Vols. 1-3*.

"Gonna Change My Way of Thinking." Copyright 1979, Special Rider Music. Appears on *Slow Train Coming*.

"Got My Mind Made Up." Written with Tom Petty. Copyright 1986, Special Rider Music and Gone Gator Music. Appears on *Knocked Out Loaded*.

"Gotta Serve Somebody." Copyright 1979, Special Rider Music. Appears on *Slow Train Coming*. This recording also appears on *Biograph*. Live recording appears on *Dylan and The Dead*.

"Go 'Way Little Boy." Copyright 1984, Special Rider Music.

"The Groom's Still Waiting at the Altar." Copyright 1981, Special Rider Music. Originally issued only as a B-side of a single, it was included on a revised *Shot of Love* album. It also appears on *Biograph*.

"Guess I'm Doin' Fine." Copyright 1964, 1966, Warner Bros. Inc.

"Gypsy Lou." Copyright 1963, 1966, Warner Bros. Inc.

"Had a Dream about You, Baby." Copyright 1988, Special Rider Music. Appears on *Down in the Groove*. Also appears on the *Hearts of Fire* soundtrack.

"Handle with Care." Written with George Harrison, Jeff Lynne, Roy Orbison and Tom Petty. Copyright 1988, Special Rider Music, Ganga Publishing B.V., SBK-Blackwood Music, Orbisongs Music and Gone Gator Music. Appears on The Traveling Wilburys' *Volume One*.

"Handy Dandy." Copyright 1990, Special Rider Music. Appears on *Under the Red Sky*.

"A Hard Rain's A-Gonna Fall." Copyright 1963, Warner Bros. Inc. Appears on *The Freewheelin' Bob Dylan*. This recording also appears on *Bob Dylan's Greatest Hits, Vol. II*. A live recording appears on *The Concert for Bangladesh*. Interestingly, a though Dylan's 1977 live album, *Hard Rain*, takes its title from this song, it does not appear on the album.

"Hard Times in New York Town." Copyright 1962, 1965, Duchess Music Corp. Appears on *The Bootleg Series, Vols. 1-3*.

"Hazel." Copyright 1973, 1974, Ram's Horn Music. Appears on *Planet Waves*.

"Heading for the Light." Written with George Harrison, Jeff Lynne, Roy Orbison and Tom Petty. Copyright 1988, Special Rider Music, Ganga Publishing B.V., SBK-Blackwood Music, Orbisongs Music and Gone Gator Music. Appears on The Traveling Wilburys' *Volume One*.

"Heart of Mine." Copyright 1981, Special Rider Music. Appears on *Shot of Love*. A live recording appears on *Biograph*.

"Her Memory." Copyright 1980, Special Rider Music.

"Hero Blues." Copyright 1963, Warner Bros. Inc. Has not appeared on an album, but was the first song performed during the 1974 tour with The Band.

"Highway 61 Revisited." Copyright 1965, Warner Bros. Inc. Appears on *Highway 61 Revisited*. Live recordings appear on *Before the Flood* and *Real Live*.

"Hurricane." Written with Jacques Levy. Copyright 1975, Ram's Horn Music. Appears on *Desire*.

"I Am a Lonesome Hobo." Copyright 1968, Dwarf Music. Appears on *John Wesley Harding*.

"I and I." Copyright 1983, Special Rider Music. Appears on *Infidels*. Concert recording appears on *Real Live*.

"I Believe in You." Copyright 1979, Special Rider Music. Appears on *Slow Train Coming*.

"I Can't Leave Her Behind." Copyright 1978, Dwarf Music. Dylan is shown singing this song in *Eat the Document*, which was filmed in 1966.

"I'd Hate to Be You on That Dreadful Day." Copyright 1964, 1967, Warner Bros. Inc. Appears on *Broadside Reunion*.

"I'd Have You Any Time." Written with George Harrison. Copyright 1970, Big Sky Music and Harrisongs Music Ltd.

"Idiot Wind." Copyright 1974, 1975, Ram's Horn Music. Appears on *Blood on the Tracks*. An outtake appears on *The Bootleg Series, Vols. 1-3*, and a live version appears on *Hard Rain*.

"I Don't Believe You." Copyright 1964, Warner Bros. Inc. Appears on *Another Side of Bob Dylan*. A live recording titled "I Don't Believe You (She Acts Like We Never Have Met)" appears on *Biograph*. A live recording also appears on *The Last Waltz*, with The Band.

"I Don't Want to Do It." Copyright 1984, Big Sky Music.

"I Dreamed I Saw St. Augustine." Copyright 1968, Dwarf Music. Appears on *John Wesley Harding*.

"If Dogs Run Free." Copyright 1970, Big Sky Music. Appears on *New Morning*.

"If I Don't Be There by Morning." Written with Helena Springs. Copyright 1978, Special Rider Music.

"If Not for You." Copyright 1970, Big Sky Music. Appears on *New Morning* and also appears on *Biograph*. An outtake, recorded with George Harrison, appears on *The Bootleg Series, Vols. 1-3*.

"If You Belonged to Me." Written with George Harrison, Jeff Lynne and Tom Petty. Copyright 1990, Special Rider Music, Ganga Publishing B.V., SBK-Blackwood Music and Gone Gator Music. Appears on The Traveling Wilburys' *Volume Three*.

"If You Gotta Go, Go Now." Copyright 1965, Warner Bros. Inc. Released as a single in Europe. This recording appears on *The Bootleg Series, Vols. 1-3*, under the title "If You Gotta Go, Go Now (Or Else You Got to Stay All Night)."

"If You See Her, Say Hello." Copyright 1974, 1975, Ram's Horn Music. Appears on *Blood on the Tracks*. An outtake appears on *The Bootleg Series, Vols. 1-3*.

"I'll Be Your Baby Tonight." Copyright 1968, Dwarf Music. Appears on *John Wesley Harding*. This recording also appears on *Bob Dylan's Greatest Hits, Vol. II* and *Biograph*.

"I'll Keep it With Mine." Copyright 1965, 1968, Warner Bros. Inc. Appears on *Biograph*. An outtake appears on *The Bootleg Series, Vols. 1-3*.

"I'll Remember You." Copyright 1985, Special Rider Music. Appears on *Empire Burlesque*.

"I Must Love You Too Much." Written with Helena Springs. Copyright 1979, Special Rider Music. Revised and retitled by Greg Lake. "Love You Too Much" credited to Dylan, Springs and Lake.

"In the Garden." Copyright 1980, Special Rider Music. Appears on *Saved*.

"In the Summertime." Copyright 1981, Special Rider Music. Appears on *Shot of Love*.

"Inside Out." Written with George Harrison, Jeff Lynne and Tom Petty. Copyright 1990, Special Rider Music, Ganga Publishing B.V., SBK-Blackwood Music and Gone Gator Music. Appears on The Traveling Wilburys' *Volume Three*.

"I Pity the Poor Immigrant." Copyright 1968, Dwarf Music. Appears on *John Wesley Harding*.

"I Shall Be Free." Copyright 1963, 1967, Warner Bros. Inc. Appears on *The Freewheelin' Bob Dylan*.

"I Shall Be Free No. 10." Copyright 1971, 1973, Special Rider Music. Appears on *Another Side of Bob Dylan*.

"I Shall Be Released." Copyright 1967, 1970, Dwarf Music. Appears on *Bob Dylan's Greatest Hits, Vol. II*. This recording also appears on *Biograph*. Live recordings appear on The Band's *The Last Waltz* and *Bob Dylan at Budokan*. A performance with The Band from the basement tapes era appears on *The Bootleg Series, Vols. 1-3*.

"Is Your Love in Vain?" Copyright 1978, Special Rider Music. Appears on *Street-Legal*. Live recording appears on *Bob Dylan at Budokan*.

"Isis." Written with Jacques Levy. Copyright 1975, 1976, Ram's Horn Music. Appears on *Desire*. Live recording appears on *Biograph*.

"It Ain't Me Babe." Copyright 1964, Warner Bros. Inc. Appears on *Another Side of Bob Dylan*. This recording also appears on *Bob Dylan's Greatest Hits* and *Biograph*. Live recordings appear on *Before the Flood* and *Real Live*.

"I Threw It All Away." Copyright 1969, Big Sky Music. Appears on *Nashville Skyline*. A live recording appears on *Hard Rain*.

"It Takes a Lot to Laugh, It Takes a Train to Cry." Copyright 1965, Warner Bros. Inc. Appears on *Highway 61 Revisited*. An outtake appears on *The Bootleg Series, Vols. 1-3*. Live recording appears on *The Concert for Bangladesh*.

"It's All Over Now, Baby Blue." Copyright 1965, Warner Bros. Inc. Appears on *Bringing It All Back Home*. This recording also appears on *Bob Dylan's Greatest Hits, Vol. II*. Live recording appears on *Biograph*.

"It's Alright, Ma (I'm Only Bleeding)." Copyright 1965, Warner Bros. Inc. Appears on *Bringing It All Back Home*. Live recordings appear on *Before the Flood* and *Bob Dylan at Budokan*.

"I Wanna Be Your Lover." Copyright 1971, 1976, Dwarf Music. Appears on *Biograph*.

"I Want You." Copyright 1966, Dwarf Music. Appears on *Blonde on Blonde*. This recording also appears on *Bob Dylan's Greatest Hits*. Live recordings appear on *Bob Dylan at Budokan* and *Dylan and The Dead*.

"I Will Love Him." Copyright 1980, Special Rider Music. Has not appeared on an album, though it was performed in concert in 1980.

"Jack O'Diamonds." Written with Ben Carruthers. Copyright 1973, Special Rider Music. Carruthers apparently used an adaptation of a poem from Dylan's notes to *Another Side of Bob Dylan*.

"Jammin' Me." Written with Tom Petty and Mike Campbell. Copyright 1989 Special Rider Music and Gone Gator Music.

"Jesus Is the One." Copyright 1981, Special Rider Music. Has not appeared on an album, though it was performed in concert in 1981.

"Jet Pilot." Copyright 1985, Special Rider Music. Originally titled "Pilot Eyes." Appears on *Biograph*.

"Joey." Written with Jacques Levy. Copyright 1975, 1976, Ram's Horn Music. Appears on *Desire*. A live recording appears on *Dylan and The Dead*.

"John Brown." Copyright 1963, 1968, Warner Bros. Inc. Appears on *Broadside Ballads*.

"John Wesley Harding." Copyright 1968, Dwarf Music. Appears on *John Wesley Harding*.

"Jokerman." Copyright 1983, Special Rider Music. Appears on *Infidels*.

"Julius and Ethel." Copyright 1983, Special Rider Music.

"Just Like a Woman." Copyright 1966, Dwarf Music. Appears on *Blonde on Blonde*. This recording also appears on *Bob Dylan's Greatest Hits* and *Biograph*. Live recordings appear on *The Concert for Bangladesh*, *Before the Flood* and *Bob Dylan at Budokan*.

"Just Like Tom Thumb's Blues." Copyright 1965, Warner Bros. Inc. Appears on *Highway 61 Revisited*. This recording also appears on *Bob Dylan's Greatest Hits, Vol. II*. A live recording appears on the B-side of the "I Want You" single.

"Knockin' on Heaven's Door." Copyright 1973, 1974, Ram's Horn Music. Appears on *Pat Garrett and Billy the Kid*. This recording also appears on *Biograph*. Live recordings appear on *Before the Flood*, *Bob Dylan at Budokan* and *Dylan and The Dead*.

"Last Night." Written with George Harrison, Jeff Lynne, Roy Orbison and Tom Petty. Copyright 1988, Special Rider Music, Ganga Publishing B.V., SBK-Blackwood Music, Orbisongs Music and Gone Gator Music. Appears on The Traveling Wilburys' *Volume One*.

"Lay Down Your Weary Tune." Copyright 1964, 1965, Warner Bros. Inc. Appears on *Biograph*.

"Lay, Lady, Lay." Copyright 1969, Big Sky Music. Appears on *Nashville Skyline*. This recording also appears on *Bob Dylan's Greatest Hits, Vol. II* and *Biograph*. Live recordings appear on *Before the Flood* and *Hard Rain*.

"Legionnaires' Disease." Copyright 1981, Special Rider Music.

"Lenny Bruce." Copyright 1981, Special Rider Music. Appears on *Shot of Love*.

"Leopard-Skin Pillbox Hat." Copyright 1966, Dwarf Music. Appears on *Blonde on Blonde*.

"Let Me Die in My Footsteps." Copyright 1963, 1965, Warner Bros. Inc. Appears on early copies of *The Freewheelin' Bob Dylan* that were withdrawn when the album was revised. Appears on *The Bootleg Series, Vols. 1-3*. Originally published under the title "I Will Not Go Down under the Ground."

"Let's Keep It between Us." Copyright 1982, Special Rider Music. Has not appeared on an album, though Dylan performed it in concert in 1981.

"License to Kill." Copyright 1983, Special Rider Music. Appears on *Infidels*. Concert recording appears on *Real Live*.

"Like A Rolling Stone." Copyright 1965, Warner Bros. Inc. Appears on *Highway 61 Revisited*. This recording also appears on *Bob Dylan's Greatest Hits* and *Biograph*. A rehearsal for this recording appears on *The Bootleg Series, Vols. 1-3*. Live recordings appear on *Self Portrait*, *Before the Flood* and *Bob Dylan at Budokan*.

"Lily, Rosemary and the Jack of Hearts." Copyright 1974, 1975, Ram's Horn Music. Appears on *Blood on the Tracks*.

"Living the Blues." Copyright 1970, Big Sky Music. Appears on *Self Portrait*.

"Lo and Behold!" Copyright 1967, 1975, Dwarf Music. Appears on *The Basement Tapes*.

"The Lonesome Death of Hattie Carroll." Copyright 1964, Warner Bros. Inc. Appears on *The Times They Are A-Changin'*. This version also appears on *Biograph*.

"Long Ago, Far Away." Copyright 1962, 1968, Warner Bros. Inc.

"Long Distance Operator." Copyright 1971, 1975, Dwarf Music. Appears on *The Basement Tapes*.

"Long Time Gone." Copyright 1963, 1968, Warner Bros. Inc.

"Lord Protect My Child." Copyright 1983, Special Rider Music. Appears on *The Bootleg*

Series, Vols. 1-3.

"Love Is Just a Four-Letter Word." Copyright 1967, Warner Bros. Inc.

"Love Minus Zero/No Limit." Copyright 1965, Warner Bros. Inc. Appears on *Bringing It All Back Home*. A live recording appears on *Bob Dylan at Budokan*.

"Love Rescue Me." Written with Adam Clayton, David Evans, Paul Hewson and Larry Mullen, Jr. Copyright 1988, Special Rider Music and Chappell Music.

"Maggie's Farm." Copyright 1965, Warner Bros. Inc. Appears on *Bringing It All Back Home*. This recording also appears on *Bob Dylan's Greatest Hits, Vol. II*. Live recordings appear on *Hard Rain*, *Bob Dylan at Budokan* and *Real Live*.

"Main Title Theme." Copyright 1973, Ram's Horn Music. Appears on *Pat Garrett and Billy the Kid*.

"Mama, You Been on My Mind." Copyright 1964, 1967, Warner Bros. Inc. Sometimes noted as "Mama, You Bin on My Mind." An alternate title is "Daddy, You Been on My Mind." Appears on *The Bootleg Series, Vols. 1-3*.

"Man Gave Names to All the Animals." Copyright 1979, Special Rider Music. Appears on *Slow Train Coming*.

"Man in a Long Black Coat." Copyright 1989, Special Rider Music. Appears on *Oh Mercy*.

"The Man in Me." Copyright 1970, Big Sky Music. Appears on *New Morning*.

"Man of Peace." Copyright 1983, Special Rider Music. Appears on *Infidels*.

"Man on the Street." Copyright 1962, 1965, Duchess Music Corp. Also known under title "The Old Man." Appears on *The Bootleg Series, Vols. 1-3*.

"Margarita." Written with George Harrison, Jeff Lynne, Roy Orbison and Tom Petty. Copyright 1988, Special Rider Music, Ganga Publishing B.V., SBK-Blackwood Music, Orbisongs Music and Gone Gator Music. Appears on The Traveling Wilburys' *Volume One*.

"Masters of War." Copyright 1963, Warner Bros. Inc. Appears on *The Freewheelin' Bob Dylan*. This recording also appears on *Biograph*. A concert recording appears on *Real Live*.

"Maybe Someday." Copyright 1986, Special Rider Music. Appears on *Knocked Out Loaded*.

"Meet Me in the Morning." Copyright 1974, 1975, Ram's Horn Music. Appears on *Blood on the Tracks*.

"Million Dollar Bash." Copyright 1967, 1975, Dwarf Music. Appears on *The Basement Tapes*. This recording also appears on *Biograph*.

"Minstrel Boy." Copyright 1970, Big Sky Music. Appears on *Self Portrait*.

"Mixed Up Confusion." Copyright 1962, 1968, Warner Bros. Inc. Though released as a single in 1962, it did not appear on an album. A different version, recorded at the same session as the single, was finally released on *Biograph*.

"Money Blues." Written with Jacques Levy. Copyright 1975, 1976 Ram's Horn Music.

"More Than Flesh and Blood." Written with Helena Springs. Copyright 1979, Special Rider Music.

"Most Likely You Go Your Way (and I'll Go Mine)." Copyright 1966, Dwarf Music. Appears on *Blonde on Blonde*. A live recording opens *Before the Flood*, and this recording is reprised on *Biograph*. On the cover and label of *Blonde on Blonde* there are no parentheses in the title.

"Most of the Time." Copyright 1989, Special Rider Music. Appears on *Oh Mercy*.

"Motorcycle Nightmare." Copyright 1964, Warner Bros. Inc. Appears on *Another Side of*

Bob Dylan, with the title spelled "Motorcycle Nitemare."

"Mozambique." Written with Jacques Levy. Copyright 1975, Ram's Horn Music. Appears on *Desire*.

"Mr. Tambourine Man." Copyright 1965, Warner Bros. Inc. Appears on *Bringing It All Back Home*. This recording also appears on *Bob Dylan's Greatest Hits* and *Biograph*. Live recordings appear on *The Concert for Bangladesh* and *Bob Dylan at Budokan*.

"My Back Pages." Copyright 1964, Warner Bros. Inc. Appears on *Another Side of Bob Dylan*. This recording also appears on *Bob Dylan's Greatest Hits, Vol. II*.

"Nashville Skyline Rag." Copyright 1969, Big Sky Music. Appears on *Nashville Skyline*. A recording with Dylan and Earl Scruggs appears on *Earl Scruggs: His Family and Friends*.

"Need a Woman." Copyright 1982, Special Rider Music. Appears on *The Bootleg Series, Vols. 1-3*.

"Neighborhood Bully." Copyright 1983, Special Rider Music. Appears on *Infidels*.

"Never Gonna Be the Same Again." Copyright 1985, Special Rider Music. Appears on *Empire Burlesque*.

"New Blue Moon." Written with George Harrison, Jeff Lynne and Tom Petty. Copyright 1990, Special Rider Music, Ganga Publishing B.V., SBK-Blackwood Music and Gone Gator Music. Appears on The Traveling Wilburys' *Volume Three*.

"New Morning." Copyright 1970, Big Sky Music. Appears on *New Morning*.

"New Pony." Copyright 1978, Special Rider Music. Appears on *Street-Legal*.

"Nobody 'Cept You." Copyright 1973, 1976, Ram's Horn Music. Appears on *The Bootleg Series, Vols. 1-3*.

"North Country Blues." Copyright 1963, Warner Bros. Inc. Appears on *The Times They Are A-Changin'*.

"Not Alone Anymore." Written with George Harrison, Jeff Lynne, Roy Orbison and Tom Petty. Copyright 1988, Special Rider Music, Ganga Publishing B.V., SBK-Blackwood Music, Orbisongs Music and Gone Gator Music. Appears on The Traveling Wilburys' *Volume One*.

"Nothing Was Delivered." Copyright 1968, 1975, Dwarf Music. Appears on *The Basement Tapes*.

"No Time to Think." Copyright 1978, Special Rider Music. Appears on *Street-Legal*.

"Obviously Five Believers." Copyright 1966, Dwarf Music. Appears on *Blonde on Blonde* as "Obviously 5 Believers."

"Odds and Ends." Copyright 1969, 1975, Dwarf Music. Appears on *The Basement Tapes*.

"Oh, Sister." Written with Jacques Levy. Copyright 1975, 1976, Ram's Horn Music. Appears on *Desire*. Live recordings appear on *Hard Rain* and *Bob Dylan at Budokan*.

"On a Night Like This." Copyright 1973, 1974, Ram's Horn Music. Appears on *Planet Waves*. This recording also appears on *Biograph*.

"On a Rainy Afternoon." Written with J. R. Robertson. Copyright 1978, Dwarf Music. Has not appeared on an album, though it is performed in the film *Eat the Document*.

"One More Cup of Coffee." Written with Jacques Levy. Copyright 1975, 1976, Ram's Horn Music. Appears on *Desire*. A live recording, under the title "One More Cup of Coffee (Valley Below)," appears on *Bob Dylan at Budokan*.

"One More Night." Copyright 1969, Big Sky Music. Appears on *Nashville Skyline*.

"One More Time." Copyright 1978, Special Rider Music.

"One More Weekend." Copyright 1970, Big Sky Music. Appears on *New Morning*.

"One of Us Must Know (Sooner or Later)." Copyright 1966, Dwarf Music. Appears on *Blonde on Blonde*.

"One Too Many Mornings." Copyright 1964, 1966, Warner Bros. Inc. Appears on *The Times They Are A-Changin'*. A live recording appears on *Hard Rain*.

"Only a Hobo." Copyright 1963, 1968, Warner Bros. Inc. Appears on *Broadside Ballads, Vol. I*. Also appears on *The Bootleg Series, Vols. 1-3*.

"Only a Pawn in Their Game." Copyright 1963, 1964, Warner Bros. Inc. Appears on *The Times They Are A-Changin'*. A live recording under the title "Ballad of Medgar Evans [Evers]" appears on *We Shall Overcome*.

"On the Road Again." Copyright 1965, Warner Bros. Inc. Appears on *Bringing It All Back Home*.

"Open the Door, Homer." Copyright 1968, 1975, Dwarf Music. Appears on *The Basement Tapes*.

"Outlaw Blues." Copyright 1965, Warner Bros. Inc. Appears on *Bringing It All Back Home*.

"Oxford Town." Copyright 1963, Warner Bros. Inc. Appears on *The Freewheelin' Bob Dylan*.

"Paths of Victory." Copyright 1964, Warner Bros. Inc. Appears on *The Bootleg Series, Vols. 1-3*.

"Patty's Gone to Laredo." Copyright 1977, 1978, Ram's Horn Music. Has not appeared on an album, though it is performed by the Rolling Thunder Revue in *Renaldo and Clara*.

"Peggy Day." Copyright 1969, Big Sky Music. Appears on *Nashville Skyline*.

"Percy's Song." Copyright 1964, 1966, Warner Bros. Inc. Appears on *Biograph*.

"Playboys and Playgirls." Copyright 1964, 1968, Warner Bros. Inc. Appears as a duet on with Pete Seeger on *Newport Broadside* under the title "Ye Playboys and Playgirls."

"Please, Mrs. Henry." Copyright 1967, 1971, Dwarf Music. Appears on *The Basement Tapes*.

"Pledging My Time." Copyright 1966, Dwarf Music. Appears on *Blonde on Blonde*.

"Political World." Copyright 1989, Special Rider Music. Appears on *Oh Mercy*.

"Poor Boy Blues." Copyright 1962, 1965, Duchess Music Corp.

"Poor House." Written with George Harrison, Jeff Lynne and Tom Petty. Copyright 1990, Special Rider Music, Ganga Publishing B.V., SBK-Blackwood Music and Gone Gator Music. Appears on The Traveling Wilburys' *Volume Three*.

"Positively 4th Street." Copyright 1965, Warner Bros. Inc. Appears on *Bob Dylan's Greatest Hits*.

"Precious Angel." Copyright 1979, Special Rider Music. Appears on *Slow Train Coming*.

"Pressing On." Copyright 1980, Special Rider Music. Appears on *Saved*.

"Property of Jesus." Copyright 1981, Special Rider Music. Appears on *Shot of Love*.

"Queen Jane Approximately." Copyright 1965, Warner Bros. Inc. Appears on *Highway 61 Revisited*. A live recording appears on *Dylan and The Dead*.

"Quinn the Eskimo (The Mighty Quinn)." Copyright 1968, Dwarf Music. Appears on *Biograph*. A live recording under the title "The Mighty Quinn" appears on *Self Portrait*.

"Quit Your Lowdown Ways." Copyright 1963, 1964, Warner Bros. Inc. Appears on *The Bootleg Series, Vols. 1-3*.

"Rainy Day Women # 12 & 35." Copyright 1966, Dwarf Music. Appears on *Blonde on*

Blonde. This recording also appears on *Bob Dylan's Greatest Hits*. A live recording appears on *Before the Flood*.

"Rambling, Gambling Willie." Copyright 1962, 1965, Duchess Music Corp. Appears on the early promotional copies of *The Freewheelin' Bob Dylan* and on *The Bootleg Series, Vols. 1-3*. Sometimes called "Gamblin' Willie's Dead Man's Hand."

"Rattled." Written with George Harrison, Jeff Lynne, Roy Orbison and Tom Petty. Copyright 1988, Special Rider Music, Ganga Publishing B.V., SBK-Blackwood Music, Orbisongs Music and Gone Gator Music. Appears on The Traveling Wilburys' *Volume One*.

"Responsibility." Written with Helena Springs. Copyright 1979, Special Rider Music.

"Restless Farewell." Copyright 1964, 1966, Warner Bros. Inc. Appears on *The Times They Are A-Changin'*.

"Ring Them Bells." Copyright 1989, Special Rider Music. Appears on *Oh Mercy*.

"Rita May." Written with Jacques Levy. Copyright 1975, 1976, Ram's Horn Music. Appears as the flip side of the single "Stuck Inside of Mobile with the Memphis Blues Again" in 1976.

"River Theme." Copyright 1973, Ram's Horn Music. Appears on *Pat Garrett and Billy the Kid*.

"Rocks and Gravel." Copyright 1963, 1966, Warner Bros. Inc. An early version of this song (under the title "Solid Road") appears on some promotional copies of *The Freewheelin' Bob Dylan*.

"Romance in Durango." Written with Jacques Levy. Copyright 1975, 1976, Ram's Horn Music. Appears on *Desire*. A live recording appears on *Biograph*.

"Sad-Eyed Lady of the Lowlands." Copyright 1966, Dwarf Music. Appears on *Blonde on Blonde*.

"Santa-Fe." Copyright 1973, Dwarf Music. Appears on *The Bootleg Series, Vols. 1-3*.

"Sara." Copright 1975, 1976, Ram's Horn Music. Appears on *Desire*.

"Saved." Written with Tim Drummond. Copyright 1980, Special Rider Music. Appears on *Saved*.

"Saving Grace." Copyright 1980, Special Rider Music. Appears on *Saved*.

"Seeing the Real You at Last." Copyright 1985, Special Rider Music. Appears on *Empire Burlesque*.

"Senor (Tales of Yankee Power)." Copyright 1978, Special Rider Music. Appears on *Street-Legal*. This recording also appears on *Biograph*.

"Series of Dreams." Copyright 1989, Special Rider Music. Appears on *The Bootleg Series, Vols. 1-3*.

"Seven Curses." Copyright 1963, Warner Bros. Inc. Appears on *The Bootleg Series, Vols. 1-3*.

"Seven Days." Copyright 1976, 1979, Ram's Horn Music. Appears on *The Bootleg Series, Vols. 1-3*.

"Seven Deadly Sins." Written with George Harrison, Jeff Lynne and Tom Petty. Copyright 1990, Special Rider Music, Ganga Publishing B.V., SBK-Blackwood Music and Gone Gator Music. Appears on The Traveling Wilburys' *Volume Three*.

"She Belongs to Me." Copyright 1965, Warner Bros. Inc. Appears on *Bringing It All Back Home*. Live recording appears on *Self Portrait*.

"Shelter From the Storm." Copyright 1974, 1975, Ram's Horn Music. Appears on *Blood on the Tracks*. Live recordings appear on *Hard Rain* and *Bob Dylan at Budokan*.

"She's My Baby." Written with George Harrison, Jeff Lynne and Tom Petty. Copyright 1990, Special Rider Music, Ganga Publishing B.V., SBK-Blackwood Music and Gone Gator Music. Appears on The Traveling Wilburys' *Volume Three*.

"She's Your Lover Now." Copyright 1971, 1976 Dwarf Music. Appears on *The Bootleg Series, Vols. 1-3*. Also known as "Just a Little Glass of Water."

"Shooting Star." Copyright 1989, Special Rider Music. Appears on *Oh Mercy*.

"Shot of Love." Copyright 1981, Special Rider Music. Appears on *Shot of Love*.

"Sign Language." Copyright 1976, Ram's Horn Music.

"Sign on the Cross." Copyright 1971, 1973, Dwarf Music.

"Sign on the Window." Copyright 1970, Big Sky Music. Appears on *New Morning*.

"Silent Weekend." Copyright 1973, 1976, Dwarf Music.

"Silvio." Written with Robert Hunter. Copyright 1988, Special Rider Music and Ice Nine Music. Appears on *Down in the Groove*.

"Simple Twist of Fate." Copyright 1974, 1975, Ram's Horn Music. Appears on *Blood on the Tracks*. Live recording appears on *Bob Dylan at Budokan*.

"Sitting on a Barbed Wire Fence." Copyright 1970, Warner Bros. Inc. Appears on *The Bootleg Series, Vols. 1-3*. Also known as "Killing Me Alive" and "Over the Cliff."

"Slow Train." Copyright 1979, Special Rider Music. Appears on *Slow Train Coming*. Live recording appears on *Dylan and The Dead*.

"Solid Rock." Copyright 1980, Special Rider Music. Appears on *Saved* and on *Biograph*.

"Someone Else's Arms." Written with Helena Springs. Copyright 1979, Special Rider Music.

"Someone's Got a Hold of My Heart." Copyright 1983, Special Rider Music. Appears on *The Bootleg Series, Vols. 1-3*. This is an early version of "Tight Connection to My Heart (Has Anybody Seen My Love?)."

"Something's Burning, Baby." Copyright 1985, Special Rider Music. Appears on *Empire Burlesque*.

"Something There Is about You." Copyright 1973, 1974, Ram's Horn Music. Appears on *Planet Waves*.

"Song to Woody." Copyright 1962, 1965, Duchess Music Corp. Appears on *Bob Dylan*.

"Spanish Harlem Incident." Copyright 1964, Warner Bros. Inc. Appears on *Another Side of Bob Dylan*.

"Stand by Faith." Copyright 1979, Special Rider Music.

"Standing on the Highway." Copyright 1962, 1965, Duchess Music Corp.

"Steel Bars." Written with Michael Bolton. Copyright 1991, Special Rider Music and Mr. Bolton's Music. Has not appeared on a Dylan album.

"Stepchild." Written with Helena Springs. Copyright 1978, Special Rider Music. Has not appeared on an album, though it was performed in concert in 1978.

"Stop Now." Copyright 1978, Special Rider Music.

"Straight A's in Love." Copyright 1985, Special Rider Music.

"Stuck Inside of Mobile with the Memphis Blues Again." Copyright 1966, Dwarf Music. Appears on *Blonde on Blonde*. This recording also appears on *Bob Dylan's Greatest Hits, Vol. II*. A live recording appears on *Hard Rain*.

"Subterranean Homesick Blues." Copyright 1965, Warner Bros. Inc. Appears on *Bringing It All Back Home. This recording also appears on *Bob Dylan's Greatest Hits*. An acoustic outtake appears on *The Bootleg Series, Vols. 1-3*.

"Suze (The Cough Song)." Copyright 1991, Special Rider Music. Appears on *The Bootleg Series, Vols. 1-3*.

"Sweetheart Like You." Copyright 1983, Special Rider Music. Appears on *Infidels*.

"Take It or Leave It." Copyright 1978, Special Rider Music.

"Talking Bear Mountain Picnic Massacre Blues." Copyright 1962, 1965, Duchess Music Corp. Appears on *The Bootleg Series, Vols. 1-3*.

"Talking Devil." Copyright 1963, Special Rider Music. Appears on *Broadside Ballads, Vol. I*.

"Talking Folkore Center." Copyright 1962, The Folklore Center.

"Talking New York." Copyright 1962, 1965, Duchess Music Corp. Appears on *Bob Dylan*.

"Talkin' Hava Negeilah Blues." Copyright 1963, 1968, Warner Bros. Inc. Appears on *The Bootleg Series, Vols. 1-3*.

"Talkin' John Birch Paranoid Blues." Copyright 1970, Special Rider Music. Appears on some early versions of *The Freewheelin' Bob Dylan* under the title "Talkin' John Birch Society Blues." Appears on *The Bootleg Series, Vols. 1-3*. First published under the title "Talking John Birch."

"Talkin' World War III Blues." Copyright 1963, 1966, Warner Bros. Inc. Appears on *The Freewheelin' Bob Dylan*.

"Tangled Up in Blue." Copyright 1974, 1975, Ram's Horn Music. Appears on *Blood on the Tracks*. This recording also appears on *Biograph*. An outtake appears on *The Bootleg Series, Vols. 1-3*. A concert recording appears on *Real Live*.

"Tears of Rage." Written with Richard Manuel. Copyright 1968, 1970, Dwarf Music. Appears on *The Basement Tapes*.

"Tell Me." Copyright 1983, Special Rider Music. Appears on *The Bootleg Series, Vols. 1-3*.

"Tell Me Momma." Copyright 1971, 1973, Dwarf Music. Has not appeared on an album, though it was performed in concert in 1966.

"Tell Me That It Isn't True." Copyright 1969, Big Sky Music. Appears on *Nashville Skyline*.

"Tell Me the Truth One Time." Written with Helena Springs. Copyright 1979, Special Rider Music.

"Temporary Like Achilles." Copyright 1966, Dwarf Music. Appears on *Blonde on Blonde*.

"10,000 Men." Copyright 1990, Special Rider Music. Appears on *Under the Red Sky*.

"The Ugliest Girl in the World." Written with Robert Hunter. Copyright 1988, Special Rider Music and Ice Nine Music. Appears on *Down in the Groove*.

"Thief on the Cross." Copyright 1982, Special Rider Music. Has not appeared on an album, though it was performed in concert in 1981.

"This Way That Way." Copyright 1978, Special Rider Music.

"This Wheel's on Fire." Written with Rick Danko. Copyright 1967, 1970, Dwarf Music. Appears on *The Basement Tapes*.

"Three Angels." Copyright 1970, Big Sky Music. Appears on *New Morning*.

"Tight Connection to My Heart (Has Anybody Seen My Love?)." Copyright 1985, Special Rider Music. Appears on *Empire Burlesque*.

"Time Passes Slowly." Copyright 1970, Big Sky Music. Appears on *New Morning* and on

Biograph.

"The Times They Are A-Changin'." Copyright 1963, 1964, Warner Bros. Inc. This recording also appears on *Bob Dylan's Greatest Hits* and *Biograph*. A live recording appears on *Bob Dylan at Budokan* and a demonstration recording appears on *The Bootleg Series, Vols. 1-3*.

"Tiny Montgomery." Copyright 1967, 1975, Dwarf Music. Appears on *The Basement Tapes*.

"To Be Alone with You." Copyright 1969, Big Sky Music. Appears on *Nashville Skyline*.

"Tombstone Blues." Copyright 1965, Warner Bros. Inc. Appears on *Highway 61 Revisited*. This recording also appears on *Biograph*. Concert recording appears on *Real Live*.

"Tomorrow Is a Long Time." Copyright 1963, Warner Bros. Inc. Live recording appears on *Bob Dylan's Greatest Hits, Vol. II*.

"Tonight I'll Be Staying Here With You." Copyright 1969, Big Sky Music. Appears on *Nashville Skyline*. This recording also appears on *Bob Dylan's Greatest Hits, Vol. II*.

"Too Much of Nothing." Copyright 1967, 1970, Dwarf Music. Appears on *The Basement Tapes*.

"To Ramona." Copyright 1964, Warner Bros. Inc. Appears on *Another Side of Bob Dylan*. This recording also appears on *Biograph*.

"Tough Mama." Copyright 1973, 1974, Ram's Horn Music. Appears on *Planet Waves*.

"Train A-Travelin'." Copyright 1968, Warner Bros. Inc. Appears on *Broadside Reunion*.

"Trouble." Copyright 1981, Special Rider Music. Appears on *Shot of Love*.

"Trouble In Mind." Copyright 1979, Special Rider Music. Has not appeared on an album, though it was the B-side of the "Gotta Serve Somebody" single.

"True Love Tends to Forget." Copyright 1978, Special Rider Music. Appears on *Street-Legal*.

"Trust Yourself." Copyright 1985, Special Rider Music. Appears on *Empire Burlesque*.

"Turkey Chase." Copyright 1973, Ram's Horn Music. Appears on *Pat Garrett and Billy the Kid*.

"T.V. Talkin' Song." Copyright 1990, Special Rider Music. Appears on *Under the Red Sky*.

"Tweeter and the Monkey Man." Written with George Harrison, Jeff Lynne, Roy Orbison and Tom Petty. Copyright 1988, Special Rider Music, Ganga Publishing B.V., SBK-Blackwood Music, Orbisongs Music and Gone Gator Music. Appears on The Traveling Wilburys' *Volume One*.

"2 x 2." Copyright 1990, Special Rider Music. Appears on *Under the Red Sky*.

"Unbelievable." Copyright 1990, Special Rider Music. Appears on *Under the Red Sky*.

"Under the Red Sky." Copyright 1990, Special Rider Music. Appears on *Under the Red Sky*.

"Under Your Spell." Written with Carole Bayer Sager. Copyright 1986, Special Rider Music and Carole Bayer Sager. Appears on *Knocked Out Loaded*.

"Union Sundown." Copyright 1983, Special Rider Music. Appears on *Infidels*.

"Up to Me." Copyright 1974, 1976, Ram's Horn Music. Appears on *Biograph*.

"The Very Thought of You." Copyright 1985, Special Rider Music.

"Visions of Johanna." Copyright 1966, Dwarf Music. Appears on *Blonde on Blonde*. Originally titled "Freeze Out." Live recording appears on *Biograph*.

"Waiting to Get Beat." Copyright 1985, Special Rider Music.

"Walkin' Down the Line." Copyright 1963, 1965, Warner Bros. Inc. Appears on *The Boot-

leg Series, Vols. 1-3.

"Walk Out in the Rain." Written with Helena Springs. Copyright 1978, Special Rider Music.

"Wallflower." Copyright 1971, 1976, Ram's Horn Music. Appears on *The Bootleg Series*.

"Walls of Red Wing." Copyright 1963, Warner Bros. Inc. Appears on *The Bootleg Series*.

"The Wandering Kind." Written with Helena Springs. Copyright 1979, Special Rider Music.

"Wanted Man." Copyright 1969, 1976, Big Sky Music.

"Watching the River Flow." Copyright 1971, Big Sky Music. Appears on *Bob Dylan's Greatest Hits, Vol. II*.

"Watered-Down Love." Copyright 1981, Special Rider Music. Appears on *Shot of Love*.

"We Better Talk This Over." Copyright 1978, Special Rider Music. Appears on *Street-Legal*.

"Wedding Song." Copyright 1973, 1974, Ram's Horn Music. Appears on *Planet Waves*.

"Went to See the Gypsy." Copyright 1970, Big Sky Music. Appears on *New Morning*.

"What Can I Do For You?" Copyright 1980, Special Rider Music. Appears on *Saved*.

"Whatcha Gonna Do?" Copyright 1963, 1966, Warner Bros. Inc.

"What Good Am I?" Copyright 1989, Special Rider Music. Appears on *Oh Mercy*.

"What Kind of Friend Is This?" Copyright 1978, Dwarf Music. Has not appeared on an album, though Dylan performs it in the film *Eat the Document*.

"What's the Matter?" Written with Helena Springs. Copyright 1979, Special Rider Music.

"What Was It You Wanted?" Copyright 1989, Special Rider Music. Appears on *Oh Mercy*.

"What Will You Do When Jesus Comes?" Copyright 1977, 1978, Ram's Horn Music. Has not appeared on an album, though it is performed in the film *Renaldo and Clara*.

"When He Returns." Copyright 1979, Special Rider Music. Appears on *Slow Train Coming*.

"When I Paint My Masterpiece." Copyright 1971, 1972, Big Sky Music. Appears on *Bob Dylan's Greatest Hits, Vol. II*.

"When the Night Comes Falling from the Sky." Copyright 1985, Special Rider Music. Appears on *Empire Burlesque*. An early attempt at the song appears on *The Bootleg Series, Vols. 1-3*.

"When the Ship Comes In." Copyright 1963, 1964, Warner Bros. Inc. Appears on *The Times They Are A-Changin'*. Demonstration recording appears on *The Bootleg Series, Vols. 1-3*.

"When You Gonna Wake Up?" Copyright 1979, Special Rider Music. Appears on *Slow Train Coming*.

"Where Are You Tonight? (Journey through Dark Heat)." Copyright 1978, Special Rider Music. Appears on *Street-Legal*.

"Where Teardrops Fall." Copyright 1989, Special Rider Music. Appears on *Oh Mercy*.

"Where Were You Last Night?" Written with George Harrison, Jeff Lynne and Tom Petty. Copyright 1990, Special Rider Music, Ganga Publishing B.V., SBK-Blackwood Music and Gone Gator Music. Appears on The Traveling Wilburys' *Volume Three*.

"Who Killed Davey Moore?" Copyright 1964, 1965, Warner Bros. Inc. A live recording from October 26, 1963 concert at Carnegie Hall was included on *The Bootleg Series*.

"Who Loves You More." Copyright 1984, Special Rider Music.

"The Wicked Messenger." Copyright 1968, Dwarf Music. Appears on *John Wesley Harding*.

"Wiggle Wiggle." Copyright 1990, Special Rider Music. Appears on *Under the Red Sky*.

"Wigwam." Copyright 1970, Big Sky Music. Appears on *Self Portrait*.

"Wilbury Twist." Written with George Harrison, Jeff Lynne and Tom Petty. Copyright 1990, Special Rider Music, Ganga Publishing B.V., SBK-Blackwood Music and Gone Gator Music. Appears on The Traveling Wilburys' *Volume Three*.

"Winterlude." Copyright 1970, Big Sky Music. Appears on *New Morning*.

"With God on Our Side." Copyright 1963, Warner Bros. Inc. Appears on *The Times They Are A-Changin'*. Live recording with Joan Baez appears on *Newport Broadside*.

"Without You." Written with Helena Springs. Copyright 1979, Special Rider Music.

"Wolf." Copyright 1984, Special Rider Music.

"Woogie Boogie." Copyright 1970, Big Sky Music. Appears on *Self Portrait*.

"Ye Shall Be Changed." Copyright 1979, Special Rider Music. Appears on *The Bootleg Series, Vols. 1-3*.

"Yonder Comes Sin." Copyright 1980, Special Rider Music. Has not appeared on an album, but played during rehearsals for the gospel tours.

"You Ain't Goin' Nowhere." Copyright 1967, 1972, Dwarf Music. Appears on *The Basement Tapes*. A later version appeared on *Bob Dylan's Greatest Hits, Vol. II*.

"You Angel You." Copyright 1973, 1974, Ram's Horn Music. Appears on *Planet Waves*. This recording also appears on *Biograph*.

"You Changed My Life." Copyright 1982, Special Rider Music. Appears on *The Bootleg Series, Vols. 1-3*.

"You'd Like Me to Go." Copyright 1978, Special Rider Music.

"You're a Big Girl Now." Copyright 1974, 1975, Ram's Horn Music. Appears on *Blood on the Tracks*. A live recording appears on *Hard Rain*. An outtake of the song appears on *Biograph*.

"You're Gonna Make Me Lonesome When You Go." Copyright 1974, 1975, Ram's Horn Music. Appears on *Blood on the Tracks*.

"Your Rockin' Chair." Copyright 1978, Special Rider Music.

"You Took My Breath Away." Written with George Harrison, Jeff Lynne and Tom Petty. Copyright 1990, Special Rider Music, Ganga Publishing B.V., SBK-Blackwood Music and Gone Gator Music. Appears on The Traveling Wilburys' *Volume Three*.

Part II: Works About Bob Dylan

Books

Aaseng, Nathan. *Bob Dylan: Spellbinding Songwriter*. Minneapolis: Lerner Press, 1987.

Amendt, Gunter. *Reunion Sundown: Bob Dylan in Europa*. Munich: Hobo Press, 1985.

Anderson, Dennis. *The Hollow Horn: Bob Dylan's Reception in the United States and Germany*. Munich: Hobo Press, 1981.

Baez, Joan. *Daybreak*. New York: The Dial Press, 1968.

———. *And a Voice to Sing With*. New York: Summit Books, 1987.

Bauldie, John. *Bob Dylan and Desire*. Romford, England: Wanted Man Press, 1982.

———. *Wanted Man: In Search of Bob Dylan*. London: Black Spring Press, 1990; New York: The Citadel Press, 1991.

Bowden, Betsy. *Performed Literature: Words and Music by Bob Dylan*. Bloomington: Indiana University Press, 1982.

Cable, Paul. *Bob Dylan: His Unreleased Recordings*. London: Scorpion Publications, Ltd./Dark Star, 1978; New York: Schirmer Books, 1980.

Cartwright, Bert. *The Bible in the Lyrics of Bob Dylan*. Romford, England: Wanted Man Press, 1985.

Cott, Jonathan. *Dylan*. New York: Rolling Stone Press/Summit Books, 1984.

Davis, Clive, with James Willwerth. *Clive: Inside the Record Business*. New York: Morrow, 1975.

Day, Aidan. *Escaping on the Run*. Romford, England: Wanted Man Press, 1984.

Denisoff, R. Serge. *Great Day Coming: Folk Music and the American Left*. Urbana: University of Illinois Press, 1972.

———. *Sing a Song of Social Significance*. Bowling Green, Ohio: Bowling Green Popular Press, 1972.

———, and Richard Peterson, eds. *The Sounds of Social Change: Studies in Popular Culture*. Chicago: Rand McNally, 1972.

De Somogyi, Mick. *Jokerman and Thieves: Bob Dylan and the Ballad Tradition*. Romford, England: Wanted Man Press, 1986.

DeTurk, David A. and A. Poulin Jr. *The American Folk Scene*. New York: Dell, 1967.

Dickstein, Morris. *Gates of Eden: American Culture in the Sixties*. New York: Basic Books, 1977.

Diddle, Gavin. *Images and Assorted Facts: A Peek Behind the Picture Frame*. Manchester, England: The Print Centre, 1983.

Dorman, James E. *Recorded Dylan*. San Francisco: Soma Press, 1982.

Dowley, Tim, and Barry Dunnage. *Bob Dylan: From a Hard Rain to a Slow Train*. New York: Hippocrene Books, 1982.

Dreau, Jean Louis and Robert Schlockoff. *Hypnotist Collectors: An International Illustrated Discography*. Paris: Media Presse, 1989.

Ducray, F., P. Manoeuvre, H. Muller, and J. Vassal. *Dylan*. Paris: Albin Michel, 1975. (Revised in 1978.)

Dundas, Glen. *Tangled Up in Tapes: A Collector's Guide to Tape Recordings of Bob Dylan*. Thunder Bay, Ontario: SMA Services, 1987.

Fong-Torres, Ben. *What's That Sound?: Readings in Contemporary Music*.

New York: Anchor Books, 1976.

Gans, Terry. *What's Real and What is Not: The Myth of Protest*. Munich: Hobo Press, 1983.

Gray, Michael. *The Art of Bob Dylan*. London: Hamlyn Press, 1981; New York: Dutton, 1973.

_____, and John Bauldie, eds. *All across the Telegraph*. London: Sidgwick and Jackson, 1987.

Goldstein, Richard. *The Poetry of Rock*. New York: Bantam Books, 1969.

Gross, Michael. *Bob Dylan: An Illustrated History*. New York: Grosset and Dunlap, 1978; rev. ed., New York: Tempo Books, 1980. (Credit reads, "Produced by Michael Gross with a text by Robert Alexander.")

_____. *Bob Dylan: Une Historie Illustree*. Paris: Albin Michel, 1980.

Hammond, John, with Irving Townsend. *John Hammond on Record*. New York: Ridge Press/Summit Books, 1977.

Hampton, Wayne. *Guerrilla Minstrels*. Knoxville: University of Tennessee Press, 1987.

Herdman, John. *Voice without Restraint: Bob Dylan's Lyrics and Their Background*. New York: Delilah Books, 1982; Edinburgh: Harris Press, 1982.

Heylin, Clinton. *Bob Dylan--Stolen Moments*. Romford, England: Wanted Man Press, 1988.

_____. *Rain Unravelled Tales: A Rumourography*. Romford, England: Wanted Man Press, 1982.

_____. *To Live Outside the Law: A Guide to Bob Dylan Bootlegs*. London: Labour of Love Productions, 1989.

_____. *Bob Dylan: Behind the Shades*. New York: Summit Books, 1991.

Hinchey, John. *Bob Dylan's Slow Train*. Romford, England: Wanted Man Press, 1982.

Hoggard, Stuart, and Jim Shields. *Bob Dylan: An Illustrated Discography*. Dumbarton, Scotland: Transmedia Express, 1979.

Humphries, Patrick, and John Bauldie. *Oh No! Not Another Bob Dylan Book*. London: Square One Books, 1991.

_____. *Absolutely Dylan*. New York: Viking Studio Books, 1991.

Karpel, Craig. *The Tarantula in Me: Behind Bob Dylan's Novel*. San Francisco: Klohn, 1973.

Klein, Joe. *Woody Guthrie: A Life* (New York: Knopf, 1985).

Kooper, Al. *Backstage Passes: Rock 'n' Roll Life in the Sixties*. New York: Stein and Day, 1977.

Kramer, Daniel. *Bob Dylan*. New York: The Citadel Press, 1967; rev. ed., 1991.

Krogsgaard, Michael. *Twenty Years of Recording: The Bob Dylan Reference Book*. Copenhagen: Scandanavian Society of Rock Research, 1980.

_____. *Master of the Tracks: The Bob Dylan Reference Book of Recording*. Copenhagen: Scandanavian Society of Rock Research, 1988.

_____. *Positively Bob Dylan: A Thirty-Year Discography, Concert and Recording Session Guide*. Ann Arbor, Mich.: Popular Culture, Ink., 1991.
Landy, Elliot. *Woodstock Vision*. Hamburg, Germany: Rowohlt, 1984.
McGregor, Craig, ed. *Bob Dylan: A Retrospective*. New York: Morrow, 1972; London: Angus and Robertson, 1980.
_____, ed. *Bob Dylan: The Early Years*. New York: Da Capo Press, 1990. (Revised edition of the above.)
Mellers, Wilfrid. *A Darker Shade of Pale*. London: Faber and Faber, 1984; New York: Oxford University Press, 1985.
Miles, Barry, ed. *Bob Dylan: In His Own Words*. New York: Quick Fox Press, 1978; London: Omnibus Press, 1978.
_____. *Bob Dylan*. London: Big O Publishing Ltd., 1978.
Pennebaker, D. A. *Bob Dylan: Don't Look Back*. New York: Ballantine Books, 1968.
Pichaske, David R. *Beaowulf to Beatles: Approaches to Poetry*. New York: Free Press, 1972.
Pickering, Stephen. *Bob Dylan Approximately: A Portrait of the Jewish Poet in Search of God*. New York: David MacKay, 1975.
Ribakove, Sy, and Barbara Ribakove. *Folk-Rock: The Bob Dylan Story*. New York: Dell, 1966.
Riley, Tim. *Hard Rain: A Dylan Commentary*. New York: Knopf, 1992.
Rinzler, Alan. *Bob Dylan: The Illustrated Record*. New York: Harmony Books, 1978.
Robinson, Earl, ed. *Young Folk Songbook*. New York: Simon and Schuster, 1963.
Rodnitzky, Jerome L. *Minstrels of the Dawn: The Folk Protest Singer as Cultural Hero*. Chicago: Nelson-Hall, 1976.
Rolling Stone editors. *Knockin' on Dylan's Door: On the Road in '74*. New York: Pocket Books, 1974.
Roques, Dominique. *The Great White Answers*. Salindres, France: Southern Live Oak Productions, 1980.
Sarlin, Bob. *Turn it Up! I Can't Hear the Words*. New York: Simon and Schuster, 1973.
Scaduto, Anthony. *Bob Dylan: An Intimate Biography*. New York: Grosset and Dunlap, 1971; London: W. H. Allen, 1972. (Updated, with an afterward by Steven Gaines. Rev. ed., New York: Signet/New American Library, 1979.
Shelton, Robert. *No Direction Home: The Life and Music of Bob Dylan*. New York: Beech Tree Books/Morrow, 1986.
Shepard, Sam. *Rolling Thunder Logbook*. New York: The Viking Press, 1977; London: Penguin, 1978.
Sloman, Larry. *On the Road with Bob Dylan: Rolling With the Thunder*. New York: Bantam Books, 1978.

Smith, Joe. *Off the Record: An Oral History of Popular Music.* New York: Warner Books, 1988.
Spitz, Bob. *Dylan: A Biography.* New York: McGraw-Hill, 1989.
Thompson, Toby. *Positively Main Street: An Unorthodox View of Bob Dylan.* New York: Coward-McCann, 1971; London: New English Library, 1972.
Thomson, Elizabeth M., ed. *Conclusions on the Wall: New Essays on Bob Dylan.* Manchester, England: Thin Man Press, 1980.
____, and David Gutman. *A Dylan Companion.* New York: Delta Books, 1991.
von Schmidt, Eric, and Jim Rooney. *Baby Let Me Follow You Down: The Illustrated Story of the Cambridge Folk Years.* New York: Anchor Books, 1979.
Weberman, A.J. *My Life in Garbology.* New York: Stonehill Press, 1980.
Williams, Don. *Bob Dylan: The Man, the Music, the Message.* Englewood Cliffs, N. J.: Fleming Revell, 1985.
Williams, Paul. *Dylan: What Happened?* San Francisco: Entwhistle Books, 1979.
____. *Dylan: One Year Later.* San Francisco: (Privately published), 1980.
____. *Performing Artist: The Music of Bob Dylan, Volume 1, 1960-1973.* Novato, California: Underwood-Miller, 1990.
Williams, Richard. *Dylan: A Man Called Alias.* New York: Henry Holt, 1992.
Wurlitzer, Rudolph. *Pat Garrett and Billy the Kid.* New York: New American Library, 1973.
Yenne, Bill. *One Foot on the Highway: Bob Dylan on Tour 1974.* San Francisco: Klohne Books, 1974.

Magazines Devoted to Bob Dylan and His Work

Isis. Edited by Derrick Barker. Published since 1986 in Grand Junction, Colorado.
Look Back. Edited by Tim Dunn and Rob Whitehouse. Published since 1984 in Chardon, Ohio.
The Telegraph. Edited by John Bauldie. Published since November 1981 in Romford, England.
The Wicked Messenger. Edited by Ian Woodward. Published since 1980, available since 1989 as a supplement to *Look Back.*

Articles in North American Journals and Literary Reviews

Campbell, Greg M. "Bob Dylan and the Pastoral Apocalypse." *Journal of Popular Culture*, 8, no. 4 (Spring 1975).
Cash, Johnny. "A Letter From Johnny Cash." *Broadside*, no. 41 (10 March 1964).

Denisoff, R. Serge. "Dylan: Hero or Villain?" *Broadside*, no. 45 (May 15, 1964).
―― and David Fandray. "The Political Side of Bob Dylan." *Popular Music and Society*, 5, no. 5 (1977).
Dunson, Josh. "Yevtushenko, Lorca and Bob Dylan." *Broadside*, no. 27 (June 1963).
Hattenhauer, Darryl. "Bob Dylan as Hero." *Southern Folklore Quarterly*, 45 (Fall 1981).
Lhamon, W. T. "Poplore and Bob Dylan." the *Bennington Review*, no. 3 (December 1978).
Lindstrom, Naomi. "Dylan: Song Returns to Poetry." *Texas Quarterly*, 19, no. 4 (Winter 1976).
Mood, John J. "On Behalf of the Later Dylan: A Study of Bob Dylan's Lyrics." *Encounter* (Autumn 1967).
Nelson, Paul. "Newport Folk Festival 1965." *Sing Out*, 15, no. 5 (November 1965): 3-8.
――. "Bob Dylan: Another View." *Sing Out* (February/March 1966).
――. "Don't Look Back." *Sing Out* (January 1968).
Ochs, Phil. "The Art of Bob Dylan's Hattie Carroll." *Broadside*, no. 48 (20 July 1964).
Pankake, John and Paul Nelson. "Bob Dylan." *Little Sandy Review*, no. 22 (1962).
Paxton, Tom. "Folk Rot." *Sing Out*, 15, no. 6 (1966): 103-4.
Poague, Leland A. "Dylan as Auteur." *Journal of Popular Culture* (Summer 1974).
Rose, Stephen C. "Bob Dylan as Theologian." *Renewal* (October/November 1965).
Scalet, Elizabeth Butler. "The Song Was There Before Me: The Influence of Traditional Music on the Songs of Bob Dylan." *Heritage of Kansas*, 8, no. 2, (1975).
Silber, Irwin. "An Open Letter to Bob Dylan." *Sing Out*, 14, no. 5 (1964): 22-3.
――. "Topical Song: Polarization Sets In." *Sing Out* (February/March 1966).
Strouse, Jean. "Bob Dylan's Gentle Anarchy." *Commonweal* (1968).
Sumner, Carolyn. "The Ballad of Dylan and Bob." *Southwest Review* (Winter 1981).
Turner, Gil. "A New Voice Singing New Songs." *Sing Out*, 12, no. 4 (October/November 1962): 5-7.
Weberman, A. J. "John Wesley Harding is Bob Dylan." *Broadside*, no. 93 (July/August 1968).
Willis, Ellen. "The Sound of Bob Dylan." *Commentary* (November 1967).
Wolfe, Paul. "The New Dylan." *Broadside*, no. 53 (December 1964).

Selected North American Magazine Articles

Altman, Billy. "Knockin' on Woody's Door." *Entertainment Weekly*, 16 November 1992.
Bangs, Lester. "Bob Dylan's Dalliance with Mafia Chic." *Creem*, April 1976.
Bloomfield, Mike. "Impressions of Bob Dylan." *Hit Parader*, June 1968.
"Bob Dylan Sings in Washington Square." *Seventeen*. September 1962.
"Bob Dylan, 22, a Folknik Hero." *Variety*, 30 October 1963.
Castin, S. "Folk Rock's Mr. Tambourine Man." *Look*, 8 March 1966.
Cocks, Jay. "Bringing Folk Back Home," *Time*, 26 October 1992.
Cott, Jonathan. "Dylan Film: Opening Night Fast on the Eye." *Rolling Stone*, 4 March 1971.
____. "I Dreamed I Saw Bob Dylan." *Rolling Stone*, 2 September 1971.
Eustis, Helen. "A Middle-Aged Mother Visits the Teen Scene." *McCall's*, August 1966.
Farina, Richard. "Baez and Dylan: A Generation Singing Out." *Mademoiselle*, August 1964.
Gant, Sandy. "A Discography of Bob Dylan." *New York*, July 1976.
Gleason, Ralph J. "The Times They Are A-Changin'." *Ramparts*, April 1965.
____. "The Children's Crusade." *Ramparts*, March 1966.
____. "We've Got Dylan Back Again." *Rolling Stone*, 26 November 1970.
Goddard, J. R. "Records: Bobby Dylan." *Village Voice*, 26 April 1962.
Goldman, Albert. "That Angry Kid Has Gone All Over Romantic." *LIFE*, 23 May 1969.
Goldstein, Richard. "Growing Up with Bob Dylan." *New York*, 28 January 1974.
Gzowski, Peter. "Dylan: An Exlosion of Poetry." *Maclean's*, 22 January 1966.
Hedgepath, William Bowling. "What Dylan Did." *Intellectual Digest*, February 1973.
Hentoff, Nat. "Folk, Folkum and the New Citybilly." *Playboy*, June 1963.
____. "The Crackin' Shakin' Breakin' Sounds." *New Yorker*, 24 October 1964.
Hopkins, Jerry. "'New' Dylan Album Bootlegged in L.A." *Rolling Stone*, 20 September 1969.
"I Am My Words." *Newsweek*, 4 November 1963.
Kael, Pauline. "The Calvary Gig." *New Yorker*, 13 February 1978.
Kittleson, Barry. "A Legend Under Construction: Folk Poet Dylan Weaves a Spell." *Billboard*, 27 April 1963.
Knobler, Peter. "Bob Dylan: A Gut Reaction." *Crawdaddy*, September 1973.
Kretchmer, Arthur. "It's All Right Ma, I'm Only Playing R&R." *Village Voice*, 5 August 1965.
Levinson, L.L. "Bob Dylan's Protest Songs Fill Carnegie With Teenster Fans." *Variety*, 30 October 1963.
Lhamon, W. T. "A Cut Above: 'Blood on the Tracks.'" *New Republic*, 5 April

1975.

———. "Bicentennial Dylan: Desire." *New Republic*, 14 February 1976.

Marcus, Greil. "Records [Devoted to *The Great White Wonder*]." *Rolling Stone*, 29 November 1969.

———. "Self Portrait No. 25." *Rolling Stone*, 23 July 1970.

McClure, Michael. "The Poet's Poet." *Rolling Stone*, 14 March 1974.

Sander, Ellen. "Bob Dylan Revisited." *Saturday Review*, 26 April 1969.

Scaduto, Anthony. "Won't You Listen to the Lambs, Bob Dylan?" *New York Times Magazine*, 28 November 1971.

Shepard, Sam. "True Dylan." *Esquire*, July 1987.

Shelton, Robert. "Dylan: The Charisma." *Cavalier*, July 1965.

Siegel, Jules. "Well, What Have We Here?" *Saturday Evening Post*, 30 July 1966.

Sloman, Larry. "Blood on the Tracks: Dylan Looks Back," *Rolling Stone*, 21 November 1974.

Smith, Patti. "Depletion behind a Positive Mask." *Creem*, April 1974.

Smucker, Tom. "Bob Dylan Meets the Revolution." *Fusion*, 31 October 1969.

Spender, Stephen and Frank Kermode. "The Metaphor at the End of the Funnel." *Esquire*, May 1972.

Stamaty, Mark Alan. "Bob Dylan: The Hottest Ticket in Town," the *New Yorker*, 2 November 1992.

Watt, Douglas. "Something is Happening Here." *The New Yorker*, 19 March 1966.

Welles, Chris. "The Angry Young Folk Singer." *LIFE*, 10 April 1963.

Weberman, A.J. "Bob Dylan's *Renaldo and Clara*." *High Times*, May 1978.

Wenner, Jann. "Dylan's Basement Tapes Should Be Released." *Rolling Stone*, 22 June 1968.

———. "The Slow Train is Coming." *Rolling Stone*, 20 September 1979.

Williams, Paul. "Understanding Dylan." *Crawdaddy*, August 1966.

Willis, Ellen. "Dylan." *Cheetah*, March 1967.

Wild, David. "Plans Set for Dylan Tribute," *Rolling Stone*, 29 October 1992.

Selected North American Newspaper Articles

Ashenmacher, Bob. "Dylan Talks." *Duluth News-Tribune and Herald*, 29 June 1986.

Bream, Jon. "The Many Faces of Bob Dylan." *Minneapolis Star and Tribune*.

Gilmore, Mikal. "Dylan Returns to the Material World." *Los Angeles Herald Examiner*, 30 October 1983.

Gleason, Ralph. "A Folk Singing Social Critic." *San Francisco Examiner*, 24 February 1964.

Goldstein, Richard. "Don't Look Back." *New York Times*, 22 October 1967.

Hilburn, Robert. "Bob Dylan at 42." *Los Angeles Times*, 30 October 1983.

Iachetta, Michael. "Scarred Bobby Dylan is Coming Back." *New York Daily News*, 8 May 1967.
Kramer, Daniel. "A Night With Bob Dylan." *New York Herald Tribune*, 12 December 1965.
Marsh, Dave. "Out of the 60's, into His 50's," the *New York Times*, 19 May 1991.
Pareles, Jon. "The Man Who Moved Rock into a New Era," the *New York Times*, 19 October 1992, p. B1.
Shelton, Robert. "A Distinctive Folk Song Stylist." *New York Times*, 29 September 1961.
_____. "Bob Dylan Sings His Compositions." *New York Times*, 13 April 1963.
_____. "Pop Singer and Songwriters Racing down Bob Dylan's Road." *New York Times*, 27 August 1965.
_____. "Dylan Hurt in Cycle Mishap." *New York Times*, 1 August 1966.
Vespiri, Maria. "Maryland Poor Hear Echo of '63 Killing." *St. Petersburg Times*, 9 June 1991.
Wyman, Bill. "Don't Think Twice." *Oakland Express*, 28 November 1986.

Mail-Order Book Finders Specializing in Dylan

My Back Pages, P.O. Box 2 (North P.D.O.), Manchester, M8 7BL, England.
Rolling Tomes, P.O. Box 1943, Grand Junction, Colorado 81502; phone: 303/245-4315

Notes

1. Clinton Heylin, *Bob Dylan: Behind the Shades* (New York: Summit Books, 1991), p. 335.
2. Anthony Scaduto, *Bob Dylan: An Intimate Biography* (New York: Grosset and Dunlap, 1971), jacket copy.
3. Robert Hilburn, "Dylan Now," the *Los Angeles Times Magazine*, 9 February 1992, p. 18.
4. Heylin, *Behind the Shades*, p. 467.
5. Michael Krogsgaard, *Positively Bob Dylan: A Thirty-Year Discopgraphy, Concert and Recording Session Guide* (Ann Arbor, Mich.: Popular Culture, Ink, 1991), documents Dylan's extensive touring schedule.
6. Hilburn, "Dylan Now," p. 42.

Part IV

Performances

Chapter 7

Recordings

BOB DYLAN'S ALBUMS HAVE NEVER BEEN out of print. Columbia Records has made sure that Dylan's music was accessible to his fans, even reissuing the albums that he made for Asylum Records. The Dylan catalog has been a steady money-maker for Columbia. Although he rarely produced a top-seller (*Desire* being an exception), his records have sold at a respectable level for an artist of his stature.

With his official releases so readily available, collectors have concentrated on trying to obtain Dylan rarities: singles released only overseas, Dylan performances on other artists' albums and recordings on obscure records under even more obscure pseudonymns. (Blind Boy Grunt is one Dylan disguise and Robert Milkwood Thomas is another.)

Since Dylan had little success as a singles artist, these old seven-inch records are sought by collectors and Dylan devotees. His first single, "Mixed Up Confusion," was released around the time of *The Freewheelin' Bob Dylan* in 1963. While the album is classic early Dylan--largely acoustic, in the folk/topical song tradition, the single is an early attempt at a rock 'n' roll sound. The single and its flip side, an alternate verison of "Corrina, Corrina," has never appeared on an American release. When the 1985 retrospective, *Biograph*, was issued, the generally excellent liner notes mistakenly cited the version of "Mixed Up Confusion" on that album as being the single, whereas actually it is an alternate take.

Some Dylan collectors are lucky enough to have early pressings of the "Positively 4th Street" single which was issued at the end of July 1965. A recording of "Can You Please Crawl Out Your Window?" was mistakenly issued with "Positively 4th Street" on the label. This version of "Can You

Please Crawl Out Your Window?" is *not* the same version of the song to be released as a single that November.

Dylan occasionally gave collectors prizes on the B-sides of singles drawn from albums. True Dylan fans probably bought *Blonde on Blonde* within moments of its arrival at their local record stores. Why would they buy "I Want You" when it was issued as a single off the album? The flip side was "Just Like Tom Thumb's Blues," which was from *Highway 61 Revisited*. Those completists who chose to buy the single (perhaps for the picture sleeve, which was an outtake from the *Blonde on Blonde* photo session) were surprised to discover a live version of "Tom Thumb's Blues" that had been recorded a month earlier, during Dylan's tour of Europe featuring a blistering performance by The Hawks.

Some other rare Dylan singles include the following: "George Jackson," his 1971 tribute to the slain Black Panther leader, has an acoustic version of the song on the A-side and a band version on the B-side. It has yet to appear on an American album. A live version of "Stuck Inside of Mobile with the Memphis Blues Again," drawn from the Rolling Thunder Revue, is backed with a Dylan-Jacques Levy composition, "Rita May," which has appeared on albums elsewhere in the world (notably in Japan, with *Masterpieces*), but not in the United States. The flip side of Dylan's first gospel single, "Gotta Serve Somebody," features "Trouble in Mind," which has yet to be collected on a Dylan album. The European single version of "Heart of Mine" includes a tribute to the Everly Brothers on the flip side: Dylan's version of "Let It Be Me," which differs from an earlier version on *Self Portrait*. A strong album track from *Infidels*, "Union Sundown," was released as a single in Europe with Dylan's version of Willie Nelson's "Angel Flying Too Close to the Ground."

These obscure recordings are prized by Dylan collectors, as are Dylan's guest appearances on albums by other artists. Some are uncredited. It has long been rumored that it is Dylan who played harmonica on George Harrison's "Apple Scruffs," from Harrison first solo album, *All Things Must Pass* (1970). More often, Dylan appeared under a pseudonymn. He was Blind Boy Grunt for a couple of albums which appeared under the aegis of *Broadside* magazine in the early 1960s. Some of these frequently bootlegged songs have been released on Dylan retrospectives ("Only a Hobo," for example, showed up on *The Bootleg Series, Vols. 1-3*). Others remain obscure. As Bob Landy (an anagram of Dylan), he appeared on the debut album of The Blues Project, a seminal 1960s rock/blues band. On a Ramblin' Jack Elliot album, he performed as Tedham Porterhouse. In the early 1970s, he showed up on a Steve Goodman album as Robert Milkwood Thomas, an allusion to Dylan Thomas's "Under Milk Wood."

Dylan also made some notable appearances under his famous performing name. Perhaps his most sustained and successful cameo appearance was on

George Harrison's *The Concert for Bangladesh*. This recording of the 1971 charity concerts at Madison Square Garden--with Dylan's performance drawn from the best versions of the songs at the matinee and evening shows--showcased Dylan doing five of his early 1960s classics: "A Hard Rain's A-Gonna Fall," "It Takes a Lot to Laugh, It Takes a Train to Cry," "Blowin' in the Wind," "Mr. Tambourine Man" and "Just Like a Woman." Backed by Harrison, Ringo Starr and Leon Russell, Dylan was in fine form. Dylan's performance at the farewell of The Band, which was released on *The Last Waltz* album, shows Dylan and his former accompanists running through "Baby, Let Me Follow You Down" (which they did twice), "I Don't Believe You (She Acts Like We Never Have Met)," "Forever Young," and, joined by the whole cast of the concert, "I Shall Be Released."

Dylan frequently blew harmonica on albums of friends ranging from Allen Ginsberg to Roger McGuinn to Warren Zevon. Dylan showed up to sing with Doug Sahm on a 1972 album and contributed background vocals on a Leonard Cohen song called "Don't Go Home with Your Hard-On." However, Dylan rarely dueted, though he apparently could do so with great success. He and Bette Midler recorded a hilarious version of "Buckets of Rain," on Midler's *Songs of the New Depression*. Dylan joined the superstar choruses for "We Are the World," a massive effort for African famine relief, and "Sun City," a recording that aimed to call consumer attention to the apartheid government in South Africa.

Dylan has contributed tracks to benefit recordings. For the Library of Congress tribute to Woody Guthrie and Huddie Ledbetter (Leadbelly), Dylan recorded "Pretty Boy Floyd." This late 1980s recording sounds like a lost outtake from his debut album, so fresh was his voice. For the Pediatric AIDS Foundation, Dylan contributed a version of the children's classic "This Old Man." Of the many artists who performed the collection of songs for and about children, Dylan was the most effective: It was simple, warm and direct.

As if these legitimate recordings were not enough, Dylan's bootleg albums were among the most sought-after. These illegal recordings--drawn from stolen tapes, concert performances, acetates, and other sources--began to appear in the late 1960s. Dylan, in fact, is the major artist to bring about the underground system. It was the news of the recordings of his basement sessions with The Hawks (later known as The Band) that created a demand for the songs. The first hugely successful bootleg, *The Great White Wonder*, was drawn largely from those sessions. Then the floodgates opened. Bootleg recordings of Dylan's 1961 performances in Minneapolis began to appear. Then came the series of bootlegs drawn from outtakes from his recording sessions, followed by live concert recordings, most notably his appearance at London's Royal Albert Hall in 1966, and finally, there were bootlegs of bootlegs. Dylan fans, to an extent that was perhaps second only to fans of The Grateful Dead, taped his concerts and shared these illicit recordings with other collectors. Each Dylan performance offered a brand-new intepretation of his classic songs, and serious collectors discuss the superior nature of the version of "One Too Many Mornings" on the 5th night of the tour to a version of the same song on the 12th.

Dylan was the first artist to learn how to fight bootleggers. Eight years after the basement sessions with The Band, he released *The Basement Tapes* on Columbia Records (1975). However, that did not stop the bootleggers of those sessions, because Dylan had not included every song that had been recorded. With *The Bootleg Series, Vols. 1-3* in 1991, Dylan again undercut them.

This chapter contains six sections: Section I is devoted to Dylan's official recordings released in the United States: the catalog, in short. Section II is a listing of significant Dylan releases in foreign markets--those not generally available in the United States. Section III is devoted to Dylan's appearances on recordings by other artists, while Section IV demonstrates some of Dylan's effect on musicians of this era. (This is a listing of recordings featuring Dylan not as a musician, but as a character.) Section V lists the artists who have performed the best known cover versions of Dylan songs. Many in Dylan's audience first heard of him through recordings by Peter, Paul and Mary, The Byrds or, perhaps, Guns n' Roses. This is not a definitive list of cover versions, but it does cite the most significant recordings. Section VI is devoted to bootlegs.

Section I:
Recordings by Bob Dylan Released in the United States

All songs are by Bob Dylan, unless indicated otherwise. Catalog numbers are listed for long-playing albums (LP), compact discs (CD) and cassettes (CS). Single records listed are those in seven-inch format, unless indicated otherwise. Singles and albums are listed in order of release (release dates refer to the original LP release).

Album: *Bob Dylan*
Columbia Records
LP: PC-8579; CD: CK-8579; CS: PCT-8579
Produced by John Hammond
Album notes by "Stacey Williams" (pseudonym of Robert Shelton); includes reprint of Shelton's *New York Times* article of 29 September 1961
Released 19 March 1962
"You're No Good" (Jesse Fuller)
"Talkin' New York"
"In My Time of Dyin'" (Blind Willie Johnson)
"Man of Constant Sorrow" (Traditional)
"Fixin' to Die" (Bukka White)

"Pretty Peggy-O" (Traditional)
"Highway 51" (Curtis Jones)
"Gospel Plow" (Traditional)
"Baby, Let Me Follow You Down" (Credited to Eric Von Schmidt)
"House of the Risin' Sun" (Traditional)
"Freight Train Blues" (John Lair)
"Song to Woody"
"See That My Grave Is Kept Clean" (Blind Lemon Jefferson)

Single: "Mixed Up Confusion"/"Corrina, Corrina" (Traditional)
Columbia 3-42656
Produced by John Hammond
Released 14 December 1962
Note: This version of "Corrina, Corrina" differs from the version on *The Freewheelin' Bob Dylan*.

Album: *The Freewheelin' Bob Dylan*
Columbia Records
LP: CL-1986; CD: CK-8786; CS: CS-8786
Produced by John Hammond, except (*) produced by Tom Wilson (uncredited)
Album notes by Nat Hentoff
Released 27 May 1963
Note: Some early promotional copies of this album include "Rambling Gambling Willie," "Rocks and Gravel" (a song by Brownie McGhee that is also known as "Solid Road" and performed as a medley with Leroy Carr's "Alabama Woman Blues"), "Let Me Die in My Footsteps" and "Talkin' John Birch Society Blues." Those copies (catalog no. CL-1986) were withdrawn. The song lineup here is the revised album.

"Blowin' in the Wind"
"Girl from the North Country" *
"Masters of War" *
"Down the Highway"
"Bob Dylan's Blues"
"A Hard Rain's A-Gonna Fall"
"Don't Think Twice, It's All Right"
"Bob Dylan's Dream" *
"Oxford Town"
"Talking World War III Blues" *
"Corrina, Corrina" (Traditional)
"Honey, Just Allow Me One More Chance" (Henry Thomas, arranged and adapted by Bob Dylan)
"I Shall Be Free"

Single: "Blowin' in the Wind"/"Don't Think Twice, It's All Right"
Columbia 4-42856
Produced by John Hammond
Released July 1963

Album: *The Times They Are A-Changin'*
Columbia Records
LP: CL-2105; CD: CK-8905; CS: CS-8905
Produced by Tom Wilson
Album notes by Bob Dylan, titled "11 Outlined Epitaphs"
Released 13 January 1964
"The Times They Are A-Changin'"
"Ballad of Hollis Brown"
"With God on Our Side"
"One Too Many Mornings"
"North Country Blues"
"Only a Pawn in Their Game"
"Boots of Spanish Leather"
"When the Ship Comes In"
"The Lonesome Death of Hattie Carroll"
"Restless Farewell"

Album: *Another Side of Bob Dylan*
Columbia Records
LP: CL-2193; CD: CK-8993; CS: CS-8993
Produced by Tom Wilson
Album notes by Bob Dylan, "Some Other Kinds of Songs . . ."
Released 8 August 1964
"All I Really Want to Do"
"Black Crow Blues"
"Spanish Harlem Incident"
"Chimes of Freedom"
"I Shall Be Free No. 10"
"To Ramona"
"Motorpsycho Nitemare"
"My Back Pages"
"I Don't Believe You"
"Ballad in Plain D"
"It Ain't Me Babe"

Album: *Bringing It All Back Home*
Columbia Records
LP: CL-2328; CD: CK-9128; CS: CS-9128
Produced by Tom Wilson
Album notes by Bob Dylan
Released 22 March 1965
"Subterranean Homesick Blues"
"She Belongs to Me"
"Maggie's Farm"
"Love Minus Zero/No Limit"
"Outlaw Blues"
"On the Road Again"

"Bob Dylan's 115th Dream"
"Mr. Tambourine Man"
"Gates of Eden"
"It's Alright Ma (I'm Only Bleeding)"
"It's All Over Now, Baby Blue"

Single: "Subterranean Homesick Blues"/"She Belongs to Me"
Columbia 4-43242
Produced by Tom Wilson
Released April 1965

Single: "Like a Rolling Stone"/"Gates of Eden"
Columbia 4-43346
Produced by Tom Wilson
Released 20 July 1965

Album: *Highway 61 Revisited*
Columbia Records
LP: CL-2389; CD: CK-9189; CS: CS-9189
Produced by Bob Johnston, except (*) produced by Tom Wilson
Album notes by Bob Dylan
Released 30 August 1965
"Like a Rolling Stone" *
"Tombstone Blues"
"It Takes a Lot to Laugh, It Takes a Train to Cry"
"From a Buick 6"
"Ballad of a Thin Man"
"Queen Jane Approximately"
"Highway 61 Revisited"
"Just Like Tom Thumb's Blues"
"Desolation Row"

Single: "Positively 4th Street"/"From a Buick 6"
Columbia 4-43389
Produced by Bob Johnston
Released 7 September 1965
Note: This single was mistakenly issued with an early take of "Can You Please Crawl Out Your Window?" on the A-side. That version was recorded with the musicians from the *Highway 61 Revisited* sessions.

Single: "Can You Please Crawl Out Your Window?"/"Highway 61 Revisited"
Columbia 4-43477
Produced by Bob Johnston
Released 30 November 1965
Note: This take of "Can You Please Crawl Out Your Window" is not the same as the one that was mistakenly issued as "Positively 4th Street." This version was recorded with the musicians later known as The Band.

Single: "One of Us Must Know (Sooner or Later)"/"Queen Jane Approximately"

Columbia 4-43541
Produced by Bob Johnston
Released February 1966

Single: "Rainy Day Women # 12 & 35"/"Pledging My Time"
Columbia 4-43592
Produced by Bob Johnston
Released April 1966

Album: *Blonde on Blonde*
Columbia Records
LP: C2L-41; CD: CK-841; CS: C2S-841
Produced by Bob Johnston
Released 16 May 1966
Note: Early CD releases of this album included trims (mostly early fades on several songs) and a verse cut from "Sad-Eyed Lady of the Lowlands." These cuts were reinstated on later versions of the CD.

"Rainy Day Women # 12 & 35"
"Pledging My Time"
"Visions of Johanna"
"One of Us Must Know (Sooner or Later)"
"I Want You"
"Stuck Inside of Mobile with the Memphis Blues Again"
"Leopard-Skin Pillbox Hat"
"Just Like a Woman"
"Most Likely You Go Your Way and I'll Go Mine"
"Temporary Like Achilles"
"Absolutely Sweet Marie"
"4th Time Around"
"Obviously 5 Believers"
"Sad-Eyed Lady of the Lowlands"

Single: "I Want You"/"Just Like Tom Thumb's Blues"
Columbia 4-43683
Produced by Bob Johnston
Released June 1966
Note: This version of "Just Like Tom Thumb's Blues" was recorded May 14, 1966, and differs from the version on *Highway 61 Revisited*.

Single: "Just Like a Woman"/"Obviously 5 Believers"
Columbia 4-43792
Produced by Bob Johnston
Released August 1966

Single: "Leopard-Skin Pillbox Hat"/"Most Likely You Go Your Way and I'll Go Mine"
Columbia 4-44069
Produced by Bob Johnston
Released March 1967

Album: *Bob Dylan's Greatest Hits*
Columbia Records
LP: KCL-2663; CD: CK-9463; CS: KCS-9463
Produced by Tom Wilson, except (*) produced by Bob Johnston and (**) produced by John Hammond
Released 27 March 1967
Note: The original LP release of this album included a poster of Dylan by graphic designer Milton Glaser.
"Rainy Day Women # 12 & 35" *
"Blowin' in the Wind" **
"The Times They Are A-Changin'"
"It Ain't Me Babe"
"Like a Rolling Stone"
"Mr. Tambourine Man"
"Subterranean Homesick Blues"
"I Want You" *
"Positively 4th Street" *
"Just Like a Woman" *

Album: *John Wesley Harding*
Columbia Records
LP: CL-2804; CD: CK-9604; CS: CS-9604
Produced by Bob Johnston
Album notes by Bob Dylan
Released 27 December 1967
"John Wesley Harding"
"As I Went Out One Morning"
"All along the Watchtower"
"I Dreamed I Saw St. Augustine"
"The Ballad of Frankie Lee and Judas Priest"
"Drifter's Escape"
"Dear Landlord"
"I Am a Lonesome Hobo"
"I Pity the Poor Immigrant"
"The Wicked Messenger"
"Down along the Cove"
"I'll Be Your Baby Tonight"

Album: *Nashville Skyline*
Columbia Records
LP: KCS-9825; CD: CK-9825; CS: PCT-9825
Produced by Bob Johnston
Album notes by Johnny Cash, "Of Bob Dylan"
Released 9 April 1969
"Girl from the North Country" (Duet with Johnny Cash)
"Nashville Skyline Rag"
"To Be Alone with You"

"I Threw It All Away"
"Peggy Day"
"Lay, Lady, Lay"
"One More Night"
"Tell Me That It Isn't True"
"Country Pie"
"Tonight I'll Be Staying Here with You"

Single: "I Threw It All Away"/"Drifter's Escape"
Columbia 4-44826
Produced by Bob Johnston
Released April 1969

Single: "Lay, Lady, Lay"/"Peggy Day"
Columbia 4-44926
Produced by Bob Johnston
Released July 1969

Single: "Tonight I'll Be Staying Here with You"/"Country Pie"
Columbia 4-45004
Produced by Bob Johnston
Released October 1969

Album: *Self Portrait*
Columbia Records
LP: C2X-30050; CD: C2K-30050; CS: C2T-30050
Produced by Bob Johnston
Released 8 June 1970
"All the Tired Horses"
"Alberta #1"
"I Forgot More Than You'll Ever Know" (Cecil A. Null)
"Days of '49" (Traditional)
"Early Mornin' Rain" (Gordon Lightfoot)
"In Search of Little Sadie"
"Let It Be Me" (M. Curtis, Pierre Delano and Gilbert Becaud)
"Little Sadie"
"Woogie Boogie"
"Belle Isle"
"Living the Blues"
"Like a Rolling Stone"
"Copper Kettle" (Albert Frank Beddoe)
"Gotta Travel On" (Paul Clayton, Larry Ehrlich, David Lazar and Tom Six)
"Blue Moon" (Richard Rodgers and Lorenz Hart)
"The Boxer" (Paul Simon)
"The Mighty Quinn (Quinn the Eskimo)"
"Take Me As I Am (Or Let Me Go)" (Boudleaux Bryant)
"Take a Message to Mary" (Felice Bryant and Boudleaux Bryant)

"It Hurts Me Too" (Tampa Red; arrangement by Elmore James)
"Minstrel Boy"
"She Belongs to Me"
"Wigwam"
"Alberta #2"

Single: "Wigwam"/"Copper Kettle" (Albert Frank Beddoe)
Columbia 4-45199
Produced by Bob Johnston
Released July 1970

Album: *New Morning*
Columbia Records
LP: KC-30290; CD: CK-30290; CS: PCT-30290
Produced by Bob Johnston
Released 21 October 1970
"If Not For You"
"Day of the Locusts"
"Time Passes Slowly"
"Went to See the Gypsy"
"Winterlude"
"If Dogs Run Free"
"New Morning"
"Sign on the Window"
"One More Weekend"
"The Man in Me"
"Three Angels"
"Father of Night"

Single: "Watching the River Flow"/"Spanish Is the Loving Tongue" (Charles Badger Clark)
Columbia 4-45409
Side A produced by Leon Russell
Side B produced by Bob Johnston
Released 3 June 1971

Single: "George Jackson" (band version)/"George Jackson" (solo version)
Columbia 4-45516
Produced by Bob Dylan
Released 4 November 1971

Album: *Bob Dylan's Greatest Hits, Vol. II*
Columbia Records
LP: KG-31120; CD: C2K-31120; CS: CGT-31120
Produced by Bob Johnston, except (*) produced by Leon Russell, (**) produced by John Hammond, (***) produced by Tom Wilson, (#) producer unknown, but probably Tom Wilson, and (##) uncredited, but probably Bob Dylan and Happy Traum
Released 17 November 1971
"Watching the River Flow" *

"Don't Think Twice, It's All Right" **
"Lay, Lady, Lay"
"Stuck Inside of Mobile with the Memphis Blues Again"
"I'll Be Your Baby Tonight"
"All I Really Want to Do" ***
"My Back Pages" ***
"Maggie's Farm" ***
"Tonight I'll Be Staying Here with You"
"She Belongs to Me" ***
"All along the Watchtower"
"The Mighty Quinn (Quinn the Eskimo)"
"Just Like Tom Thumb's Blues"
"A Hard Rain's A-Gonna Fall" **
"If Not for You"
"It's All Over Now, Baby Blue" ***
"Tomorrow Is a Long Time" #
"When I Paint My Masterpiece" *
"I Shall Be Released" ##
"You Ain't Goin' Nowhere" ##
"Down in the Flood (Crash on the Levee)" ##

Album: *Pat Garrett and Billy the Kid*
Columbia Records
LP: KC-32460; CD: CK-32460; CS: PCT-32460
Produced by Gordon Carroll
Released 13 July 1973
Note: Album credit reads "Bob Dylan/Soundtrack"
"Main Title Theme (Billy)"
"Cantina Theme (Workin' for the Law)"
"Billy 1"
"Bunkhouse Theme"
"River Theme"
"Turkey Chase"
"Knockin' on Heaven's Door"
"Final Theme"
"Billy 4"
"Billy 7"

Single: "Knockin' on Heaven's Door"/"Turkey Chase"
Columbia 4-45913
Produced by Gordon Carroll
Released August 1973

Album: *Dylan*
Columbia Records
LP: PC-32747; CS: PCT-32747

Produced by Bob Johnston
Released 16 November 1973
Note: Credit reads "original sessions produced by Bob Johnston." The version of "Spanish Is the Loving Tongue" differs from the single release of 1971. This album has not been issued on compact disc in the United States.

"Lily of the West" (Traditional, arranged by E. Davies and J. Peterson)
"Can't Help Falling in Love" (George Weiss, Hugo Peretti and Luigi Creatore)
"Sarah Jane" (Traditional)
"The Ballad of Ira Hayes" (Peter LaFarge)
"Mr. Bojangles" (Jerry Jeff Walker)
"Mary Ann" (Traditional)
"Big Yellow Taxi" (Joni Mitchell)
"A Fool Such as I" (Bill Trader)
"Spanish Is the Loving Tongue" (Charles Badger Clark)

Single: "A Fool Such as I" (Bill Trader)/"Lily of the West" (Traditional, arranged by E. Davies and J. Peterson)
Columbia 4-33259
Produced by Bob Johnston
Released December 1973

Album: *Planet Waves*
Asylum Records
LP: S-7E-1003
Producer uncredited, but probably Bob Dylan and The Band; Robbie Robertson credited for "special assistance."
Album notes by Bob Dylan
Released 17 January 1974
This album was reissued by Columbia Records in April 1982
LP: PC-37637; CD: CK-37637; CS: PCT-37637
"On a Night Like This"
"Going Going Gone"
"Tough Mama"
"Hazel"
"Something There Is about You"
"Forever Young" (version one)
"Forever Young" (version two)
"Dirge"
"You Angel You"
"Never Say Goodbye"
"Wedding Song"

Single: "On a Night Like This"/"You Angel You"
Asylum 11033
Producer uncredited
Released February 1974

Single: "Something There Is about You"/"Going Going Gone"
Asylum 11035

Producer uncredited
Released March 1974

Album: *Before the Flood*
Asylum Records
LP: S-201
Producer uncredited, but probably Bob Dylan and The Band, assisted by engineers Phil Ramone and Rob Fraboni
Released 20 June 1974
This album was reissued by Columbia Records in August 1982
LP: KG-37661; CD: C2K-37661; CS: CGT-377661
Note: The album is credited to "Bob Dylan/The Band." The opening song includes different punctuation in the title than the original version on *Blonde on Blonde*.

"Most Likely You Go Your Way (and I'll Go Mine)"
"Lay, Lady, Lay"
"Rainy Day Women # 12 & 35"
"Knockin' on Heaven's Door"
"It Ain't Me Babe"
"Ballad of a Thin Man"
"Up on Cripple Creek" (J. R. Robertson)
"I Shall Be Released"
"Endless Highway" (J. R. Robertson)
"The Night They Drove Old Dixie Down" (J. R. Robertson)
"Stage Fright" (J. R. Robertson)
"Don't Think Twice, It's All Right"
"Just Like a Woman"
"It's Alright, Ma (I'm Only Bleeding)"
"The Shape I'm In" (J. R. Robertson)
"When You Awake" (J. R. Robertson and Richard Manuel)
"The Weight" (J. R. Robertson)
"All along the Watchtower"
"Highway 61 Revisited"
"Like a Rolling Stone"
"Blowin' in the Wind"

Single: "Most Likely You Go Your Way (And I'll Go Mine)"/"Stage Fright"
    (J. R. Robertson)
Asylum 11043
Producer uncredited
Released July 1974
A-side performed by Bob Dylan and The Band
B-side performed by The Band

Single: "All along the Watchtower"/"It Ain't Me Babe"
Asylum E-45212
Producer uncredited
Released August 1974

Album: *Blood on the Tracks*
Columbia Records
LP: PC-33235; CD: CK-33235; CS: JCT-33235
Produced by Bob Dylan (uncredited)
Album notes by Pete Hamill
Released 17 January 1975
Note: A November 1974 test pressing of the album (PC-33235) was recorded with New York musicians. Dylan rerecorded five songs with Minneapolis musicians on 27 and 30 December 1974, thus delaying the album's release.

"Tangled up in Blue"
"Simple Twist of Fate"
"You're a Big Girl Now"
"Idiot Wind"
"You're Gonna Make Me Lonesome When You Go"
"Meet Me in the Morning"
"Lily, Rosemary and the Jack of Hearts"
"If You See Her, Say Hello"
"Shelter from the Storm"
"Buckets of Rain"

Single: "Tangled up in Blue"/"If You See Her, Say Hello"
Columbia 3-10106
Produced by Bob Dylan
Released February 1975

Album: *The Basement Tapes*
Columbia Records
LP: C2-33682; CD: C2K-33682; CS: CGT-33682
Produced by Bob Dylan and The Band
Album notes by Greil Marcus
Released 26 June 1975
Note: The album is credited to Bob Dylan and The Band. Other credits read, "Compiled by Robbie Robertson" and "Recorded in the basement of Big Pink, West Saugerties, N.Y., 1967."

"Odds and Ends"
"Orange Juice Blues (Blues for Breakfast)" (Richard Manuel)
"Million Dollar Bash"
"Yazoo Street Scandal" (J. R. Robertson)
"Going to Acapulco"
"Katie's Been Gone" (J. R. Robertson and Richard Manuel)
"Lo and Behold"
"Bessie Smith" (Rick Danko and J. R. Robertson)
"Clothes Line Saga"
"Apple Sucking Tree"
"Please, Mrs. Henry"
"Tears of Rage" (Bob Dylan and Richard Manuel)
"Too Much of Nothing"
"Yea! Heavy and a Bottle of Bread"

"Ain't No More Cane" (Traditional)
"Crash on the Levee (Down in the Flood)"
"Ruben Remus" (J. R. Robertson and Richard Manuel)
"Tiny Montgomery"
"You Ain't Goin' Nowhere"
"Don't Ya Tell Henry"
"Nothing Was Delivered"
"Open the Door, Homer"
"Long Distance Operator"
"This Wheel's on Fire" (Bob Dylan and Rick Danko)

Single: "Million Dollar Bash"/"Tears of Rage" (Bob Dylan and Richard Manuel)
Columbia 3-10217
Produced by Bob Dylan and The Band
Released July 1975

Single: "Hurricane, Part I" (Bob Dylan and Jacques Levy)/"Hurricane, Part II" (Bob Dylan and Jacques Levy)
Columbia 3-10245
Produced by Don DeVito
Released November 1975

Album: *Desire*
Columbia Records
LP: PC-33893; CD: CK-33893; CS: JCT-33893
Produced by Don DeVito
Album notes by Bob Dylan; liner notes by Allen Ginsberg
Released 16 January 1976
Note: The producer's credit reads, "This record could have been produced by Don DeVito."
"Hurricane" (Bob Dylan and Jacques Levy)
"Isis" (Bob Dylan and Jacques Levy)
"Mozambique" (Bob Dylan and Jacques Levy)
"One More Cup of Coffee"
"Oh, Sister" (Bob Dylan and Jacques Levy)
"Joey" (Bob Dylan and Jacques Levy)
"Romance in Durango" (Bob Dylan and Jacques Levy)
"Black Diamond Bay" (Bob Dylan and Jacques Levy)
"Sara"

Single: "Mozambique" (Bob Dylan and Jacques Levy)/"Oh, Sister" (Bob Dylan and Jacques Levy)
Columbia 3-10298
Produced by Don DeVito
Released February 1976

Single: "Hurricane" (Bob Dylan and Jacques Levy)/"Mozambique" (Bob Dylan and Jacques Levy)

Columbia 13-33324
Produced by Don DeVito
Released March 1976

Album: *Hard Rain*
Columbia Records
LP: PC-34349; CD: CK-34349; CS: PCT-34349
Produced by Don DeVito and Bob Dylan
Released 10 September 1976
Note: This album was a companion to the NBC television special of the same name broadcast 14 September 1976. The special was drawn from a concert at Fort Collins, Colorado, on 23 May 1976. Five tracks on the album were recorded at that concert. The four remaining tracks are from a Fort Worth, Texas, concert on 16 May 1976.

"Maggie's Farm"
"One Too Many Mornings"
"Stuck Inside of Mobile with the Memphis Blues Again"
"Oh, Sister" (Bob Dylan and Jacques Levy)
"Lay, Lady, Lay"
"Shelter from the Storm"
"You're a Big Girl Now"
"I Threw It All Away"
"Idiot Wind"

Single: "Rita May" (Bob Dylan and Jacques Levy)/"Stuck Inside of Mobile with the Memphis Blues Again"
Columbia 3-10454
Produced by Don DeVito
Released November 1976
A-side studio recording
B-side concert recording

Album: *Street-Legal*
Columbia Records
LP: JC-35453; CD: CK-35453; CS: PCT-35453
Produced by Don DeVito
Released 15 June 1978
Note: Producer's credit reads, "Captain in Charge: Don DeVito."

"Changing of the Guards"
"New Pony"
"No Time to Think"
"Baby Stop Crying"
"Is Your Love in Vain?"
"Senor (Tales of Yankee Power)"
"True Love Tends to Forget"
"We Better Talk This Over"
"Where Are You Tonight? (Journey through Dark Heat)"

Single: "Baby Stop Crying"/"New Pony"
Columbia 3-10805

Produced by Don DeVito
Released June 1978

Single: "Changing of the Guards"/"Senor (Tales of Yankee Power)"
Columbia 3-10851
Produced by Don DeVito
Released September 1978

Album: *Bob Dylan at Budokan*
Columbia Records
LP: PC2-36067; CD: G2K-36067; CS: CGT-36067
Produced by Bob Dylan
Album notes by Bob Dylan
Released 23 April 1979
"Mr. Tambourine Man"
"Shelter from the Storm"
"Love Minus Zero/No Limit"
"Ballad of a Thin Man"
"Don't Think Twice, It's All Right"
"Maggie's Farm"
"One More Cup of Coffee (Valley Below)"
"Like a Rolling Stone"
"I Shall Be Released"
"Is Your Love in Vain?"
"Going Going Gone"
"Blowin' in the Wind"
"Just Like a Woman"
"Oh, Sister" (Bob Dylan and Jacques Levy)
"Simple Twist of Fate"
"All along the Watchtower"
"I Want You"
"All I Really Want to Do"
"Knockin' on Heaven's Door"
"It's Alright, Ma (I'm Only Bleeding)"
"Forever Young"
"The Times They Are A-Changin'"

Album: *Slow Train Coming*
Columbia Records
LP: FC-36120; CD: CK-36120; CS: PCT-36120
Produced by Jerry Wexler and Barry Beckett
Released 18 August 1979
"Gotta Serve Somebody"
"Precious Angel"
"I Believe in You"
"Slow Train"
"Gonna Change My Way of Thinking"

"Do Right to Me Baby (Do unto Others)"
"When You Gonna Wake Up?"
"Man Gave Names to All the Animals"
"When He Returns"

Single: "Gotta Serve Somebody"/"Trouble in Mind"
Columbia 1-11072
Produced by Jerry Wexler and Barry Beckett
Released September 1979

Single: "Man Gave Names to All the Animals"/"When You Gonna Wake Up?"
Columbia 1-11168
Produced by Jerry Wexler and Barry Beckett
Released November 1979

Single: "Slow Train"/"Do Right to Me Baby (Do unto Others)"
Columbia 1-11235
Produced by Jerry Wexler and Barry Beckett
Released January 1980

Album: *Saved*
Columbia Records
LP: FC-36553; CD: CK-36553; CS: PCT-36553
Produced by Jerry Wexler and Barry Beckett
Released 20 June 1980
Note: The original album cover featured a painting of the hand of God (presumably) reaching down to annoint Dylan on stage. Later pressings of the album and the compact disc release featured a painting of Dylan in performance.
"A Satisfied Mind" (Red Hayes and Jack Rhodes)
"Saved" (Bob Dylan and Tim Drummond)
"Covenant Woman"
"What Can I Do for You?"
"Solid Rock"
"Pressing On"
"In the Garden"
"Saving Grace"
"Are You Ready?"

Single: "Solid Rock"/"Covenant Woman"
Columbia 1-11318
Produced by Jerry Wexler and Barry Beckett
Released June 1980

Single: "Saved" (Bob Dylan and Tim Drummond)/"Are You Ready?"
Columbia 1-11370
Produced by Jerry Wexler and Barry Beckett
Released August 1980

Album: *Shot of Love*
Columbia Records
LP: TC-37496; CD: CK-37496; CS: PCT-37496
Produced by Chuck Plotkin and Bob Dylan, except (*) produced by Chuck Plotkin, Bob Dylan and Bumps Blackwell
Released 12 August 1981
Note: A later version of this album, released in the summer of 1985, included "The Groom's Still Waiting at the Altar" as the sixth track.

"Shot of Love" *
"Heart of Mine"
"Property of Jesus"
"Lenny Bruce"
"Watered-Down Love"
"Dead Man, Dead Man"
"In the Summertime"
"Trouble"
"Every Grain of Sand"

Single: "Heart of Mine"/"The Groom's Still Waiting at the Altar"
Columbia 18-02510
Produced by Chuck Plotkin and Bob Dylan
Released 11 September 1981

Album: *Infidels*
Columbia Records
LP: QC-38819; CD: CK-38819; CS: PCT-38819
Produced by Bob Dylan and Mark Knopfler
Released 1 November 1983

"Jokerman"
"Sweetheart Like You"
"Neighborhood Bully"
"License to Kill"
"Man of Peace"
"Union Sundown"
"I and I"
"Don't Fall Apart on Me Tonight"

Single: "Union Sundown"/"Sweetheart Like You"
Columbia 38-04301
Produced by Bob Dylan and Mark Knopfler
Released December 1983
Note: This single was rereleased in January 1984 with "Sweetheart Like You" as the A-side. It carried the same catalog number.

Single: "Jokerman"/"Isis" (Bob Dylan and Jacques Levy)
Columbia 18-02510
A-side produced by Bob Dylan and Mark Knopfler
B-side from the soundtrack of *Renaldo and Clara*
Released April 1984

Album: *Real Live*
Columbia Records
LP: FC 39944; CD: CK-39944; CS: FCT-39944
Produced by Glyn Johns
Released 3 December 1984
"Highway 61 Revisited"
"Maggie's Farm"
"I and I"
"License to Kill"
"It Ain't Me Babe"
"Tangled Up in Blue"
"Masters of War"
"Ballad of a Thin Man"
"Girl From the North Country"
"Tombstone Blues"

Single: "Tight Connection to My Heart (Has Anybody Seen My Love?)"/"We Better Talk This Over"
Columbia 38-04933
A-side probably produced by Bob Dylan and Arthur Baker
B-side produced by Don DeVito
Released May 1985

Album: *Empire Burlesque*
Columbia Records
LP: FC 40110; CD: CK-40110; CS: FCT-40110
No producer credited, although Arthur Baker is credited with remixing the album.
Released 27 May 1985
"Tight Connection to My Heart (Has Anybody Seen My Love?)"
"Seeing the Real You at Last"
"I'll Remember You"
"Clean Cut Kid"
"Never Gonna Be the Same Again"
"Trust Yourself"
"Emotionally Yours"
"When the Night Comes Falling From the Sky"
"Something's Burning, Baby"
"Dark Eyes"

Single: "Emotionally Yours"/"When the Night Comes Falling From the Sky"
Columbia 38-05697
Probably produced by Bob Dylan and Arthur Baker
Released October 1985

Album: *Biograph*
Columbia Records
LP: C5X-38830; CD: C3K-38830; CS: CXT-38830
Compiled and supervised by Jeff Rosen
Original producer credits noted with each song
Album notes by Cameron Crowe (booklet and liner notes)
Released 28 October 1985
Note: This anthology collected a number of songs that had never been released. Indicated are previously unreleased songs (*), previously unreleased live versions (**), and rare singles finally included on an album (***). This is the sequence of songs for the five-LP boxed set. In the CD and cassette sets, "Jet Pilot" follows "Isis."

"Lay, Lady, Lay" (Produced by Bob Johnston)
"Baby, Let Me Follow You Down" (Credited to Eric Von Schmidt) (Produced by John Hammond)
"If Not for You" (Produced by Bob Johnston)
"I'll Be Your Baby Tonight" (Produced by Bob Johnston)
"I'll Keep It with Mine" (Produced by Bob Dylan) *
"The Times They Are A-Changin'" (Produced by Tom Wilson)
"Blowin' in the Wind" (Produced by John Hammond)
"Masters of War" (Produced by John Hammond)
"The Lonesome Death of Hattie Carroll" (Produced by Tom Wilson)
"Percy's Song" (Produced by Tom Wilson) *
"Mixed Up Confusion" (Produced by John Hammond) ***
"Tombstone Blues" (Produced by Bob Johnston)
"Groom's Still Waiting at the Altar" (Produced by Chuck Plotkin and Bob Dylan) ***
"Most Likely You Go Your Way (And I'll Go Mine)" (Producer uncredited, but probably Bob Dylan and The Band)
"Like a Rolling Stone" (Produced by Tom Wilson)
"Jet Pilot" (Produced by Bob Johnston) *
"Lay Down Your Weary Tune" (Produced by Tom Wilson) *
"Subterranean Homesick Blues" (Produced by Tom Wilson)
"I Don't Believe You (She Acts Like We Never Have Met)" (Producer uncredited) **
"Visions of Johanna" (Producer uncredited) **
"Every Grain of Sand" (Produced by Chuck Plotkin and Bob Dylan)
"Quinn the Eskimo" (Produced by Bob Dylan and The Band) **
"Mr. Tambourine Man" (Produced by Tom Wilson)
"Dear Landlord" (Produced by Bob Johnston)
"It Ain't Me Babe" (Produced by Tom Wilson)
"You Angel You" (Producer uncredited, but most likely Bob Dylan and The Band)
"Million Dollar Bash" (Produced by Bob Dylan and The Band)
"To Ramona" (Produced by Tom Wilson)
"You're a Big Girl Now" (Producer uncredited) *
"Abandoned Love" (Produced by Don DeVito) *
"Tangled Up in Blue" (Producer uncredited)
"It's All Over Now, Baby Blue" (Producer uncredited) **

"Can You Please Crawl Out Your Window?" (Produced by Bob Johnston) ***
"Positively Fourth Street" (Produced by Bob Johnston)
"Isis" (Producer uncredited) ***
"Caribbean Wind" (Produced by Chuck Plotkin and Bob Dylan) **
"Up to Me" (Producer uncredited) *
"Baby, I'm in the Mood for You" (Produced by John Hammond) *
"I Wanna Be Your Lover" (Produced by Bob Johnston) *
"I Want You" (Produced by Bob Johnston)
"Heart of Mine" (Produced by Chuck Plotkin and Bob Dylan) **
"On a Night Like This" (Producer uncredited, but probably Bob Dylan and The Band)
"Just Like a Woman" (Produced by Bob Johnston)
"Romance in Durango" (Bob Dylan and Jacques Levy) (Producer uncredited) **
"Senor (Tales of Yankee Power)" (Produced by Don DeVito)
"Gotta Serve Somebody" (Produced by Jerry Wexler and Barry Beckett)
"I Believe in You" (Produced by Jerry Wexler and Barry Beckett)
"Time Passes Slowly" (Produced by Bob Johnston)
"I Shall Be Released" (Producer uncredited, but probably Bob Dylan and Happy Traum)
"Knockin' on Heaven's Door" (Produced by Gordon Carroll)
"All along the Watchtower" (Producer uncredited, but probably Bob Dylan and The Band)
"Solid Rock" (Produced by Jerry Wexler and Barry Beckett)
"Forever Young" (Producer uncredited) *

Single: "Band of the Hand"/"Theme from Joe's Death" (Michael Malone)
MCA Records MCA-52811 (12-inch single MCA-23633)
Produced by Bob Dylan and Tom Petty
Released April 1986
B-side not performed by Bob Dylan

Album: *Knocked Out Loaded*
Columbia Records
LP: OC-40439; CD: CK-40439; CS: OCT-40439
No producer credited
Released 8 August 1986
"You Wanna Ramble" (Herman Parker, Jr.)
"They Killed Him" (Kris Kristofferson)
"Driftin' Too Far from Shore"
"Precious Memories" (J. B. F. Wright, arranged by Bob Dylan)
"Maybe Someday"
"Brownsville Girl" (Bob Dylan and Sam Shepard)
"Got My Mind Made Up" (Bob Dylan and Tom Petty)
"Under Your Spell" (Bob Dylan and Carole Bayer Sager)

Album: *Down in the Groove*
Columbia Records
LP: OC-40957; CD: CK-40957; CS: OCT-40957
No producer credited
Released 31 May 1988
"Let's Stick Together" (Wilbert Harrison)
"When Did You Leave Heaven?" (Walter Bullock and Richard Whiting)
"Sally Sue Brown" (J. Alexander, E. Montgomery and T. Stafford)
"Death Is Not the End"
"Had a Dream about You, Baby"
"Ugliest Girl in the World" (Bob Dylan and Robert Hunter)
"Silvio" (Bob Dylan and Robert Hunter)
"Ninety Miles an Hour (Down a Dead End Street)" (Hal Blair and Don Robertson)
"Shenandoah" (Traditional)
"Rank Strangers to Me" (A. Brumley)

Single: "Silvio" (Bob Dylan and Robert Hunter)/"Driftin' Too Far from Shore"
Columbia 38-0790
Producer uncredited
Released June 1988

Album: *Dylan and the Dead*
Columbia Records
LP: OC-45056; CD: CK-45056; CS: OCT-45056
Produced by Jerry Garcia and John Cutler
Released 6 February 1989
"Slow Train"
"I Want You"
"Gotta Serve Somebody"
"Queen Jane Approximately"
"Joey" (Bob Dylan and Jacques Levy)
"All along the Watchtower"
"Knockin' on Heaven's Door"

Album: *Oh Mercy*
Columbia Records
LP: OC-45281; CD: CK-45281; CS: OCT-45281
Produced by Daniel Lanois
Released 22 September 1989
"Political World"
"Where Teardrops Fall"
"Everything Is Broken"
"Ring Them Bells"
"Man in a Long Black Coat"
"Most of the Time"
"What Good Am I?"

"Disease of Conceit"
"What Was It You Wanted?"
"Shooting Star"

Cassette single: "Everything Is Broken"/"Dead Man, Dead Man"
Columbia 38T-73062
A-side produced by Daniel Lanois
B-side concert recording; producer uncredited
Released 18 October 1989
Note: This was Dylan's first cassette single. It was not released in the standard seven-inch format.

Album: *Under the Red Sky*
Columbia Records
LP: C-46794; CD: CK-46794; CS: CT-46794
Produced by Don Was, David Was and Jack Frost
Released 11 September 1990
"Wiggle Wiggle"
"Under the Red Sky"
"Unbelievable"
"Born in Time"
"T.V. Talkin' Song"
"10,000 Men"
"2 x 2"
"God Knows"
"Handy Dandy"
"Cat's in the Well"

Album: *The Bootleg Series, Vols. 1-3*
Columbia Records
CD: C3T-47382; CS: C3K-47382
Produced by John Hammond, except (*) produced by Tom Wilson, (**) produced by Bob Johnston, (***) producer uncredited, (#) produced by Bob Dylan and Mark Knopfler, (##) produced by Bob Dylan and Chuck Plotkin. Other producer credits noted with the song. Credits identify Johnston as "Bob Johnson."
Album notes by John Bauldie (booklet)
Released 26 March 1991
Note: This was the first Dylan album that was not released on LP. Only a few songs on this album had ever been released before. (Four had appeared on early copies of *The Freewheelin' Bob Dylan* and one had appeared as a single in Europe.) By far, most of this album was made up of outtakes and alternate versions. Unlike *Biograph*, the recordings on this set were arranged in chronological order.
"Hard Times in New York Town" ***
"He Was a Friend of Mine" (Traditional)
"Man on the Street"
"No More Auction Block" (Traditional) ***
"House Carpenter" (Traditional)
"Talkin' Bear Mountain Picnic Massacre Blues"
"Let Me Die in My Footsteps"

"Rambling Gambling Willie"
"Talkin' Hava Negeilah Blues"
"Quit Your Lowdown Ways"
"Worried Blues" (Traditional)
"Kingsport Town" (Traditional)
"Walkin' Down the Line" ***
"Walls of Red Wing"
"Paths of Victory" *
"Talkin' John Birch Paranoid Blues" ***
"Who Killed Davey Moore?" ***
"Only a Hobo" *
"Moonshiner" (Traditional) *
"When the Ship Comes In" ***
"The Times They Are A-Changin'" ***
"Last Thoughts on Woody Guthrie" ***
"Seven Curses" *
"Eternal Circle" *
"Suze (The Cough Song)" *
"Mama, You Been on My Mind" *
"Farewell, Angelina" *
"Subterranean Homesick Blues" *
"If You Gotta Go, Go Now (Or Else You Got to Stay All Night)" *
"Sitting on a Barbed-Wire Fence" *
"Like a Rolling Stone" *
"It Takes a Lot to Laugh, It Takes a Train to Cry" *
"I'll Keep It with Mine" **
"She's Your Lover Now" **
"I Shall Be Released" ***
"Santa-Fe" ***
"If Not for You" **
"Wallflower" ***
"Nobody 'Cept You" ***
"Tangled Up in Blue" ***
"Call Letter Blues" ***
"Idiot Wind" ***
"If You See Her, Say Hello" ***
"Golden Loom" (Produced by Don DeVito)
"Catfish" (Bob Dylan and Jacques Levy) (Produced by Don DeVito)
"Seven Days" ***
"Ye Shall be Changed" (Produced by Jerry Wexler and Barry Beckett)
"Every Grain of Sand" ***
"You Changed My Life" ##
"Need a Woman" ##

"Angelina" ##
"Someone's Got a Hold of My Heart" #
"Tell Me" #
"Lord Protect My Child" #
"Foot of Pride" #
"Blind Willie McTell" #
"When the Night Comes Falling from the Sky" ***
"Series of Dreams" (Produced by Daniel Lanois)

Album: *Good as I Been To You*
Columbia Records
CD: CK-53200; CS: CT-53200
Produced by Debbie Gold
Released 3 November 1992
Note: Production credit reads "Production Supervised by Debbie Gold for The Gold Network."
"Frankie and Albert" (Traditional)
"Jim Jones" (Traditional)
"Blackjack Davey" (Traditional)
"Canadee-I-O" (Traditional)
"Sittin' on Top of the World" (Traditional)
"Little Maggie" (Traditional)
"Hard Times" (Traditional)
"Step it Up and Go" (Traditional)
"Tomorrow Night" (Traditional)
"Arthur McBride" (Traditional)
"You're Gonna Quit Me" (Traditional)
"Diamond Joe" (Traditional)
"Froggie Went A-Courtin'" (Traditional)

Section II:
Recordings by Bob Dylan Not Issued in the United States

All songs by Bob Dylan, unless indicated otherwise. Composers' names are in parenthesis after song titles. Catalog numbers are listed for long-playing albums (LP), compact discs (CD) and cassettes (CS). Single records listed are those in seven-inch format. Singles and albums are listed in order of release.

Single: "If You Gotta Go, Go Now"/"To Ramona"
CBS 2921
Produced by Tom Wilson
Released July 1967 in Belgium, the Netherlands and Luxembourg

Album: *Masterpieces*
CBS/Sony
LP: 57AP-875/6/7
Producer credits noted with each song
Released March 1978 in Japan, Australia and New Zealand
Previously unreleased songs are indicated (*) and songs never included on an album before are indicated (**).
"Knockin' on Heaven's Door" (Produced by Gordon Carroll)
"Mr. Tambourine Man" (Produced by Tom Wilson)
"Just Like a Woman" (Produced by Bob Johnston)
"I Shall Be Released" (Producer uncredited, but probably Bob Dylan and Happy Traum)
"Tears of Rage" (Bob Dylan and Richard Manuel) (Produced by Bob Dylan and The Band)
"All along the Watchtower" (Produced by Bob Johnston)
"One More Cup of Coffee" (Produced by Don DeVito)
"Like a Rolling Stone" (*Self-Portrait* version) (Produced by Bob Johnston)
"The Mighty Quinn (Quinn the Eskimo)" (*Self-Portrait* version) (Produced by Bob Johnston)
"Tomorrow Is a Long Time" (Producer uncredited, but probably Tom Wilson)
"Lay, Lady, Lay" (*Hard Rain* version) (Produced by Don DeVito and Bob Dylan)
"Idiot Wind" (*Hard Rain* version) (Produced by Don DeVito and Bob Dylan)
"Mixed Up Confusion" (Produced by John Hammond) *
"Positively 4th Street" (Produced by Bob Johnston)
"Can You Please Crawl out Your Window?" (Produced by Bob Johnston)
"Just Like Tom Thumb's Blues" (Produced by Bob Johnston) **
"Spanish Is the Loving Tongue" (Produced by Leon Russell) **
"George Jackson" (band version) (Produced uncredited) **
"Rita May" (Bob Dylan and Jacques Levy) (Produced by Don DeVito) **
"Blowin' in the Wind" (Produced by John Hammond)
"A Hard Rain's A-Gonna Fall" (Produced by John Hammond)
"The Times They Are A-Changin'" (Produced by Tom Wilson)
"Masters of War" (Production credited to John Hammond, but actually produced by Tom Wilson)
"Hurricane" (Bob Dylan and Jacques Levy) (Produced by Don DeVito)
"Maggie's Farm" (*Hard Rain* version) (Produced by Don DeVito and Bob Dylan)
"Subterranean Homesick Blues" (Produced by Tom Wilson)
"Ballad of a Thin Man" (Produced by Bob Johnston)
"Mozambique" (Bob Dylan and Jacques Levy) (Produced by Don DeVito)
"This Wheel's on Fire" (Bob Dylan and Rick Danko) (Produced by Bob Dylan and The Band)
"I Want You" (Produced by Bob Johnston)
"Rainy Day Women # 12 & 35" (Produced by Bob Johnston)
"Don't Think Twice, It's All Right" (Produced by John Hammond)
"Song to Woody" (Produced by John Hammond)
"It Ain't Me Babe" (Produced by Tom Wilson)
"Love Minus Zero/No Limit" (Produced by Tom Wilson)

"If You See Her, Say Hello" (Producer uncredited, but probably Bob Dylan, assisted by Phil Ramone)
"Sara" (Produced by Don DeVito)

Album: *Bob Dylan at Budokan*
CBS/Sony
LP: 40 AP-1100-1
Produced by Bob Dylan
Album notes by Bob Dylan
Recorded February-March 1978 in Tokyo and released in Japan in July 1978. This album was created for the Japanese market, and its success inspired its release in the United States the following year. This version is identical to the album released in the United States. (See song listing in Section A of this discography.)

Single: "Heart of Mine"/"Let it Be Me" (M. Curtis, G. Becaud and P. Delano)
CBS A-1406
Produced by Chuck Plotkin and Bob Dylan
Released 1 September 1981 in Great Britain and Europe

Single: "Union Sundown"/"Angel Flying Too Close to the Ground" (Willie Nelson)
CBS A-3916
Produced by Bob Dylan and Mark Knopfler
Released 28 October 1983 in Great Britain and Europe

Section III:
Recordings by Other Artists On Which Bob Dylan Appears

This listing does not include the catalog information in Sections I and II. Title, artist and recording company are listed. Songs on which Dylan played are listed and his contribution is noted. Unless otherwise indicated, Dylan sang and accompanied himself on guitar and harmonica. Indicated are songs written by Bob Dylan (*); songs written by Bob Dylan and Jacques Levy (**); songs written by Dylan, George Harrison, Roy Orbison, Jeff Lynne and Tom Petty (#); and songs written by Dylan, Harrison, Lynne and Petty (##).

Album: *Midnight Special*
Harry Belafonte
RCA Victor Records
LP: LMP/LSP 2449
Released March 1962
"Midnight Special"
Dylan plays harmonica.

Album: *Carolyn Hester*
Carolyn Hester
Columbia Records

LP: CL-1796; CS: CS-8596
Released 14 May 1962
"I'll Fly Away"
"Swing and Turn Jubilee"
"Come Back, Baby"
Dylan plays harmonica.

Album: *Broadside Ballads, Vol. I*
Various Artists
Broadside/Folkways Records
LP: BR-301
Released September 1963
"John Brown" *
"Let Me Die in My Footsteps" *
"Only a Hobo" *
"Talkin' Devil" *
Dylan appears in the credits as Blind Boy Grunt.

Album: *The Blues Project*
Various Artists
Elektra Records
LP: EKL/EKS 7264
Released June 1964
"Downtown Blues"
Dylan plays piano. Credits list him as Bob Landy.
Note: This recording was made in mid-1963.

Album: *Evening Concerts at Newport, Vol. I*
Various Artists
Vanguard Recording Society
LP: VRS-9148/VSD-79148
Released May 1964
"Blowin' in the Wind" *
"We Shall Overcome"
Note: These live recordings were made July 1963 at the Newport Folk Festival. Dylan joins several other performers for "We Shall Overcome," the concert finale.

Album: *Newport Broadside*
Various Artists
Vanguard Recording Society
LP: VRS-9144/VSD-79144
Released May 1964
"Playboys and Playgirls" *
"With God on Our Side" *
Dylan duets with Pete Seeger on "Playboys and Playgirls," and with Joan Baez on "With God on Our Side."
Note: Both performances were recorded in July 1963 at the Newport Folk Festival.

Album: *Jack Elliott*
Jack Elliott
Vanguard Recording Society
LP: VSD-79151
Released June 1964
"Will the Circle Be Unbroken"
Dylan plays harmonica. Credits list him as Tedham Porterhouse.

Album: *Three Kings and a Queen*
Victoria Spivey
Spivey Records
LP: LP-1004
Released October 1964
"Sitting on Top of the World"
"Wichita"
Dylan plays harmonica and sings backing vocals.
Note: These performances were recorded in October 1961.

Album: *We Shall Overcome*
Various Artists
Folkways Records
LP: FH-5592
Released Winter 1964
"Only a Pawn in Their Game" *
Note: This song was recorded live at the March on Washington, August 1963. It was known then as "The Ballad of Medgar Evers."

Album: *Dick Farina and Eric von Schmidt*
Dick Farina and Eric von Schmidt
Folklore Records
LP: LEUT-7
Released 1967, only in Great Britain
"Glory, Glory"
"Overseas Stomp"
"You Can Always Tell"
"Xmas Island"
"Cocaine"
"London Waltz"
Dylan plays harmonica and sings background. Credits list him as Blind Boy Grunt.
Note: These recordings were made in January 1963.

Album: *Earl Scruggs Performing with His Family and Friends*
Earl Scruggs
Columbia Records
LP: KC-30584
Released Summer 1971
"East Virginia Blues"
"Nashville Skyline Rag" *
Dylan plays acoustic guitar.

Album: *Broadside Reunion*
Various Artists
Folkways Records
LP: FR-5315
Released November 1971
"Train A-Travelin'" *
"I'd Hate to Be You on That Dreadful Day" *
"The Death of Emmett Till" *
"Ballad of Donald White" *
Dylan appears as Blind Boy Grunt.
Note: These performances were recorded in 1962.

Album: *The Concert for Bangladesh*
George Harrison
Apple Records
LP: STCX-3385
Released 20 December 1971
"A Hard Rain's A-Gonna Fall" *
"It Takes a Lot to Laugh, It Takes a Train to Cry" *
"Blowin' in the Wind" *
"Mr. Tambourine Man" *
"Just Like a Woman" *
Dylan is backed by Harrison, Leon Russell and Ringo Starr at the charity concert, which was recorded August 1, 1971 at Madison Square Garden in New York City.

Album: *A Tribute to Woody Guthrie, Part One*
Various Artists
Columbia Records
LP: KC-31171
Released 12 January 1972
"Grand Coulee Dam"
"Dear Mrs. Roosevelt"
"I Ain't Got No Home"
Dylan is backed by The Band in these recordings from the tribute concert recorded in January 1968 at Carnegie Hall in New York City.

Album: *Three Kings and a Queen, Vol. II*
Victoria Spivey
Spivey Records
LP: LP-1014
Released July 1972
"It's Dangerous"
Dylan plays harmonica.
Note: This performance was recorded in October 1961.

Album: *Somebody Else's Troubles*
Steve Goodman
Buddah Records
LP: BDS-5121
Released mid-September 1972
"Somebody Else's Troubles"
Dylan plays piano and sings backing vocals. Credits list him as Robert Milkwood Thomas.

Album: *Roger McGuinn*
Roger McGuinn
Columbia Records
LP: KC-31-946
Released December 1972
"I'm So Restless"
Dylan plays harmonica.

Album: *Doug Sahm and Band*
Doug Sahm
Atlantic Records
LP: SD-7254
Released December 1972

"Wallflower" *
"Blues Stay Away from Me"
"(Is Anybody Going to) San Antone?"
Dylan sings backing vocals and duets with Sahm on "Wallflower."

Album: *Chronicles*
Booker T. and Priscilla Jones
A&M Records
LP: ST-4413
Released 1973
"The Crippled Crow"
Dylan plays harmonica.

Album: *Texas Tornado*
Doug Sahm
Atlantic Records
LP: SD-7287
Released October 1973
"Tennessee Blues"
"Ain't That Loving You"
"I'll Be There"
Dylan plays harmonica, guitar and organ.

Album: *Barry Goldberg*
Barry Goldberg
Atco Records
LP: SD-7040
Released December 1973
"Stormy Weather Cowboy"
"Silver Moon"
"Minstrel Show"
"Big City Woman"
"It's Not the Spotlight"
"(I've Got to Use My) Imagination"
Dylan plays percussion and sings backing vocals. Credits list him as co-producer.
Note: "(I've Got to Use My) Imagination" was released as a single (ATCO 45-6946) in 1973.

Album: *Disconnected*
The Dial-A-Poem Poets
Giorno Poetry Systems
LP: GPS-003
Released 1974
"Jimmy Berman Rag" (Allen Ginsberg and Bob Dylan)
Dylan plays acoustic guitar.
Note: This performance was recorded in November 1971.

Album: *The Essential Steve Goodman*
Steve Goodman
Buddah Records
LP: BDS-5665-2
Released 1974
"Election Year Rag"
Bob Dylan plays piano and sings under the name Robert Milkwood Thomas.
Note: This was released as a single (Buddah BDA-326) in 1973.

Album: *Com'n Back for More*
David Blue
Asylum Records
LP: 7E-1043
Released 1975
"Who Love"
Dylan plays harmonica.

Album: *Songs for the New Depression*
Bette Midler
Atlantic Records
LP: SD-18155
Released January 1976
"Buckets of Rain" *
Dylan duets with Midler.

Album: *No Reason to Cry*
Eric Clapton
RSO Records
LP: RS1-3004
Released September 1976
"Sign Language" *
Dylan duets with Clapton.

Album: *Death of a Ladies Man*
Leonard Cohen
Warner Bros. Records (reissued on compact disc by Columbia Records in 1988)
LP: BS-3125; CD: CK-44286
Released 1977
"Don't Go Home With Your Hard-On"
Dylan sings backing vocals.
Note: This session was produced by Phil Spector

Album: *4 Songs from Renaldo and Clara*
Bob Dylan and the Rolling Thunder Revue
Columbia Records
EP: CBS XSM-164035
Released January 1978
"People Get Ready"
"Never Let Me Go"
"Isis" **
"It Ain't Me Babe" *
Dylan performs with the Rolling Thunder Revue.
Note: This promotional record featured material recorded in the fall of 1975.

Album: *The Last Waltz*
The Band
Warner Bros. Records
LP: 3WS-3146; CD: 3146-2
Released 7 April 1978
"Baby, Let Me Follow You Down" (two versions)
"I Don't Believe You" *
"Forever Young" *
"I Shall Be Released" *

Dylan performs with The Band, and joins the whole cast of *The Last Waltz*--including Van Morrison, Neil Diamond, Joni Mitchell, Neil Young and others--on "I Shall Be Released," the concert's finale.
Note: These performances were recorded on Thanksgiving Day, 1976.

Album: *So You Wanna Go Back to Egypt*
Keith Green
Pretty Good Records
LP: PGR-1
Released 7 May 1980
"Pledge My Head to Heaven"
Dylan contributes harmonica.

Album: *First Blues*
Allen Ginsberg
John Hammond Records
LP: W2X-37673
Released February 1983
"Jimmy Berman Rag" (Allen Ginsberg and Bob Dylan)
"Vomit Express" (Allen Ginsberg and Bob Dylan)
"Going to San Diego"
Dylan plays guitar and organ.
Note: These performances were recorded in November 1971.

Album: *We Are the World*
Various Artists
Columbia Records
LP: CL-40043
Released April 1985
"We Are the World"
Dylan is part of the all-star chorus on the title song of this album, which was intended to raise money for African famine relief. The single release (Columbia US7-04839) was a Top 10 hit.

Album: *Language Barrier*
Sly and Robbie
Island Records
LP: 90286
Released 5 August 1985
"No Name on the Bullet"
Dylan plays harmonica.

Album: *Sun City*
Artists United against Apartheid
Manhattan Records
LP: ST-53019
Released December 1985
"Sun City"
Dylan again joins an all-star chorus for this record, which was intended to call world attention to South Africa's racial policy of apartheid. The single (b50017) was released in mid-November 1985.

Album: *Kingdom Blow*
Curtis Blow
Mercury Records
LP: 830-215-1
Released September 1986
"Street Rock"
Dylan sings backing vocals and raps.

Album: *Sentimental Hygiene*
Warren Zevon
Virgin America Records
LP: 7-90603-1
Released August 1987
"The Factory"
Dylan plays harmonica.

Album: *Hearts of Fire*
Film Soundtrack
Columbia Records
LP: SC-40870; CD:
Released 20 October 1987
"The Usual"
"Had a Dream about You, Baby" *
"Night After Night" *
Note: Dylan starred in this film about a pop singer.

Album: *Folkways: A Vision Shared*
Various Artists
Columbia Records
LP: OC-44034; CD: CK-44034
Released 24 August 1988
"Pretty Boy Floyd"
Dylan contributes a track to this tribute to Woody Guthrie and Leadbelly.

Album: *Volume One*
The Traveling Wilburys
Wilbury Records (Warner Bros. Records)
LP: 9 25796-1; CD: 9 25796-2; CS: 9 25796-4
Released 18 October 1988
"Handle With Care" #
"Dirty World" #
"Rattled" #
"Last Night" #
"Not Alone Anymore" #
"Congratulations" #
"Heading for the Light" #
"Margarita" #
"Tweeter and the Monkey Man" #
"End of the Line" #
Note: The first single from the album, "Handle with Care"/"Margarita" (7-27732; CS: 9-277324-4; CD: 2-27732), was released 18 October 1988. The second single, "End of the Line"/"Congratulations" (7-27637; CS: 9-27637-4; CD: 2-27637) was released in late January 1987.

Album: *Flashback*
Original Motion Picture Soundtrack
WTG Records
LP: 46042; CD: NK-46042
Released 30 January 1990
"People Get Ready"
Dylan contributed a track to the Dennis Hopper/Keifer Sutherland film.

Album: *Nobody's Child: Romanian Angel Appeal*
Various Artists
Warner Bros. Records
CD: 9 26280-2; CS: 9 26280-4
Released 24 July 1990
"Nobody's Child"
Dylan and the other Traveling Wilburys contributed a track for this benefit album, organized by Olivia Arias, wife of George Harrison, and actress Barbara Bach, wife of Ringo Starr.

Album: *The Byrds*
The Byrds
Columbia Legacy Records
CD: CK-46773; CS: CS-46773
Released 23 October 1990
"Mr. Tambourine Man"
Dylan joins a reunited Byrds trio--Roger McGuinn, David Crosby and Chris Hillman--for several verses of this song, which was recorded live at a tribute concert for Roy Orbison. Dylan's arrival is announced by huge ovation from the audience. The performance was recorded in early 1990.

Album: *Volume Three*
The Traveling Wilburys
Wilbury Records (Warner Bros. Records)
LP: 9 26324-1; CD: 9 26324-2; CS: 9 26324-4
Released 23 October 1990
"She's My Baby" ##
"Inside Out" ##
"If You Belonged to Me" ##
"The Devil's Been Busy" ##
"Seven Deadly Sins" ##
"Poor House" ##
"Where Were You Last Night?" ##
"Cool, Dry Place" ##
"New Blue Moon" ##
"You Took My Breath Away" ##
"Wilbury Twist" ##

Album: *For Our Children*
Various Artists
Disney Records
CD: 60616-2; C: 60616-2
Released May 1991
"This Old Man"
This album benefited the Pediatric AIDS Foundation and included a number of well-known artists (Paul McCartney, Bruce Springsteen, Sting, Barbra Streisand, Meryl Streep, Jackson Browne and others) supposedly singing children's songs. Many of the artists seemed to miss the point, singing songs that only the dreariest child would find interesting. Dylan,

however, contributed the most delightful moment on the album with his rendition of the traditional children's singalong. It was one of the few unpretentious moments on a pretentious album.

Section IV: Recordings by Other Artists in Which Bob Dylan Appears as a Character

Bob Dylan not only inspired other artists to launch careers in music, he also inspired some of their songs. This is a partial listing of songs in which Dylan is mentioned or alluded to. The songs are listed with the albums on which they initially appeared, with the name of the artist, record company and date of original release of the album. In some cases, there may have been a lapse between the appearance of a song as a single and its inclusion on an album, and we have chosen to list the album release date. Songs are listed in the order of release.

"American Pie"
American Pie
Don McLean
United Artists Records
Released October 1970
This song about "the day the music died" seemed to be an attempt to write the whole history of pop music. McLean's manic melodrama begins with the death of Buddy Holly and follows the increasingly apocalyptic turns in the 1960s. The Byrds, The Beatles, The Rolling Stones and Bob Dylan all appear in various guises throughout the song. Dylan appears as "the jester," taking the mantle of youth idol from James Dean. Later on, in a reference to Dylan's 1966 motorcycle accident, he is referred to as being in a cast.

"God"
Plastic Ono Band
John Lennon
Apple Records
Released December 1970
In this song, a denunciation of all but the self, Lennon offers a litany of nonbelief. Among the things in which he no longer believes he includes Elvis Presley, Bob Dylan and The Beatles.

"To Bobby"
Come from the Shadows
Joan Baez
A&M Records
Released June 1972
This paean to Bob Dylan was an attempt to rouse him from his life as a country gentleman in the aftermath of *Nashville Skyline* and *Self Portrait*. Baez asks her former lover to listen to the cries of those who waited for his words. Whether Dylan took her words to heart or whether it was an accident of timing, his first release after Baez's plea was "George Jackson," his angry eulogy for the murdered Black Panther leader.

"The Seeker"
Meaty, Beaty, Big and Bouncy
The Who
Track Records
Released September 1972

Peter Townshend, lead guitarist and principal songwriter for The Who, like many of his generation, went on a spiritual quest in the late 1960s. Townshend's led him to guru Meher Baba. This song is essentially about that quest for enlightenment, in which the narrator, a "seeker" asks "Bobby" Dylan and The Beatles for the answer to life's questions. Alas, Townshend concludes, rock 'n' roll artists do not have the answers.

"Let Freedom Ring"
Street Language
Rodney Crowell
Columbia Records
Released March 1986

This song is another history-of-the-1960s piece, a bit uncharacteristic for Crowell, whose songs of love and relationships are usually highly personal and intense. Crowell, who is perhaps the best exponent of the New Traditionalists who took over country music in the 1990s, refers to a Dylan concert as a high point of his early life.

"You Ain't Goin' Nowhere"
Will the Circle Be Unbroken, Vol. II
The Nitty Gritty Dirt Band (Roger McGuinn and Chris Hillman are guests on the recording of this song)
Universal City Records
Released May 1989

This song was written by Dylan, but its lyrics change with every recording. It has been like a ping-pong ball passed between Dylan and McGuinn for several years. It was recorded first by Dylan and The Band in 1967 for what was eventually released as *The Basement Tapes* in 1975. Early in 1968, The Byrds released a version as the lead-off song of their influential album, *Sweetheart of the Rodeo*, which gave birth to country rock music. Dylan took the song back, recording it with Happy Traum for *Bob Dylan's Greatest Hits, Vol. II*, in 1971. He addressed one verse of the song to Roger McGuinn. When McGuinn and Hillman joined The Nitty Gritty Dirt Band for their tribute to the "new" Nashville, *Will the Circle Be Unbroken, Vol. II*, McGuinn returned the favor, addressing one verse to the songwriter.

Section V:
Artists Known for Interpretations of Songs by Bob Dylan

What follows is a listing of selected artists who have done significant interpretations of songs by Dylan. For those who found Dylan's rough voice too coarse for listening pleasure, a number of artists, ranging from rock 'n' roll bands to easy-listening lounge singers. Most of Dylan's songs could survive these varied intepretations, but critics often wrote that the smoothed-over versions of Dylan's songs paled next to the original recordings.

This listing of cover versions is by no means complete. These are merely the most important of such recordings. Artists are listed alphabetically.

Joan Baez
One of Dylan's earliest interpreters has also remained one of the best throughout her career. Baez introduced Dylan to her audience and shared her fame with him. She was always supportive, and her early albums included a generous sampling of Dylan songs.

At the beginning of the 1970s, Baez released a two-record set entirely devoted to Dylan's writing, *Any Day Now*. The album included songs from every phase of Dylan's career to that point. One of the most touching performances by Baez, Dylan's former lover, is of "Sad-Eyed Lady of the Lowlands," Dylan's tribute to Sara Lowndes, the woman for whom he left Baez.

Baez's and Dylan's careers have crossed many times during their three decades of fame. Perhaps no artist has been more tireless in his or her devotion to a songwriter as Baez has been to Dylan.

The Band
Dylan's collaborators on the road in 1966 when they were still The Hawks, they became his in-studio backing band during the recordings that became *The Basement Tapes*. These musicians--Jaime Robbie Robertson, Richard Manuel, Rick Danko, Garth Hudson and Levon Helm--were a superb rock 'n' roll band when they accompanied Dylan on his 1966 world tour. After Dylan's motorcycle accident, they moved to West Saugerties, New York, near their boss' home in Woodstock. Several members of the group lived there in a house they called Big Pink. There, they met with Dylan to record the new songs he was writing during his recuperation. Bootlegged for years, these 1967 recordings were finally released in 1965.

Calling themselves The Band, the former Hawks released an album in 1968 that reverberated through the music industry. At a time when rock 'n' roll bands were doing increasingly strange things in the studio, *Music from Big Pink* was a simple, straight-ahead rock 'n' roll album with heavy twinges of country music. It came with a cover painting by Bob Dylan and three new Dylan songs: "Tears of Rage," an epic of adolescent independence cowritten by Richard Manuel, the mysterious "This Wheel's on Fire," written with Rick Danko, and the lovely prison prayer, "I Shall Be Released." The presence of the Dylan songs certainly helped The Band gain media attention, but the quality of the music deserved the attention of the listeners.

Robbie Robertson, who in the early days billed himself as "J. R. Robertson," was an outstanding songwriter. Many critics consider him to be one of the greatest writers of the rock 'n' roll era. The second and third albums by the group, *The Band* and *Stage Fright* contained all original material. The Band recorded a brand-new Dylan tune, "When I Paint My Masterpiece" for

Cahoots, their fourth album.

The Band performed with Dylan on Dylan's 1973 *Planet Waves* and backed him on the world tour chronicled in *Before the Flood*. He is featured in the film and album documenting The Band's farewell to performing, *The Last Waltz*, in which he joins his former backing musicians on "I Shall Be Released."

The Beach Boys

Known in the early 1960s for hedonistic songs of cars and girls, The Beach Boys began exploring more adult and personal themes in 1965, when they began recording the classic *Pet Sounds*. That album took a long time to make and the record company wanted another album in the interim. The Beach Boys went into the studio, pretended they were having a party at home with the microphone on, and produced *Beach Boys Party*, which turned out to be their farewell to youth and huge popularity. Along with popping corks, laughter, and the sounds of eating, the album featured a somewhat comical recording of "The Times They Are A-Changin'." The song was a harbinger of what was coming for the band.

Michael Bolton

Bolton, a songwriter who began recording with great success in the 1980s, collaborated with Dylan on "Steel Bars," the finale on Bolton's hugely successful 1991 album, *Time, Love and Tenderness*.

The Byrds

Perhaps the first rock 'n' roll band to achieve great acclaim using the works of Bob Dylan, these five musicians hit the top of the music charts in 1965 with Dylan's "Mr. Tambourine Man." Throughout their stormy career and prolific personnel changes, The Byrds remained devout Dylan interpreters. Indeed, most of the group's hits and high points came as a result of collaboration with Dylan. After The Byrds had disbanded, Columbia Records released an anthology called *The Byrds Sing Dylan*.

After their tremendous success with "Mr. Tambourine Man," The Byrds recorded "All I Really Want to Do," "Chimes of Freedom" and "Spanish Harlem Incident" for their first album, *Mr. Tambourine Man*. They scored a major hit with the title song of their second album, *Turn! Turn! Turn!*, a Pete Seeger song that was drawn from the Book of Ecclesiastes. That album contained two Dylan compositions, "Lay Down Your Weary Tune" and "The Times They Are A-Changin'." Other Dylan songs were recorded, but not released for nearly two decades. The Byrds were confident enough as songwriters not to include any Dylan compositions on their third album, *5D*, but their recording of "My Back Pages" was the high point of *Younger than Yesterday*, the 1967 album that saw the dissolution of the original Byrds. (Gene

Clark had left in the middle of *5D.*) *Younger Than Yesterday*, which took its title from the refrain of "My Back Pages," was the last Byrds album to feature Jim McGuinn, David Crosby, Chris Hillman and Michael Clarke.

Dylan wrote two songs for the revamped Byrds lineup that recorded *Sweetheart of the Rodeo*, the seminal country rock album, which was released in 1968. Jim McGuinn had changed his name to Roger McGuinn and had enlisted Gram Parsons from the International Submarine Band, a group that had been experimenting with a merger of country music with rock 'n' roll. The opening song on the album was Dylan's "You Ain't Goin' Nowhere," and the closing song was another Dylan composition, "Nothing Was Delivered."

Parsons left The Byrds and Chris Hillman went with him, to form The Flying Burrito Brothers. This band recorded Dylan's "If You Gotta Go, Go Now" on its *Burrito Deluxe* album in 1970. McGuinn continued The Byrds for another five years with a number of other talented musicians. He continued to cover Dylan songs, including "This Wheel's on Fire," "Positively 4th Street," a live version of "Mr. Tambourine Man," "It's All Over Now, Baby Blue," and made several recordings that were not immediately released.

The original members of The Byrds regrouped in 1972, and then McGuinn retired the name. Largely to protect the name from copyright infringement, McGuinn, Hillman and Crosby began performing again as The Byrds in the late 1980s and early 1990s. When Columbia Records began putting together a four-CD retrospective of the group's work, McGuinn unearthed many recordings of Dylan songs that had never been released, including "Lay, Lady, Lay" and an earlier version of "It's All Over Now, Baby Blue." These were included on *The Byrds*, along with two live recordings, one of which ("Mr. Tambourine Man") included a guest appearance by Dylan. Of four new songs recorded by McGuinn, Hillman and Crosby for the set, one was Dylan's "Paths of Victory" from the early 1960s.

Dylan is said to have contributed the key verse to "Ballad of Easy Rider," a song that McGuinn performs on the soundtrack of the 1969 film *Easy Rider*. Filmmakers Dennis Hopper and Peter Fonda wanted a Dylan song, but Dylan did not participate in the soundtrack. Instead, McGuinn performed "It's Alright Ma (I'm Only Bleeding)" solo, and then sang the new song, which credits him as sole songwriter, apparently at Dylan's request. McGuinn rerecorded the song with The Byrds on the 1969 album, *Ballad of Easy Rider*.

Johnny Cash

Dylan's admiration for the legendary country singer was well known. Cash had a hit with a Mexicali version of "It Ain't Me Babe." After his collaboration with Dylan for *Nashville Skyline*, Cash was the recipient of a new Dylan song, "Wanted Man," which he recorded on the *Johnny Cash at San Quentin* album and on the soundtrack album for the 1970 film *Little Fauss and Big Halsey*, starring Robert Redford and Michael J. Pollard.

Cher
At the height of her fame as a duo with husband Sonny Bono, Cher recorded Dylan's "All I Really Want to Do." The song competed with The Byrds' version on the charts, and Cher's recording won.

Judy Collins
This folk-turned-pop singer has recorded Dylan songs throughout her career. Early on, she included Dylan songs on most of her records. However, as she became more of a pop artist in the 1970s and 1980s, she rarely included a track written by Dylan. Among her recordings are "Daddy, You've Been on My Mind" and "Time Passes Slowly."

Coulson, Dean, McGuinness, Flint
This obscure British band recorded a slew of little-known Dylan songs in the early 1970s for an album called *Lo and Behold*. Early songs such as "Let Me Die in My Footsteps" were given honorable treatments, and the band mined the bootlegged basement tapes for a number of gems that would not be released until *The Basement Tapes* was made public in 1975.

The Everly Brothers
Donald and Philip Everly grew up in show business. They were seasoned veterans by the time they were teen-agers and had a run of rock 'n' roll hits in the late 1950s. They influenced The Beatles, Simon and Garfunkel, and Bob Dylan, all of whom were adolescents when The Everly Brothers enjoyed their early success.

In late 1968, Dylan offered The Everly Brothers the song "Lay, Lady, Lay." The brothers turned it down. Phil Everly later said they thought the key line of the song was "lay across my *big breasts, babe*," and felt it was too weird to record.

After a 10-year hiatus from recording together, The Everly Brothers regrouped in the mid-1980s and finally recorded "Lay, Lady, Lay" on their *EB '84* album.

"Lay, Lady, Lay" was an adequate performance, but two years later they recorded a fine version of a long-lost Dylan song that was only recently resurrected on *Biograph*. Their version of "Abandoned Love," complete with Irish pipes, stands as one of their finest recordings, which is quite a testament considering the high quality of their work. It appeared on their 1986 album, *Born Yesterday*.

Guns 'n' Roses
This inexplicably popular hard rock band of the 1990s had one of its biggest hits with Dylan's dirge, "Knockin' on Heaven's Door." Afterward, Dylan

asked the group's lead guitar player, known as Slash, to play on *Under the Red Sky*.

George Harrison
The former Beatle and Dylan met at Dylan's Woodstock home in 1970 to write songs together. The only collaboration ever released, "I'd Have You Any Time," opened Harrison's massive *All Things Must Pass* album. Harrison also performed Dylan's "If Not for You." Harrison's arrangement was copied, nearly note-for-note, by Olivia Newton-John, who scored her first hit with the song.

Jimi Hendrix
Dylan himself said that Hendrix did a brilliant cover of "All along the Watchtower," turning this quiet and ominous song into a noisy and ominous one. Hendrix's recording shows what a fine singer he was. His guitar mastery usually overshadowed the distinctive singing. Hendrix also recorded "Like a Rolling Stone" at the Monterey Pop Festival in 1967, and his performance was released as one side of an album in 1971. The flip side was made up of Otis Redding's performance at the same festival. Dylan so much liked Hendrix's arrangement of "Watchtower" that he began performing it in concert in the Hendrix style. He said of his later performances of "Masters of War" that he was also doing that song just as Hendrix would have done it.

The Hollies
This superb British band emerged in the wake of "Beatlemania" with a number of great pop hits. The group, which took its name from Buddy Holly, was known for the blended voices of Allan Clark, Tony Hicks and Graham Nash.

As the 1960s neared its end, The Hollies struggled to find a direction. The group decided to record an album of Bob Dylan songs, but Nash revolted. This was not the time, he told his bandmates, to record songs by other people. The audience expected bands to do only original songs. Consequently, in 1969, Nash left to become a member of Crosby, Stills and Nash (occasionally known as Crosby, Stills, Nash and Young), and The Hollies recorded *Words and Music by Bob Dylan*. It is too bad Nash left when he did: The only complaint a listener could make about this album is that Nash's high harmony is absent. It is a selection of cleverly arranged and performed Dylan songs. Some were radical reworkings of his early material. "When the Ship Comes In" became a banjo-strumming stomp behind Clark's rich vocal, while "Blowin' in the Wind" became a theaterpiece, performed like a Broadway showstopper.

Manfred Mann

This British group had a number of hits at the height of the British Invasion in the mid-1960s, but perhaps the greatest hit was "The Mighty Quinn." This Dylan song, which in later years has become known as "Quinn the Eskimo," is a product of the *Basement Tapes* era. It was an international hit in 1969. A recording of "If You Gotta Go, Go Now" met with less success.

Terry Melcher

One of the stranger cover versions of a Dylan song is Melcher's inclusion of "Like a Rolling Stone" as a part of a medley on his eponymous 1973 album. Melcher, the son of singer Doris Day, produced several classic albums by The Byrds and frequently wrote and produced records by The Beach Boys in the late 1980s.

Bette Midler

Midler's cover version of "Buckets of Rain" is unusual because it features a duet with the song's composer. The slow, contemplative number takes on a bossa nova element on Midler's 1975's *Songs for the New Depression*.

Rick Nelson

As a child, Ricky Nelson was the adorable kid on "The Adventures of Ozzie and Harriet," the radio and television program that starred his parents. As a teenager, Nelson became one of the most successful early rock 'n' roll stars. Long criticized for merely being a safer, more clean-cut version of Elvis Presley, it is obvious, looking back, that Nelson made fine pop records. He began calling himself Rick Nelson when he turned 21, and moved on to a career in movies. The music career slowed, though Nelson's mid-1960s recordings were prototypes of country rock.

Nelson's comeback hit in 1969 was Dylan's "She Belongs to Me." Backed with The Stone Canyon Band, Nelson had considerable chart success with this song. The followup album, *Rick Nelson in Concert*, showcased that tune as well as a rollicking version of "If You Gotta Go, Go Now." With a new audience and new respect, Nelson was interested in showing his maturation as a writer, so he followed that success with *Rick Sings Nelson*, his first album of all-original material. The follow-up to that record, *Rudy the Fifth*, was primarily original material but did include two Dylan cover versions. Nelson's "Just Like a Woman" was accurate, but it was odd to hear "little Ricky" sing of amphetamines. His performance of the other song, "Love Minus Zero/No Limit," was superb. It may be the best version of a Dylan song another artist has recorded. Nelson also recorded "Tonight I'll Be Staying Here with You," but had greater success with "Garden Party," his lament on fleeting fame.

The Neville Brothers
This New Orleans group achieved mass acclaim (after years of cult status) with their 1989 album, *Yellow Moon*. Aaron Neville's quavering voice was perfect for Dylan's "With God on Our Side." New verses were added with references to the Vietnam War, which was still in the early stages when Dylan wrote the song. The album was produced by Daniel Lanois, who so impressed Dylan that he used him to produce *Oh Mercy* later that year.

Olivia Newton-John
The Australian singer's first hit was with Dylan's "If Not for You," in 1971. Her arrangement was identical to that of George Harrison.

Nilsson
Singer Harry Nilsson teamed with John Lennon and an all-star rock 'n' roll band in 1973 to record the *Pussycats* album. Included was a maniacal, cacophonic version of "Subterranean Homesick Blues."

The Persuasions
This a cappella band did wonderful versions of two *New Morning* songs on their 1971 record, *Spread the Word*: "The Man in Me" and "Father of Night."

Peter, Paul and Mary
Bob Dylan made the pop charts as a songwriter thanks to Peter Yarrow, Noel Paul Stookey and Mary Travers. This trio was at the forefront of the folk music boom in the early 1960s. They recorded traditional folk songs, yet were quick to recognize Dylan's revolutionary songs and give them wide appeal. "Blowin' in the Wind" was their first hit, and the trio recorded Dylan's songs throughout their career. Among their recordings are "Bob Dylan's Dream," "Don't Think Twice, It's All Right" and "Too Much of Nothing."

Elvis Presley
Of all the cover versions of his songs, Dylan said he was proudest of Elvis Presley's recording of "Tomorrow Is a Long Time." Presley included this on the soundtrack of *Speedway*, his 1966 film.

Linda Ronstadt
While still a member of The Stone Poneys, Ronstadt recorded a bluesy bar-band version of "I'll Be Your Baby Tonight." (Actress Goldie Hawn also recorded this song on her one-and-only attempt at music stardom.)

The Earl Scruggs Revue
The legendary banjo player, his sons and other assorted musicians enjoyed some acclaim as a crossover act in the early 1970s. They recorded

"Nashville Skyline Rag" with Dylan on *His Family and Friends* and included "Most Likely You Go Your Way (And I'll Go Mine)" on *Live at Kansas State*.

Bruce Springsteen

One of the "new Dylans" touted by critics and record companies, Springsteen has commercially released only one Dylan song. "Chimes of Freedom" was the centerpiece of Springsteen's live 1988 mini-album, which was drawn from his *Tunnel of Love* tour. He prefaced the song with an announcement of a tour with Sting, Peter Gabriel and other artists on behalf of Amnesty International. The line about those individuals who are "misplaced" in jails drew a rousing response from the audience.

The Turtles

This band had success similar to that of The Byrds in getting Dylan's songs into the top ten. The vehicle was "It Ain't Me Babe," which sounded great with the harmonies of Howard Kaylan and Mark Volman. The Turtles had many other hits, including "Happy Together" and "You Baby." Kaylan and Volman also performed under the name The Phlorescent Leech and Eddie, which they then shortened to Flo and Eddie.

U2

The Irish quartet was one of the most popular bands in the 1980s. Dylan performed onstage with the group and appears on two tracks on their *Rattle and Hum* album. That album also featured a blistering version of "All along the Watchtower."

Stevie Wonder

Beginning his musical career as a child prodigy named "Little Stevie Wonder," this successful Motown Records artist embraced Dylan's music in the mid-1960s with a soulful, reworked version of "Blowin' in the Wind" which became one of his biggest hits of the era.

Section VI: Bootlegs

Dylan is among the most bootlegged of popular musicians. It would be nearly impossible to list all his bootlegged recordings, since many of them are bootlegs of other bootlegs, and are, by their illegal nature, of unknown origin and date. This lists major sources of these recordings and lists titles of representative bootleg albums.

Minnesota Tapes, 1960-1961

These tapes (from a 1960, a May 1961 party and a December 1961 session in a Minneapolis hotel room) contain some of his earliest recordings. The December 1961 songs were taped after Dylan had spent time in New York. One of his original songs (though, of course, it was based on an old folk melody) was--appropriately enough--"Hard Times in New York Town," eventually released as the opening track on *The Bootleg Series, Vols. 1-3*. Most of the rest of the songs taped in this era were standard folk and blues numbers, including some Woody Guthrie songs. A partial listing includes "Hard Times in New York Town," "I Ain't Got No Home," "Ramblin' Round," "Man of Constant Sorrow," "Wade in the Water," "Gospel Plow," "See That My Grave is Kept Clean," "VD Blues," "VD Waltz," and "Stealin'."

Notable bootleg albums:

Number One. Recorded in 1960, this album features traditionals and talking blues.

Minnesota 1961. The party tape includes standards, as well as one of Dylan's earliest songs, "Why'd You Cut My Hair?"

John Birch Society Blues. Although this album includes later outtakes from studio albums, some of the tracks are drawn from the Minnesota tape.

Carnegie Chapter Hall, 4 November 1961

Dylan's first major New York concert had only 53 persons in the audience, but at least one of them had the foresight to bring a tape recorder. Dylan performed several traditional tunes and tried on a high, pretty voice for "A Long Time A-Growin'," a Scotch ballad.

Notable bootleg album:

Acoustic Troubadour. In addition to seven tracks from the concert, this album includes two songs from the Concert for Bangladesh in 1971, and a couple of early versions of songs from *Blood on the Tracks*.

Columbia Outtakes, 20-22 November 1961

There were a lot of leftovers for the John Hammond-produced sessions for *Bob Dylan*. A partial listing includes "He Was a Friend of Mine," "Man on the Street," "House Carpenter" and "Connecticut Cowboy," a spoken introduction to Jesse Fuller's "You're No Good" (a song that did make it on the album).

Coffee Houses and Night Clubs, 1961-1963

Several of Dylan's performances at Greenwich Village clubs were recorded. The earlier the performance, the more likely that the set included traditionals. By the end of the coffee house period, Dylan's performances were almost exclusively original material.

Notable bootleg albums:

Acoustic Set (NYC, 1963). Includes several songs that were recorded but never made it onto albums in the era ("Walls of Red Wing," "New Orleans Rag," "Hero Blues"). Despite the date in the title, part of this album was obviously recorded at a later date, since it includes songs from *Bringing It All Back Home* and *Blonde on Blonde*.

Documents of Bob Dylan. Four volumes exist of these early performances at The Gaslight Club in New York and The Finjan Club in Montreal.

Gaslight Tapes. At least two excellent albums exist, taken from Dylan's 1962 performances at The Gaslight Club.

Finjan Club. This is a superior recording from the Montreal club.

Exclusive. Although this album contains studio outtakes, much of it comes from performances at Gerde's Folk City in New York and The Bear in Chicago.

Cynthia Gooding Tape

Dylan taped an hourlong interview and mini-concert with Gooding on 11 March 1962, performing Hank Williams's "Lonesome Whistle," Woody Guthrie's "Hard Travelin'," and a few originals, including "The Death of Emmett Till" and "Hard Times in New York Town." The tape was most notable for Dylan's stories of traveling with carnivals and his life on the road. He also predicted he would never be rich and famous.

Notable bootleg album:

Folksinger's Choice. This contains the whole program with Dylan, including all of the interview segments.

Radio Performances, 1962

Dylan's performances from his broadcasts were much bootlegged. A couple of songs eventually appeared on *Broadside Reunion*. Some of the songs Dylan performed included "Baby, Let Me Follow You Down," "Talkin' John Birch Society Blues," "The Death of Emmett Till," "Make Me a Pallet on the Floor," "Denise," "Dusty Old Fairgrounds" and "Black Cross."

Notable bootleg albums:

Back to the Roots. Dylan mixes originals and standards. A couple of the tracks were music demos.

Columbia Outtakes, 1962-1963

These sessions for *The Freewheelin' Bob Dylan* were held in Columbia Studios in New York City. They were scattered throughout the year--one date in April, another in July, two days in October, three days in November, a date in early December and a followup session in late April of the following year. This was a fruitful time for Dylan. It resulted in the rare "Mixed Up Confusion" single--so rare it was a staple on Dylan bootlegs for years--and several songs that finally appeared on *The Bootleg Series, Vols. 1-3*.

The fact that the *Freewheelin'* album was altered soon after release made rarities of the four songs that were bumped from the first version of the album. They were bootlegged for years before their inclusion on *The Bootleg Series*. These songs are "Talkin' John Birch Society Blues," "Rocks and Gravel," "Let Me Die in My Footsteps" and "Ramblin' Gamblin' Willie." Two songs from these sessions, which have long been bootlegged, appeared on *Biograph*: "Mixed Up Confusion" (alternate take of the single) and "Baby, I'm in the Mood for You." Other songs that eventually made it onto *The Bootleg Series* include "Talkin' Bear Mountain Picnic Massacre Blues," "Quit Your Lowdown Ways," "Kingsport Town" and "Talkin' Hava Negeilah Blues."

Other songs at the session that still have not appeared on a commercial release include "Milk Cow Blues," "Wichita Blues," "Going to New Orleans," an early version of "Ballad of Hollis Brown," "Hero Blues," "Lonesome Whistle," and an alternate version of "The Death of Emmett Till."

Notable bootleg album:

Talkin' Bear Mountain Massacre Picnic Blues. Although many albums range over this material, this record is perhaps the best representative set taken from the session. It also includes a sampling of the December 1961 Minneapolis tape.

The Broadside Sessions, October 1962-March 1963

Most of these appeared on Folkways records, with Dylan performing on some under his Blind Boy Grunt pseudonym. Since these recordings were not widely available, they were prime material for bootlegs. A partial listing includes "Only a Hobo," "Paths of Victory," "John Brown," "Let Me Die in My Footsteps," "Cuban Missile Crisis." Selections from these sessions appeared on several bootlegs.

Publishing Demos, 1962-1964

During the years that Dylan's music was published by M. Witmark and Sons, he recorded a number of songs in his publisher's office. Earlier, when he had briefly been signed with Leeds Music, he made a few similar tapes. Some of the songs appeared on *The Bootleg Series*: "Walkin' Down the Line," "When the Ship Comes In" and "The Times They Are A-Changin'." Most of the rest of the songs eventually appeared on Dylan albums. These are simple recordings, usually with only Dylan's guitar, piano and voice.

Notable bootleg albums:

He Was a Friend of Mine. This album contains the Leeds demos and some outtakes from *Freewheelin'*.

Ceremonies for the Horsemen. This album is the most extensive collection of these recordings, including "Only a Hobo," "All Over You," "Tomorrow is a Long Time," "Hero Blues" and "The Rise and Fall of Hollis Brown."

Demo Tapes. In addition to the standard fare, this album includes "Lost

Highway" (written by Leon Payne) and "I'm So Lonesome I Could Cry" (written by Hank Williams).

Witmark Demos. This six-sided vinyl album includes nearly everything Dylan recorded for his publisher.

Columbia Outtakes, August-October 1963

The sessions for *The Times They Are A-Changin'* also produced "Percy's Song" and "Lay Down Your Weary Tune," which showed up on *Biograph*, and several songs that appeared on *The Bootleg Series, Vols. 1-3*. These songs are "Suze (The Cough Song)," "Moonshiner," "Only a Hobo," Seven Curses," "Eternal Circle," "Walls of Red Wing" and "Paths of Victory." Other songs that were recorded include "California" (an early version of "Outlaw Blues") and "Hero Blues," the song Dylan resurrected to open his 1974 tour with The Band.

Notable bootleg albums:

Bob Dylan. Several tracks on this album ("Long John," "Milk Cow Calves Blues" and "Going to New Orleans") remain unreleased.

Columbia Outtakes, 1964

These sessions for *Another Side of Bob Dylan* also produced "Mama, You Been on My Mind," which eventually appeared on *The Bootleg Series, Vols. 1-3*. Other outtakes include "Denise," "Farewell," "East Laredo Blues," "New Orleans Rag," "That's All Right (Mama)," "Sally Free and Easy" and an early version of "Mr. Tambourine Man."

Notable bootleg album:

Twelve Curses. This is the best collection from these sessions, including a bonus track: an early 1970s recording from Dylan's telephone answering machine.

Concert Recordings, 1964-1965

Recordings of performances in this era showed Dylan moving into larger venues. The 1964 and early 1965 performances were all-acoustic. Later 1965 shows featured a rock band.

Notable bootleg albums:

All Hallow's Eve 1964. This bootleg, originally released on vinyl, is drawn from Dylan's concert at Philharmonic Hall and includes two duets with Joan Baez. Dylan performs "If You Gotta Go, Go Now" as a solo acoustic number and offers an early version of "Gates of Eden." Most of the remaining material is from *The Times They Are A-Changin'* and *Another Side of Bob Dylan*. Another version of the bootleg is title *Halloween Masque*.

All Hallow's Eve and More 1964. This includes the best of the material on the earlier bootleg, supplemented with four tracks from an earlier Philadelphia performance.

Now Ain't the Time for Your Tears. One of Dylan's final all-acoustic concerts forms the basis of this bootleg, recorded in Manchester on May 7, 1965. The complete 77-minute show is in much the same style as the performances in the film *Don't Look Back.*

Newport/Forest Hills, 1965

These two legendary concerts were taped. Dylan's band chugs through a racuous "Maggie's Farm" at Newport. After a symphony of boos, Dylan returns with an acoustic "Mr. Tambourine Man."

The Forest Hills tape, a month after Newport, is more complete, with much of the *Bringing It All Back Home* material and a few tastes of electricity from *Highway 61 Revisited*. The acoustic "I Don't Believe You" is retooled as a rock 'n' roll song.

Notable bootleg albums:

Live in Newport 1965. The controversial live set that enraged the folk crowd is the centerpiece of this album.

Forest Hills 1965. The controversial show is featured in its entirety, supplemented with three songs from the 1974 Friends of Chile benefit concert with Arlo Guthrie and Pete Seeger.

World Tour with The Hawks, 1966

Shows at Manchester and at Royal Albert Hall during Dylan's tour with The Hawks were recorded and released under bootlegs that traveled under some variation of the "Royal Albert Hall" name.

These performances include Dylan's celebrated confrontations with audiences unhappy with his new electric music. The tension elevated the performances of Dylan and The Hawks. The "Like a Rolling Stone" on these bootlegs is a performance without equal.

In addition to the Manchester and London recordings, Dylan's concerts in Dublin, Bristol, Liverpool and Belfast were also bootlegged. Dylan and The Hawks perform "Tell Me, Momma" on many of these tapes. It was a song Dylan frequently used to open shows but which he never released.

Notable bootleg albums:

He's Your Lover Now. These rehearsals for the tour include "Midnight Train," "I Wanna Be Your Lover" and "Number One." Mike Bloomfield and Al Kooper are also featured.

Adelphi Theatre Dublin. The acoustic portion of the Dylan/Hawks tour is featured.

Royal Albert Hall 1966. This live recording earned reviews in *Rolling Stone* and other above-ground publications. Some critics, asked to compile "best of" lists periodically, list this bootleg as one of the finest records ever made, even though it was not commercially released. This bootleg was bootlegged and appears under many titles, including *Bob Dylan and The Band*

Live in England and *Bob Dylan and The Band in the Royal Albert Hall.*

Bob Dylan and The Band, Al Kooper and Mike Bloomfield. This album includes some 1966 tour recordings, matched with 1964 studio outtakes and 1965 studio work with Bloomfield and Kooper.

Burn Some More. This collection includes many oddities: "Who You Really Are," "All Over You," "You Don't Do Me Like You Used to Do" and "Goin' Back to Rome."

"Big Pink" Sessions, West Saugerties, New York, June-October 1967

These famous recordings from the basement of a big pink house rented by members of The Band produced rock 'n' roll's first best-selling bootleg, *The Great White Wonder.* A number of the songs were eventually released on Dylan and The Band's counter-bootleg, *The Basement Tapes.* "The Mighty Quinn (Quinn the Eskimo)" was released on *Biograph*, and "Santa Fe" showed up on *The Bootleg Series, Vols. 1-3.* Acetates of several songs for Dylan's new music publisher, Dwarf Music, were copied and fed to bootleggers.

Other songs from the sessions that were not commercially released include "Get Your Rocks Off," "I'm Not There (1956)," "Sign on the Cross," "Bonnie Ship the Diamond," "The Hills of Mexico," "People Get Ready," "All You Have to Do Is Dream," "A Fool Such as I" and "Bourbon Street."

Notable bootleg albums:

The Great White Wonder. Although this album was technically a career retrospective, it was the first place most collectors heard the basement tapes.

Million Dollar Bash. Most of the material on this bootleg was eventually released commercially on *The Basement Tapes.*

More Music From Big Pink. This representative bootleg contains the songs recorded but left off of *The Basement Tapes*: "All I Have to Do is Dream," "I Can't Make It Alone," "Bonnie Ship the Diamond," "Young But Daily Growing," "One Man's Loss," "The Hills of Mexico," "One For the Road," "One Single River," "Try Me Little Girl," "I Don't Hurt Anymore," "People Get Ready," "Baby, Ain't That Fine," "A Night Without Sleep," "A Fool Such As I," "Gonna Get You Now" and "Stones That You Throw."

Isle of Wight, 1969

Dylan left American concertgoers to waddle in the mud near his home for the "three days of peace, music and love" at the Woodstock festival in August 1969. Dylan and his family went to Europe, where Dylan and The Band performed at a comparatively more civilized festival on the Isle of Wight.

Recordings from this show were released on *Self Portrait*, showing the performance to have been somewhat ragged. A planned commercial release of a live album was scrapped, so the bootleggers profited from that performance.

Dylan and The Band performed "The Mighty Quinn," recently a hit for Manfred Mann, and "Minstrel Boy," Dylan's one new composition for the show. They also did the traditional "Wild Mountain Thyme." Most of the remaining songs were drawn from his 1965-1969 albums.

Notable bootleg album:

Isle of Wight. Several different recordings of the concert have appear, most with a variation on this title. An exception was the album *Minstrel Boy*.

Unreleased Recordings, 1969-1970

During this period of seclusion, Dylan made some studio and living-room demos with Johnny Cash and George Harrison.

Notable bootleg albums:

Nashville Sunset. Several recordings of album outtakes and warmup songs (Carl Perkins's "Matchbox" and "That's All Right, Mama") make up this album.

Bob Dylan Meets George Harrison and Johnny Cash. This album includes traditionals ("Good Old Mountain Dew"), rock 'n' roll standards ("Da Do Ron Ron"), as well as songs associated with Dylan ("One Too Many Mornings"), Cash ("I Still Miss Someone") and The Beatles ("Yesterday"). This is a truly varied collection.

Soundtrack Recordings, 1973

Dylan recorded a lot of material for the film *Pat Garrett and Billy the Kid* that was not released on the soundtrack album.

Notable bootleg album:

Alias. This was made up of leftovers and alternate versions.

SNACK Benefit, 1975

Dylan's performance with Neil Young, Rick Danko, Levon Helm and members of Young's band produced a couple of bootlegs. The only Dylan song was "I Want You." The other tunes were associated with Young or The Band.

Notable bootleg albums:

Bob Dylan and Neil Young in Concert.

Dollar Snack.

"Infidels" Sessions, 1983

Two songs left off of the 1983 release, "Blind Willie McTell" and "Foot of Pride," were widely bootlegged, leading to fans to speculate why Dylan would not release such brilliant work.

Notable bootleg albums:

Outfidels. This album was the primary source for "Blind Willie McTell" until Dylan allowed its commercial release in 1991.

Down in the Flood. Largely alternate versions of *Infidels* songs, this album also features "I Ain't Goin' Back" (the bootlegger's title for "Foot of Pride") and "No American Can Sing the Blues Like Blind Willie McTell" (another apparent bootlegger's variation on a title).

Idiot Wind. As the *Blood on the Tracks* era title suggests, this compilation features the New York recordings from the earlier album, along with the usual *Infidels* outtakes.

Last Infidels Outtakes. Includes some of the usual material, along with a little-heard Dylan song, "Julius and Ethel," about the Rosenbergs. It also includes Sonny Boy Williamson's "Don't Start Me to Talkin'" and "Someone's Got a Hold of My Heart," the early version of "Tight Connection to My Heart."

"Empire Burlesque" Sessions, 1985

Some of the material recorded has yet to be released commercially and a few of the songs were extensively reworked.

Notable bootleg album:

Empire Burlesque Outtakes. In addition to alternate versions, this album includes "Waiting to Get Beat," "Crazy Love," "The Very Thought of You," "Who Loves You More" and "New Danville Girl" (eventually released as "Brownsville Girl").

Live Aid, 1985

Dylan's performance with Ron Wood and Keith Richards of The Rolling Stones fared better without the visual distraction of the worldwide television performance.

"Oh Mercy" Sessions, 1989

Working with producer Daniel Lanois in New Orleans, Dylan produced too much material for a single album, so bootleggers released the extra songs.

Notable bootleg albums:

The Bootleg Series, Vol. 4. Most of these were *Oh Mercy* outtakes, with an early version of "Born in Time" (to appear on *Under the Red Sky*) and a song called "Dignity." A live recording of "Desolation Row" was also tagged on. A nearly identical album was titled *No Mercy*.

Concert Recordings, 1974-1990

Since Dylan's comeback tour with The Band in 1974, his concerts have been widely bootlegged. During his gospel tours in the early 1980s, Dylan performed a number of original new songs in concert that he never used on albums. Collectors therefore prize their stashes of concert tapes.

Tours that were particularly popular with bootleggers and collectors include The Rolling Thunder Revue, 1975 (first leg); The Vegas Tour/The Alimony Tour, 1978; The *Shot of Love* Tour, 1981; The "True Confessions" Tour with Tom Petty and the Heartbreakers, 1986; The Tour with the Grateful Dead, 1987; and The Never-Ending Tour, 1987--.

Notable bootleg albums:

Bob Dylan/The Band. A complete show from the 1974 tour, this bootleg is a counter release to *Before the Flood*.

Brothers of the Flood. This album was drawn from the Dylan/Band show in Boston on January 14, 1974.

High Voltage. This recording from the 1974 tour is most notable for a 29 minute version of "Like a Rolling Stone."

Get Ready! Tonight Bob's Staying Here With You. This clumsily titled double album includes all of the Dylan songs from a November 1975 performance in Boston, early in the Rolling Thunder Revue.

Believe What You Heard. A Rolling Thunder Revue bootleg, this album includes performances taped in Boston and Providence in the fall of 1975.

Dark as a Dungeon. This Rolling Thunder show from Toronto in November 1975 features most of Dylan's songs from the set, leaving out the performances by other members of the Revue's cast.

Hurricane Carter Benefit. This album is drawn from the "Night of the Hurricane" show at Madison Square Garden on December 8, 1975.

Clearwater. This album is drawn from the second leg of the Rolling Thunder Revue, recorded in April 1976 for Dylan's aborted television special. It includes "Rita May" and "Hold Me in Your Arms."

Hold the Fort for What It's Worth. Recorded late in the second leg of the Rolling Thunder Revue tour, this concert was also the source for a few tracks on the *Hard Rain* album.

By the Time We Got to Blackbushe. Originally an eight-sided album, this set is drawn from the *Street Legal* tour in 1978, with Dylan's big-band sound.

I Was Young When I Left Home. Another bootleg drawn the *Street Legal* tour, this album was recorded in Toronto.

Highway 80 Revisited. This recording from the *Saved* tour shows Dylan beginning to incorporate his older songs into his gospel repertoire. It includes "Let's Keep it Between Us," "Abraham, Martin and John" and "Caribbean Wind."

Nearer to the Fire. This is a representative bootleg from the 1978-1980 era, including "Thief on the Cross," "Repossession Blues," and "Ain't Gonna Go to Hell for Anybody."

Dreams for Sale. This 1981 performance from the *Shot of Love* tour includes "Let It Be Me," "Here Comes the Sun" and "Barbara Allen."

Barcelona. Recorded during the 1984 European tour that produced *Real Live*, this album features most of the songs that appeared on the commercial album, as well as "Every Grain of Sand," "Senor (Tales of Yankee Power)" and "Jokerman."

His Master's Voice. The original vinyl album had six sides drawn from the 1984 European tour, featuring Carlos Santana on guitar for a couple of tracks.

The Byrd and the Sparrow. These recordings from the 1984 European toiur feature former Byrds leader Roger McGuinn on several tracks.

Bob Dylan Featuring Tom Petty. Highlights from Dylan's 1986 Far East True Confessions Tour with Tom Petty and The Heartbreakers, variations of this bootleg travel under many names, including *Precious Memories* and *Duelling Banjos*. Most of these are superb live recordings.

Osaka. The other Dylan/Petty bootlegs were highlights. This album was nearly a complete concert, including Dylan-less performances by Petty and his band, as well as such oddities as "Money, Money, Money" and Rick Nelson's "Lonesome Town."

Bob Dylan and The Grateful Dead. A counter album to the commercial release, this album features the standard set from the short joint tour in 1987.

Bob Dylan and The Grateful Dead: Studio Sessions. The bootleggers released two albums of rehearsals for the 1987 tour.

Bob Dylan and Triumph. Another bootleg of Dylan with The Grateful Dead, this album includes a rare live performance of "Watching the River Flow."

Days of '49. This album collects a number of Dylan oddities and cover versions from 1989 concerts, including "The Lakes of Pontchairtrain," "Across the Borderline," "Give My Love to Rose" and "Buffalo Skinners."

All the Way Down to Italy. Recorded with the G. E. Smith-led band in Italy during 1989, this album includes the old Eddy Arnold tune "You Don't Know Me" and Townes Van Zandt's "Pancho and Lefty."

Live at Toad's. The original vinyl bootleg contained eight sides of Dylan's concert-tour warmup at a bar called Toad's Place in New Haven, Connecticut. In addition to recent and rarely performed-in-concert tunes, Dylan did a number of unusual covers, including Bruce Springsteen's "Dancing in the Dark," Joe South's "Walk a Mile in My Shoes," and Ry Cooder's "Across the Borderline."

A Night at the Festival. Recorded in June 1990, this set includes live performances from the *Oh Mercy* tour.

Balance of Tryst. Another show from June 1990, with the standard set.

Career Retrospectives

Some bootleggers gathered tapes from various points in Dylan's career to assemble parallel-universe anthologies on the scale of *Biograph* or *The Bootleg Series*. These lavishly produced (by bootleg standards) sets may have spurred Dylan's counter-bootleg effort in the 1990s.

The Great White Wonder. This 1969 album established the bootleg industry. Drawn from early tapes of Dylan performances, it also included some of the material recorded with The Band and later released on *The Basement Tapes*. Perhaps as poetic justice, the bootleggers who produced *The Great White Wonder* found their album pirated frequently.

Blind Boy Grunt and The Hawks. Several bootlegs were compilations of Dylan's early recordings in New York City and his sessions with The Hawks in Woodstock. These were, in part, bootlegs of the *Great White Wonder* bootlegs, but these albums mined the "basement tapes" sessions more extensively than the earlier bootleg or *The Basement Tapes*.

Bob Dylan in Concert. This album was drawn from performances on the 1966 tour, the Isle of Wight concert in 1969 and unidentified concert performances of "Sitting on a Barbed Wire Fence" (titled "Killing Me Alive") and "If You Gotta Go, Go Now."

Could You Start Again Please? Following the same concept as *Bob Dylan in Concert*, this album traces Dylan's concert performances with shows from 1975, 1978, 1981 and 1984.

Over the Cliff. Although not an extensive examination of his career, this album samples various stages in his development, including Dylan and The Hawks in the studio, performing "Seems Like a Freeze Out" and "Over the Cliff," outakes from the *Times They Are A-Changin'* session, and alternate tracks recorded with Emmylou Harris for *Desire*.

Aspects. Many outtakes that later appeared on *The Bootleg Series* as well as a few rare concert performances are coupled with several songs recorded during the 1974 tour with The Band.

Rarities. Before *Biograph* and *The Bootleg Series*, these two volumes collected obscure singles and outtakes. Most of the tunes were eventually released on the Dylan-sanctioned retrospectives.

Dylan. The original vinyl bootleg had 40 sides from various stages in Dylan's career in the studio and on the stage.

Dr. Zimmerman's Original Old-Time Hootenany. This album, largely drawn from a Canadian television broadcast and home recordings, documents the early phase of Dylan's career.

Ten of Swords. This is less-exhausting than *Dylan*, but is otherwise the most thorough and highly regarded of Dylan's bootleg albums. Released not long after *Biograph*, the ten original vinyl sides were reviewed in major music magazines and whetted the appetite for the material that would appear five years later on *The Bootleg Series*. Some of this material still has not been commercially released.

Chapter 8

Film, Television and Video

BOB ZIMMERMAN'S FAMILY OWNED TWO THEATERS in Hibbing, and film always held a fascination for him. Bob Dylan has acknowledged movies as inspiration, with his song "Brownsville Girl" being an obvious result. In the song, the protagonist is standing in line to see *The Gunfighter*, with Gregory Peck, and ruminates on the place of art in the modern world.

John Bauldie has the found roots of Dylan's writing in a lot of films. The title character of George Stevens' *Shane* says, "I don't mind leaving; I'd just like it to be my idea." In Tennessee Williams's *Cat on a Hot Tin Roof* we hear another familiar phrase: "You don't know what love means. To you it's just another four-letter word." In *Sirocco*, Humphrey Bogart says, "I've got to move fast--I can't with you around my neck," while the following statement appears in *All through the Night*: "What would a sweetheart like that Hamilton dame be doing in a dump like this?"[1]

Sitting in the darkened movie theaters of the 1950s, Bob Zimmerman may have heard these lines, and they may have percolated through his head until they came out transformed years later. His first idols were Hank Williams and Little Richard. However, the images of Marlon Brando (particularly in motorcycle leathers in *The Wild One*) and James Dean were vital to his rebellion and his eventual discovery of his own identity, which was made from the components of others.

Brando and Dean were strong screen presences. Even in mediocre (or, in the case of Brando, weak) films, the two actors were magnetic. When other actors shared a screen with either of them, they were engaged in a battle for the audience's attention, so electrifying were these actors. Other performers noted the same quality with Dylan: *He* was the one whom people watched.

He drew the attention of audiences, even standing still. He may have sensed the power that he had as a visual presence and sought to enhance it. A film career would naturally exploit that.

However, Dylan never actively pursued a movie career. The 1967 documentary (filmed in 1965), *Don't Look Back*, showed his intensity on film. Although some of the cinema verite touches appear dated a quarter-century later, it still stands as a remarkable document of an artist in transition. When the film was released, however, Dylan was in seclusion, recovering from his motorcycle accident and becoming a family man. His recording schedule was light and his concert calendar nonexistent. He had the time but perhaps not the inclination to jump into motion pictures.

He appeared in Murray Lerner's *Festival* (released in 1967), which showed Dylan and a number of other performers in scenes shot at the 1964 and 1965 Newport Folk Festivals. Unfortunately, this little-seen documentary never earned a wide release. Footage of the 1966 world tour had been shot by D. A. Pennebaker and when Dylan was finally finished editing it five years later, *Eat the Document* was released but never distributed outside the major cities on the coasts. Pennebaker created his own version of the film, titled *Something Is Happening*, but it has been shown only at film festivals and at Pennebaker's lectures to college campuses and cinema societies. By contrast, Dylan's performance in *The Concert for Bangladesh* was widely released and remains available on home video.

However, none of these were starring performances. Dylan did not appear as an actor on film until the 1973 *Pat Garrett and Billy the Kid*, Sam Peckinpah's revisionist western. That film's failure at the box office was in large part due to the studio's tinkering with the final print before release, which rendered the film incomprehensible. Dylan earned good notices, but the "movie moguls" did not come knocking at his door.

Dylan's major foray into film was a project that was under his control, the epic *Renaldo and Clara*, which was filmed during the Rolling Thunder Revue tour in 1975-1976. When released in its original four-hour version in 1978, it was mercilessly attacked by critics and was not distributed nationwide. A two-hour version was similarly squelched. When Dylan finally returned to the screen a decade later, it was in an attempt at a conventional Hollywood film, *Hearts of Fire*, a Cinderella story of a young woman wanting to be a rock 'n' roll star. Dylan played an older man, a reclusive singer drawn out of retirement to help the girl, with whom he soon falls in love. His face, 20 years after *Don't Look Back*, was lined and sad where it had once been smooth and anarchistic. However, even in this weak film, Dylan showed his power over audiences. He had learned from Woody Guthrie and Robert Johnson, but he had also learned from Marlon Brando and James Dean. The magnetism of his voice on record could be matched with that of his face on screen.

Dylan's experiments with film have been largely unsuccessful. *Don't Look*

Back was a superior documentary of its time. *The Last Waltz* was a well-crafted, affectionate look at rock 'n' roll. However, his two theatrical films, *Pat Garrett and Billy the Kid* and *Hearts of Fire* are both deeply flawed. *Renaldo and Clara*, for all the brilliance of the concert scenes, suffers from pretentiousness.

Television has not played a large role in Dylan's career either. After a few bad experiences, notably with Steve Allen, Dylan refused many interview requests. He performed with Johnny Cash in 1969, a celebrated appearance notable for Dylan's taciturn nature. He also performed on "Saturday Night Live" and did such a memorable set on "Late Night with David Letterman" in 1984 that he was invited back for the program's tenth anniversary concert, at Radio City Music Hall. There were only two celebrity guests on the program: actor Bill Murray, who had been the first guest on the first show, and Dylan, whom Letterman described as his most memorable musical guest. Dylan earned a huge ovation when he walked on stage wearing an unconventional tuxedo. He was backed by an all-star band, including Chrissie Hynde and Steve Vai on guitars, Doc Severinson on trumpet, and Paul Shaffer, the show's musical director, on piano. Dylan signaled, and the band kicked into "Like a Rolling Stone." The musicians copied the original 1965 arrangement note-for-note, but were playing with more energy. Musicians not known for their ebullience were apparently delighted to be playing such a great song with a top-notch band.

The sole exception, of course, was Bob Dylan. Again--as he had on the Grammy Awards the previous year--he seemed to be mumbling, merely going through the motions. He sneered, he bared his teeth, he blinked, as if trying to keep awake. It was only when he was joined on the chorus by back-up singers--a superstar ensemble of Mavis Staples, Rosanne Cash, Michelle Shocked, Nanci Griffith and Emmylou Harris--that Dylan seemed to come to life, possibly realizing these talented musicians had come together to play what was his greatest song, and perhaps rock 'n' roll's greatest song. Mavis Staples initiated a gospel-tinged call-and-response with Dylan and kicked the performance into higher gear. With her help, Dylan finished the song with a show of strength that had been missing from previous television performances.

Whether the confused performance was intended to do so, it was the aspect of the Letterman anniversary show that dominated conversations about the program. Even when being deliberately uncommercial, Dylan could still steal the show.

In the first section that follows, Dylan's major films are discussed. Plot details are offered and critical assessments noted. In the second section, his television performances are noted, along with titles of the songs performed.

Section I: Films and Video

Film: *Don't Look Back*
Leacock-Pennebaker Films
Released 17 May 1967
Starring Bob Dylan
Supporting cast includes Joan Baez, Bob Neuwrith, Albert Grossman, Alan Price, Allen Ginsberg and Donovan.
Produced by Albert Grossman and John Court
Assistants: Howard Alk and Jones Alk
Directed by D. A. Pennebaker
Running time: 93 minutes
Note: The title on screen omits the apostrophe
Available on Paramount Home Video

This documentary of the 1965 tour of Great Britain shows Dylan at a critical point in his career. He has a large following, most of whom seem to be enamored with his protest songs, yet he has just recorded his first rock 'n' roll album, *Bringing It All Back Home*. The audience clamors for "The Times They Are A-Changin'," but he wants to sing "Maggie's Farm."

The film opens with a video. (It was not called a video back in 1967, when the film was released.) Dylan is shown holding cards with the keywords from "Subterranean Homesick Blues" on them, and dropping them after the word is heard. Poet Allen Ginsberg lurks in the background. This clip became a video plugging the release of *Biograph* in 1985.

After this opening, the film recounts the adventures of Dylan and his entourage--manager Albert Grossman and his wife Sally, attendant Bob Neuwirth, and lover Joan Baez--during a brief concert tour. During the tour, Dylan befriends musician Alan Price (who has just quit The Animals) and the "Welsh Dylan," Donovan, who becomes the butt of many of Dylan's jokes.

Dylan is at a peak. Musically, he is bursting with ideas. His sense of humor is endearing. In concert, he is an engaging performer, and he is a master of manipulation with the press. Throughout the film, we see him toying with reporters. A journalist wants to know his real message. "Keep a good head and always carry a light bulb," Dylan says. Accused of being an angry protest singer, Dylan says, "I'm not angry. I'm delightful."

During some interviews he is attentive. A journalist from the African Service of the British Broadcasting Corporation appears to have Dylan's full attention. However, another young reporter, who claims that he is "not really a journalist" but rather a science student, is devastated after a ten-minute conversation with Dylan, during which the singer challenges the student on every point of his conversation. Dylan is merely trying to amuse himself before taking the stage, but the student appears hurt and belittled.

There are many memorable sequences in the film:
* In the movie's oldest scene, Dylan is briefly shown singing "Only a Pawn in Their Game" during a voter registration rally in 1963. Though it occurred

less than a year before, we see how he has changed from the proletariat singer/songwriter in just a few months.

* Dylan rushes through his classics in concert, even the deeply felt "Lonesome Death of Hattie Carroll." Apparently, those songs are part of a past that is holding Dylan back from his head-first spiral into the future.

* Dylan and Neuwirth ham it up, like beatniks-come-lately, snapping fingers and jiving to what a cocktail party crowd considers to be "cool jazz."

* Dylan composes on a typewriter amid the din in his hotel suite while Joan Baez sings "Love Is Just a Four-Letter Word," Grossman holds court, and English singer Marianne Faithfull looks over Dylan's shoulder.

* Dylan greets by the sheriff's high lady of Birmingham, who tells him, "You're really a good example for our youth," while he squirms in embarrassment and humility.

* Dylan berates the London correspondent from *Time* magazine, whom he tells, "I know more about what you do than you will ever know about me." He also informs the writer, "I'm just as good a singer as Caruso."

* The final concert segment at Royal Albert Hall shows segments of his performances of new songs: "It's Alright, Ma (I'm Only Bleeding)," "Gates of Eden" and "Love Minus Zero/No Limit."

The lasting impression from this film is Dylan's humor. It is one of the funniest films of this type. It is also a fine documentary of an artist at work. Pennebaker generally gives a close, honest view of Dylan.

The was a long delay between the shooting of the film and its release, owing to Dylan's reluctance to grant Pennebaker permission to show it. Although it was ready in 1966, Dylan deliberated a year before acquiescing. By 1967, he was a different man from the kid of spring 1965. In the *New York Times*, Richard Goldstein complained that the film was "a finely wrought antique which offers no insight into Bob Dylan in 1967."[2]

Critics responded more to the film's subject than its director. Andrew Sarris, in the *Village Voice*, suggested that Pennebaker was only a good filmmaker if he had a good subject. He was not an artist himself, but he could adequately record the lives and works of artists. Furthermore, a good subject has to be an exhibitionist. Sarris wrote: "Dylan is performing in front of a camera. What Pennebaker records is not Bob Dylan as he really is--whatever that means--but rather how Bob Dylan responds to the role imposed on him by the camera. Compared to most of the public figures of his time, Dylan responds very well indeed."[3]

Pennebaker retains a fondness for both the film and its subject. Twenty years later, he said:

[Dylan] had to be extraordinary where most of us settle for just being adequate. *Don't Look Back* is about the sixties, and the man who got us through them. Bob Dylan is more than just a folk singer touted by the record industry, more than the songwriter whose poetry is the only kind many of us remember, more than the Kerouac-kid who haunts our best writing. He is a force that blew us out of one era and into another ... he remains the influential voice of our times.[4]

Film: *Eat the Document*
Leacock-Pennebaker Films
Released 8 February 1971
Starring Bob Dylan, J. R. Robertson, Rick Danko, Richard Manual, Garth Hudson, Mickey Jones
Filmed by D. A. Pennebaker
Edited by Bob Dylan, Howard Alk and Robbie Robertson
Directed by D. A. Pennebaker
Running time: 54 minutes
Not available on videocassette

This was the episode of ABC Television's "Stage 67" series that Dylan had been offered in late 1965. The series, which lasted one season, was an anthology program that included live stage performances, documentaries and television plays. Nothing was off-limits, not even Bob Dylan.

Pleased with the Pennebaker experience, Dylan and Grossman secured the filmmaker for the ABC program. Pennebaker hooked up with Dylan and company in May 1966, at the beginning of the controversial English leg of his world tour. From the start, Dylan and Pennebaker argued about the nature of the film, with Pennebaker seeing it as an extension (in color) of *Don't Look Back* and Dylan (prefiguring *Renaldo and Clara* by a decade) wanting to include actors' improvisations. Initially, it appears that the concert special for ABC and the Pennebaker film were separate projects, but they were combined in order to help all the participants concentrate their efforts.[5]

Pennebaker could also tell that the drugs were far out in the open in May 1966--more than they had been the previous year during the *Don't Look Back* tour. Pennebaker said:

> When I met up with them, there was an enormous amount of grass being smoked--it seemed like pounds of it. Also, Bob was taking a lot of amphetamines and who-knows-what-else, and he was scratching all the time. He was very edgy, very uptight, and he stayed up for days on end without sleep.[6]

There was confusion over the content of the film throughout. Pennebaker thought he was directing the film, while Dylan apparently thought he was there as a cameraman and that he, Dylan, would direct the project. One of the major scenes that Dylan directed involving a number of people emerging individually from a closet. Dylan had not fully formed his concept of the film, but the scenes were shot anyway. Pennebaker tried to convince Dylan that the film he needed to make was a documentary of the madness of a rock 'n' roll tour. The intimacy of the *Don't Look Back* tour was gone, and Dylan was at the head of a revolutionary movement. Dylan discouraged any filming during concerts, yet Pennebaker did manage to record one evening in Glasgow by walking on the stage, among Dylan and The Hawks.[7] He filmed a couple of other shows during which the audience heckled Dylan repeatedly. He also capture some offstage scenes, such as Dylan and Richard Manuel of The Hawks trying to purchase a girl from her boyfriend.

Pennebaker was frustrated. "Making home movies ... simply doesn't interest me very much," he said. "I'm not sure how to ... make other people's home movies for them."[8] When Pennebaker was away, his assistant Howard Alk took over the filming, capturing some strong anti-Dylan reaction from concertgoers.

In June 1966, Pennebaker and Dylan's road companion, Bob Neuwirth, had begun assembling the film for broadcast on ABC that fall. Dylan's motorcycle accident intervened, and the film was set aside for a while. Eventually, Dylan, Neuwirth and Robbie Robertson took turns editing the footage. It was edited, as Dylan said, "fast on the eye," so as to duplicate the amphetamine-driven pace of the tour.

The film was rejected by ABC and never shown on "Stage 67," with the network declaring it "too rough, too bleak and lurid" for their viewers.[9] Reportedly, Dylan retains the rights to the concert scenes that Pennebaker filmed but has not sanctioned their release beyond the tantalizing moments that he, Alk and Robertson put into the jumbled *Eat the Document*. Never widely shown, the film appeared at a few film festivals in the early 1970s and has been broadcast only once to date: on a local New York City station in 1979. Dylan has apparently come to feel that his experiment was something of a failure. "That film was a project we did to rescue a bunch of garbage footage ABC shot on our 1966 tour," Dylan said.[10]

Film: *The Concert for Bangladesh*
Apple Films
Released 23 March 1972
Starring George Harrison
Featuring Bob Dylan, Eric Clapton, Billy Preston, Leon Russell, Ravi Shankar and Ringo Starr
Music Recording Produced by George Harrison and Phil Spector
Produced by George Harrison and Allen Klein
Directed by Saul Swimmer
Running time: Approximately 101 minutes
Available on Warner Home Video

This was simply a recording of the August 1, 1971 benefit concert in Madison Square Garden. Former Beatle George Harrison learned of the plight of Bangladesh through his friend and sitar teacher, Ravi Shankar, and organized two concerts to raise money for food and health supplies for the famine victims. It was the first major charity effort by rock 'n' roll artists. The mere presence of George Harrison rendered the concert a media event. The quietest member of The Beatles, he had the year before issued *All Things Must Pass*, a boxed three-record set of orchestral rock music. He signed on a superstar band that included Leon Russell, Eric Clapton, Billy Preston and Ringo Starr. John Lennon had been scheduled to appear but he backed out when he feared the presence of three members of The Beatles might create pressure for a reunion of the group, which had disbanded the year before.

Bob Dylan's name was not announced before the concert, yet his appearance was not a total surprise as his association with Harrison was well known. Still, Harrison could not be sure that he would participate. "It was very difficult to try and get him to come out," Harrison said. "In fact, right up to the moment he stepped on stage I wasn't sure if he was going to come on."[11] Harrison had a set list written down. After "Here Comes the Sun," he had written *Bob?* He and Dylan had rehearsed "If Not for You," but of course Dylan did not play it, though it had appeared on both his and Harrison's latest albums. Harrison and the other musicians had no idea what Dylan would play. In fact, Harrison had asked Dylan at a rehearsal, "Do you think you could sing . . . 'Blowin' in the Wind'? The audience would just love it." Dylan snapped back, "Are you gonna sing, 'I Want to Hold Your Hand'?" Consequently, when Dylan sang "Blowin' in the Wind," Harrison was just as surprised as the audience.[12] Dylan did no new songs; the most recent was nearly six years old. Harrison, Russell and Starr performed backup on the songs, improvising as Dylan played. Harrison and Russell even harmonized with Dylan, once they figured out what he was playing.

Despite this lack of rehearsal, at both concerts (and in the film edited from both concert performances) Dylan's appearance is the high point. Harrison's voice nearly catches as he says, "I'd like to bring on a friend of us all, Mr. Bob Dylan." The ovation is tremendous. Dylan performed four songs at the matinee and evening performances: "A Hard Rain's A-Gonna Fall," "Blowin' in the Wind," "It Takes a Lot to Laugh, It Takes a Train to Cry" and "Just Like a Woman." He sang "Love Minus Zero/No Limit" at the afternoon concert and replaced it with "Mr. Tambourine Man" in the evening set. The evening show's performance was included in the film and on the soundtrack album, along with a brief run-through of "If Not for You" in a before-concert rehearsal with Harrison.

Intended as a television special and blown up to wide screen size, the film is particularly grainy, yet Dylan's performance was "one of Bob's finest hours, not only because it was his first time on an American stage in five years, but also because his performance was so aggressive and exciting."[13]

The documentary form of the rock concert had been raised to a higher level with Michael Wadleigh's *Woodstock* (1970), his split-screen, multilevel record of the 1969 music festival. By comparison, *The Concert for Bangladesh* was a simple film of a concert. However, the performances were so powerful, that the critics were won over. The *Village Voice* wrote: "Someone has written than audiences are feminine. If that's correct, Shankar embraced it, Harrison made love to it, and Dylan took it by force."[14]

Film: *Pat Garrett and Billy the Kid*

Metro-Goldwyn Mayer
Released May 1973
Starring James Coburn and Kris Kristofferson
Supporting cast includes Jason Robards, Bob Dylan, Richard Jaeckel, John Beck, Katy Jurado, Slim Pickens, Dub Taylor, Elisha Cook, Paul Fix, Jack Elam, Rita Coolidge and Chill Wills.
Screenplay by Rudolph Wurlitzer
Produced by Gordon Carroll
Directed by Sam Peckinpah
Running time: 122 minutes
Available on Warner Home Video (restored director's cut)

This film was Dylan's first serious attempt at acting. Originally hired to do the music, he knew so many people involved in the production that a role was expanded to give him a chance to test his abilities as an actor. It was the often-told story of William Bonney, also known as Billy the Kid, and his association with Pat Garrett. Garrett had been an outlaw but became a lawman who then pursued his old friend. Sam Peckinpah, the film's director, was an Old West revisionist, and several of his films, including *The Wild Bunch* (1968), were notable for their violence, which deglamorized the style of older western films.

The battles over the film were legendary, and Peckinpah lost them. After his death, his original version--called the "restored director's cut"--was released. The original, chaotic version may have used some of Dylan's music better than the final version, but the director's cut is a more coherent film. Dylan's music is the first thing we hear, as sepia-toned images introduce the characters and the credits pop onto the screen in blood-red type. The music, like the editing, anticipates violence.

Dylan first shows up wearing an apron, silent, grimacing, and squinting, apparently bewildered. Was it acting or was that how he felt on the Durango set? Whatever the case, it suited the character he played.

"Who are you?" asks James Coburn, as Pat Garrett.

"That's a good question," Dylan answers. Soon, we learn that his name is "Alias." Pressed further, he says, "Alias Anything-you-please."

Dylan is a man of quick and easy violence in the film, and he kills a man with a knife. He is also a good hand with a rope, lassoing a turkey. He speaks like a hard-bitten cowboy, which contrasts with his fidgety and nervous demeanor. In addition, Dylan has the most memorable scene in the film. He is at a cantina run by character actor Chill Wills. Garrett suddenly enters, looking for Billy or news of him. As he questions one of Billy's mates, he wants to stay aware of Alias's whereabouts, so he sends Dylan to the pantry and tells him to read the labels on the "store boughts" (cans) that he finds there. As Dylan reads, "Beans. Dried beans. *Carrots*," and so on, Garrett slowly tortures and kills the others.

Dylan wrote "Billy," a long ballad in the western tradition, as the theme for the film. Unfortunately, both versions of the film mutilate it. His "Knockin' on Heaven's Door" was perfectly married to the scene it described in the original theatrical release of the film, yet it is absent in the subsequent version. Instead, Dylan only hums the tune.

Pat Garrett and Billy the Kid was an ambitious film, yet it was not successful financially or artistically, perhaps owing to the strain under which it was made (the severe financial and creative limits on Peckinpah). Dylan, however, was difficult to ignore on screen. In the company of a distinguished group of seasoned performers, he still held the attention, playing Fool to Billy the Kid's King Lear.[15]

Critics, however, were not uniformly kind to the film, and Clive Davis, president of Columbia Records, suggested that Dylan not issue the soundtrack album. Dylan did so however, and the album was modestly successful.

Television Film: *Hard Rain*
NBC Television
Broadcast 14 September 1976
Starring Bob Dylan
Featuring members of the Rolling Thunder Revue
Produced and Directed by Top Value Television
Running time: approximately 44 minutes
Not available on videocassette

This television special deserves being included as a film, even though it has not been released on videocassette. As a long-form document of a Bob Dylan concert, it is rightfully considered part of his film and video testament. Dylan had contracted with NBC for a television special but rejected the program that rock-television impresario Burt Sugarman had drawn from his performances at the Belleview Biltmore Hotel in Clearwater, Florida. Having done so, Dylan was obligated to hire another production unit to complete the special. Top Value Television was signed for the task, and they recorded the last performance of the Rolling Thunder Revue, on May 23, 1976.

Little of the revue's vitality was left by this final performance, and Dylan was distracted with marital difficulties. Nevertheless, he and the backing band roared through reinterpretations of several old songs and included a few surprises in the set. To acknowledge Guthrie's influence, Dylan sang "Deportee" as well as a traditional song, "Railroad Boy." He reached back to *The Freewheelin' Bob Dylan* for "Blowin' in the Wind" and "A Hard Rain's A-Gonna Fall." The latter song, which opened the television special, was an appropriate choice, considering the steady drizzle visible throughout the program. (Dylan called the soundtrack album *Hard Rain* as well, though the song did not appear.) Most of the other songs had been staples of the Revue, but his performances of "Shelter from the Storm" and "Idiot Wind" were particularly fierce.

Dylan did not warm to the camera. He was distant, angry and uncommunicative, looking surly in do-rag and leathers. Joan Baez said he appeared to have "viper eyes," and some critics called it an antispecial. Other critics called it "painfully artless," while one called it a "debacle." A few critics praised it. The *Boston Phoenix* said it was "perhaps the most extraordinary and moving film of a concert ever made."[16] Dylan promoted the special heavily, though, even giving an interview to *TV Guide*, among other publications.

Film: *Renaldo and Clara*
Lombard Street Films, distributed by Circuit Films
Released 25 January 1978
Starring Bob Dylan, Joan Baez, Sara Dylan, Ronee Blakely, Ronnie Hawkins, Roger McGuinn and Sam Shepard
Written by Bob Dylan, with scenes by Sam Shepard
Edited by Bob Dylan and Howard Alk
Directed by Bob Dylan
Running time: 232 minutes
Note: A short version (approximately half the length of the original film) was released in late 1978
Not available on videocassette

Whatever can be said about this film, it was a commercial disaster. There were some critics who considered it an artistic triumph, an adventure of a brave artist in search of the concept of self. Others found it egocentric. Dylan's biographer and friend, Robert Shelton, called it "a candidate for artistic suicide."[17] Filmed during the tour of the Rolling Thunder Revue, the film included songs by Dylan, Baez, McGuinn and the other performers, along with improvised scenes involving those performers and a number of others, including Sara Dylan. The improvised scenes puzzled viewers. Bob Dylan was Bob Dylan, right? He was greeted on screen as Bob Dylan. However, near the end of the film, he was revealed as Renaldo. Rockabilly singer Ronnie Hawkins, it turns out, was Bob Dylan, or was he? Moreover, Sara was not Sara but Clara. Actress Ronee Blakely played "Mrs. Dylan."

Few could be confused by the quality of the concert performances. Some critics vented their anger at all of the tight close-ups, which they saw as the manifestation of Dylan's apparently large ego. However, the closeups of his face on stage, as he sang "Tangled Up in Blue," were intense. His blue eyes bore through the screen and he sang with a frightening urgency. Guitarless, he gripped his harmonica, batting it across his lips, and blowing furiously. These scenes of Dylan in rabid performance gave the film its value. He had never been shown quite so frenzied, even during the punk-style march of "Shelter From the Storm" in *Hard Rain*. The dramatic scenes, however, were not as satisfying. The film had apparently been invented as the Rolling Thunder Revue went along, and Dylan was left to try and construct a film from hours of amateurishly performed and largely unscripted vignettes between nonactors.

The *Village Voice* sent seven critics (Dylan called them a "firing squad") to review the film, and almost all the reviews were extremely negative.[18] Dylan swam against the current, offering himself for interviews in a vain effort to promote the movie. He tied his participation to a stipulation that he be featured on the magazine's cover. *New Times* magazine agreed, but ran a mock-memo with the photo: "Dear Mr. Dylan: Here is the cover we promised you."[19] The article inside was not about the film but rather about Dylan's desperate efforts to promote the movie and control the press.

New Yorker film critic Pauline Kael was particularly caustic. Kael seemed to feel betrayed. She had admired Dylan as an artist and as a film presence in *Don't Look Back*. However, in *Renaldo and Clara*, which she called "a shocking miscalculation," Dylan was merely a star out of control; all ego, and no message. Dylan was "a surly mystic tease" who "has given himself more tight close-ups than any actor can have had in the whole history of movies." At one point in the film, Dylan remarks that he wants to be buried in an unmarked grave. "Of course," Kael writes, "that's why he's made a four-hour movie about himself...." She challenges the assertion that he "directed" the film. "Nobody did," she concludes.[20]

Film: *The Last Waltz*
Warner Bros. Pictures
Released April 1978
Starring The Band (Rick Danko, Levon Helm, Garth Hudson, Richard Manuel and Robbie Robertson)
Featuring Eric Clapton, Neil Diamond, Bob Dylan, Joni Mitchell, Van Morrison and Neil Young
Produced by Robbie Robertson
Directed by Martin Scorsese
Running time: 117 minutes
Available on Warner Home Video

This documentary by Martin Scorsese is the best film ever made about rock 'n' roll. Scorsese is known for intense dramas: *Mean Streets*, *Taxi Driver*, *Raging Bull*, *Good Fellas* and *Cape Fear* among many others. However, he also has good music credentials, having been a camera operator on *Woodstock*. The film centers on The Band. After eight years of playing bars and another eight years of playing stadiums, members of The Band decided to retire before "the road" took them, as it had taken so many artists. To say farewell, promoter Bill Graham arranged a show at San Francisco's Winterland. A number of artists associated with The Band appeared.

However, Scorsese went beyond documenting the concert. He interviewed members of the group and elicited from them tremendously funny stories and anecdotes. Pianist Richard Manuel talked about their shoplifting techniques in the early days when the musicians could not afford to buy groceries.

Beautifully filmed studio footage was also included, as The Staples Singers joined The Band for their greatest song, "The Weight," with the latter group generously passing off verses to Mavis and Roebuck "Pop" Staples. In another studio sequence, The Band performs "Evangeline" with Emmylou Harris. The majority of the film, however, shows the concert, as Van Morrison, Muddy Waters, Ronnie Hawkins, Eric Clapton, Neil Diamond, Joni Mitchell, Neil Young and others perform songs with The Band.

Although the film soundtrack album gives an entire side to Dylan's performances, only three songs show up in the film: "Forever Young," "Baby, Let Me Follow You Down" and, with the ensemble, "I Shall Be Released." Many of the performers seemed uncharacteristically stiff and formal. However, Dylan, who had reached the end of the long Rolling Thunder Revue tour, was loose, and wore a white hat that covered ringlets tumbling from under the brim. "While ostensibly... about The Band, Scorsese's editing makes no bones about how much a Dylan event it became," one critic wrote. "Everything else disappears behind his presence. Scorsese... does nothing to hide or minimize this effect."[21]

Television Film: *Hard to Handle*
HBO Productions
Broadcast 21 June 1986
Starring Bob Dylan and Tom Petty
Featuring Mike Campbell, Howie Epstein, Stan Lynch and Benmont Tench
Also featuring The Queens of Rhythm (Debra Byrd, Queen Esther Marrow, Madelyn Quebec and Elisecia Wright)
Director of Photography: Don McAlpine
Edited by John Scott
Sound Mixed by Don Smith
Produced by Wolfboy Productions; executive producer: Elliot Rabinowitz; associate producers: Carole Childs and Jeff Rosen; line producer/Australia: Greg Ricketson
Directed by Gillian Armstrong
Running time: 55 minutes
Available on CBS/Fox Home Video

This lovingly filmed concert video first appeared on pay television and was then sold in record and video stores. Filmed in Australia in 1985, it documents the successful tour Dylan made there with Tom Petty and The Heartbreakers. The association with Petty included performances on Dylan albums by Petty and his band, some collaborative songwriting, and the creation of The Traveling Wilburys as another outlet for the talents of the two men.

Gillian Armstrong, the young Australian director of *My Brilliant Career*, shows obvious affection for Dylan and his art in this film. The camera is at times slightly above and behind Dylan, placing him center frame and heroic before the audience. The music is ably recorded (it was recorded in stereo and simulcast when it first appeared on television), and the band is exceptional. The Heartbreakers rivaled Bruce Springsteen's E Street Band as the best straight forward rock 'n' roll band of the 1980s. Their playing here is superb. It was rather early in the collaboration between Dylan and the younger musicians, and their awe of him is evident as they watch him on stage in this film.

It is Dylan's speaking voice we hear first. A top-hatted Petty lurks in the background as Dylan, as gregarious as he gets, says to the audience:

> I want to do a song about my hero. Everybody's got their own hero. I don't know who your hero is. Maybe . . . Mel Gibson. [Cheers from the audience.] All right! Let's hear it for Mel Gibson. Maybe it would be Michael Jackson. Bruce Springsteen. Anyway, I don't care nothin' 'bout none of those people. I have my own hero. I'm going to sing to you about my hero now.

Dylan then launches into "In the Garden," from *Saved*. With a backup vocal from The Queens of Rhythm, Dylan punches the song more pointedly than he did on the album version. The song selection is interesting and varied, representing most points in Dylan's career. Benmont Tench's piano introduction to "Just Like a Woman" is as piercing as the guitar introduction on the original version of the song. Stan Lynch's drumming renders the ballad almost a march and Dylan, at the front of the stage, moves almost like a marionette. He stands stiff-legged, as in the James Cagney dance style. At one point, he turns around and smiles at The Heartbreakers, as if pleased with the power and precision of this excellent band. This is the best live recording made of this classic song.

Armstrong's camera is about two feet above and in front of Dylan at the beginning of "Like a Rolling Stone." It is an odd angle, but it allows us to watch Dylan's from up close as he sings his most famous song. The camera moves right into Dylan's face, and we see him singing intensely, with the emotion he would offer a new song, not churning it out like a hack at an oldies review. Tench's brilliant keyboard work annotates the work on the original by Al Kooper and Paul Griffin.

The finale is "Knockin' on Heaven's Door," which become less a funeral march and more a celebration with the gospel-group backing. At one point, Dylan says to the singers, "Oh! Tell me about it!" Dylan's variation on the lyric includes the phrase, "Just like so many times before," which he uses to punch the effect of the ending. It also serves as his commentary on the concert and the experience of being a performer. He has performed these songs often, yet he still manages to do so with passion. As the song moves to its majestic conclusion, Dylan points two fingers to the audience, Vegas-style, and says, "All right! Thanks a lot!" Then he strolls back to the drum riser while The Heartbreakers continue to play, and puts on a muffler and sunglasses. He accepts a rose and holds it aloft while striding across the front of the stage, his audience up for inspection. The band keeps playing and Dylan exits.

Hard to Handle is a great presentation of latter-era Dylan. Armstrong shows him with respect and affection, but stops short of deifying the musician. The camera work and sound are superb.

Film: *Hearts of Fire*
Lorimar Motion Pictures
Released 9 October 1987
Starring Fiona, Rupert Everett and Bob Dylan
Supporting cast includes Richie Havens, Ron Wood, Ian Dury
Musical score by John Barry
Musical director: Beau Hill
Written by Scott Richardson and Joe Eszterhas
Produced by Richard Marquand, Jennifer Miller and Jennifer Alward; co-producer: Iain Smith; executive producers: Gerald Abrams and Doug Morris
Directed by Richard Marquand
Running time: 96 minutes
Note: The release date refers to the film's English premiere. It was never released in theaters in the United States.
Available on Warner Home Video

This rags-to-rock-riches story was filmed in 1986 and was held three years until its release in America, though it was released in Great Britain in 1987. In America, it was whisked directly to videocassette, a sign that the film was an utter loss. However, *Hearts of Fire* is a film of considerable charm. It is not a triumph of cinematic art, but it is a pleasant, if predictable, saga of a young woman who yearns to become a rock 'n' roll star.

Fiona, a pop singer, plays the starring role of Molly Maguire, an 18-year-old toll collector on the Pennsylvania Turnpike who plays guitar and sings with a bar band. She wants to perform original material, but the owner of the club in which she plays wants only cover versions of well-known tunes. Consequently, Molly and her group churn out "Proud Mary," "Cinnamon Girl" and other bar-band classics.

Molly doesn't particularly like her day job at the tollbooth, but she tries to dispatch her duties in a friendly way, despite the occasionally obnoxious driver. One driver makes sexual suggestions to her. Her supervisor berates her and tells her to turn down the music to which she listens constantly, and a leather-clad man on a motorcycle (invisible behind a helmet) paying his toll also insults her musical taste. She is listening to a cassette by pop idol James Colt when a distinctive, grave voice informs her, "It sucks."

However, we do not see Dylan's face until later. As Molly and her band perform in a bar, we see him enter but the camera shows him only from the waist down, revealing only black boots, with pointed white toes. "Need a beer," he informs the bartender. From the stage, Molly recognizes the retired rock 'n' roll star, Billy Parker. Parker is rumored to have settled near town, but no one sees much of him. Parker realizes Molly has seen him and leaves the bar, but Molly follows. He gets in his pickup truck, but she manages to talk to him for a few moments. He is distant and reserved. Later, she tells her roommate, "I met Billy Parker."

"What's he like?" the roommate asks.

"He sucks," Molly says.

Parker shows up again to watch the band and when the organist asks for requests, Parker yells out the title of one of his great hits, "'The Usual'." Molly coaxes Parker on stage and they sing the song together, and so begins their friendship. Parker is clearly in love with Molly, but is hesitant because of their age difference. He tries to broach the subject of taking a trip with her: He tells her he has contracted to go to England for an oldies concert ("kind of like a freak thing at a carnival") and that he has an extra plane ticket. She begs off, but clearly enjoys Parker's company. She takes him skinny dipping, although Parker jumps into the lake with all of his clothes on.

Molly is incensed when the other members of her band agree to a steady gig at the lounge of the local Holiday Inn. "I don't play lounge music," she tells them, and quits. Things are not going well on her other job, either. When the obnoxious driver who had earlier made a sexual suggestion to her accuses her of short changing him, Molly's supervisor takes the driver's side in the argument. Molly walks off the job and runs to find Parker, who is on his way to London.

Parker sits on a bench at the bus station, blowing blues on his harmonica and waiting for Molly. The driver gives Parker an ultimatum to get on the bus or stay behind. He does get on, but after driving a couple of blocks, Parker spots Molly running toward the bus with her luggage. The driver refuses to stop, so Parker pulls out a harmonica and holds it at the driver's neck (pretending it's a gun) until he opens the door.

In London, Parker is reunited with some other old-time rock 'n' roll stars (played by Ron Wood of The Rolling Stones and Richie Havens), and Molly becomes disgusted with them as they rehearse for the oldies concert. Parker, in particular, seems not to care about the quality of his performance, and Molly accuses him of ripping off his audience. As he goes on stage, Parker says, "I'm going to sing this song for the millionth time. I'm so sick of it I could puke, but I'll sing it anyway." He then launches into "Had a Dream about You, Baby." He slogs through the song and the audience seems generally pleased, but Molly wants him to do better, so she joins him on stage and her energetic performance makes Parker try harder.

Parker's presence in London draws a lot of attention, and pop star James Colt requests an audience. Colt, played by Rupert Everett, makes synthesized pop music in the style of David Bowie. (The Colt character seems to draw heavily on Bowie's persona.) At Colt's house, the younger pop star nearly fawns in admiration of Parker. He shows Molly a videotape of a much younger Parker at his prime, performing a blistering piece of rock 'n' roll. (Interestingly, the video is of Dylan's performance in *The Concert for Bangladesh* in 1971, in which he played acoustic guitar, while the accompanying music is "When the Night Comes Falling From the Sky," a hard-rock production number from the 1980s. Dylan fans would be certain to notice the discrepancy.) Parker angrily shuts off the video. "Got any Johnny Cash records?" he asks Colt.

Colt and Parker are both uninspired. Colt has writer's block and has difficulty trying to record. A reference is made to a plane crash that Parker survived but that drove him away from his career as a performer. (He settled in Pennsylvania after an uncle died, leaving him his farm.) Colt tries to commiserate with Parker. He asks him about his attitude toward music: "You don't believe in magic anymore?"

"I never did," Parker tells him.

Parker watches Molly become involved with the young, handsome James Colt. Parker obviously loves her, but realizes he is too old for her to take seriously as a lover. She considers him her musical mentor, choosing Parker's organic rock 'n' roll to Colt's synthesized pop music. Parker and Molly begin performing around London. The punk audiences do not warm easily to the music and, at one point in a show, Parker says to Molly, "Fuck 'em if they can't take a joke," and dives into the audience.

Recording offers come for Molly, but she does not want to work without Parker. Parker begs off, reminding her that he walked away from a performing career of his own free will and that he is a farmer, not a musician. He warns her about falling into a trap.

"If I'm good," Molly says, "it can't be a trap."

"It is," Parker tells her. "The better you are, the bigger the trap."

As they take a moonlight walk in the English countryside during a visit to Colt's estate, Molly talks about wanting to be a big star.

"There's no such thing as a big star," Parker says. "There's just starlight. The stars died a million years ago." Referring to Colt, Parker says, "I used to have everything he's got. Boys and girls used to follow me around like I was the pied piper."

Nevertheless, Parker goes back to performing in order to aid Molly's career. Although he does not tell Molly of his love for her, he tries to warn her about Colt, whom he says is using her. Colt appears to be using Parker as well. Before the first major performance of the band Molly and Parker have put together, Colt tells Parker, "Can't you dye your hair or something?"

At a press conference before the concert, Colt and Molly solemnly discuss "guitar picking," but Parker changes the subject to nose picking. Colt is infuriated with Parker and his attitude. When he refers to the older man as a "retired rock star," Parker slugs Colt. Parker is devoted to Molly, but he is obviously leery of getting involved in the music world again. "Nobody's shootin' me out of any damn cannon," he tells Molly. "My life ain't no circus." He trashes his hotel room, tossing everything out the window, and then picks up his bag and walks out, with Molly following. As Parker gets in the cab that will take him to Heathrow Airport, he looks out the window and tells Molly, "Aw, shit. I love you."

Molly becomes an international star and launches a tour of America with Colt, whose own career is revitalized by his involvement with her. Molly's music is less the simple rock 'n' roll of the old days and includes more heavy production numbers, like Colt's music. As Molly and Colt tour, they are followed by a blind fan who, Colt says, has been pursuing him for as long as he can remember, showing up at every concert. After a show in Philadelphia, the fan threatens Colt with a gun and then shoots herself.

There is one last concert left on the tour, back in Molly's home town of Dunston, Pennsylvania. Colt goes into hiding and Molly drives back home, going directly to Parker's farm. Molly is disillusioned by fame, having witnessed the bloody suicide of Colt's devoted fan, but Parker urges her to continue. "Now that you've got it," he tells her, "you can't piss it away." She asks him to perform with her, but he refuses. "I'm a farmer now," he says. Now, as the retired rock 'n' roll veteran, he lectures her about the responsibility of entertainment. "You got a lot of folks waiting to hear you tonight. You can't let 'em down now."

Although Parker had refused to play with her, he and Colt show up during the opening number of her performance that night. After the concert, she talks to Colt briefly but cannot find Parker backstage. She goes to his farm, and they spend the night together in the barn. At dawn, Molly awakens to find Parker kneeling at her feet, strumming a guitar and singing about an older man's love for a younger woman. Molly gives Parker a passionate kiss and then leaves. At the end of the driveway to Parker's house, Molly finds Colt asleep in his car. She talks to him about her disappointment with him and then rides away on Parker's motorcycle. We sense that the relationship with Colt is over, while the relationship with Parker will last.

Hearts of Fire is far from a great film, but it is amusing and modestly entertaining. It suffers from the same problem as most other films about rock 'n' roll: the standard cliches of the music business bog down the simple story. Much disbelief must be suspended in order for viewers to accept the story's premise. Molly strides on stage and begins playing with Parker, for example, without stopping to plug in her electric guitar. The same happens when Parker and Colt surprise her on stage. However, for those who have followed Dylan's career, *Hearts of Fire* is a fascinating film. The role was written for him and his acceptance of it implies some kind of sanction. He would have to realize that many in the audience would assume Billy Parker was Bob Dylan, and he must have been willing to accept that fans would draw certain conclusions. Indeed, there is much of Dylan in the role. In Parker's barn we see one of his album covers displayed: a photo from the back of Dylan's *Bringing It All Back Home*. Dylan's performance in *The Concert for Bangladesh* is shown as depicting Parker at the peak of his fame. Some of the music ("When the Night Comes Falling from the Sky") was not written for the film but had already appeared on a Dylan album.

Consequently, viewers may assume that some of the things that Dylan says as Parker are agreeable to the artist. His attitude toward performing, "not pissing away" fame, and the responsibility to the audience may indeed be statements that Dylan could make convincingly. Similarly, his dialog about not caring about music anymore might reflect the lethargy behind his late-1980s albums which parallel the film (*Knocked Out Loaded* and *Down in the Groove*).

Dylan looks his age in this film, but that is not bad. A joke in the script makes light of the gray hair in Dylan's curls, and he uses self-deprecating humor to deal with the issue of a man pushing 50 in love with a girl of 18. Dylan is clean-shaven and apparently in good physical condition, though he moves stiffly. He delivers his lines tentatively, but they do not seem forced. As was the case with *Pat Garrett and Billy the Kid*, Dylan is irresistible on screen and dominates when the other actors try to share it with him. He is extremely likable in this film, and plays the part of Billy Parker agreeably.

Dylan and Fiona perform "The Usual," a John Hiatt song, in one of the early bar scenes. During the oldies concert, Dylan sings "Had a Dream about You, Baby," a Dylan original that appeared on *Down in the Groove*. He is not seen performing "When the Night Comes Falling from the Sky," though that is portrayed (poorly) as emanating from his mouth during the *Bangladesh* set. Near the end, when Molly finds Parker asleep in the barn after the concert, Parker is listening to the playback of a Dylan original, "Night after Night." This song is on the film soundtrack but has not appeared on a Dylan album. The song Parker sings to Molly at sunrise, "Couple More Years," was written by Shel Silverstein, the popular songwriter ("Sylvia's Mother," "Cover of *Rolling Stone*," among other tunes) and author (*The Giving Tree*, *The Missing Piece* and other books for children). That song appears neither on the soundtrack album or on a Dylan record.

260 / BOB DYLAN

Film: *Back Track*
Vestron Pictures
Released October 1990
Starring Jodie Foster, Dennis Hopper, Joe Pesci, Dean Stockwell, Charlie Sheen, Fred Ward, John Turturro, Vincent Price and Bob Dylan
Musical score by Michel Colombier
Written by Rachel Kronstadt Mann and Louise Bardach
Produced by Dick Clark and Dan Paulson; line producer: Paul Lewis
Directed by Dennis Hopper
Running time: 102 minutes
Note: Released theatrically in Europe, this film made its American debut on Showtime, a premium cable network. The film is also known under the titles *Catchfire* and *Do it the Hard Way*.
Available on Vestron Video

Conceptual artist Jodie Foster witnesses a Mafia execution managed by mobster Joe Pesci. Pesci then hires hitman Dennis Hopper to track down Foster and kill her. While following her, Hopper becomes obsessed with his prey and he and Foster become lovers.

Although Dylan's appearance is a mere cameo, he is memorable. On-screen for 30 seconds, Dylan plays an artist who sculpts wood with a chainsaw.

Section II: Television

"The Madhouse on Castle Street"
BBC Television (Great Britain)
January 1963
Dylan sings and acts in this drama.

"Songs of Freedom"
WNEW-TV (New York City)
30 July 1963
Dylan sings "Blowin' in the Wind" and "Only a Pawn in Their Game."

"The Tonight Show"
NBC Television (United States)
July 1963
Dylan sings and chats with host Johnny Carson

"Quest"
CBC Television (Canada)
1 February 1964
This program, subtitled "Bob Dylan Sings Bob Dylan," showed him performing six songs: "The Times They Are A-Changin'," "Talking World War III Blues," "The Lonesome Death of Hattie Carroll," "Girl from the North Country," "A Hard Rain's A-Gonna Fall" and "Restless Farewell."

"The Steve Allen Show"
NBC Television (United States)
25 February 1964
Dylan performs "The Lonesome Death of Hattie Carroll." Allen tried briefly to interview

Dylan, with pathetic results. Allen was serious but Dylan was putting him on.

"Tonight"
BBC Television (England)
8 May 1964
Dylan performs "With God on Our Side."

"Hallelujah"
ATV Television (England)
8 May 1964
Dylan performs "The Times They Are A-Changin'," "Blowin' in the Wind" and "Chimes of Freedom."

"The Les Crane Show"
WABC-TV (New York City)
17 February 1965
Dylan sings "It's Alright Ma (I'm Only Bleeding)" and "It's All Over Now, Baby Blue," accompanied by Bruce Langhorne on electric guitar. Dylan chats with Crane.

"Bob Dylan"
BBC Television (England)
June 1965
Dylan is seen performing "Ballad of Hollis Brown," "Mr. Tambourine Man," "Gates of Eden," "If You Gotta Go, Go Now," "The Lonesome Death of Hattie Carroll," "It Ain't Me, Babe," "Love Minus Zero/No Limit," "One Too Many Mornings," "Boots of Spanish Leather," "It's Alright Ma (I'm Only Bleeding)," "She Belongs to Me" and "It's All Over Now, Baby Blue."

"Johnny Cash: The Man and His Music"
NET Television (United States)
16 May 1969
Dylan performs two duets with Cash: "Girl from the North Country" and "One Too Many Mornings."

"The Johnny Cash Show"
ABC Television (United States)
7 June 1969
Dylan performs "Girl from the North Country" as a duet with Cash. He also sings "Living the Blues" and "I Threw It All Away."

"Earl Scruggs: His Family and Friends"
NET Television (United States)
10 January 1971
Dylan joins Scruggs and his band (including sons Gary and Randy) on "Nashville Skyline Rag" and the traditional "East Virginia Blues." The session was filmed (and recorded for album release) at the home of Thomas B. Allen in Carmel, New York.

"Freetime"
PBS Television (Channel 13, New York City)
October 1971
Dylan appears on an episode called "Allen Ginsberg and Friends."

"Soundstage"
PBS Television (United States)
13 December 1975

Dylan performs three songs in an episode called "The World of John Hammond," a tribute to the Columbia Records producer who introduced Dylan's work to a mass audience. With Rob Stoner on bass, Howie Wyeth on drums and Scarlet Rivera on violin, Dylan sings "Hurricane," "Oh, Sister" and "Simple Twist of Fate."

"Hard Rain"
NBC Television
14 September 1976
Dylan and the Rolling Thunder Revue in performance. For more detail, see the *Hard Rain* entry under Section I of this chapter.

"Saturday Night Live"
NBC Television
20 October 1979
Dylan performs "Gotta Serve Somebody" "I Believe in You" and "When You Gonna Wake Up?" (from *Slow Train Coming*) on the late-night comedy program. The backup band is the usual gang from the gospel tours.

"The 1980 Grammy Awards"
CBS Television (United States)
27 February 1980
Dylan performs "Gotta Serve Somebody" with his band and receives a Grammy for the song.

"The 1981 Grammy Awards"
CBS Television (United States)
28 February 1984
Dylan and Stevie Wonder present the award for the song of the year.

"Late Night with David Letterman"
NBC Television (United States)
22 March 1984
Dylan performs three songs, "Don't Start Me to Talkin'," "License to Kill" and "Jokerman." Letterman approaches Dylan after the last song and asks if he would like to come back and play every week. Dylan laughs, but says nothing.

"Clancy Brothers and Tommy Makem"
WNET-TV (New York)
Date unknown, 1984
Dylan is interviewed in this documentary about the Irish singers.

"Live Aid Concert"
Worldwide Television
13 July 1985
At Robert F. Kennedy Stadium in Philadelphia, Dylan performs "The Ballad of Hollis Brown," "When the Ship Comes In" and "Blowin' in the Wind," backed by Keith Richards and Ron Wood of The Rolling Stones.

"Farm Aid"
The Nashville Network (United States)
22 September 1985
Backed by Tom Petty and The Heartbreakers, Dylan (apparently in great spirits), performs "Clean Cut Kid," "Shake," "I'll Remember You," "Trust Yourself," "That Lucky Old Sun" and "Maggie's Farm."

FILM, TELEVISION AND VIDEO / 263

"20/20"
ABC Television (United States)
10 October 1985
Dylan is interviewed by Bob Brown of the popular television magazine program, on *Biograph*'s release.

"The Old Grey Whistle Test"
BBC Television (England)
22 November 1985
Dylan is interviewed by host Andy Kershaw.

"An All-Star Celebration Honoring Martin Luther King, Jr."
NBC Television (United States)
20 January 1986
Dylan performs with Stevie Wonder and Wonderlove on "The Bells of Freedom," "I Shall Be Released" and "Blowin' in the Wind." He joins the cast of the program for "Happy Birthday," Wonder's tribute to King.

"Hard to Handle"
HBO Television (United States)
June 1986
An hour-long concert special taken from a show in Sydney, Australia. For details, see Section I of this chapter.

"Omnibus"
BBC Television (England)
19 September 1987
Dylan is interviewed by journalist Christopher Sykes during the filming of *Hearts of Fire*.

"The 1991 Grammy Awards"
CBS Television (United States)
20 February 1991
Dylan was honored with a lifetime achievement award presented by actor Jack Nicholson, who offered a clever and humorous tribute to "Uncle Bobby." A brief film biography was shown, largely drawn from *Don't Look Back*, *Eat the Document*, *Renaldo and Clara* and *Hard Rain*. Dylan crashed through a nearly demented version of "Masters of War" and then received the award from Nicholson. Dylan was jocular, unmanageable and downright hilarious.

"Late Night with David Letterman's 10th Anniversary Special"
NBC Television (United States)
6 February 1992
This 90-minute prime-time special celebrated the innovative post-midnight variety show hosted by David Letterman. Most of the program was made up of clips from old shows. Dylan and his all-star band perform "Like a Rolling Stone."

"The Music of Bob Dylan"
Pay-Per-View Television (United States)
16 October 1992
This four-hour broadcast celebrates Dylan's three decades of music. Sponsored by Columbia Records, the telecast featured performances before a live audience in Madison Square Garden. Artists include Eric Clapton, George Harrison, John Mellencamp, Tom Petty and The Heartbreakers and Neil Young.

Notes

1. John Bauldie, *Wanted Man: In Search of Bob Dylan* (New York: Citadel Underground Press, 1991), p. 203.
2. Richard Goldstein, "Don't Look Back," the *New York Times*, 22 October 1967, in Craig McGregor, ed., *Bob Dylan: The Early Years* (New York: DaCapo Press, 1990), p. 206.
3. Andrew Sarris, "Don't Look Back," the *Village Voice*, 21 September 1967, in Elizabeth Thomson and David Gutman, eds., *The Dylan Companion* (New York: Delta Books, 1991), p. 88.
4. Patrick Humphries and John Bauldie, *Absolutely Dylan* (New York: Viking Studio Books, 1991), p. 79.
5. Bob Spitz, *Dylan: A Biography* (New York: McGraw-Hill, 1989), p. 350.
6. Ibid.
7. Clinton Heylin, *Bob Dylan: Behind the Shades* (New York: Summit Books, 1991), p. 167.
8. Ibid.,
9. Spitz, *Dylan*, p. 365.
10. Larry Sloman, "Bob Dylan and Friends on the Bus: Like a Rolling Thunder," *Rolling Stone*, 4 December 1975, in Thomson and Gutman, *Dylan Companion*, p. 198.
11. Humphries and Bauldie, *Absolutely Dylan*, p. 197.
12. Heylin, *Behind the Shades*, p. 215.
13. Spitz, *Dylan*, p. 406. Spitz notes that the pre-Isle of Wight guest appearance with The Band did not count since Dylan played under the name "Elmer Johnson."
14. Tom Costner, the *Village Voice*, 23 March 1972, cited in Robert Shelton, *No Direction Home: The Life and Music of Bob Dylan* (New York: Beech Tree Books/Morrow, 1986), p. 485.
15. Neil Sinyard, "Bob Dylan and Billy the Kid," in Thomson and Gutman, *Dylan Companion*, p. 150.
16. Shelton, *No Direction Home*, p. 544.
17. Ibid., p. 546.
18. Ibid.
19. Spitz, *Dylan*, p. 519.
20. Pauline Kael, "The Calvary Gig," the *New Yorker*, 13 February 1978, in Thomson and Gutman, *Dylan Companion*, p. 230.
21. Terry Curtis Fox, "The Last Waltz," the *Village Voice*, 29 April 1978, cited in Shelton, *No Direction Home*, p. 546.

Chapter 9

Concerts

A BOB DYLAN SONG IS NEVER REALLY FINISHED: Dylan's long career has accentuated the schizophrenic nature of his work. His songs are both permanent and ever-changing, definitive and incomplete. We have his legendary recordings, which for much of his audience would define Dylan as an artist. These albums, many of which sold millions of copies, would seem to be definitive versions. However, Dylan has never regarded his work as sacred and above tampering.

Much of Dylan's work as a performer is elusive. The performance of "Tangled Up in Blue" that opens *Blood on the Tracks*, for example, is quite different from the song he recorded for--and then removed from--an early version of that album. (He released the first recording 16 years later.) In concert, the song has mutated wildly. On a mid-1980s performance on *Real Live*, we find the lyric changed from the third to the first person. Many of the details of the story have been similarly altered in subsequent concert appearances.

Thus, although his fans may regard his work as something that is too good to be altered, Dylan himself is not afraid to make changes. He has refused to deify his work: The ominous, relentless "Masters of War" offers a good example. It would be difficult to find a song more powerful than the recording on Dylan's second album. The arrangement is simple: Dylan and guitar. It would seem easiest and most effective to retain that style of performance. Presumably, since the audience is familiar with the recording, that would be the sort of performance the fans would want.

However, that is not what Dylan does. Enamored with the late Jimi Hendrix's recording of "All along the Watchtower" on his 1968 release, *Electric Ladyland*, Dylan adopted the frenetic Hendrix style for his version of that song. Carrying the tribute further, in the 1980s, Dylan began performing "Masters of War" the way he assumed Hendrix would play the song, had he lived. Although the lyrics remain the same, the added instrumentation changes the flavor of the song. In the recording, the young Dylan is angry, but also pious and hectoring. It is the perfect pose for a young man with a sermon. The older Dylan, however, churns an apocalyptic guitar line and shouts the words, usually with the accompaniment of a chaotic, crashing rock 'n' roll band. Now he is not lecturing; he is threatening.

Again, many rock 'n' roll performers have learned not to tamper with a successful formula. The Rolling Stones, for all their skill as a band, rarely alter their songs, which are performed in the same style in which they were recorded. The Beach Boys, whose career spans all of Dylan's, long ago reverted to a strict oldies act, trying desperately (but often in vain) to match their sublime recorded performances during concert appearances. However, Dylan's fans attend successive concert tours wondering what new twist Dylan will add to "Like a Rolling Stone." Dylan collectors live for bootlegged recordings of the various mutations of his songs.

Why does he do it? One answer appears obvious. Perhaps he would simply become bored with a performance that only recreates a studio recording, changing song arrangements and lyrics because he discovers new directions in his words or allows the song's story to grow with the years. Many other artists performing popular music went to great lengths to ensure that their live performances would echo their records note for note. This was not so with Dylan, who chose--for whatever reason--to reinterpret his works radically in concert. In any case, Dylan's body of work is enlarged with every concert, because he is a performing artist. His art is not static.

Scholar Betsy Bowden wrote her dissertation at the University of California at Berkeley on the subject of Bob Dylan as an interpreter of his work.[1] Her focus, naturally, was on the evolution of Dylan's performances through 20 years of concerts. (Her study concerned only the 1960s and 1970s.) She found textual variants in nearly all Dylan's major concert pieces and cited "Idiot Wind" as one song that seemed to develop, reproduce, and nearly emerge as another song altogether.

Paul Williams has also chosen to focus on Dylan as a performer. Williams, a pioneer in the criticism of rock 'n' roll music, was the founder and editor of *Crawdaddy*. Dylan is one of Williams's favorite subjects and is the featured attraction in *Performing Artist* (Novato, Calif.: Underwood-Miller, 1990). Williams's respect for Dylan as an artist who respects and values growth is reflected in a story Williams tells on himself. Dylan was appearing in San Francisco and Williams planned to speak with him before the show. Williams showed Dylan an art book, a collection of Pablo Picasso's paintings that was part of a retrospective at the Museum of Modern Art. Williams showed Dylan a spread from the book that demonstrated Picasso's series of 11 lithographs stemming from the same inspiration. Each showed something new, a variation or a nuance missing in the other work, as if Picasso was showing how his mind turned, studied, felt and examined a thought. It was, Williams thought, a fitting analogy to Dylan's treatment of his songs. Dylan studied the pictures, pointed to the second lithograph in the series and said, "He should have stopped at that one." However, after studying the artwork closely, he said, "But I see why he had to keep going."[2]

Dylan's embrace of the stance of working-class hero at the beginning of his professional career made concert performing a relatively simple affair. He performed without regular accompaniment until mid-1965, when he became a rock 'n' roll star. Then, however, touring became much more complicated. Collectors have long circulated recordings of early Dylan performances, which were relatively simple affairs. He sang traditional songs, spoke to the audience in his husky pseudo-Okie drawl, and effectively mimicked his idols, such as Woody Guthrie and Cisco Houston. Dylan's confidence and self-assurance are worth noting, and appear to be those of the older performers whom he is emulating.

Critics noted his stage presence. There was something nearly Chaplinesque about his movements. With just guitar, harmonica, stool and a glass of water, Dylan showed an engaging ability to maintain an audience's attention even when he was not speaking or singing. He became more aloof and toned down the banter when he began performing more original material, much of which was of a serious nature that had heretofore been seldom heard in popular music.

This aloofness was enhanced as Dylan "went electric." His famous bouts with audiences during the 1965-1966 tours may have contributed to his withdrawal from the road until 1974 and his general taciturnity after that. During the May 17, 1966 concert in the British Isles (appearing on the *Royal Albert Hall* bootleg), a young man shouted "Judas!" at Dylan, on stage with The Hawks. "I don't believe you," Dylan shouted back, as the group begins playing. "You're a liar!" he yelled. Aloofness worked for Dylan. During the 1974 tour with The Band, he rarely spoke. He might mutter a couple of dozen words, but rarely did he say anything by way of greeting or patter between songs: That was not the Dylan way.

What follows is an attempt to document Dylan's concert appearances. Much about his early performing career is sketchy, although this listing is generally reliable from 1966 onward. The backing musicians and repertoire are noted. Significant guest appearances and single-performance benefits are also indicated. The listing is chronological and some years are missing. In 1967, for example, and again in 1972 and 1973, Dylan did not appear in concert.

1961

Dylan's performances included appearances at various New York City cafes and night clubs. He appeared at the Riverside Church on July 29 for a program broadcast on WRVR-FM. His other appearances were at the Gaslight Cafe and Gerde's Folk City. His first major appearance was at Carnegie Chapter Hall on November 4, 1961. An audience of approximately 53 listened as Dylan offered a program of traditionals.

Tapes exist of Dylan's Carnegie concerts as well as night club and cafe appearances. He was also a frequent entertainer at parties, and fellow celebrants recorded those performances as well.

1962

Dylan broadened his performing sphere from New York City to Montreal, where his appearance at the Finjan Club was recorded. His repertoire now included many original compositions, highlighted by "Blowin' in the Wind." With the issue of his eponymous debut album in March, Dylan was moving beyond the nonpaying coffeehouse circuit to more legitimate venues. By the time of that album's release, his shows contained nearly an equal number of originals and traditional tunes.

He was writing songs at an incredibly prolific pace. Recordings made at the offices of *Broadside* magazine appeared on radio broadcasts and on *Broadside* albums issued by Folkways Records. Aside from club appearances, Dylan appeared with Pete Seeger at a Carnegie Hall hootenanny on September 22, during which he performed "Talkin' John Birch Paranoid Blues," "Ballad of Hollis Brown" and "A Hard Rain's A-Gonna Fall."

1963

Dylan's first major appearance as a headliner of a New York concert was on April 12, when he performed at Town Hall. Columbia Records taped this performance for an album to be called *Bob Dylan in Concert*. A catalog number was assigned to the album but it was never issued. Two of the performances eventually made it onto his albums: "Tomorrow Is a Long Time" on *Bob Dylan's Greatest Hits, Vol. II*, and his nervous reading of the poem "Last Thoughts on Woody Guthrie," on *The Bootleg Series, Vols. 1-3*. With the exception of a blending of two Guthrie songs that were used to open the program, Dylan played original material. Only two of the songs were to appear on albums ("Masters of War" and "With God on Our Side"), although several of the songs were later issued on anthologies and career retrospectives. It would have made a superb third album for Dylan. Dylan now appeared on the national coffee-house circuit and tapes exist of performances in The Bear (in Chicago) and at the Newport Folk Festival in July. His appearance at a voter registration rally at Silas Magee's farm in Greenwood, Mississippi on July 6 was used in the film *Don't Look Back*.

By the late summer, he was making guest appearances on the program at Joan Baez's concerts. He and Baez sang "Only a Pawn in Their Game" at the March on Washington on August 28.

1964

Dylan was a big enough star by now to warrant concert tours. A complete itinerary does not exist, but we know that he spent the spring performing in Ohio, Kentucky, Georgia, Colorado and California. Several of these dates were as the guest star on a Joan Baez concert. Often, his solo dates were in auditoriums or small concert halls.

In April, he performed in Boston's Symphony Hall and in Club 47 in Cambridge, Massachusetts. He also played at the University of Massachusetts and Brandeis University. He made an appearance at the Monterey Folk Festival in California before heading to England for a May 17 date at the Royal Festival Hall in London. He was back to the American Midwest in early July and spent July 24-26 at the Newport Folk Festival. In October and November, he crisscrossed the country and slipped into Canada for a date in Toronto. His concert tours were not extensive, just widespread.

1965

Tour of the United States
Dylan's tours were now more involved--and better documented. (From this point on, the concert listing is relatively complete.)

March 5: Philadelphia, Pennsylvania; 6: New Haven, Connecticut; other dates that month in Trenton, New Jersey, Newark, New Jersey and Buffalo, New York; 24: Pittsburgh, Pennsylvania (two shows); 27: Santa Monica, California; 28: Berkeley, California.
April 3: Berkeley, California, and Seattle, Washington; 9: Vancouver, British Columbia.

Tour of England
Dylan's brief trip to the British Isles was immortalized in D. A. Pennebaker's documentary, *Don't Look Back*. Dylan was in the process of changing. In America, he was having problems offering his new rock 'n' roll persona to a crowd that wanted him to remain a folk singer. In England, his popularity

was based almost entirely on his old work: the *Freewheelin'* and *Times They Are A-Changin'* albums.
April 30: Sheffield, England.
May 1: Liverpool, England; **2:** Leicester, England; **5:** Birmingham, England; **6:** Newcastle, England; **7:** Manchester, England; **9-10:** London, England.

Tour of North America
Dylan introduced rock 'n' roll to the old fans at the Newport Folk Festival and then inaugurated his first tour with a group, many of the members of which were later to be known as The Band. Robbie Robertson, The Band's lead guitarist, was the only musician to appear with Dylan on all the 1965-1966 dates. Levon Helm, later drummer for The Band, quit the tour in November and was replaced by Bobby Gregg. The performances forsook the early folk favorites and relied on material from Dylan's first two rock 'n' roll albums, *Bringing It All Back Home* and *Highway 61 Revisited*. (This concert listing is not complete.)
July 24-25: Newport, Rhode Island.
August 28: Forest Hills, New York.
September 3: Los Angeles, California; **24:** Austin, Texas; **25:** Dallas, Texas.
October 1: New York City; **2:** Newark, New Jersey; **10:** Atlanta, Georgia; **16:** Worcester, Massachusetts; **22:** Providence, Rhode Island; **23:** Burlington, Vermont; **24:** Detroit, Michigan; **29:** Boston, Massachusetts; **30:** Hartford, Connecticut; **31:** Boston, Massachusetts.
November 5: Minneapolis, Minnesota; **6:** Buffalo, New York; **12:** Cleveland, Ohio; **14-15:** Toronto, Ontario; **18:** Cincinnati, Ohio; **19:** Columbus, Ohio; **20:** Rochester, New York; **21:** Syracuse, New York; **26-27:** Chicago, Illinois; **28:** Washington, D.C.
December 1: Seattle, Washington; **3-4:** Berkeley, California; **5:** San Francisco, California; **7:** Long Beach, California; **8:** Santa Monica, California; **9:** Pasadena, California; **10:** San Diego, California; **11:** San Francisco, California; **12:** San Jose, California; **18:** Pasadena, California; **19:** Santa Monica, California.

1966

World Tour with The Hawks
Most of The Hawks (The Band) were back: Robertson, Richard Manuel, Rick Danko and Garth Hudson. Helm's replacement, Bobby Gregg, was much in demand for recording sessions, and was replaced for the February and March dates by Sandy Konikoff. Mickey Jones became the drummer for the April and May dates, including the controversial appearances in Manchester and London so often bootlegged. (This listing is not complete.)
February 4: Louisville, Kentucky; **5:** White Plains, New York; **6:** Pittsburgh, Pennsylvania; **10:** Memphis, Tennessee; **11:** Richmond, Virginia; **13:** Norfolk, Virginia; **19:** Ottawa, Ontario; **20:** Montreal, Quebec; **20:** Vancouver, British Columbia; **24-25:** Philadelphia, Pennsylvania; **26:** Hempstead, New York.
March 3: Miami Beach, Florida; **11:** St. Louis, Missouri; **12:** Lincoln, Nebraska; **13:** Denver, Colorado; **24:** Tacoma, Washington; **25:** Seattle, Washington; **26:** Vancouver, British Columbia.
April 9: Honolulu, Hawaii; **13:** Sydney, Australia; **15:** Brisbane, Australia; **16:** Sydney, Australia; **19-20:** Melbourne, Australia; **22:** Adelaide, Australia; **23:** Perth, Australia; **29:** Stockholm, Sweden.
May 1: Copenhagen, Denmark; **5:** Dublin, Ireland; **6:** Belfast, North Ireland; **10:** Bristol, En-

gland; **11:** Cardiff, Wales; **12:** Birmingham, England; **14:** Liverpool, England; **15:** Leicester, England; **16:** Sheffield, England; **17:** Manchester, England; **19:** Glasgow, Scotland; **20:** Edinburgh, Scotland; **21:** Newcastle, England; **24:** Paris, France; **26-27:** London, England.

1968

Woody Guthrie Memorial Concert
After a long layoff from the road following his 1966 motorcycle accident, Dylan returned to the stage, but only for a brief set. Dylan was one of the reasons why the Guthrie memorial concert was held. After Guthrie's death the previous fall, Dylan called the singer's former manager and said that if there was to be such a memorial, he wanted to participate. Luring the elusive Dylan back to the stage would be a coup for the concert organizers. He had released *John Wesley Harding* a month before but had made no plans to tour. The Guthrie concert would be his only stage performance from May 1966 until August 1969.

Dylan, backed by The Band (in this incarnation known as The Crackers), performed three Guthrie songs: "I Ain't Got No Home," "Dear Mrs. Roosevelt" and "The Grand Coulee Dam." With the other performers (including Pete Seeger, Arlo Guthrie, Judy Collins, Odetta and others), Dylan performed "This Train Is Bound for Glory" and "This Land Is Your Land." There were afternoon and evening performances, and Dylan's songs were released on a Guthrie tribute album.
January 20: New York City.

1969

The Isle of Wight Festival
Dylan chose to flee his home near the site of the massive Woodstock Music and Arts Fair (which drew 500,000 fans) in order to perform at this festival, which he assumed would be smaller and more intimate. The concert drew 200,000 fans. Dylan was again backed by The Band, which was, by this time, a successful recording act on its own. Visibly nervous, Dylan took the stage hours after his appointed time due to the delays inherent with music festivals. Dylan's 17-song set sampled from all areas of his career and included "Quinn the Eskimo (The Mighty Quinn)," which he had not released before, and "Minstrel Boy," a brand-new song. He also performed the traditional "Wild Mountain Thyme." The shaky performance was recorded by Columbia Records, and four of the songs showed up on *Self Portrait* the next year.
August 31: Ryde, England.

1971

The Concert for Bangladesh
Former Beatle George Harrison organized this charity concert at Madison Square Garden. The proceeds were to benefit the refugees in Bangladesh. It took a long time for the money to get to the victims of the war for independence, but eventually more than $200,000 raised at the concert was sent to Bangladesh. Harrison was the star of the show, but he managed to recruit a band that included Ringo Starr, Eric Clapton, Leon Russell and Billy Preston. Each took a solo turn. However, it was Dylan's appearance that made the shows newsworthy. He came out of his self-imposed seclusion to perform five songs at both the afternoon and evening performances. The evening performance appeared in the album and film *The Concert for Bangladesh*.
August 1: New York City (two shows).

1974

On Tour with The Band
This blockbuster tour signaled Dylan's return to concert performance. The shows usually began with six- or seven songs by Dylan and The Band. The Band then did a set without Dylan, who rejoined them for three or four songs before an intermission. Afterward, Dylan performed three or four songs solo then was joined by the group for several tunes. Several concerts opened and closed with the same song: "Most Likely You Go Your Way (and I'll Go Mine)." The sets drew heavily on material from 1962 through 1966, along with a few songs from his then-new album, *Planet Waves*. The centerpiece of the solo set, "It's Alright Ma (I'm Only Bleeding)," drew tremendous cheers with its reference to the president of the United States not being above the law. It was heady stuff for a Watergate-era audience. The concerts at the Forum in Los Angeles on February 13-14 were the source of most of *Before the Flood*, the document of the tour.
January 3-4: Chicago; **6-7:** Philadelphia, Pennsylvania (two shows on 6 January); **9-10:** Toronto, Ontario; **11-12:** Montreal, Quebec; **14:** Boston, Massachusetts (two shows); **15-16:** Largo, Maryland; **17:** Charlotte, North Carolina; **19:** Hollywood, Florida (two shows); **21-22:** Atlanta; **23:** Memphis, Tennessee; **25:** Fort Worth, Texas; **26:** Houston, Texas (two shows); **28-29:** Nassau, New York; **30-31:** New York City (two shows on 31 January).
February 2: Ann Arbor, Michigan; **3:** Bloomington, Indiana; **4:** St. Louis, Missouri (two shows); **6:** Denver (two shows); **9:** Seattle, Washington (two shows); **11:** Oakland; **13-14**: Inglewood, California (two shows on 14 February).

The Friends of Chile Benefit Concert
This performance at the Felt Forum in Madison Square Garden was organized by Dylan's compadre in protest from the early 1960s, Phil Ochs.

Dylan joined Arlo Guthrie on Woody Guthrie's "Deportee," then sang his "North Country Blues," which remarkably, paralleled the Chilean experience. With Guthrie, Ochs, Dave Van Ronk, Pete Seeger and others, Dylan performed "Spanish Is the Loving Tongue" and "Blowin' in the Wind."
May 9: New York City.

1975

The SNACK Benefit
Dylan joined Neil Young's band, the Stray Gators, for a set at Kezar Stadium to benefit San Francisco public schools. (SNACK stood for Students Need Athletic And Cultural Kicks.") Dylan played only two of his songs ("I Want You" and "Knockin' on Heaven's Door"), but joined in on several tunes by Young and The Band.
March 23: San Francisco, California.

The Rolling Thunder Revue, Part I
The Chile benefit and Dylan's return to New York had led him into the company of his friends from the early 1960s. He launched an informal theater tour that soon became a big draw at stadiums and coliseums. The standard set for the early performances of the Rolling Thunder Revue began with 10 to 15 songs by the group. Bob Neuwirth, Rob Stoner, Mick Ronson, Ronee Blakely and Ramblin' Jack Elliot, among others, did one or two solo numbers. Dylan did five or six songs with the group before intermission. The second part of the shows began with an acoustic set by Dylan and Joan Baez. A few songs each by Baez, the group and Dylan led to a closing set by Dylan and the group.
October 30-31: Plymouth, Massachusetts.
November 1: Dartmouth, Massachusetts; **2:** Lowell, Massachusetts; **4:** Providence, Rhode Island (two shows); **6:** Springfield, Massachusetts (two shows); **8:** Burlington, Vermont; **9:** Durham, New Hampshire; **11:** Waterbury, Connecticut; **13:** New Haven, Connecticut (two shows); **15:** Niagara Falls, New York (two shows); **17:** Rochester, New York (two shows); **19:** Worcester, Massachusetts; **20:** Cambridge, Massachusetts; **21:** Boston, Massachusetts (two shows); **22:** Waltham, Massachusetts; **24:** Hartford, Connecticut; **26:** Augusta, Maine; **27:** Bangor, Maine; **29:** Quebec City, Quebec.
December 1-2: Toronto, Ontario; **4:** Montreal, Quebec; **7:** Clinton, New Jersey; **8:** New York City (a benefit for boxer Rubin "Hurricane" Carter, this Madison Square Garden show was billed as "The Night of the Hurricane").

1976

The Rolling Thunder Revue, Part I (Continued)
After a month and a half off for the holidays, Dylan and company resumed the first leg of the tour. The performance in Houston on January 25 was in

tended as another benefit for Carter, but ended up as a financial fiasco. Dylan lost thousands of dollars and played to a largely empty Astrodome.

January 23: West Los Angeles, California; **25:** Houston, Texas (a second benefit, called "Night of the Hurricane II," at the Astrodome). **28:** Austin, Texas (Dylan joins Joni Mitchell during one of her concerts).

The Rolling Thunder Revue, Part II

After a three-month hiatus, Dylan and members of the revue returned to the road. The shows for Rolling Thunder II followed the same basic outline as in Rolling Thunder I, with the major difference being a boost in scale. The shows in Part I had played theaters and smaller halls. Part II was more of an arena show. The concept of intimacy that had led to the creation of the Rolling Thunder Revue was lost. Rolling Thunder II gave a larger role to Roger McGuinn, the former leader of The Byrds and a longtime Dylan interpreter and collaborator.

The Clearwater, Florida, show of April 22 was filmed for a television special, but it was not broadcast. The Fort Collins, Colorado, show of May 23 was the basis for the *Hard Rain* NBC television special on September 14. That show, at Colorado State University, was played in the midst of a rainstorm, hence the title of the television program. The song "A Hard Rain's A-Gonna Fall" appears in the television special but not on the companion album, which was recorded at Fort Collins and Fort Worth.

April 18: Lakeland, Florida; **20:** St. Petersburg, Florida; **21:** Tampa, Florida; **22:** Clearwater, Florida (two shows); **23:** Orlando, Florida; **25:** Gainesville, Florida; **27:** Tallahassee, Florida; **28:** Pensacola, Florida; **29:** Mobile, Alabama (two shows).
May 1: Hattiesburg, Mississippi; **3:** New Orleans (two shows); **4:** Baton Rouge, Louisiana; **8:** Houston, Texas; **10:** Corpus Christi, Texas; **11:** San Antonio, Texas; **12:** Austin, Texas; **15:** Gatesville, Texas; **16:** Fort Worth, Texas; **18:** Oklahoma City, Oklahoma; **19:** Wichita, Kansas; **23:** Fort Collins, Colorado; **25:** Salt Lake City, Utah.

The Last Waltz

Dylan performed at the Thanksgiving Day concert by The Band at San Francisco's Winterland. This was the Band's farewell to the stage. Several artists made guest appearances, including Van Morrison, Neil Young and Joni Mitchell. Dylan performed "Baby, Let Me Follow You Down" (twice), "Hazel," "Forever Young" and "I Don't Believe You (She Acts Like We Never Have Met)." He joined the ensemble for "I Shall Be Released."

November 25: San Francisco, California

1978

The Vegas Tour/The Alimony Tour

Dylan never played Las Vegas on his tours of 1978, but he adopted a new stage presence. Appearing in a shiny three-piece suit that called to mind images of Wayne Newton and Sergio Franchi, Dylan looked markedly different.

The sound was different too. He incorporated brass into the band and used a "girl group" as backing singers. Some fans dubbed this the "Vegas Tour" because of the slickness of the band and Dylan's bantering. Others, noting the divorce settlement with Sara Dylan (which was rumored to be devastating), called it "The Alimony Tour." The bookings were so extensive, some wags said, because he had to come up with a lot of cash for the settlement.

Another difference was the between-song banter. The normally close-mouthed Dylan was now gregarious. "I'm just an entertainer," he told the press when asked about his new persona. The sets for these tours incorporated much of the *Blood on the Tracks/Desire* music as well as radical reinterpretations of his classic songs from the 1960s. He had often altered arrangements of his greatest hits, but the revisions for this tour rendered some of his better known work unrecognizable for several verses.

February 20-23: Tokyo, Japan; **24-26:** Hirakata City, Japan; **28:** Tokyo, Japan.
March 1-4: Tokyo, Japan; **9:** Auckland, New Zealand; **12-15:** Brisbane, Australia; **18:** Adelaide, Australia; **20-22:** Melbourne, Australia; **25, 27-28:** Perth, Australia.
April 1: Sydney, Australia.
June 1-7: Los Angeles; **15-20:** London; **23:** Rotterdam, The Netherlands; **26-27:** Dortmund, West Germany; **29:** West Berlin.
July 1: Nurnburg, West Germany; **3-6, 8:** Paris; **11-12:** Goteborg, Sweden; **15:** Camberly, England.
September 15: Augusta, Maine; **16:** Portland, Maine; **17:** New Haven, Connecticut; **19:** Montreal, Quebec; **20:** Boston, Massachusetts; **22:** Syracuse, New York; **23:** Rochester, New York; **24:** Binghampton, New York; **26:** Springfield, Massachusetts; **27:** Uniondale, New York; **29-30:** New York City.
October 3: Norfolk, Virginia; **4:** Baltimore, Maryland; **5:** Largo, Maryland; **6:** Philadelphia, Pennsylvania; **7:** Providence, Rhode Island; **9:** Buffalo, New York; **12:** Toronto, Ontario; **13:** Detroit, Michigan; **14:** Terre Haute, Indiana; **15:** Cincinnati, Ohio; **17-18:** Chicago; **20:** Richfield, Ohio; **21:** Toledo, Ohio; **22:** Dayton, Ohio; **24:** Louisville, Kentucky; **25:** Indianapolis, Indiana; **27:** Kalamazoo, Michigan; **28:** Carbondale, Illinois; **29:** St. Louis, Missouri; **31:** St. Paul, Minnesota.
November 1: Madison, Wisconsin; **3:** Kansas City, Missouri; **4:** Omaha, Nebraska; **6:** Denver, Colorado; **9:** Portland, Oregon; **10:** Seattle, Washington; **11:** Vancouver, British Columbia; **13-14:** Oakland, California; **14:** Inglewood, California; **17:** San Diego, California; **18:** Tempe, Arizona; **19:** Tuscon, Arizona; **21:** El Paso, Texas; **23:** Norman, Oklahoma; **24:** Fort Worth, Texas; **25:** Austin, Texas; **26:** Houston, Texas; **28:** Jackson, Mississippi; **29:** Baton Rouge, Louisiana.
December 1: Memphis, Tennessee; **2:** Nashville, Tennessee; **3:** Birmingham, Alabama; **5:** Mobile, Alabama; **7:** Greensboro, North Carolina; **8:** Savannah, Georgia; **9:** Columbia, South Carolina; **10:** Charlotte, North Carolina; **12:** Atlanta, Georgia; **13:** Jacksonville, Florida; **15:** Lakeland, Florida; **16:** Hollywood, Florida.

1979

The Gospel Tours

Dylan's tours of 1979-1980 reflected his Christian-influenced albums of the era. The shows often opened with six gospel songs performed by his backing singers (Helena Springs, Regina Havis and Mona Lisa Young) and then a long set of all new material by Dylan and his backing band. The shows were difficult. Dylan's determination to sing only his new songs offended some and by the second leg (year) of the tour, he was included some of his best-known older material. Dylan complained about the crowds during these tours, for shouting sexual insults at the backing singers. Dylan was also criticized for his comments between songs, which resembled preaching to some critics.

November 1-4, 6-11, 13-16: San Francisco, California; **18-21:** Santa Monica, California; **25-26:** Tempe, Arizona; **27-28:** San Diego, California.
December 4-5: Albuquerque, New Mexico; **8-9:** Tucson, Arizona.

1980

The Gospel Tours, Continued
January 11-12: Portland, Oregon; **13-15:** Seattle, Washington; **16:** Portland, Oregon; **17-18:** Spokane, Washington; **21-23:** Denver, Colorado; **25-26:** Omaha, Nebraska; **27-29:** Kansas City, Missouri; **31:** Memphis, Tennessee.
February 1: Memphis, Tennessee; **2-3:** Birmingham, Alabama; **5-6:** Knoxville, Tennessee; **8-9:** Charleston, West Virginia.
April 17-20: Toronto, Ontario; **22-25:** Montreal, Quebec; **27-28:** Albany, New York; **30:** Buffalo, New York.
May 1: Buffalo, New York; **2-3:** Worcester, Massachusetts; **4-5:** Syracuse, New York; **7-8:** Hartford, Connecticut; **9-10:** Portland, Maine; **11-12:** Providence, Rhode Island; **14-16:** Pittsburgh, Pennsylvania; **17-18:** Akron, Ohio; **20:** Columbus, Ohio; **21:** Dayton, Ohio.
November 9-13, 15-19, 21-22: San Francisco, California; **24:** Tuscon, Arizona; **26:** San Diego, California; **29-30:** Seattle, Washington.
December 2: Salem, Oregon; **3-4:** Portland, Oregon.

1981

The "Shot of Love" Tour
In form, Dylan's 1981 shows were an extension of the Gospel Tours. The shows began with gospel tunes by the backing singers and Dylan's sets leaned heavily on the material from *Slow Train Coming* and *Saved*. Near the end of the 1980 shows, Dylan began including older material, and by the time of these concerts in 1981, he had fully incorporated the gospel material into sets that sampled liberally from each of his artistic periods. Back in the show after a three-year absence were many of his standards, including "Maggie's Farm," "Simple Twist of Fate," "Girl from the North Country" and "Mr. Tambourine Man," among others.

Although the *Shot of Love* album is often recognized as completing Dylan's Christian trilogy, most of it deals with secular themes. A masterful song such as "Every Grain of Sand" could have appeared on any other Dylan album without immediately being categorized as a religious song. The opening segment by the gospel trio was dropped, although the supporting singers were generally spotlighted with a number mid-show. Veterans of the gospel tours fleshed out Dylan's stage band. For the American dates in October and November, Dylan was joined by Al Kooper on keyboards. Although the shows often began with "Gotta Serve Somebody," Dylan's opening staple from the gospel tours, the concerts begin to evolve into more of a full-career retrospective. Interesting songs covered on the tour, included Jimmy Webb's "Let's Begin," George Harrison's "Here Comes the Sun," the popular film theme "The Rose," "Abraham, Martin and John" and a Chuck Berry tune called "No Money Down," on which Dylan played saxophone.

June 10: Hoffman Estates, Illinois; **11-12:** Clarkston, Michigan; **14:** Columbia, Maryland; **21:** Toulouse, France; **23:** Colombes, France; **26-30:** London, England.
July 1: London, England; **4-5:** Birmingham, England; **8:** Stockholm, Sweden; **9-10:** Drammen, Norway; **12:** Copenhagen, Denmark; **14-15:** Bad Segeberg, West Germany; **17:** St. Goarshausen, West Germany; **18:** Mannheim, West Germany; **19-20:** Munich, West Germany; **21:** Vienna, Austria; **Basel, Switzerland; 25:** Avignon, France.
October 16-17: Milwaukee, Wisconsin; **18:** Madison, Wisconsin; **19:** Merrillville, Indiana; **21:** Boston, Massachusetts; **23:** Philadelphia, Pennsylvania; **24:** State College, Pennsylvania; **25:** Bethlehem, Pennsylvania; **27:** East Rutherford, New Jersey; **29:** Toronto, Ontario; **30:** Montreal, Quebec; **31:** Kitchener, Ontario.
November 2: Ottawa, Ontario; **4-5:** Cincinnati, Ohio; **6:** Lafayette, Indiana; **7-8:** Ann Arbor, Michigan; **10-11:** New Orleans, Louisiana; **12:** Houston, Texas; **14:** Nashville, Tennessee; **15-16:** Atlanta, Georgia; **19-20:** Miami, Florida; **21:** Lakeland, Florida.

1982

Peace Sunday
Dylan appeared with Joan Baez at a benefit for the antinuclear movement. They duetted on "With God on Our Side," Jimmy Buffett's "A Pirate Looks at Forty" and "Blowin' in the Wind."
June 6: Pasadena, California.

1983

Guest Appearance
Dylan joined former Band members Levon Helm and Rick Danko at their Lone Star Cafe concert. Dylan played and sang on tunes by Hank Williams, Leadbelly and Johnny Otis, among others.
February 16: New York City

1984

European Tour
Dylan and Joan Baez were reunited on this tour, although they rarely shared the stage. Baez was the opening act and then Santana played, followed by Dylan. Occasionally, Dylan and Baez duetted on the encores. Dylan's group was pared down from previous tours. Ex-Rolling Stone Mick Taylor played

lead guitar and Ian MacLagan, formerly of Small Faces, played keyboards. Bassist Greg Sutton sang a lead vocal at some shows. The drummer was Colin Allen.

May 28-29: Verona, Italy; **31:** Hamburg, West Germany.
June 2: Basel, Switzerland; **3:** Munich, West Germany; **4, 6:** Rotterdam, The Netherlands; **7:** Brussels, Belgium; **9:** Goteborg, Sweden; **10:** Copenhagen, Denmark; **11:** Offenbach, West Germany; **13:** West Berlin; **14:** Vienna, Austria; **16:** Cologne, West Germany; **17:** Nice, France; **19-21:** Rome, Italy; **24:** Milan, Italy; **26:** Madrid, Spain; **28:** Barcelona, Spain; **30:** Nantes, France.
July 1: Paris, France; **3:** Grenoble, France; **5:** Newcastle, England; **7:** London, England; **8:** Slane, Ireland.

1985

Live Aid
The whole philanthropic spirit behind the massive Live Aid benefit for African relief owed a great debt to Dylan and his humanitarian work. It seemed fitting that Dylan be the solo artist who was chosen to conclude the massive two-continent concert. Dylan was backed by Keith Richards and Ron Wood of the Rolling Stones, and the performance was sloppy and rather anticlimactic. Dylan strummed an acoustic guitar and sang "Ballad of Hollis Brown," "When the Ship Comes In" and "Blowin' in the Wind." Richards and Wood also strummed guitars, but it was not readily apparent what song they were playing.
July 13: Philadelphia, Pennsylvania.

Farm Aid
Backed by Tom Petty and The Heartbreakers (and by Willie Nelson on one song), Dylan played a brief set--two oldies ("That Lucky Old Sun" and "Shake") and a few of his compositions--"Clean Cut Kid," "I'll Remember You," "Trust Yourself" and "Maggie's Farm."
September 22: Champaign, Illinois.

1986

Martin Luther King Day
To celebrate the first national holiday honoring the slain civil rights leader, Dylan and many other entertainers performed in a gala at the John F. Kennedy Center for the Performing Arts. Dylan joined Stevie Wonder on Wonder's composition, "The Bells of Freedom." He sang "I Shall Be Released," backed by Wonder and his band, and, with Wonder, joined Peter, Paul and Mary for "Blowin' in the Wind." With an all-star chorus that included Harry Belafonte, Elizabeth Taylor, Diana Ross and others, Dylan sang Wonder's "Happy Birthday," a song urging the nation to honor King

with a holiday.
January 20: Washington, D.C.

The True Confessions Tour
Dylan found an agreeable younger partner in Tom Petty. Petty, who was a full decade younger than Dylan, was atypical for rock 'n' rollers of his generation. Although he matured in the 1970s, an era dominated by synthetic disco music, Petty and a few others (notably Bruce Springsteen) were keepers of a more traditional rock 'n' roll flame. Petty was already a headliner when he and his superb band, The Heartbreakers, joined Dylan for a series of dates in 1986. The Heartbreakers were Dylan's best accompaniment since The Band, and Petty and Dylan's tastes complimented one another. Some of the Australian dates were filmed for the Home Box Office television special, *Hard to Handle*.

February 5: Wellington, New Zealand; **7:** Auckland, New Zealand; **10-13:** Sydney, Australia; **15:** Adelaide, Australia; **17-18:** Perth, Australia; **19:** Melbourne, Australia [Dylan appears at a Dire Straits concert and performs four songs with the band]; **21-22:** Victoria, Australia; **24-25:** Sydney, Australia; **28:** Queensland, Australia.
March 1: Queensland, Australia; **5:** Tokyo, Japan; **6:** Osaka Fu, Japan; **8:** Nagoya, Japan; **10:** Tokyo, Japan.
June 9: San Diego, California; **11:** Reno, Nevada; **12:** Sacramento, California; **13:** Berkeley, California; **16-17:** Costa Mesa, California; **18:** Phoenix, Arizona; **20:** Houston, Texas; **21:** Austin, Texas; **22:** Dallas, Texas; **24:** Indianapolis, Indiana; **26:** Minneapolis, Minnesota; **27:** East Troy, Wisconsin; **29:** Hoffman Estates, Illinois; **30:** Clarkston, Michigan.
July 1: Clarkston, Michigan; **2:** Akron, Ohio [joined by The Grateful Dead]; **4:** Buffalo, New York [joined by The Grateful Dead]; **6-7:** Washington, D.C. [joined by The Grateful Dead on July 6]; **8-9:** Mansfield, Massachusetts; **11:** Hartford, Connecticut; **13:** Saratoga Springs, New York; **15-17:** New York City; **19-20:** Philadelphia, Pennsylvania; **21:** East Rutherford, New Jersey; **22:** Mansfield, Massachusetts; **24:** Bonner Springs, Kansas; **26-27:** Morrison, Colorado; **29:** Portland, Oregon; **31:** Tacoma, Washington.
August 1: Vancouver, British Columbia; **3:** Inglewood, California; **5:** Mountain View, California; **6:** Paso Robles, California.

1987

On Tour with The Grateful Dead
These six concerts began with The Grateful Dead performing two hours of songs from their vast repertoire. Dylan then joined the band and played 12 or 13 songs, with the Dead's backing. Dylan and The Dead performed the encores together. Dylan's performances drew from all phases of his career. He even pulled out an obscure song from the early 1960s that he had never released: "John Brown." Other unusual inclusions--songs rarely performed in concert--included "The Wicked Messenger," "The Ballad of Frankie Lee and Judas Priest" and "Watching the River Flow." The dates were recorded, and *Dylan and The Dead* exists as a document of the tour.

July 4: Foxboro, Massachusetts; **10:** Philadelphia, Pennsylvania; **12:** East Rutherford, New Jersey; **19:** Eugene, Oregon; **24:** Oakland, California; **26:** Anaheim, California.

The Temples-in-Flames Tour of Europe

Dylan and Tom Petty and The Heartbreakers reunited and were joined by Roger McGuinn, former leader of The Byrds. The shows began with a solo set by McGuinn. Petty and the band joined McGuinn for several songs. Petty and the band did a few songs by themselves before an intermission. Dylan, Petty and the band performed 14 or 15 songs and all appeared together for the encores.

September 5: Tel-Aviv, Israel; **7:** Jerusalem, Israel; **10:** Basel, Switzerland; **12:** Modena, Italy; **13:** Turin, Italy; **15:** Dortmund, West Germany; **16:** Nurnburg, West Germany; **17:** East Berlin, East Germany; **19:** Rotterdam, The Netherlands; **20:** Hanover, West Germany; **21:** Copenhagen, Denmark; **23:** Helsinki, Finland; **25:** Goteborg, Sweden; **26:** Stockholm, Sweden; **28:** Frankfurt, West Germany; **29:** Stuttgart, West Germany; **30:** Munich, West Germany.
October 1: Verona, Italy; **3:** Rome, Italy; **4:** Milan, Italy; **5:** Locarno, Italy; **7:** Paris, France; **8:** Brussels, Belgium; **10-12:** Birmingham, England; **14-17:** London, England.

1988

Guest Appearance

Dylan joined former Band drummer Levon Helm for a couple of songs during Helm's concert at the Lone Star Cafe. They performed "The Weight" and Chuck Berry's "Nadine."
May 29: New York City

The Never-Ending Tour, Part I

Dylan began four years of touring with a tight three-piece band led by G. E. Smith, former lead guitarist for Hall and Oates and the bandleader on *Saturday Night Live*. The stripped-down sound was a major change from the Petty tours (which had been augmented by three female backup singers known as The Queens of Rhythm), the claustrophobic sound of The Grateful Dead, and the massive big-band approach of the Vegas/Alimony tours. Smith was a brilliant guitarist but he was also a driving force for the band, which included Christopher Parker on drums and various bass guitarists. Marshall Crenshaw, a young artist whose work reflected a 1960s sensibility, had been announced as the original bass player, but he was replaced by Kenny Aaronson. Later, Tony Garnier replaced Aaronson. The sets were short and packed with hits. Occasional traditionals were thrown in ("The Lakes of Pontchartrain," "Man of Constant Sorrow," "Barbara Allen") and some songs that Dylan rarely (if ever) played in concert were performed: "Boots of Spanish Leather," "Absolutely Sweet Marie" and "Watching the River Flow."

June 7: Concord, California; **9:** Sacramento, California; **10:** Berkeley, California; **11:** Mouintain View, California; **13:** Park City, Utah; **15:** Denver, Colorado; **17:** St. Louis, Missouri; **18:** East Troy, Wisconsin; **21:** Cuyahoga Falls, Ohio; **22:** Cincinnati, Ohio; **24-25:** Holmdel, New Jersey; **26:** Saratoga Springs, New York; **28:** Canandaigua, New York; **30:** Wantagh, New York.
July 1: Wantagh, New York; **2:** Mansfield, Massachusetts; **3:** Old Orchard Beach, Maine; **6:**

Philadelphia, Pennsylvania; **8:** Montral, Quebec; **9:** Ottawa, Ontario; **11:** Hamilton, Ontario; **13:** Charlevoix, Michigan; **14:** Hoffman Estates, Illinois; **15:** Indianapolis, Indiana; **17-18:** Rochester Hills, Michigan; **20:** Columbia, Maryland; **22:** Nashville, Tennessee; **24-25:** Atlanta, Georgia; **26:** Memphis, Tennessee; **28:** Dallas, Texas; **30:** Mesa, Arizona; **31:** Costa Mesa, California.
August 2-4: Hollywood, California; **6:** Carlsbad, California; **7:** Santa Barbara, California; **19:** Portland, Oregon; **20:** George, Washington; **21:** Vancouver, British Columbia; **23:** Calgary, Alberta; **24:** Edmonton, Alberta; **26:** Winnipeg, Manitoba; **29:** Toronto, Ontario; **31:** Syracuse, New York.
September 2: Middletown, New York; **3:** Manchester, New Hampshire; **4:** Bristol, Connecticut; **7:** Essex Junction, Vermont; **8:** Binghamton, New York; **10:** Stanhope, New Jersey; **11:** Fairfax, Virginia; **13:** Pittsburgh, Pennsylvania; **15:** Chapel Hill, North Carolina; **16:** Columbia, South Carolina; **17:** Charlotte, North Carolina; **18:** Knoxville, Tennessee; **19:** Charlottesville, Virginia; **22:** Tampa, Florida; **23:** Miami, Florida; **24:** Gainesville, Florida; **25:** New Orleans, Louisiana.
October 13-14: Upper Darby, Pennsylvania; **16-19:**1 New York City.

1989

The Never-Ending Tour, Part II

This resumption of the tour traveled to Europe for the summer of 1989. The backing trio included Smith, Aaronson and Parker until an illness forced Aaronson off the road. He was replaced by Tony Garnier on bass.

May 27: Andrarum, Sweden; **28:** Stockholm, Sweden; **30:** Helsinki, Finland.
June 3-4: Dublin, Ireland; **6:** Glasgow, Scotland; **7:** Birmingham, England; **8:** London, England; **10:** The Hague, The Netherlands; **11:** Brussels, Belgium; **13:** Frejus, France; **15:** Madrid, Spain; **16:** Barcelona, Spain; **17:** San Sebastian, Spain; **19:** Milan, Italy; **20:** Rome, Italy; **21:** Cava Dei Tirreni, Italy; **22:** Livorno, Italy; **24:** Istanbul, Turkey; **26:** Patras, Greece; **27:** Athens, Greece.
July 1: Peoria, Illinois; **2:** Hoffman Estates, Illinois; **3:** Milwaukee, Wisconsin; **5-6:** Rochester, Michigan; **8:** Noblesville, Indiana; **9:** Cuyahoga Falls, Ohio; **11:** Harrisburg, Pennsylvania; **12:** Allentown, Pennsylvania; **13:** Mansfield, Massachusetts; **15:** Old Orchard Beach, Maine; **16:** Bristol, Connecticut; **17:** Stanhope, New Jersey; **19:** Columbia, Maryland; **20:** Atlantic City, New Jersey; **21:** Holmdel, New Jersey; **23:** Wantagh, New York; **25:** Canandaigua, New York; **26:** Saratoga Springs, New York; **28:** Pittsburgh, Pennsylvania; **29:** Maple, Ontario; **31:** Quebec, Canada.
August 3: St. Paul, Minnesota; **4:** Madison, Wisconsin; **5:** Grand Rapids, Michigan; **6:** Columbus, Ohio; **8:** Toledo, Ohio; **9:** St. Louis, Missouri; **10:** Cincinnati, Ohio; **12:** Doswell, Virginia; **13:** Charlotte, North Carolina; **15-16:** Atlanta, Georgia; **18:** Louisville, Kentucky; **19:** Springfield, Illinois; **20:** Nashville, Tennessee; **22:** Bonner Springs, Kansas; **23:** Oklahoma City, Oklahoma; **25:** New Orleans, Louisiana; **26:** Houston, Texas; **27:** Dallas, Texas; **29:** Las Cruces, New Mexico; **31:** Englewood, Colorado.
September 1: Park City, Utah; **3:** Berkeley, California; **5:** Santa Barbara, California; **6:** San Diego, California; **8:** Costa Mesa, California; **9-10:** Hollywood, California.
October 10-13: New York City; **15-16:** Upper Darby, Pennsylvania; **17-18:** Washington, D.C.; **20:** Poughkeepsie, New York; **22:** Kingston, Rhode Island; **23-25:** Boston, Massachusetts; **27:** Troy, New York; **29:** Ithaca, New York; **31:** Chicago, Illinois.
November 1: Ann Arbor, Michigan; **2:** Cleveland, Ohio; **4:** Indiana, Pennsylvania; **6:** Blackburg, Pennsylvania; **7:** Norfolk, Virginia; **8:** Durham, North Carolina; **10:** Atlanta, Georgia; **12-13:** Miami, Florida; **14-15:** Tampa, Florida.

1990

The Never-Ending Tour, Part III

The same personnel made the tour with Dylan in 1990, and the sets varied little from the 15 or 20 song sets of the previous years. The one variation was the 12 January date at Toad's Place in New Haven, Connecticut, where Dylan and his band performed for four hours as a warm-up for the tour, covering Joe South's "Walk a Mile in My Shoes," Kris Kristofferson's "Help Me Make It through the Night" and "Across the Borderline" by Ry Cooder and John Hiatt. He also did a lot of material from *Oh Mercy*, his new album. (Only one or two *Oh Mercy* songs were performed in concert during the rest of the tour.)

January 12: New Haven, Connecticut; **14:** State College, Pennsylvania; **15:** Princeton, New Jersey; **18:** Sao Paolo, Brazil; **25:** Rio de Janiero, Brazil; **29-31:** Paris, France.
February 1: Paris, France; **3-8:** London, England.
May 29: Montreal, Quebec; **30:** Kingston, Ontario.
June 1-2: Ottawa, Ontario; **4:** London, Ontario; **5-7:** Toronto, Ontario; **9:** East Troy, Wisconsin; **10:** Davenport, Iowa; **12:** LaCrosse, Wisconsin; **13:** Sioux Falls, South Dakota; **14:** Fargo, North Dakota; **15:** Bismarck, North Dakota; **17-18:** Winnipeg, Manitoba; **25:** Reykjavik, Iceland; **29:** Roskilde, Denmark; **30:** Sandvika, Norway.
July 1: Turku, Finland; **3:** Hamburg, Germany; **4:** Berlin, Germany; **7:** Torhout, Belgium; **8:** Werchter, Belgium; **9:** Montreaux, Switzerland.
August 12-13: Edmonton, Alberta; **15-16:** Calgary, Alberta; **18:** George, Washington; **19:** Victoria, British Columbia; **20:** Vancouver, British Columbia; **21:** Portland, Oregon; **24:** Pueblo, Colorado; **26:** Des Moines, Iowa; **27-28:** Merrillville, Indiana; **29:** St. Paul, Minnesota; **31:** Lincoln, Nebraska.
September 1: Lampe, Missouri; **2:** Hannibal, Missouri; **4:** Tulsa, Oklahoma; **5:** Oklahoma City, Oklahoma; **6:** Dallas, Texas; **8:** San Antonio, Texas; **9:** Austin, Texas; **11:** Santa Fe, New Mexico; **12:** Mesa, Arizona.
October 11: Brookville, New York; **12:** Springfield, Massachusetts; **13:** West Point, New York; **15-19:** New York City; **21:** Richmond, Virginia; **22:** Pittsburgh, Pennsylvania; **23:** Charleston, West Virginia; **25:** Oxford, Mississippi; **26:** Tuscaloosa, Alabama; **27:** Nashville, Tennessee; **28:** Athens, Georgia; **30:** Boone, North Carolina.
November 2: Lexington, Kentucky; **3:** Carbondale, Illinois; **4:** St. Louis, Missouri; **6:** DeKalb, Illinois; **8:** Iowa City, Iowa; **9:** Chicago, Illinois; **10:** Milwaukee, Wisconsin; **12:** East Lansing, Michigan; **13:** Dayton, Ohio; **14:** Normal, Illinois; **16:** Columbua, Ohio; **17:** Cleveland, Ohio; **18:** Detroit, Michigan.

1991

The Never-Ending Tour, Part IV

The tour had finally ended for G. E. Smith in October 1990, and his place had been taken by a succession of guitarists. By the time Dylan was ready to begin his spring world tour in 1991, the band included two additional guitarists: John Jackson and Cesar Diaz. Tony Garnier was still on bass and Ian Wallace, from the *Street-Legal* days, was the drummer. The early 1991 shows are notable for their inclusion of more recent material and some old songs rarely performed in concert, such as "Bob Dylan's Dream."

January 28: Zurich, Switzerland; **30:** Brussels, Belgium; **31:** Utrecht, The Netherlands.
February 2-3: Glasgow, Scotland; **5:** Dublin, Ireland; **6:** Belfast, Northern Ireland; **8-10, 12-13, 15-17:** London, England; **21:** Williamsport, Pennsylvania; **22:** Owings Mills, Maryland; **25, 27:** Guadalajara, Mexico.
March 1-2: Mexico City.
October 24: Corpus Christi, Texas; **25:** Austin, Texas; **26:** San Antonio, Texas; **28:** Lubbock, Texas; **30:** Tulsa, Oklahoma; **31:** Wichita, Kansas.
November 1: Kansas City, Missouri; **2:** Ames, Iowa; **4:** Evanston, Illinois; **5:** Madison, Wisconsin; **6:** South Bend, Indiana; **8:** Louisville, Kentucky; **9:** Dayton, Ohio; **10:** Indianapolis, Indiana; **12:** Detroit, Michigan; **13:** Akron, Ohio.

1992

The Never-Ending Tour, Part V

Dylan's appearances included the same stage band as in 1990 and ventured to the Pacific Basin, including his first-ever concerts in Hawaii.

Dylan once explained the rationale of the Never-Ending Tour to British journalist Adrian Deevoy: "It works out better for me that way. You can pick and choose better when you're just out there all the time and your show is already set up. You know, you just don't have to start it up and end it. It's better just to keep it out there with breaks, you know, with extended breaks."[3]

Jackson, Garnier and Wallace remained at the core of Dylan's band, but he added steel guitarist Bucky Baxter, from Steve Earle's backing band, and a second drummer, Winton Watson. The content of Dylan's sets still varied radically from show to show, his unpredictability endearing him even more to his fans. Here is a representative set from a performance in the fall: Dylan opened with Muddy Waters's "I Can't Be Satisfied," followed with an "If Not for You" that borrowed the melody from "Someone's Got a Hold of My Heart." "All Along the Watchtower" followed, then the rarely heard-in-concert for years "Simple Twist of Fate" appeared, augmented with Baxter's mandolin. Then came several surprises: "Drifter's Escape," "Under the Red Sky," "Silvio," and two solo performances, "Mama, You Been on My Mind" and "Boots of Spanish Leather." Rejoined by the band, he did "Mr. Tambourine Man" (with a new melody, to thwart those who wanted to sing along) and "Don't Think Twice, It's All Right." Garnier played acoustic bass on these numbers. With the drummers and Baxter back, the band ripped through "Unbelievable," then Baxter's slide guitar added the appropriately spooky touches to "Man in the Long Black Coat." After "The Times They Are A-Changin'," Dylan ended with a blistering, drum-driven "Maggie's Farm." For his encores, Dylan chose two *Oh Mercy* songs: the delicate "Shooting Star" and "Everything is Broken." The band left Dylan solo. He turned his revisionism on "It Ain't Me Babe," then stood at the edge of the stage and studied the faces in the audiences before leaving.

Some nights, Dylan's shows resemble greatest-hits sets. On this night, however, one-third of the songs came from the previous four years, and many of the older songs selected were tunes rarely performed in concert ("Mama, You Been on My Mind" and "Drifter's Escape," for example). Dylan was determined not to become predictable.

March 18: Perth, Australia; **21:** Adelaide, Australia; **23-25:** Sydney, Australia; **28:** Brisbane. Australia; **29:** Canberra, Australia.
April 1-3, 5-7: Melbourne, Australia; **10:** Launceton, Australia; **11:** Hobart, Australia; **14-16:** Sydney, Australia; **18:** Auckland, New Zealand; **22:** Maui, Hawaii; **24:** Waikiki, Hawaii; **27-28:** Seattle, Washington; **30:** Eugene, Oregon.
May 1: Red Bluff, California; **2:** Santa Rosa, California; **4-5:** San Francisco, California; **7-8:** Berkeley, California; **9:** San Jose, California; **11:** Santa Barbara, California; **13-14, 16-17, 19-21:** Los Angeles, California; **23:** Las Vegas, Nevada.
June 26: Lule, Sweden; **28:** Goteborg, Sweden; **30:** Dunkerque, France.
July 1: Reims, France; **2:** Belfort, France; **4:** Genoa, Italy; **5:** Correggio, Italy; **7:** Merrano, Italy; **8:** Aosta, Italy; **10:** Leysin, Switzerland; **12:** Juan les Pins, France.
August 17-18: Toronto, Ontario; **20:** Meadeville, Pennsylvania; **21:** Hamilton, Ontario; **22:** Ottawa, Ontario; **23:** Sudbury, Ontario; **25:** Sault Ste. Marie, Ontario; **27:** Thunder Bay, Ontario; **29-31:** Minneapolis, Minnesota.
September 2-3: Minneapolis, Minnesota; **5:** Omaha, Nebraska; **6:** Kansas Cit, Missouri; **8:** Little Rock, Arkansas; **9:** Jackson, Mississippi; **11:** Birmingham, Alabama; **12:** Pensacola, Florida; **13:** Lafayette, Louisiana.
October 9: Pittsburgh, Pennsylvania; **10:** Lock Haven, Pennsylvania; **11:** Rochester, New York; **12:** Binghamton, New York; **16:** New York City (tribute concert celebrating "The Music of Bob Dylan"); **23:** Newark, Delaware; **24:** Storrs, Connecticut; **25:** Providence, Rhode Island; **27:** Burlington, Vermont; **28:** Springfield, Massachusetts; **30:** Beverly, Massachusetts.
November 1: Wilkes-Barre, Pennsylvania; **2:** Youngstown, Ohio; **3:** Cincinnati, Ohio; **6:** Gainesville, Florida; **8:** Coral Gables, Florida; **9:** Sarasota, Florida; **11:** Clearwater, Florida; **13:** Sunrise, Florida; **15:** West Palm Beach, Florida; **16:** Jacksonville, Florida.

Notes

1. Betsy Bowden, *Performed Literature: Words and Music by Bob Dylan* (Bloomington: Indiana University Press, 1982).
2. Paul Williams, *Bob Dylan: Performing Artist* (Novato, Calif.: Underwood-Miller, 1990), p. xvi.
3. Adrian Deevoy, "The Wanted Man," *Q*, December 1989, p. 72.

Part V

Chronology

Chapter 10

Bob Dylan's Life-in-Progress

BOB ZIMMERMAN INVENTED BOB DYLAN nearly 35 years ago and, as he as often said of himself, "I'm only Bob Dylan when I want to be." Early in his career as an entertainer, this allowed him to mask much of his identity. He was not so much running from his past or hiding his midwestern upbringing; he was simply telling the truth. As Bob Zimmerman, he was a boy from the North Country with a rather conventional upbringing. As Bob Dylan, he was busy being born and had a whole new life: one he could invent and reinvent, as he has done throughout his public career. Being Bob Dylan is probably a difficult job. It is a legacy he has carried for a long time. Whether he has carried it well is a subject of debate among those who consider his work important. Dylan once said:

> People ask me if it's hard being me. I answer, "To a degree, but it's not any more difficult than being George Michael." You can't really complain about who you are. You just have to make the most of it and that's all that can be expected of you.[1]

Dylan may shrug it off, but his legacy is the most intimidating in rock 'n' roll. Even major artists like Paul McCartney and Mick Jagger do not bear such burdens. They were members of bands, while Dylan has generally worked alone. However, rather than rest on his considerable laurels and restire to his estates in Minnesota or California, Dylan chooses to remain an active artist. Sometimes he fails to enhance his reputation. Other times, he succeeds--often, spectacularly so. Reports of his wildly varied concert performances and his odd (in both senses of the word) television appearances divide the community of Dylan followers. Some believe, and state emphatically, that Dylan wants to keep the mass audience at bay and uses whatever forum he can to protect the integrity of his art for those in the smaller group who understand it.

"Bob Dylan has always been a pop outsider," Robert Hilburn wrote, "and there are few signs, as he enters his sixth decade, that he is surrendering his independence."[2]

As Dylan reevaluates his career with projects such as *Biograph* and the volumes of *The Bootleg Series*, he nonetheless continues to create new work that can stand alongside his old. Critics cite the material on *Oh Mercy* as some of his best writing, and his vocals on *Under the Red Sky* and *Good As I Been to You* as being masterful blues singing. Although his concerts may frequently take on the sound of career retrospectives, Dylan sends a message that he will continue to write as long as his powers of imagination allow him to do so.

What follows are some of the facts and figures of Bob Zimmerman's life and Bob Dylan's career.

1941

May 24: Robert Allen Zimmerman is born at 9:05 p.m., in Duluth, Minnesota, to Abraham and Beatty Zimmerman. He weighs 7 pounds, 13 ounces.

1945

May: Bobby Zimmerman makes his first public performance, singing "Accentuate the Positive" for his grandmother at a family reunion.

1947

Abe and Beatty Zimmerman, with their sons Robert and David, move to Hibbing, Minnesota, where Abe Zimmerman buys into Micka Electric Company.

1951

May: Bob, age 10, write his first creative literary work: a poem for his mother.

1954

Spring: Bob Zimmerman is bar mitzvahed.

1955

Bob gets his first guitar. He first hears the music of Hank Williams, Little Richard and Johnnie Ray.
Fall: Zimmerman sees James Dean in *Rebel without a Cause* four times. He adopts the Dean persona and mourns the actor's death on September 30.

1956

Fall: Bob decides he wants to be a musician. He forms a band, The Golden Chords, which fails the audition for a variety show at Hibbing Junior College.

1957

Bob plays in a succession of bands after The Golden Chords, including The Shadow Blasters, The Satin Tones and Elston Gunn & The Rock Boppers.

1959

January 31: Zimmerman sees the Winter Dance Party tour of Buddy Holly, Richie Valens and the Big Bopper, three nights before the performers perished in a plane crash.
Summer: Plays piano in Bobby Vee's backing band.
Fall: Zimmerman enrolls at the University of Minnesota and begins hanging out at coffeehouses in Dinkytown, the area near campus that is frequented by the Bohemian crowd. He begins performing under the name Bob Dillon, eventually altering the spelling to *Dylan*.

1960

Fall: He makes his first recordings. In a Minneapolis studio, Dylan performs several talking blues and traditional songs.

1961

February-March: At the East Orange, New Jersey, home of Bob and Sid Gleason, Dylan records several traditional songs as well as some well-known works of Woody Guthrie. Confident in the face of his idol, he sings an early version of "Song to Woody."
May: Back in Minneapolis, Dylan records several traditional songs and Guthrie tunes that will be the source of bootleg albums in the decades to come. This legendary "Minnesota Tape" includes versions of "Pastures of

Plenty," "Pretty Polly," "Will the Circle Be Unbroken?" and "This Land is Your Land."

June: In New York, he contributes harmonica to Harry Belafonte's recording of "Midnight Special" for the RCA Victor album, *Midnight Special*, which is released in March 1962. It is Dylan's first professional recording session.

July 29: Dylan performs five songs at Riverside Church in New York in a concert broadcast live over WRVR-FM.

September 29: Robert Shelton's article, "Bob Dylan: A Distinctive Folk-Song Stylist," appears in the *New York Times*.

September 30: At his second professional recording session, Dylan plays harmonica on three songs with Carolyn Hester.

October 21: Dylan backs up Victoria Spivey, Big Joe Williams and Lonnie Johnson on a recording of several blues numbers. Some of the recordings will be released in November 1964, but others will not be released until July 1972. (For information on this and any other recording references, see Section III of the discography.) A photograph of Dylan and Spivey taken this day is used on the back cover his *New Morning* album in 1970.

November 4: The Folklore Center presents Bob Dylan "in his first New York concert" at Carnegie Chapter Hall. Songs include "Pretty Peggy-O," "In the Pines," "Gospel Plow," "1913 Massacre," "Backwater Blues," "Long Time A-Growin'" and "Fixin' to Die."

November 20 and 22: Dylan records the songs for his first album at Columbia Studios in New York. John Hammond produces. Two original songs are included on the album, "Talkin' New York" and "Song to Woody."

1962

March: Dylan performs two original compositions, "Ballad of Donald White" and "The Death of Emmett Till" on "The Broadside Show" on WBAI-FM. These recordings are released a decade later on *Broadside Reunion*, with Dylan credited under one of his many pseudonyms, Blind Boy Grunt.

Spring: Dylan is writing furiously and makes demonstration recordings for his music publisher, M. Witmark and Sons, of these new songs: "Blowin' in the Wind," "The Ballad of Hollis Brown," "Tomorrow Is a Long Time," "Masters of War," "When the Ship Comes In" and "A Hard Rain's A-Gonna Fall."

March 19: His first album, *Bob Dylan*, is released by Columbia Records.

July: Begins recording sessions that will produce *The Freewheelin' Bob Dylan*, to be released the following spring.

November 14: Dylan's first single, "Mixed Up Confusion," backed with "Corrina, Corrina," is released by Columbia Records. It fails miserably.

1963

January 14 and 15: Dylan is in London, backing up friends Richard Farina and Eric von Schmidt for their recording sessions for a duo album. When the album finally appears in 1964, Dylan again is credited as Blind Boy Grunt.
Late winter: Dylan records four originals, "John Brown," "Only a Hobo," "Talkin' Devil" and "Let Me Die in My Footsteps," as Blind Boy Grunt. They make up part of an anthology called *Broadside Ballads*, which is released in September.
May 27: Dylan's second album, *The Freewheelin' Bob Dylan*, is released. Early promotional copies of the album include "Let Me Die in My Footsteps," "Rambling, Gambling Willie," "Rocks and Gravel" and "Talkin' John Birch Society Blues." These songs are removed from the album and replaced with four others.
July 6: At a voter registration rally in Greenwood, Mississippi, Dylan sings his song about Medgar Evers, "Only a Pawn in Their Game."
July 26-28: Dylan appears at the Newport Folk Festival in Newport, Rhode Island. He performs "With God on Our Side" and "Blowin' in the Wind," and joins with all the performers for a finale of "We Shall Overcome."
August: On a television documentary about protest singers, Dylan sings "Blowin' in the Wind" and "Only a Pawn in Their Game."
August 28: At the March on Washington, D. C., Dylan performs "Only a Pawn in Their Game."
August-October: Dylan records 24 songs for his next album. Only 11 make the final cut.

1964

January 13: Dylan's third album, *The Times They Are A-Changin'*, is released.
February 25: Dylan performs "The Lonesome Death of Hattie Carroll" on "The Steve Allen Show."
June 9: Dylan records his next album in one day at Columbia Studios in New York.
August 8: Dylan's fourth album, *Another Side of Bob Dylan*, is released.

1965

January 14: Most of Dylan's fifth album is recorded at Columbia Studios in New York.
February 17: Dylan sings "It's All Over Now, Baby Blue" and "It's Alright, Ma (I'm Only Bleeding)" on "The Les Crane Show" on WABC-TV.
March 22: Dylan's first rock 'n' roll album, *Bringing It All Back Home*, is released.

April-May: Filmmaker D. A. Pennebaker and his assistants film Dylan during his tour of England. This is the last of the folk tours and is documented in *Don't Look Back*, released in 1967.
June: Dylan and backing musicians begin recording the tracks for his next album.
July 19: Dylan records "Tombstone Blues," "It Takes a Lot to Laugh, It Takes a Train to Cry" and "Positively 4th Street" at Columbia Studios in New York.
July 25: Dylan performs at the Newport Folk Festival. With members of the Paul Butterfield Blues Band, Dylan sings "Maggie's Farm," "Like A Rolling Stone" and "It Takes a Lot to Laugh, It Takes a Train to Cry." Solo, he sings "It's All Over Now, Baby Blue" and "Mr. Tambourine Man."
July 29: Dylan releases "Positively 4th Street."
August 28: Dylan and members of The Hawks perform at Forest Hills Tennis Stadium. The songs are from *Bringing It All Back Home* and the forthcoming *Highway 61 Revisited*, with the exception of new rock 'n' roll versions of "I Don't Believe You" and "It Ain't Me Babe."
August 30: Dylan's sixth album, *Highway 61 Revisited*, is released.
September 23: Dylan and The Hawks begin their North America tour in Austin, Texas.
November 22: Robert Allen Zimmerman marries Sara Shirley Lowndes in a private civil ceremony.
November 30: Dylan's new single, "Can You Please Crawl out Your Window," is released.
December 3: Interviewed by a television reporter, Dylan says he thinks of himself as a "song and dance man."

1966

January-March: Dylan is in Nashville, recording what will become *Blonde on Blonde*.
February 9: Reporter Nora Ephron breaks the story of Dylan's marriage in the *New York Post* under the headline, "Hush! Bob Dylan Is Wed."
February: Dylan and The Hawks tour America.
April-May: Dylan and The Hawks tour the world.
May 16: Dylan's first two-record set (his seventh album) is released. *Blonde on Blonde* is the first Dylan album not to carry the name or title on the front cover.
May 27: Dylan's electric sound still outrages some of his fans. At a Royal Albert Hall show in London, a fan shouts "Judas!" at Dylan and The Hawks onstage. Dylan spits back, "I don't believe you ... you're a *liar*!" Then, turning to The Hawks, he says, "Play it fucking louder." The performance, bootlegged for years, marked the end of Dylan's concert touring until 1974.
June 29: Dylan is injured in a motorcycle accident near his home in Wood-

stock, New York.
July 1: In an article about Dylan's hit single, "Rainy Day Women # 12 & 35," *Time* magazine notes: "In the shifting, multi-level jargon of teenagers, to 'get stoned' does not mean to get drunk, but to get high on drugs . . . . [A] 'rainy day woman,' as any junkie knows, is a marijuana cigarette."
July 29: Dylan is seriously injured in a motorcycle accident in upstate New York. He begins a long period of seclusion.

1967

May 17: D. A. Pennebaker's documentary of the last folk tour, *Don't Look Back*, is released.
June-October: Dylan and various members of the group to become famous as The Band record dozens of songs in the basement of a house in West Saugerties, New York. Much bootlegged, these recordings are eventually released commercially in 1975.
August 21: Columbia Records announces that it has re-signed Bob Dylan. (Dylan had been courted by MGM Records.)
October 3: Woodrow Wilson Guthrie, one of Bob Dylan's idols and inspirations, dies of Huntington's chorea.
December 27: The first album since the accident, *John Wesley Harding*, is released.

1968

January 20: Dylan makes his first public appearance since the 1966 motorcycle accident. Backed by The Band, he performs four songs ("Grand Coulee Dam," "This Train," "Dear Mrs. Roosevelt" and "I Ain't Got No Home") at the Woody Guthrie Memorial Concert at Carnegie Hall. The memorial concert had been Dylan's idea.

1969

February 13-14, 17: Dylan and studio veterans record *Nashville Skyline* in Music City, U. S. A.
April 9: *Nashville Skyline* is released.
July 14: Introduced as "Elmer Johnson," Dylan performs three songs with The Band at the Mississippi River Festival in Edwardsville, Illinois.
August 31: Dylan and The Band perform at the Isle of Wight Festival in England. They do 17 songs, a mixture of new and old material, including three songs he had not previously released: "Wild Mountain Thyme," "The Mighty Quinn (Quinn the Eskimo)" and "Minstrel Boy."
Late fall: At Columbia Studios in New York, Dylan records a miscellany of

songs, from The Beatles' "Yesterday" to the girl-group classic, "I Met Him on a Sunday." These recordings have not been released, but they are harbingers of what is to come the following summer.

1970

March: Dylan is in Nashville, recording some of the basic tracks for what will become *Self Portrait*.
May: At home in Woodstock, Dylan is visited by George Harrison. They write and record two songs together: "Every Time Somebody Comes to Town" and "I'd Have You Any Time."
June 8: Dylan's second two-record set (the first, *Blonde on Blonde*, set a high standard) is released. *Self Portrait* is uniformly panned by the critics. Greil Marcus of *Rolling Stone* begins his review, "What is this shit?"
September: Dylan moves back to New York City after four years in Woodstock.
October 21: Dylan releases *New Morning*. Most critics vow to forgive the lapse of judgment that was *Self Portrait*.

1971

March 14: Critic Marion Meade, writing in the *New York Times*, says of Dylan's "Just Like a Woman," that the song "defines women's natural traits as greed, hypocrisy, whining and hysteria."
March 16: Working with Leon Russell as producer, Dylan records "Spanish Harlem," "That Lucky Old Sun" and "Watching the River Flow" at Blue Rock Studios in New York.
May: *Tarantula* is published by Macmillan.
August 1: Dylan performs at the Concert for Bangladesh, former Beatle George Harrison's benefit for famine victims, which is held at Madison Square Garden in New York. Dylan sings "A Hard Rain's A-Gonna Fall," "Blowin' in the Wind," "Love Minus Zero/No Limit" and "Just Like a Woman" at the matinee performance, and replaces "Love Minus Zero" with "Mr. Tambourine Man" in the evening set.
September 24: Dylan records "When I Paint My Masterpiece" at Blue Rock Studios in New York.
October: Dylan records some of his basement tape songs in Woodstock, New York, for inclusion on an upcoming two-record anthology. Assisted by Happy Traum, Dylan performs "You Ain't Goin' Nowhere," "I Shall Be Released" and "Crash on the Levee" (alternately known as "Down in the Flood").
November 4: Dylan releases a strong ballad about a slain Black Panther leader called "George Jackson." The song is banned from many radio station playlists for the use of the word *shit* as much as its political content.

November 17: In time for the Christmas market, Columbia Records releases *Bob Dylan's Greatest Hits, Vol. II*, a two-record set that includes a few newly recorded songs as well as some old recordings in the Columbia vaults. The oldest such recording is "Tomorrow Is a Long Time," from Dylan's April 12, 1963 concert at Town Hall in New York.

1972

September: Dylan records with Steve Goodman at Bell Sound Studio in New York. Under the pseudonymn Robert Milkwood Thomas, Dylan plays piano and sings on two Goodman compositions.
October: Dylan offers an original song, "Wallflower," to Doug Sahm and sings duet on the number for Sahm's album. Dylan performs on three other tunes with Sahm and his band.
November: Dylan begins filming *Pat Garrett and Billy the Kid* in Durango, Mexico.

1973

January: Dylan journeys to Mexico City to record some of the soundtrack music for *Pat Garrett and Billy the Kid*. Only one of these recordings is eventually used in the film.
February-March: Dylan works to finish scoring the film.
May: Sam Peckinpah's film, *Pat Garrett and Billy the Kid*, starring James Coburn, Kris Kristofferson and Bob Dylan, is released.
November 5-6, 9: Dylan and The Band record *Planet Waves* at Malibu and begin rehearsing for a national tour.
November 16: To punish the artist for leaving the label, Columbia Records releases an album of outtakes called *Dylan*.
December: *Writings and Drawings* is published.

1974

January 3: Dylan and The Band kick off their tour in Chicago. The opening song is an obscure Dylan song he has not recorded, "Hero Blues."
January 17: *Planet Waves* is released by Asylum Records.
February 14: The Dylan/Band tour ends with the last of three nights at The Forum in Los Angeles.
May 9: Dylan and several inebriated friends perform at a Chilean benefit at Madison Square Garden. Dylan duets with Arlo Guthrie on "Deportees," solos on "North Country Blues" and "Spanish Is the Loving Tongue," and joins the ensemble for "Blowin' in the Wind."
June 20: Asylum Records releases *Before the Flood*, a faithful chronicle of

the tour with The Band.
September 12: With New York studio musicians, Dylan records much of *Blood on the Tracks*. He will later re-record many of the tracks in Minneapolis, thereby delaying the album's release.

1975

January 17: Back home at Columbia Records, Dylan releases *Blood on the Tracks*. The last-minute rerecording does not allow the Minneapolis musicians to be credited.
March 23: With Neil Young, Dylan performs at the SNACK Benefit at Kezar Stadium in San Francisco. They perform several of Young's songs, including "Helpless" and "Are You Ready for the Country?" and only a few of Dylan's: "I Want You" and "Knockin' on Heaven's Door."
June 26: *The Basement Tapes* is released.
July-October: Dylan records the songs that will soon appear on *Desire*. Several outtakes of the era include "Rita May," "Abandoned Love" and "Seven Days."
September 10: Dylan performs three songs on "The World of John Hammond" television documentary: "Hurricane," "Oh, Sister" and "Simple Twist of Fate."
October: Dylan joins Bette Midler to record "Buckets of Rain" for Midler's album, *Songs for the New Depression*.

1976

January 16: *Desire* is released.
April-May: Second leg of the Rolling Thunder Revue tour takes Dylan and company through the Southeast and up through the Great Plains.
April 22: Dylan and his band tape a concert at the Belleview Biltmore Hotel in Clearwater, Florida, for an NBC television special. The show was not broadcast.
May 23: Dylan's concert at Colorado State University in Fort Collins is filmed.
September 10: The live album *Hard Rain* is released.
September 14: The film of the May 23 concert, *Hard Rain* is broadcast by NBC. Critics are generally disappointed with the result.
November 25: At San Francisco's Winterland, Dylan performs six songs with The Band at their farewell concert, "The Last Waltz." Dylan does two versions of "Baby Let Me Follow You Down," "Hazel," "I Don't Believe You (She Acts Like We Never Have Met)" and "Forever Young." Dylan leads all the concert performers in "I Shall Be Released." All of these songs except "Hazel" will later be released in *The Last Waltz*, Martin Scorsese's docu-

mentary of the concert.
June 28: Dylan and Sara Shirley Lowndes Dylan are divorced.

1977

December 30: Dylan begins rehearsals for his world tour, to begin in February.

1978

February-March: In Tokyo, Dylan performs several shows at the Budokan, for a live album released that fall.
April: Recording sessions for *Street-Legal*.
June 15: *Street-Legal* is released.
June-July: After a week-long stand at the Universal Amphetheater in Los Angeles, Dylan embarks on a tour of Europe.
September-December: Dylan goes on tour in the United States and Canada.
November: *Bob Dylan at Budokan* released in Japan by CBS/Sony.

1979

April 23: *Bob Dylan at Budokan* is released in the United States.
May: Recording sessions in Muscle Shoals, Alabama.
August 18: *Slow Train Coming* is released.
October 20: Dylan appears on NBC Television's "Saturday Night Live," performing "Gotta Serve Somebody," "When You Gonna Wake Up?" and "I Believe in You."

1980

June 20: *Saved* is released.

1981

May: Recording sessions yield the contents of the *Shot of Love* album, including "The Groom's Still Waiting at the Altar," which appears on later editions of the record. Other songs recorded are "Yonder Comes Sin," "I Need a Woman," "Angelina" and the Everly Brothers' classic, "Let It Be Me."
August 12: *Shot of Love* is released.

1982

June 6: During the "Peace Sunday" concert at the Rose Bowl in Pasadena, California, Dylan sings "With God on Our Side," "Blowin' in the Wind" and Jimmy Buffett's "A Pirate Looks at Forty."

1983

August: In addition to the songs that will appear on *Infidels*, Dylan records "When the Night Comes Falling from the Sky," "This Was My Love," "Foot of Pride," "Clean Cut Kid," "Julius and Ethel," "Death Is Not the End," "Someone's Got a Hold of My Heart," "Lord, Protect My Child" and "Blind Willie McTell." Some of these appear on *Empire Burlesque* and others show up on *The Bootleg Series, Vols. 1-3*.
November 1: *Infidels* is released.

1984

March 22: Dylan and a hard rock trio blister through "Don't Start Me to Talkin'," "Jokerman" and "License to Kill" on NBC Television's "Late Night with David Letterman." The host gets the dour-faced musician to smile.
November 29: *Real Live* is released.

1985

Late winter: In addition to the songs that will appear on *Empire Burlesque*, Dylan records these tunes: "Is It Worth It?" "Yes Sir, No Sir," "Was It Magic?" "You're a Child to Me," "Wind Blowing on the Water," "All the Way Home," "On Borrowed Time," "I Want You to Know I Love You," "On a Rocking Boat," "It's Dangerous to Me," "Wait and See," "Drifting Too Far From Shore," "Go Away, Little Boy," "Straight A's in Love," "The Very Thought of You" and others.
May 27: *Empire Burlesque* is released.
July 13: Dylan, backed by Ron Wood and Keith Richards of The Rolling Stones, performs three songs at the worldwide Live Aid benefit. At Robert F. Kennedy Stadium in Philadelphia, he sings "The Ballad of Hollis Brown," "When the Ship Comes In" and "Blowin' in the Wind." He makes a suggestion that results in the Farm Aid benefit that fall.
September 22: Dylan performs six songs at the Farm Aid benefit in Champaign, Illinois. Energetic and happy, he rips through "Clean Cut Kid," "Shake," "I'll Remember You," "Trust Yourself," "That Lucky Old Sun" and "Maggie's Farm."
October 10: An interview with Dylan at his Malibu home is broadcast on

ABC Television's "20/20." Journalist Bob Brown is the correspondent.
November 4: The massive retrospective, *Biograph*, is released.
December: *Lyrics, 1962-1985* is published.

1986

January 20: At a tribute to Martin Luther King, Jr. at the Kennedy Center for the Performing Arts in Washington, D. C., Dylan joins Stevie Wonder for "Song of Hope" and "Blowin' in the Wind." He also sings "Happy Birthday" and "I Shall Be Released."
January 25: His former manager, Albert Grossman, dies of a heart attack.
February 5: A tour with Tom Petty and The Heartbreakers begins in Wellington, New Zealand.
March: Back in the states, Dylan begins recording his next album.
March 31: Dylan receives the Founder's Award from ASCAP.
June: Dylan's North American tours begins. On several dates, Dylan, Petty and the Heartbreakers are joined by The Grateful Dead.
July 14: *Knocked Out Loaded* is released.
August 17: Dylan is part of a London press conference to announce the beginning of filming for *Hearts of Fire*.
October: Filming begins in the Ontario countryside, which is used to double for Pennsylvania in the film.

1987

February 19: Dylan performs on a Los Angeles nightclub stage with George Harrison, John Fogerty and Taj Mahal.
February 28: In a more unusual collaboration, Dylan joins Michael Jackson on a duet at Elizabeth Taylor's 55th birthday party.
March 11: Dylan sings a little known George Gershwin ballad, "Soon," at a tribute to the composer at the 50th anniversary of his death.
April 20: Dylan performs onstage with U2 at their Los Angeles concert.
October 9: *Hearts of Fire* has its world premiere in London. Dylan is in town, but he passes up the festivities.

1988

January 20: Bob Dylan is inducted to the Rock and Roll Hall of Fame at the Waldorf-Astoria in New York. The Beatles and The Beach Boys are also inducted, so the end-of-the-evening jam includes classics by those groups, but it moves to its conclusion with "Like a Rolling Stone."
Early April: George Harrison, in need of a song to fill out a four-song single, drops by Dylan's house, bringing along Tom Petty, Roy Orbison and Jeff

Lynne. "Handle with Care" becomes the first song by The Traveling Wilburys.
May 29: Dylan joins ex-Band mate Levon Helm for a show at the Lone Star Cafe in New York.
May 31: *Down in the Groove* is released.
June: Dylan begins a tour with a minimalist band: G. E. Smith on lead guitar, Kenny Aaronson on bass and Christopher Parker on drums. At the first few shows, the band includes guest guitarist Neil Young.
July 15: Dylan makes an after-midnight visit to James Dean's grave in Fairmount, Indiana.
October: Dylan's collaboration with U2 ("Love Rescue Me") is released on the band's *Rattle and Hum* album.
November: Dylan, under the guise of Lucky Wilbury, releases *Volume One*, the first album with the Traveling Wilburys.

1989

February 6: *Dylan and The Dead*, a live album from the tour with The Grateful Dead in 1987, is released.
March: Dylan is in New Orleans, recording with producer Daniel Lanois and members of The Neville Brothers' rhythm section.
September 19: *Oh Mercy* is released.
September 24: A surprise appearance on the Chabad Telethon in Los Angeles: Dylan, son-in-law Peter Himmelman, and actor Harry Dean Stanton, calling themselves Chopped Liver, perform "Hava Naghila."
November 20: At John Mellencamp's studio near Bloomington, Indiana, Dylan records Curtis Mayfield's "People Get Ready" for the soundtrack of the film *Flashback*. During his stay, Mellencamp directs a promotional video for "Political World," the first single from *Oh Mercy*.

1990

January: Begins recording *Under the Red Sky*.
January 12: Dylan and his touring band play for five and half hours at Toad's Place in New Haven, Connecticut, readying for the next leg of The Never-Ending Tour.
January 30: Dylan is awarded the medal of the *Commandeur de Arts et des Lettres* by the French Ministry of Culture. It is the highest cultural honor that can be bestowed on a foreigner.
March: Dylan becomes a recording company executive when he forms Strikin' it Rich Records and releases a compilation album called *Christmas Party With Eddie G*. It bombs.
September 11: *Under the Red Sky* is released.
September: *Life* magazine calls Dylan one of the 20th century's "100 Most In-

fluential Americans."

1991

February 20: Actor Jack Nicholson makes a moving tribute in giving Dylan his lifetime achievement award on the broadcast of the Grammy Awards on CBS Television. The show is filled with flag waving for the U. S. troops fighting the Persian Gulf War, but Dylan chooses to sing "Masters of War." Alas, only a few can make out the mumbled words.
March 26: Dylan's three-disc retrospective, *The Bootleg Series, Volumes 1-3*, is released.
May 24: Bob Dylan turns 50.

1992

February 6: With an all-star band, Dylan performs "Like a Rolling Stone" at Radio City Music Hall on the tenth anniversary program of "Late Night with David Letterman."
October 16: Dylan is honored with an all-star concert in Madison Square Garden. George Harrison, Neil Young, Eric Clapton, Stevie Wonder, John Mellencamp, Johnny Cash and Tom Petty, among others, sing Dylan's songs and offer tributes. After three hours of such praise, Dylan is introduced. He sings an ode to his hero, "Song to Woody."
November 3: The day Bill Clinton is elected president, Bob Dylan releases his 37th album, *Good As I Been to You*.

1993

January 17: Dylan makes a surprise appearance at a pre-inaugural concert at the Lincoln Memorial in Washington, D.C. A surprised President-elect Clinton grins broadly when Dylan walks onstage, giving the singer a "thumbs up" signal. Dylan performs "Chimes of Freedom."

Notes

1. Joe Smith, *Off the Record: An Oral History of Popular Music* (New York: Warner Books, 1988), p. 165.
2. Robert Hilburn, "Dylan Now," *The Los Angeles Times Magazine*, 9 February 1992, p. 18.

Index

Aaronson, Kenny, 280
ABC Television, 39, 41, 45, 51, 246-247
Alk, Howard, 244, 246-247, 251
Alk, Jones, 244,
And a Voice to Sing With (Baez), 148-149, 172
Another Side of Bob Dylan (album), 31-33, 188, 291
Artes, Mary Alice, 67
Asylum Records, 57, 60, 195-196, 295

Baby Let Me Follow You Down (von Schmidt), 148, 175
Backstage Passes (Kooper), 149, 173
Baez, Joan, 23-26, 34, 37, 44, 50, 63, 71-72, 92, 95, 106, 117, 139, 148-149, 172, 212, 244-245, 251, 269, 274, 278,
Band, The, 44, 46, 50, 51, 54, 57-60, 64-65, 185, 195-196, 197-198, 216-217, 252-253, 293, 295-296
  farewell concert of, 64-65, 185, 216-217, 252-253, 296
  1974 tour with Dylan, 59-60, 196, 295
  recording sessions with Dylan, 41, 189, 195-196, 197-198, 216-217, 295
Bangladesh, benefit concert for, 51-52, 214, 247-249, 272, 294
Basement Tapes, The (album), 62, 107-108, 139, 154, 186, 197-198, 225, 235, 240, 296
Beatles, The, 28, 32-33, 37-38, 42, 43, 58, 62, 72, 76, 87, 97, 123, 129, 130, 131, 137-138, 143, 144, 146, 220, 226, 248
Beckett, Barry, 67, 200-201
Beecher, Bonnie, 10-13, 18, 88
Before the Flood (album), 60, 105-106, 196, 272, 295-296
Beggars Banquet (album), 43
Belafonte, Harry, 16, 72, 211, 290
Berry, Chuck, 6, 10, 92, 114, 126-127
Bikel, Theodore, 24
Biograph (album), 74, 75, 104, 114-115, 204-205, 207, 299
Blake, Norman, 100
Blakley, Ronee, 251
Blonde on Blonde (album), 39-40, 48, 51, 96-97, 101, 139, 153, 184, 190, 292
Blood on the Tracks (album), 4, 61-62, 64, 70, 78, 93, 106-107, 108, 109, 114, 118, 130, 153, 197, 265, 296
Bloomfield, Michael, 35, 36
Bob Dylan (album), 17, 86-87, 186-187, 290
Bob Dylan: An Intimate Biography (Scaduto), 140, 174
Bob Dylan at Budokan (album), 66, 110-111, 200, 211, 297
Bob Dylan's Greatest Hits (album), 41, 42, 97-98, 191,
Bob Dylan's Greatest Hits, Vol. II (album), 50, 102-103, 193-194, 295
bootleg Dylan recordings, 49-50, 62, 78, 185-186, 229-240
Bootleg Series, The (albums), 78, 118-119, 184, 207-209, 301
Born to Run (album), 62
Bound for Glory (Guthrie), 13
Bowie, David, 70, 257
Brando, Marlon, 5, 7, 8, 241, 242
Bringing It All Back Home (album), 33-34, 36, 38, 92-93, 188-189, 244, 270, 291, 292
Bringing It All Back Home (album notes), 79, 85, 138, 139, 188

Broadside, 18, 19, 150, 175-176, 212, 213, 231, 232
Bucklen, John, 9
Byrds, The, 38, 41, 43, 51, 62, 91, 93, 97, 102, 114, 219, 280

Cahn, Rolf, 13
Carnegie Hall, 16, 26, 27, 230, 268, 290, 293
Carter, Rubin "Hurricane," 62, 63, 108
Cash, Johnny, 45, 79, 100, 191, 224-225, 257, 261, 301
CBS Television, 21-22, 262, 263, 301
Clapton, Eric, 51, 216, 247-248, 252, 301
Coburn, James, 52, 249
Collins, Judy, 17, 19, 225
Columbia Records, 16, 18, 20, 22, 57, 60, 131, 183, 186-211, 290,
Concert for Bangladesh, The (album), 51-52, 214
Concert for Bangladesh, The (film), 52, 242, 247-249
concert tours, Dylan's, 34, 38, 40, 58-59, 62-64, 65-67, 69-70, 71-72, 73, 74-75, 76, 77, 78, 233-235, 237-239, 266-283,
Costello, Elvis, 70
Cott, Jonathan, 144, 172
Crane, Les, 260
Crenshaw, Marshall, 280
Crowe, Cameron, 74, 115, 204

Dandy, Jim, 10, 12
Daniels, Charlie, 100
Danko, Rick, 44, 107, 168, 197-198, 222
Davis, Clive, 22, 42, 58
Daybreak (Baez), 148, 172
Dean, James, 7, 8, 9, 242
Desire (album), 62-63, 108-109, 145, 152, 172, 183, 198, 296
DeVito, Don, 198, 199, 200, 203, 204, 205, 208, 210, 211
Diamond, Neil, 65, 66, 252-253
Dire Straits, 68, 70, 111
Donovan, 244
Don't Look Back (film), 34, 79, 244-246, 293
Down in the Groove (album), 76, 115-116, 206, 300
Drummond, Tim, 112, 201
Dylan (album), 58, 103-104, 194-195, 295
Dylan: A Biography (Spitz), 40, 141
Dylan, Bob:
  albums of, 184-209
  Beecher, Bonnie, and, 10-13, 18, 88
  birth of, 4
  childhood and adolescence of, 4-11
  Columbia Records and, 15-16, 42, 57-58
  concerts by, 265-284
  divorce of, 65
  family background of, 4-5
  films of, 241-250
  Greenwich Village and, 13-17, 62-63
  Guthrie's influence on, 13-15
  Hammond's relationship with, 15-18
  Helstrom, Echo, and, 8-12, 45
  marriage of, 39
  motorcycle accident of, 40
  name changed of, 12
  protest/topical songs by, 17, 19, 21-22, 23-25, 27-28, 87-91, 128-129
  recordings of, 183-240
  rock 'n' roll affected by, 35-40, 127-130
  songs by, 154-171
  television appearances of, 26-263
  tribute concert for, 131-133, 301
Dylan, Sara Lowndes, 34, 35, 38, 39, 40, 45, 46, 53, 61, 64, 65, 97, 105, 109, 251-252, 275, 292, 297
Dylan and the Dead (album), 116, 206, 279, 300
Dylan Liberation Front, 48

East of Eden (film), 7, 9
East Village Other, 49
Eat the Document (film), 51, 52, 79, 246-247
Elliot, Ramblin' Jack, 15, 212
Ellis, Terry, 145
Emergency Civil Liberties Committee, 26-27
Empire Burleque (album), 74, 114, 203, 298
Europe, Dylan's tours of, 34-35, 38-40, 71-72, 269-271, 277-278, 280
Everett, Rupert, 75, 255-259
Everly Brothers, 225
Evers, Medgar, 24, 165, 213

Farina, Mimi, 24, 50
Farina, Richard, 213
Farm Aid, 73, 262, 278, 298
Fielding, Jerry, 53-54
Finnegans Wake (Joyce), 138
Flanagan, Fiona, 75, 255-259
folk music, 9-19, 35-36, 86-91, 128-129
folk-rock music, 36-38
Folkways Records, 15, 212, 213
Freewheelin' Bob Dylan, The (album), 18-21, 24, 25, 27, 87-89, 187, 29-291
Friends of Chile Benefit Concert, 60, 272-273, 295

Gallo, Joey, 62, 108, 62
garbology, 49, 149
Garcia, Jerry, 116, 206
Garnier, Tony, 281-283
Geffen, David, 57, 60

INDEX / 305

Getaway, The (film), 53
Ginsberg, Allen, 51, 185, 215, 244
Gleason, Bob, 14
Gleason, Ralph J., 48
Gleason, Sidsel, 14
Golden Chords, The, 7-8, 77
Good as I Been to You (album), 119-120, 209
Gooding, Cynthia, 231
Goodman, Steve, 51, 184, 215, 295
Graham, Bill, 58, 65
Grammy Awards, 79-81, 131, 262, 263, 301
Grateful Dead, The, 76, 116, 206, 279
Gray, Michael, 146, 173
Great White Wonder, The (bootleg album), 185, 239
Greenwich Village, 14-18
Grossman, Albert, 19, 20, 21, 26, 27, 33, 34, 36, 38, 40, 42, 43, 51, 66, 70, 244-245
Grossman, Sally, 33
Gunfighter, The (film), 241
Gunn, Elston (Dylan pseudonymn), 10
Guthrie, Arlo, 14, 271
Guthrie, Woody, 3, 10, 11, 13, 14, 15, 17, 17, 19, 21, 27, 43, 45, 51, 60, 86, 88, 118, 120, 128, 129, 139, 147, 185, 214, 218, 267, 268, 271, 289, 293

Hammond, John, Jr., 15
Hammond, John, Sr., 15, 16, 17-18, 19, 20, 21, 27, 32, 148, 173, 186, 187, 191, 193, 204-205, 207, 217, 261, 290
Hard Rain (album), 64, 109, 199, 251, 296
Hard Rain (TV special), 64, 250-251, 296
Hard Rain (Riley), 146, 155
Harris, Emmylou, 62, 108
Harrison, George, 51, 76-77, 87, 132, 214, 218, 219, 226, 247-249, 272, 294, 299, 301
Hawks, The, 39-42, 270-271
Heartbreakers, The, 73, 74-75, 132, 239, 278, 279, 280
Hearts of Fire (album), 218, 259
Hearts of Fire (film), 75-76, 242-243, 255-259, 299
Helm, Levon, 38, 270, 277, 280
Helstrom, Echo, 8, 9, 10, 11, 12, 19, 45, 88
Hendrix, Jimi, 226
Hentoff, Nat, 31, 39, 187
Hester, Carolyn, 15-16, 211-212
Heylin, Clinton, 141-142, 145, 173
Hiatt, John, 259
Highway 61 Revisited (album), 36-37, 94-96, 189, 292
Hunter, Robert, 206

Infidels (album), 71, 113, 202, 298

Isle of Wight festival, 46, 101, 271, 293

Johnson, Elmer (Dylan pseudonym), 46, 293
Johnson, Robert, 3, 33, 10
Johnston, Bob, 36-37, 189-193, 195, 204-205, 207
John Wesley Harding (album), 42-43, 98-99, 191, 293
Jones, Mickey, 270

Kael, Pauline, 37, 252
Knocked Out Loaded (album), 75, 76, 115, 205, 299
Knopfler, Mark, 68, 70, 111, 202, 207
Kooper, Al, 35, 36, 48, 94, 97, 102, 131, 149, 173, 234
Kristofferson, Kris, 39, 52, 53, 132, 205, 249

Landau, Jon, 86, 99
Lanois, Daniel, 78, 116, 119, 206, 207, 209, 228
Last Waltz, The (album), 216-217, 296
Last Waltz, The (film), 252-253, 296
"Late Night with David Letterman," 71, 243, 262, 263, 298, 301
Leadbelly (pseudonymn of Huddie Ledbetter), 10, 120, 218
Letterman, David, 71, 243, 262, 263, 298, 301
Levy, Jacques, 62, 108, 184, 198, 199, 200, 202, 205, 208, 210
Little Richard (pseudonymn of Penniman, Richard), 6, 7, 8, 10, 127
Live Aid, 72-73, 237, 278, 298
Lowndes, Sara, *see* Dylan, Sara
Lynch, Stan, 74-75
Lynne, Jeff, 76, 77
Lyrics, 1962-1985 (Dylan), 74, 138-139, 153

McCartney, Paul, 72, 219
McCoy, Charlie, 95-96
McGuinn, Roger, 62, 63, 93, 132, 187, 220, 226, 228, 229, 231, 232, 246, 251, 275, 280
MacLeish, Archibald, 48, 102
"Madhouse on Castle Street," 260
Manuel, Richard, 44, 107, 196, 197, 198, 252-253
Marcus, Greil, 86, 100, 101, 102, 108, 151, 152, 178, 197
Marquand, Richard, 75, 255
MGM Records, 42
Midler, Bette, 185, 216, 227
Midnight Cowboy (film), 45,
Minneapolis tapes (bootleg recordings), 230

Music from Big Pink (album), 44, 222

Nashville Skyline (album), 45, 46, 99-100, 191-192, 293
Nelson, Willie, 132, 278
Neuwirth, Bobby, 63, 244-245
Neville Brothers, 77-78, 228
New Morning (album), 48, 51, 102, 193, 294
Newport Folk Festival, 25, 31, 36, 42, 212, 242, 269, 270, 291, 292
No Direction Home (Shelton), 140-141, 174

Ochs, Phil, 60, 64
O'Connor, Sinead, 132
Oh Mercy (album), 78, 116-118, 206-207, 282, 283, 300
Orbison, Roy, 76, 77

Parker, Christopher, 280, 281
Pat Garrett and Billy the Kid (album), 53, 103, 194, 295
Pat Garrett and Billy the Kid (film), 52-54, 103, 249-250, 295
Paxton, Tom, 33, 43, 176
Peace Sunday concert, 277
Peck, Gregory, 50, 242
Peckinpah, Sam, 52-54, 249-250
Pennebaker, D. A., 34, 39, 42, 51, 242, 244-247
Penniman, Richard, *see* Little Richard
Peter, Paul and Mary, 19, 21, 25, 228
Petty, Tom, 73, 74-75, 76, 132, 239, 278, 279, 280
Planet Waves (album), 58, 59, 60, 61, 104-105, 195, 295
Porco, Mike, 14-15
Presley, Elvis, 6, 8, 20, 21, 123, 125, 126, 127, 138, 227, 228

Queens of Rhythm, 253-254

Raeben, Norman, 60-61
Real Live (album), 72, 113-114, 203, 298
Rebel without a Cause (film), 7
Renaldo and Clara (film), 65, 79, 130, 202, 242, 251-252
Richards, Keith, 72-73, 237
Riley, Tim, 146, 155
Rimbaud, Arthur, 15, 91, 106, 130,
Rivera, Scarlet, 63, 108
Robertson, Robbie (J. R. Robertson), 41, 51, 54, 57, 60, 62, 65, 78, 104, 105, 195, 196, 197, 222, 246, 247, 252, 270
Rock and Roll Hall of Fame, 76, 299
Rolling Stone, 45, 46, 47, 48, 71, 75, 78, 100, 101, 102, 117, 131, 144, 145, 149, 150, 151, 173, 158, 159, 160, 259, 294
Rolling Thunder Logbook (Shepard), 148, 174
Rolling Thunder Revue, 63, 64, 65, 75, 77, 108, 109, 114, 115, 141, 148, 149, 238, 242, 250, 251, 252, 253, 261, 273-274, 296
Rotolo, Suze, 18-19, 25, 26
Russell, Leon, 51, 185, 193, 214, 294

Sahm, Doug, 51, 214-215
Sandburg, Carl, 28
Santana, Carlos, 62, 71, 277
"Saturday Night Live," 68, 243, 261, 297
Saved (album), 69, 111-112, 201, 276
Scaduto, Anthony, 11, 140, 141, 174
Scorsese, Martin, 252-253
Scratch (play), 48, 102
Seeger, Pete, 14, 19, 23, 24, 25, 36, 43
Self Portrait (album), 47-48, 58, 100-102, 103, 192-193, 210, 294
Sgt. Pepper's Lonely Hearts Club Band (album), 42
Shelton, Robert, 11, 14, 15, 16, 18, 26, 44, 86, 91, 92, 93, 94, 95, 96, 98, 104, 106
Shepard, Sam, 40, 75, 76, 115, 148, 152, 174, 178, 205, 251
Shot of Love (album), 69, 70, 112-113, 202, 276, 297
Silber, Irwin, 150, 176
Simon and Garfunkel, 101
Sing Out!, 150, 176
Slow Train Coming (album), 67, 68, 70, 111, 112, 145, 200-201, 276
Smith, G. E., 77, 280, 281, 282
SNACK Concert, 61-62, 236, 273, 296
Something is Happening Here (film), 51
South, Joe, 97, 282
Spector, Phil, 35, 216
Spitz, Bob, 40, 47, 141, 175
Spivey, Victoria, 48, 213, 214, 290
Springs, Helena, 67, 68
Springsteen, Bruce, 62, 72, 73, 76, 124, 130, 131, 229
Street-Legal (album), 66, 109-110, 199, 297
Sweetheart of the Rodeo (album), 43, 224

Tarantula (Dylan), 39, 40, 49-50, 138, 153
Taylor, Mick, 71-72, 113, 277
Telegraph, 145
Ten O'Clock Scholar, 11-12
Times They Are A-Changin', The (album), 27, 89-91, 188, 291
Toad's Place, 282
Tom Paine Award, 26-27
Traum, Happy, 51, 193
Traveling Wilburys, 76, 77, 218, 219, 300
Travers, Mary, 61, 228

Under the Red Sky (album), 78, 118, 207, 300

Vee, Bobby, 10
von Schmidt, Eric, 148, 175, 187, 204

Was, David, 78, 118, 207
Was, Donald, 118, 207
Waters, Muddy (pseudonymn of McKinley Morganfield), 283
Weberman, A. J., 48-49, 149
Wexler, Jerry, 67, 200-201
Wild One, The (film), 241
Williams, Hank, 5, 7, 8
Williams, Paul, 142, 266-267

Wonder, Stevie, 131, 229
Writings and Drawings (Dylan), 138, 139, 153
Wurlitzer, Rudy, 52, 249

Yellow Moon (album), 228
Young, Neil, 61-62, 132, 236, 252-253, 273, 296

Zappa, Frank, 10
Zimmerman, Abraham, 4-5, 10-11, 44
Zimmerman, Beatty Stone, 4-5, 10-11
Zimmerman, David, 5, 61
Zimmerman, Robert, *see* Dylan, Bob

About the Author

WILLIAM McKEEN is Associate Professor at the University of Florida College of Journalism and Communications. His publications include *Hunter S. Thompson* (1991), *The Beatles: A Bio-Bibliography* (Greenwood Press, 1989), and his *Tom Wolfe* is scheduled for publication in 1995.

**Recent Titles in
Popular Culture Bio-Bibliographies**

Charlie Chaplin: A Bio-Bibliography
Wes D. Gehring

Hank Williams: A Bio-Bibliography
George William Koon

Will Rogers: A Bio-Bibliography
Peter C. Rollins

Billy the Kid: A Bio-Bibliography
Jon Tuska

Errol Flynn: A Bio-Bibliography
Peter Valenti

W.C. Fields: A Bio-Bibliography
Wes D. Gehring

Elvis Presley: A Bio-Bibliography
Patsy Guy Hammontree

Charles A. Lindbergh: A Bio-Bibliography
Perry D. Luckett

The Marx Brothers: A Bio-Bibliography
Wes D. Gehring

Mae West: A Bio-Bibliography
Carol M. Ward

The Beatles: A Bio-Bibliography
William McKeen

Laurel & Hardy: A Bio-Bibliography
Wes D. Gehring

John Wayne: A Bio-Bibliography
Judith M. Riggin